P9-DMS-961

Also by Steve Fiffer

SO YOU'VE GOT A GREAT IDEA

HOW TO WATCH BASEBALL

AGAINST THE GRAIN
(with Eugene "Mercury" Morris)

A SEASON FOR JUSTICE

The Life and Times of Civil Rights Lawyer Morris Dees

Morris Dees

with Steve Fiffer

A TOUCHSTONE BOOK
Published by Simon & Schuster
New York   London   Toronto   Sydney   Tokyo   Singapore

TOUCHSTONE
Simon & Schuster Building
Rockefeller Center
1230 Avenue of the Americas
New York, New York 10020

Copyright © 1991 by Morris Dees and Steve Fiffer

All rights reserved
including the right of reproduction
in whole or in part in any form.
First Touchstone Edition, 1992
Published by arrangement with Charles Scribner's Sons, a
division of Macmillan, Inc.
TOUCHSTONE and colophon are registered trademarks
of Simon & Schuster Inc.
Manufactured in the United States of America

1 3 5 7 9 10 8 6 4 2

Library of Congress Cataloging in Publication Data
Dees, Morris.
    A season for justice : the life and times of civil rights lawyer
Morris Dees / Morris Dees with Steve Fiffer.—1st
Touchstone ed.
        p. cm.
    "A Touchstone book."
    Includes index.
    1. Dees, Morris. 2. Lawyers—Southern States—
Biography. 3. Civil rights workers—Southern States—
Biography. 4. Civil rights movements—Southern States—
History. I. Fiffer, Steve. II Title.
[KF373.D43A3 1992]
342.73′085′092—dc20
[B]
[347.30285092]
[B]   91-47206
                                                                  CIP

ISBN: 0-671-77875-7

The following names have been changed for purposes of
protection: "Cliff Tisdale," "Mary Ann Womack," "Annie
Jenkins," "Donna," and "Valerie Martin."

Photo credits appear on page 353.

FOR DADDY

I have lived my life and I have fought my battles, not against the weak and poor—but against power, injustice, against oppression.

Clarence Darrow

ACKNOWLEDGMENTS

Without Steve Fiffer there would be no book. It was his idea. He has gained my respect, admiration, and friendship. I would sit second chair to him at a trial any day. There is no higher compliment a trial lawyer can give.

I owe my partner, Richard Cohen, special thanks for his impartial eye, astutely keeping Steve and me focused and credible. He is by far the best writer and editor I know. His name should be on the book jacket.

To our Scribners editors, Ned Chase and Hamilton Cain, and literary agent, Carol Mann, I also give thanks for guidance and support.

There are so many more whose unselfish help made possible my keeping an active trial schedule while at the same time writing: Dave Watson, for his computer layout of the photographs; Linda Stringer, for printing the finished manuscript; Pam Parker, for transcribing hours of my taped recollections; Joe Levin, Sara Bullard, Beth Boyd, Danny Welch, Joe Roy, and Sharon Fiffer, for constructive editorial criticism; and Judy Bruno, for keeping Steve and me coordinated.

The most important and helpful person has been my dear mother. We spent hours discussing my childhood, my daddy, and life on our farm. She shared things I had never known, some painful, some joyous. My reward for writing this book has been to relive the most wonderful childhood imaginable, this time with my elderly mother at my knee.

A SEASON
FOR JUSTICE

PROLOGUE

July 1947   Mount Meigs, Alabama

Daddy called for me to get my cotton basket as he headed for his green Studebaker pickup. Billy Lucas had asked if he would bring the field hands who lived on our small farm to help him finish picking what he hoped would be the first bale harvested in Montgomery County for 1947. He had planted early in hope of reaping the extra five hundred dollars it would bring at auction.

Billy was rushing to beat the Belser brothers, owners of a large plantation with over fifty hands. He had dreams of using the extra money to repay past-due debts. It was also a great honor to be pictured on the front of the *Montgomery Advertiser* with your freshly ginned bale of cotton and the merchant who made the highest bid.

This honor usually went to the big planters—the Belsers, the McLemores, Gus Dozier, Gene Handey, or the Olivers. The eight black folks and me would give Billy and his family an even chance to ride his mule-powered wagon across the scales ahead of everyone. I was only ten, but I added fifty pounds that day to the fifteen hundred he needed for the winning bale.

Robert Belser's face was redder than its usual sunburnt hue as he cussed Daddy. "Why the goddamn hell did he have to help that nigger beat me out of the first bale?" he demanded. He ranted for ten minutes to the small group of white farmers sitting around my uncle Lucien Dees's country store.

My uncle didn't speak up for Daddy. I got a soda from the cooler and slipped quietly away from the store. Daddy stood at the gin, waiting to take Billy's bale to Court Square in downtown Montgomery.

It would be many years before I understood why my father was

1

different from most other white men in Mount Meigs when it came to black folks. It would be nearly a lifetime before I could appreciate the influence his examples had in shaping my decision to fight legal battles for underdogs like Billy Lucas.

December 1984   Rolling Hills Ranch

My daughter Ellie found the Christmas ornaments, and we set about decorating the big cedar I'd cut and hauled halfway across the farm. The tree's scent was powerful enough to fill the room and to fill me with memories of past Christmases when all our kin in Montgomery County would gather at my grandmother Dees's old rambling frame house in Mount Meigs. We'd trim the tree and then sit down to a dinner of home-raised turkey with cornbread dressing, sweet potatoes, black-eyed peas, and greens from her garden.

Tonight there was just the two of us. Three, if you counted E. T. Davis, who moved back and forth through the house trying to make himself as scarce as possible. For someone carrying a submachine gun and a two-way radio, he did a pretty good job of fading into the woodwork.

"Did I ever tell you how I tried to sell mistletoe?" I asked Ellie, watching her pull a red elf from the ornament box.

"I thought you sold holly wreaths." She moved to the window behind the tree and looked out. It was a crisp, cloudless night. Stars filled the slate gray sky.

"I sold the wreaths later," I said. "Don't stand over there, sugar."

Ellie nodded and returned to the ornaments. She combed through colored glass balls, Santas, and stars until she found what she was looking for. She held up an angel made of white lace. "The tree's so tall. Think you'll be able to get this on top?" she asked.

"Always have. If not—"

"Jesus Christ, there's someone out here," cried a voice over E. T.'s radio: It was Tom Summers, the outside guard. "Do you read me, E. T.? There's someone on the property."

"Ellie!" I grabbed my Beretta from the bookcase and found my Browning .22 pistol. Ellie took it without a word.

E. T.—rock-solid, blue eyes hidden behind sunglasses at all hours— swept into the room. He was the best of the round-the-clock corps of private guards who'd been patrolling the farm and my offices at the Southern Poverty Law Center. He'd been a policeman once, but as another guard had told me, "E. T.'s just too violent and hot-tempered to be a cop." I liked him.

E. T. rushed us into the pantry designated as the safe room. "Stay on the floor and don't come out until I tell you," he told us, shutting the door.

Tom's voice came back over the radio. "There were two of them. I think I see one in the bushes."

"Shoot the bastard," E. T. said.

Ellie and I found a spot beside some empty boxes. She huddled against me. I put my arm around her and told her everything would be all right.

"I had my light on him," Tom was saying. "He was by the bushes near the driveway. He's armed. Some kind of rifle. Maybe an AR-fifteen."

"Shoot him!" E. T. and I shouted at the same time.

"I don't know," Tom said.

"Jesus," E. T. said. I heard him pick up the phone and call his supervisor. "Get the FBI and sheriff out here ASAP."

Tom spoke again. "I can see his boots." There was a pause, then: "Sir, would you please step out so I can escort you off the property?"

"What's this escort bullshit?" E. T. radioed. "Tom, shoot him fast before he moves."

I wished E. T. were out there instead of Tom. I wished I were out there. Two weeks earlier an FBI agent had called to warn me a group of white supremacists were plotting to kill me. He had suggested I leave the country for a few months. I had refused, explaining that leaving wasn't my style and that I was in the middle of two of the most important cases I'd ever had. If all went well, one case would shut down the Carolina Knights of the Ku Klux Klan's sophisticated paramilitary operations, and the other would bring Bobby Shelton's United Klans of America to its knees.

"I don't want to shoot," said Tom. "What if it's a hunter?"

"It's almost midnight," I yelled. "That's no hunter!"

Ellie shuddered.

"You okay, sugar?" I asked.

She nodded. She held her gun in one hand and the angel in the other. This was a hell of a spot for a fourteen-year-old high-school freshman.

"First they burn down your law office, now they come after you. Why do you do the cases you do, Daddy? I don't understand. Why can't you just practice regular law?" She was trembling.

"Just hold on to me and close your eyes, and it'll be over in a little while. I promise."

"E. T.?" Tom called. It sounded like he had come in the back door.

"What the hell did you leave your post for?" E. T. exploded.

Tom was so terrified of E. T. that it took him a minute to answer. He finally explained that he'd been sitting in his truck with the lights off when he'd seen two men walking down the road toward the house, each carrying a gun. Apparently they hadn't seen him at first. But when he drove the truck toward them, they ran into the woods. That's when he had called E. T.

"You're lucky they didn't blow you away," said E. T. "Now get the hell back out there and see if you can find them. And this time shoot."

"If you want to go out there with him, we'll be okay," I told E. T. through the door.

He refused, reminding me his post was the house and he was the last line of defense.

Ellie still shivered. "Hang in there, darlin'," I said.

I held her silently in the darkness, and then all of a sudden she stopped shaking. "Dad, you know I can handle this," she said in an unconvincingly firm voice. "We're reading *The Diary of Anne Frank* in school, and this is nothing compared to what she and all those children had to face in the war."

I couldn't say anything through my tears. I kissed her on the forehead.

The farm is out in the country about twenty miles south of Montgomery. It was half an hour before the FBI and two sheriff's deputies arrived and E. T. told us it was safe to come out. One of the deputies showed me a piece of camouflage cloth he'd found along the driveway. An FBI agent put it in a paper sack and said something about fibers. We all agreed that it would be pointless searching the thick woods in the dark. The sheriff sent his men in cars along the roads on all sides of the farm. They looked for strangers coming out of the woods, but didn't see anybody.

I lost track of Ellie during all the police talk. When the FBI and deputies left, it was after 1 A.M. I said good night to E. T. and went down the hall to the bedrooms. Ellie was asleep in her room.

When I climbed into my bed, I saw that she had tied the Christmas angel to the headboard over my pillow. *God, what a child.* I sat on the edge of my bed, fighting back tears.

Sleep did not come easy: I kept thinking of the question Ellie had asked. Why risk my life, or, worse, the lives of my loved ones and colleagues at the Center? I was forty-eight years old, healthy, blessed with wonderful children and a home that I had only dreamed about when I was a young boy picking cotton for two cents a pound.

I didn't have to try these cases—or any cases at all. I was financially secure through business ventures begun long before Joe Levin and I had founded the Center in Montgomery in 1971. I could hunt or fish or take my motorcycle on that trip around the world I'd never had time for. And if I was so set on working, I could open a comfortable, private practice or return to the kind of cases the Center had been involved in before 1980—important cases challenging the segregation of the Alabama State Troopers and the Montgomery YMCA and the exclusion of minorities from juries. Those cases had prompted some angry folks to try to smear my reputation. But, in suing governmental bodies and private institutions, I'd never felt my life was in danger.

That had all changed when I'd taken on the Klan.

I went back down the hall. I stood in the doorway and watched Ellie as she slept. My little girl was growing up. In the morning, I would tell her that I wanted her to come to court when I sought justice for Beulah Mae Donald, a black woman who had lost her son to a Klansman's noose. "I'm not sure if you can ever know a person, Ellie, even your own dad," I whispered, then listened to her soft breathing.

CHAPTER 1

May 1981   Houston, Texas

Louis Beam, the Grand Dragon of the Texas Knights of the Ku Klux Klan, was, depending on the way I looked at it, breathing fire or blowing smoke. Three weeks earlier the Southern Poverty Law Center had sued the Klan and Beam, a college-educated extremist with his own paramilitary organization, in order to prevent them from terrorizing the members of the Vietnamese Fishermen's Association in Galveston Bay. Now we were sitting across a table from each other in a jury room in Houston's federal courthouse while Beam's lawyer, Sam Adamo, took the deposition of one of my clients, Col. Nguyen Van Nam.

Beam was a short, slight man in his mid-thirties with a pockmarked face. He had a dark moustache that curved down around his lips and greasy black hair slicked across his head like Adolf Hitler. On this day he was holding a book with the word *Exorcism* printed in large type on the front cover. For the better part of an hour, he chanted something I couldn't make out. Then he fixed his demonic black eyes on me and began to mouth something all too clear:

"You die, you die, you die. . . . You die, you die, you die. . . ."

I took him seriously. This was a man with a string of arrests for violent acts committed in the name of Christianity and "the American way." A year earlier, he had been arrested for trying to strangle Deng Xiaoping when the Chinese leader had visited Texas. State grand juries had also indicted him for blowing up a Communist party headquarters and bombing a left-wing radio station. That these charges had eventually been dropped did little to make me feel comfortable about Beam.

When he wasn't wearing his Klan robe, he often sported a tie tack with the word *Never* written in bold letters. He explained that this meant "Never let any race but the white race rule the country."

"We'll set up our own state here in Texas and announce to all nonwhites that they have twenty-four hours to leave. Lots of people won't believe it or won't believe us when we say we'll have to get rid of them, so we'll have to exterminate a lot of them the first time around," he had told a reporter who had gone undercover to investigate the Klan in 1980.

The means for extermination was already in place. On the first and third Sundays of every month, members of Beam's Texas Emergency Reserve would gather in Deer Park, a Houston suburb, where they boarded an army-surplus troop carrier for an hour-long ride to a training camp located on private property in the swampy flatlands northwest of Galveston Bay. Carrying sidearms or assault rifles and dressed in fatigues, heavy boots, web gear, and cloth caps, the men were taught military tactics in a Quonset hut and then led through field maneuvers by Beam, his face smudged with charcoal, and a Korean War veteran known as Cap'n Bob. Newspaper reports quoted Beam, a highly decorated Vietnam helicopter door gunner, telling his men he wanted "kill zones" guaranteeing the annihilation of the enemy. He added that the maneuvers were "a lot more fun than watching jungle bunnies run up and down and toss balls"—a reference to black basketball players.

This was no operation to be laughed at or dismissed. Cap'n Bob said that some five hundred people had gone through training. Beam boasted that active-duty military personnel from Fort Hood also belonged to the Texas Emergency Reserve. There were other reports that Civil Air Patrol cadets—schoolchildren—had received instruction in hand-to-hand combat at the camps.

A few days before Colonel Nam's deposition, Beam had shown up at his own deposition wearing a white Klan robe. A black-robed Aryan Covenant Church "chaplain" called Father Joseph accompanied him. Beam pulled out a cross, placed it on the table, and the two men prayed together.

We were sitting in a long conference room in the Houston bank building where Beam's attorneys had their offices. A large rectangular table filled most of the space. Beam, Father Joseph, and the Klan's lawyers, including Sam Adamo, sat on one side of the table. I sat across from them with Colonel Nam, three other Vietnamese clients, and Randall Williams and Mike Vahala, Center investigators helping with the case.

When the praying ended and the deposition finally began, the Grand Dragon was evasive. As Beam lamely tried to explain how the Fifth Amendment protected him from stating his name, Colonel Nam whispered that he had seen a gun under the robe.

"Are you sure?" I asked.

The colonel, who had spent twenty-two years in the Vietnamese military, nodded.

I looked Beam over. There was a bulge under his right arm suggesting a shoulder holster, but I couldn't see a gun. Then he leaned back. Tucked in his waistband was a revolver with an ivory handle.

Ignore it, I thought. *He can't be planning on using it here. Not in a public place. He's like all those macho Texans you read about. He just wants to be ready in case somebody draws on him.*

No. Louis Beam was not a typical Texan. He was a violent nut, just crazy enough to pull out the revolver, if not use it. It was important to stop that before it happened and important to get it on the record that he had come to his deposition armed.

I leaned over to Randall and Mike. "Beam's got a gun under his robe," I whispered without emotion. "I'm going to tell Adamo."

Randall, a thirty-year-old liberal idealist from a dirt-poor east Alabama family, sneaked a quick glance at Beam.

Mike, an Indiana native and recent graduate of Yale, had volunteered to work at the Center for a year before going to law school. His round face paled when I mentioned the gun. He and Randall were in good shape, but they were not street fighters. I wondered if they were up to what I had in mind.

"You guys be ready to shove the table into Beam if he makes a move for the gun," I continued. "Then we'll turn it over on the bastard."

Their eyes widened.

I turned to Adamo: "Would you determine whether your witness is armed?"

Shocked, he looked at his client. Beam jumped to his feet, glaring at me. "You don't have permission to search my body unless you've got a permit," he said, leaving the room.

I stopped the deposition. When reporters questioned Beam about the incident, he scoffed at the suggestion he had been armed. He said he carried a Bible under his robe, not a gun.

When we resumed the deposition a few days later, Beam resorted to religious imagery to make it clear what he thought of me. "Demon Dees," he called me, eyes locked on mine. He barked out his lines in military fashion. "No Antichrist Jew should be allowed to ask a Christian anything for a court of law. . . . So the issue is not Louis Beam opposed to the Vietnamese. It's Louis Beam versus Morris Dees, Antichrist Jew."

I'm not the Antichrist. Hell, I'm not even Jewish. I've got sandy blond hair and blue eyes and look a lot more like the "ideal Aryan warrior" than Louis Beam does. Maybe that's what made him so angry. Maybe he figured I should have been on his side of the table. Instead, here I was with Colonel Nam standing up for a bunch of Asian refugees whose efforts to fish in Galveston Bay had driven the "genuine American" fishermen to call in the Klan.

Now, as Adamo took Colonel Nam's deposition, Beam continued chanting: "You die. You die. You die." I didn't take my eyes off him until the deposition was over.

After the deposition, Vahala went down to the underground garage near the Federal Building to get our car and run a lunchtime errand. As he neared our parking space, he spotted Beam. The Grand Dragon quickly moved to another car in the garage, paused for a moment, and then hurried to the elevator.

Mike was scared. He bent down to the pavement and looked under the car. Had Beam planted a bomb?

Everything seemed in order. Mike got into the car. He held his breath, turned the key, then thanked God that the car hadn't exploded. After finishing his errand, he took the car to an outdoor lot with a parking attendant.

We took more depositions in the afternoon. As a defendant, Beam had the right to be present, but he did not appear. After the last deposition, Mike and I left the courthouse for the parking lot. Halfway down the block, we realized we were being followed. Turning around, we saw Beam. We didn't know where he'd come from.

We quickened our pace and entered the parking lot. Beam stopped down the street. He stood motionless on the corner watching us.

The attendant brought our car. Beam again headed toward us. Mike moved quickly into the driver's seat. I hurried into the passenger side. I looked out the window and saw that Beam was carrying a brown paper bag in his left hand. He was moving faster now, just a few feet from the car. He reached into the bag with his right hand, then bent down into a firing position.

"Mike!" I cried. "Floor it!"

We screeched out of the lot before I could see if he had a gun. It didn't matter. I'd had enough. Back in our motel room, I drafted a motion seeking the court's protection from this madman, just as I had the day Colonel Nam had spied the gun. This time, for good measure, I asked the court to order a mental examination so that we could "seek commitment of Mr. Beam to an appropriate mental hospital should the report indicate that Defendant Beam is legally insane or that his mental condition is such that he poses a great likelihood of danger to plaintiffs or their counsel."

"Klan Official Is 'Deranged,' Viets' Lawyer Charges" ran the front-page headline in the *Houston Chronicle* the next day. Beam was furious and embarrassed. That was fine with me. I didn't need a revolver to fight this battle. I'd use the law.

I wasn't surprised that the proceedings had turned so ugly and dangerous. I'm sure there were quite a few people across the country who would have been shocked to learn that the Ku Klux Klan was still in business in 1981. Many probably thought that its heyday of hate was long past and that its members lived in a rest home for beer-drinking rednecks without high-school diplomas. But it was the violence of the Klan that had brought me down to Texas, and it had been the violence of the Klan a couple of years earlier in Decatur, Alabama, that had led me to point the Southern Poverty Law Center in a new direction and to start taking on those cases that would worry my Ellie so.

On May 26, 1979, about sixty protesters had marched through the streets of Decatur, a city of about forty thousand in the northern part of the state. Almost half a century earlier, in 1931, the nine black young men known as the Scottsboro Boys had been tried in Alabama for the rape of a white woman. Eight had been convicted and then sentenced to death. This flagrant miscarriage of justice had attracted national publicity, reinforcing the belief that little had changed since the Civil War. Forty-eight years later, many felt a twenty-six-year-old black man named Tommy Lee Hines had also been denied justice.

In 1978, Hines had been arrested in connection with a series of black-on-white rapes in Decatur. The rapes had terrified and angered the community, pressuring the police to find the culprit. They came up with Hines, who was mentally retarded. Those who knew Hines thought that, in their haste to solve the crime, the police had picked up the wrong man.

Two days after the arrest, eighty blacks held a church rally to protest. The rally was followed by the first major march by blacks in Decatur's history. Over the next weeks, blacks staged a sit-in at the courthouse and erected a tent city at City Hall. Dr. Joseph Lowery of the Southern Christian Leadership Conference, Dr. Martin Luther King, Jr.'s old organization, came and addressed three hundred of Hines's supporters. But in the end the protests had little effect. An all-white jury convicted Hines.

The May 26 march was to commemorate the one-year anniversary of Hines's arrest. As the protesters gathered, so, too, did a large group of Klansmen in robes and hoods, armed with clubs and guns.

A police line had been created to let the marchers pass safely through Decatur's streets, but the police were no match for the anonymous thugs chanting "Nigger, go home!" The Klansmen burst into the street. The police followed. Some marchers ran for cover; some stayed to defend themselves and their families. Shots were fired. Two blacks and two Klansmen were wounded.

Four Klansmen were arrested—three for assaulting a police officer and one for unlawfully discharging a weapon. Curtis Robinson, a black man who had been watching the march, was also arrested—for shooting David Kelso, a Klan leader. Robinson admitted that he had fired a weapon but insisted he had only been defending himself from the Klan. He was eventually indicted for assault with intent to commit murder.

When Clint Brown, the Alabama Legal Services director in Decatur, called and asked if the Center would represent Curtis Robinson, I explained that we didn't take this kind of case; the criminal cases we took focused on challenging the death penalty. Clint then put Curtis on the phone. His account of his arrest so moved me that I agreed to help.

I went up to Decatur and met Curtis. He was a short, solid man of fifty. A thin moustache hugged his lip. He spoke softly, but confidently. I liked him. Married with five children, he worked as a maintenance man at City Hall. He had never caused any serious trouble. Twenty years earlier, he had been in a singing group that imitated the Coasters, whose big hits had included "Poison Ivy," "Yakity Yak," and "Charlie Brown." In his baritone voice, he had sung the memorable refrain: "Why's everybody always picking on me?"

It was over a year before we went to trial. During that time, Center investigator Bill Stanton learned just about everything there was to know about the Klan by attending rallies, finding undercover informers, and talking with Klansmen, their families and friends.

Since its founding in 1865 by six young ex-Confederates, the Klan had experienced a number of rises and falls. Yankee Reconstruction had created the perfect environment for the ascension of night-riding vigilantes. Then, after a lengthy dormant period, the Klan had thrived in the years after World War I, largely in response to the massive wave of immigration that had brought twenty-three million "aliens" to our shores—aliens who threatened "the American way," according to Klan leaders. At its height in the mid-1920s, the "Invisible Empire" had counted four to five million members.

Opposition by clergy, the press, and politicians had eventually weakened the Klan, but it began to spread its evil again in the 1950s and '60s with the birth of the civil rights movement. Churches were burned. Nonviolent activists, black and white, were beaten and murdered.

In 1964, the FBI finally undertook a major effort to infiltrate the Klan. Congress also took action, calling Klan leaders to Capitol Hill to testify, then holding them in contempt when they refused to answer questions. A number of Klansmen, including the United Klans' Bobby Shelton, chose to go to jail rather than reveal the secrets of the Invisible Empire. A leadership vacuum was created, and by the end of the '60s, the Klan had declined again.

The events in Decatur opened our eyes to the Klan's comeback. It made sense. Hard times often inspired the Klan's rebirth, and we were in hard times. Jobs were scarce. Inflation pushed up the price of everything. To many people mired in what President Jimmy Carter called a "malaise," it seemed that minorities were getting all the breaks through affirmative action programs. The rhetoric of savvy new Klan leaders like Don Black in Alabama and Bill Wilkinson and David Duke in Louisiana—that Jews controlled the pie and that blacks, Hispanics, and refugees were getting the biggest pieces— struck a responsive chord with an increasing number of whites hungry for a better life.

From the beginning, the Free Tommy Hines movement had served as a lightning rod for Klan activity. After the black protesters' sit-in at City Hall, Klansmen had burned a cross. Then, in July of 1978, some thirty-five hundred men and women came to Decatur for the first major Klan rally since Congress had passed the Civil Rights Act of 1964. There they heard Bill Wilkinson, the clean-cut, articulate Imperial Wizard of the Invisible Empire Knights of the Ku Klux Klan (there are several major competing organizations with slightly different names), predict a race war. Three weeks later a white woman who reportedly dated a black man was killed in Decatur. Police found the imprint of a burned cross in her yard. The next night another Klan rally drew between five and ten thousand people. At the end of the first week of the Hines trial, the Klan burned a forty-foot cross. Two days later Wilkinson announced that his Invisible Empire intended to fight for the repeal of the Civil Rights Act and proclaimed that federal judges should be shot for treason.

Decatur was not the only site of renewed Klan activity around the country. In April of 1979, twenty members of Bobby Shelton's United Klans of America had been arrested after waging a campaign of terror in the Alabama towns of Sylacauga and Childersburg. That November a group of Klansmen and Nazis opened fire on members of the Communist Workers party who were peacefully demonstrating against the Klan in Greensboro, North Carolina; five of the Workers were killed. In April of 1980, a Klan splinter group gunned down five black women on a street in Chattanooga, Tennessee. At the same time, Beam was organizing the Texas Emergency Reserve. "When the shooting starts, we're gonna win it just like we did in Greensboro," he announced. Juries had acquitted the defendants in Greensboro and Chattanooga.

We thought Curtis Robinson had a strong case for self-defense. We had found a videotape of the riot showing Klansman Kelso provoking Curtis with a club before Curtis had drawn his gun. Despite the evidence, the all-white jury convicted him. Based on the jury's recommendation, the judge gave Curtis two years' probation.

Although the sentence was relatively lenient, I was furious. As Curtis's wife and children cried in the courtroom, I told the press, "This verdict makes history in this state and this nation because it's the first time a black man has ever been convicted of shooting a robed Klansman who advanced on him with a raised club."

I wasn't ready to let go of the case. On the ride back to Montgomery, I told Bill that we would not only appeal the conviction, we'd figure out some way to haul the Klan into court for violating the civil rights of the Decatur marchers—something the federal government should have done from the start.

I had something else in mind, too: Klanwatch. We would set up a system at the Center to monitor the Klan's activities and to sue KKK groups and members who violated the rights of others. The Klan was certainly entitled to exercise its First Amendment rights of speech and assembly; but it wasn't entitled to take to the streets and harass, club, or shoot other people.

There was some reluctance at the Center when I circulated a memo proposing Klanwatch. No one disagreed with the notion that the Klan should be monitored and, when necessary, sued. Some of the attorneys felt that the Southern Poverty Law Center, with its small staff of five lawyers and two investigators, didn't have the resources to take on the KKK all over America. Others didn't think that the Center should shift what they perceived to be its focus and begin fighting the Klan. We should fight against employment discrimination, for equal rights for women, for greater minority representation in government, they argued.

I didn't see that taking on the Klan was a radical shift in focus. One of our earliest cases had involved suing the state of Alabama to integrate the Alabama State Troopers. We hoped not only to win jobs for blacks, but also to use the case to stop the pattern of abuse directed at blacks by the all-white force. Suing the Klan wasn't that different.

I persuaded my colleagues to explore the idea of creating Klanwatch. In less than four weeks, we filed our first suit in federal court in Birmingham against the Invisible Empire, Bill Wilkinson, and a dozen other Klansmen for turning the peaceful Decatur march into a riot. We wanted a monetary award for the marchers whose rights had been violated and an injunction preventing the Klan and its members from violating civil rights in the future. In April of 1981, we filed our second suit—in Houston, against the Texas Knights of the Ku Klux Klan, Louis Beam, and his cohorts.

The case against Beam was typical of many of the cases the Center took on. Colonel Nam and the Vietnamese Fishermen's Association didn't find us. We found them.

At first glance Col. Nguyen Van Nam seemed an unlikely Texas shrimper. He had led a unit of ten thousand Vietnamese troops in combat, had served in the Airborne, in Special Forces, and in the Political Welfare Department. When Saigon fell in April 1975, he had reluctantly given up his command. Knowing that the victorious North Vietnamese would severely punish high-ranking career officers, he had fled to America along with tens of thousands of other South Vietnamese.

Nam's story was typical of many Southeast Asian refugees. Arriving with no money and few possessions, he joined his brother in San Antonio, Texas. He took a job at a car wash. Soon he was pumping gas and working as a mechanic, trying to save enough money to start his own business.

In January 1979, the colonel moved to Seabrook, Texas, a town of thirty-five hundred on the west shore of Galveston Bay about twenty-five miles southeast of Houston. Much of Vietnam is coastline and the area around Saigon is delta country. The towns along the Gulf of Mexico, reminiscent of home, immediately attracted refugees—some fifty thousand Indochinese.

Seabrook has long been the most productive shrimping area on the Texas Gulf Coast. With the money he had managed to save, the financial backing of his brother, and a loan from a bank, Colonel Nam bought a shrimping boat and some property on the waterfront. Full of ambition, the colonel planned to shrimp and build a fish house where he would buy the daily catch of the bay fishermen and then sell it both retail and wholesale. Because of his status in Vietnam, the colonel quickly became a leader of the refugees around Galveston Bay.

Shrimping isn't terribly complicated. Once the boat is maneuvered into the right area, the shrimper drops a large, pouch-shaped net, then drags it over the sea bottom. Although it's not complicated to be a shrimper, that doesn't mean it's easy. The life of those "harvesting" shrimp reminds me a lot of my daddy's life farming cotton. He ran a good, efficient operation, but sometimes that wasn't enough. The boll weevil and armyworm could destroy a year's crop, and so could the weather. Pollution, heavy rains, and hurricanes created the same dangers for the Gulf fishermen.

The uncertainties of the business might have made some Americans think twice about shrimping, but it didn't stop the Vietnamese. By the time Colonel Nam came to Seabrook, there were about twenty-five Vietnamese boats in the water. Soon the size of the fleet working out of Clear Creek Channel—both Texans and Vietnamese—had doubled. Naturally, the locals who had long fished the area were not happy with the increased competition for a finite number of shrimp. Overfishing had been a problem even before the Vietnamese came.

The way in which the new competition fished also concerned the Americans. As strangers in a new land, the Vietnamese did not know all the laws and customs governing the bay. Sometimes they didn't give other boats room to maneuver. Sometimes they tried to slip their boats into circles of boats already working an area. While these breaches were usually innocent, they still heightened tensions with the natives. There were shouting matches between American and Vietnamese boats, and sometimes the Americans would weave their boats in front of the refugees to emphasize their anger.

Nineteen hundred seventy-nine, Colonel Nam's first year on the water, was not a good year for any shrimper. Not only were there more boats, but also it rained so much that the salinity of the bay—essential for the shrimp to flourish—was threatened. Tension mounted. In nearby Seadrift, an American fisherman was shot and killed; two Vietnamese fishermen were charged with murder. A jury acquitted them, finding justifiable homicide, but in the aftermath several Vietnamese boats were burned.

The Texans began to sound jingoistic, calling the places where the Vietnamese docked their boats "Saigon Harbor" or "Pearl Harbor." Some said that the Vietnamese had an unfair advantage because they were being subsidized by welfare. Some said that controversial Reverend Sun Myung Moon, the Korean founder of the Unification Church, was supporting them. Neither allegation was true, of course.

If anything, the Vietnamese, with less experience and inferior boats, should have been at a disadvantage. But their work ethic and willingness to accept deprivation without complaint helped them through the hard times.

Vietnamese families were willing to share houses or apartments to cut down on expenses. Some of the Americans resented the fact that the Vietnamese ate differently. "They live off whatever they take from the water. Hell, the water's a supermarket for them. They eat what we throw away. They don't throw nothing back. Even the littlest crab, they make some kind of sauce from it," said Gene Fisher, the fisherman who eventually asked Beam and the Klan to intervene. Keeping the food metaphor alive, Fisher concluded, "I've just had enough. They're getting my part of the American pie."

Despite their differences, all the fishermen agreed that there were simply too many boats for the bay. After a special meeting to discuss the crisis, a coalition of Vietnamese and Americans drafted a sixteen-item "gentlemen's agreement." The most critical item read: "The Vietnamese agree to discourage other Vietnamese against moving into Seabrook or buying any more boats." At the same time, the Americans said they would work to limit boats in the Clear Creek Channel area.

Unfortunately this gentlemen's agreement was without legal standing or mechanism for enforcement. Both the Texans and the Vietnamese wanted the state of Texas to draft a law barring entry into the shrimping business in the area, but Governor Clements pointed out that when Texas had enacted such a statute in 1959, the Supreme Court declared it an unlawful restraint of free trade.

Although the agreement had no teeth, most fishermen tried to abide by it. Things were relatively peaceful in 1980 except for the increasingly nationalistic rhetoric of a few Americans, most notably Fisher. A burly ex-con in his mid-thirties, he had refused to join the coalition. "What I want to know is when the refugees are going to stop coming," he told one reporter. "You say you've never seen a good thing come from violence? Once upon a time, some men put on Indian clothes and dumped some tea off some boats, and that's how this country came about." Fisher seemed to have forgotten that the American colonists were themselves immigrants or at least descendants of recent immigrants.

As 1981 began, legislators contemplated limiting the number of licenses, imposing a daily 2 P.M. fishing curfew to prevent overfishing, and strongly enforcing existing regulations.

Others contemplated more drastic action. Terming the situation on the bay "potentially explosive," Governor Clements told resettlement agencies to stop placing Southeast Asians on the coast. The governor also suggested that the agencies try to persuade those Vietnamese already settled there to move elsewhere.

Despite being treated so inhospitably, the refugees continued to be reasonable. In January, Vietnamese fishermen in the Rockport and Fulton area, down the coast from Seabrook, signed a petition pledging to limit the number of their boats in the water. A week later, two Vietnamese boats were burned.

Colonel Nam stood up for his people, saying that it wasn't fair to blame them for the problems of the last two years, that weather had been the real villain. He also pointed out that it was unfair of the Americans to sell boats to the refugees and then get angry at them for plying their trade. Still, he said, 60 percent of the Vietnamese fishermen were willing to leave if they could sell their boats.

This Vietnamese response and the solutions offered by state officials were not good enough for the more militant local fishermen. Gene Fisher had reached his boiling point. It was time to call that infamous protector of the rights of true Americans—the Ku Klux Klan.

Our investigation would later show that people started gathering at Jody Collins's place in Sante Fe, not too far from Seabrook, at dusk on February 14. Many were Texas fishermen, including Collins, his brother David, Gene Fisher, and Jim Stanfield. Stanfield, a member of the Texas Knights of the Ku Klux Klan, had paid one dollar to lease the property for the evening. He wore a Klan uniform, like several others present. The press had come, too. The crowd would later be estimated at between 250 and 750 people.

As the moon was rising over Galveston Bay, the featured speaker arrived with his entourage. Louis Beam wore his white Klan robe with four green stripes on each sleeve and a cross over the heart. His thirteen-man security force was dressed in olive green military garb.

Gene Fisher smiled proudly. A few weeks earlier he had formed the American Fishermen's Association to fight for the rights of the natives. It had been his idea to call on Beam.

While Fisher wasn't a member of the Klan, he had admired Beam for a long time. Almost every Saturday he made a pilgrimage to the small white building, decorated with the American and Confederate flags and crosses, that housed Beam's Public Information Bookstore in the Houston suburb of Pasadena. The store offered racist literature, and many of its patrons wore camouflage fatigues.

On January 24, Fisher had managed to get an audience with Grand Dragon Beam and told him about the situation on the bay. Fisher hoped the Klan would help the American fishermen. He felt the Klan was the one organization with the courage to stand by its convictions. If its involvement didn't scare the Vietnamese so that they'd pack up and leave, Fisher thought, it would at least generate the publicity needed to force the state to act decisively before the fishing season began on May 15.

Beam was sympathetic to Fisher's dilemma, if not rational. A few days later, when his Klan gathered for a convention in Cleveland, Texas, Beam called on Governor Clements to appoint a committee of Vietnam veterans to remove "the Vietcong" from the Texas coast. (He somehow had it in his mind that many of the refugees were Communists.) He also asked Clements to declare a technical state of war with Vietnam.

At the February 14 Santa Fe rally, Beam wasn't *asking* for anything. He was telling. He began by granting federal and state authorities a ninety-day "Grand Dragon's dispensation" to do something about the problem on the bay. It just so happened that the dispensation would end on May 14, the eve of the fishing season. If authorities didn't do anything by then, Beam warned, "this entire Gulf Coast is going to be a difficult place to live."

There was no hemming and hawing about what that threat meant. "It's going to be a hell of a lot more violent than it was in Korea or Vietnam," Beam explained. The crowd was excited now. "If you want our country for the whites, you're going to have to get it the way our founding fathers got it—with blood, blood, blood." It would be necessary to "fight, fight, fight." Toward that end, Beam offered to train

American fishermen in his paramilitary camps. "When you come out of there, you'll be ready for the Vietnamese," he said, smiling.

Someone had brought an old shrimp boat to the rally. Someone else had painted the words *USS Vietcong* on its hull. A third person now doused the boat with five gallons of diesel fuel. Beam set a torch to it. "This is the right way to burn a shrimp boat," he shouted. "This is in-service training." The flames shot up into the starry night, silhouetting the robed figure against the Texas sky. As the fire consumed the boat, the crowd cheered, "Fight, fight, fight."

Fisher also spoke. He couldn't match Beam's pyrotechnics, but his words were just as hot. "I'll be here fishing five to ten years from now, even if I have to run over every gook in my way," he said.

Over the next month life became more and more dangerous for the Vietnamese fishermen and the Americans who were their friends or business associates or rented them space to dock their boats: Two crosses were burned, one in the yard of a Vietnamese shrimper, one near a marina in the town of Kemah where several refugees docked their boats; Fisher told Emery Waite, another dock owner, that the only way to deal with the refugees was to "drop a bomb in Saigon Harbor," the nickname given American Jim Craig's Old Seafood Harbor; two men approached American fisherman Leon Bateman and offered to burn Vietnamese boats; the Anderwall family received phone threats, Klan cards in the mailbox, and two visits from American fishermen who threatened to burn their house and the Vietnamese boat docked at their wharf unless they forced the owner, Mr. Khang, to move his boat; David Collins brandished an AR-15 semiautomatic rifle for the press and announced he'd have armed members of the Klan on shrimping boats when the season began; a Vietnamese boat was burned.

Understandably, the Vietnamese grew increasingly fearful and disillusioned. "I'm glad I got out of Vietnam, but I'm sorry I came here, because the people are against us," shrimper Dyen Troung told a reporter. Colonel Nam told a group of seventy-five shrimpers at a meeting arranged by the governor's task force on refugees, "If you no like me to stay, yes sir, I leave."

These events attracted little notice outside the Houston area, but that's no great surprise. Ronald Reagan had just been inaugurated; the men and women held hostage in Iran by the Ayatollah had just come home. The nation and the media were interested in other things than the plight of some Vietnamese fishermen.

It wasn't until March 15 that Beam's outfit did something outrageous enough to attract national publicity. On that morning, a group including American fishermen and fifteen Klan members gathered at the Seabrook dock and boarded Jody Collins's shrimp boat. Some, like Jim Stanfield, wore robes and hoods; others wore black Ku Klux Klan T-shirts; a few were dressed in army fatigues. They were well armed. Some had shotguns; some had semiautomatic assault weapons.

They carried an odd cargo—one cannon and one mock human figure that they quickly hanged by the neck in effigy on the rigging at the boat's stern. Beam was not present. David Collins took the helm, guiding his brother's boat from the pier.

The boat moved slowly along the Seabrook side of Clear Creek Channel until it came to Colonel Nam's home. Collins pulled up to the dock and stopped the boat. Somebody on board started gesturing toward the house. The colonel and his wife were not home. The boat remained at the dock for five minutes. Phuong Pham, the colonel's thirteen-year-old sister-in-law, was in the house baby-sitting Nam's little girl. Phuong looked out the window and saw the men in robes and hoods. She saw their weapons, saw the figure hanging from the back of the boat. She grabbed her niece and ran from the house.

Collins motored back into Galveston Bay. About a mile offshore, somebody on board placed a blank round into the cannon and fired it. It was heard up and down the coast, shattering the Saturday morning tranquility. "Let's hear it for the American fishermen," Collins shouted. His passengers cheered.

The boat moved on through the channel, stopping at Jim Craig's Old Seafood Harbor where some refugees were working on their boats. Mr. Hoy, a Vietnamese shrimper, was terrified. Craig came out; he, too, was shaken to see the armed Klan members.

After several hours of such maneuvers on the water, Collins finally docked the boat.

I read about the Klan's boat ride in the *New York Times*. This wasn't the first I'd heard about the problems on the Gulf Coast. Klanwatch, although in its infancy and nothing like the sophisticated operation it is today, was aware that the Klan had established a beachhead on Galveston Bay. But not until we learned of this terror on Clear Creek Channel did we think that we might have a chance to battle Mr. Beam.

We had begun to keep a file on Klan figures, writing down what we knew about them on three-by-five-inch file cards. Like Bill Wilkinson and David Duke, Beam was touted as one of the new breed of Klansmen. The Klan was changing its rhetoric and its approach to capitalize on the political shift to the right evidenced by Reagan's election. Some extremists were beginning to turn in their robes for combat boots, creating paramilitary organizations to complement traditional Klan activities, and talking about establishing their own whites-only homeland by whatever means.

I read all the information we had about Beam. "He may look different from some of those old-timers like Bobby Shelton, and he may talk different, too," I told Vahala, "but he smells the same. When it comes right down to it, they're all yellow-bellied sons of bitches."

The article in the *Times* hadn't described all the incidents on the bay, but it had mentioned that Colonel Nam was the leader of the Vietnamese Fishermen's Association. It sounded to me as though he could use our help. I picked up the phone and dialed information in Seabrook, Texas.

CHAPTER 2

"This is the place," said John Hayslip, the lawyer Colonel Nam had referred me to.

I stopped my rental car in front of a modest white frame house sitting on pillars along Clear Creek Channel. Three Vietnamese men stood by the front steps. They watched us closely as we got out of the car.

"After that Klan boat came by, these fellows just appeared and started guarding the colonel. They really respect him down here," explained Hayslip, a stout man in his late thirties with a small law practice in nearby Texas City. He had done a lot of work for the Vietnamese refugees. When I had suggested taking the Klan to court, he had been enthusiastic.

Colonel Nam met us at the front door, a handsome man in his late forties with shiny black hair combed straight back. His greeting was courteous but reserved. He carried himself like an officer.

We followed the colonel to his den which looked out over the calm, blue channel. I could see the colonel's boat docked at the end of a short wooden pier. I was no expert on shrimping vessels, but this one didn't look too seaworthy. A coat of paint couldn't disguise its age and battle scars.

The colonel pointed to a VCR and told us he had taped everything concerning the conflict that had been on the news. He wanted to show the tape to me, but I asked him to wait a bit. I let him talk about himself, his business, his problems. I like to do that with all potential clients. It's important to get a feel for them, to gauge their honesty and resolve.

Resolve would be particularly important if we were to sue Beam and the Klan. A lawsuit would probably intensify the threats and intimidation. Hayslip had said the Vietnamese fishermen were already thinking about leaving town instead of standing their ground. If we got into the middle of a case and the heat scared the refugees, it could be fatal.

It was clear from our conversation that the colonel had backbone. He proudly told me that he had battled the North Vietnamese until the last American was safely out of Vietnam. "And now this Louis Beam say *we* are Communists," said the colonel.

"Colonel Nam," I said, "Beam is a dangerous man. I'd like to talk to you about stopping him."

Colonel Nam's baby daughter toddled into the room. The colonel's wife hurried in and picked her up, bowed politely to me and Hayslip, and left without a word.

The colonel shook his head. "We don't want to cause no trouble, Mr. Dees. We appreciate being in America."

"You're not the ones causing trouble," I said.

The colonel rose and motioned for us to follow him. We walked out onto his pier. He pointed to several Vietnamese-owned boats nearby. Few looked seaworthy. All bore *For Sale* signs. "Many people think it's best if we let the Klan have its way," he sighed.

"I don't think *you* do," I said.

He shook his head.

I explained what we had in mind. We wanted to get an injunction in federal court in Houston preventing Beam and the rest of his crew from ever intimidating the Vietnamese and interfering with their right to fish. But because it might take several months to hold a hearing on this permanent injunction, we wanted to secure a preliminary injunction before the fishing season began to prevent Beam and the Klan and Fisher and the American Fishermen's Association from carrying out their threats of violence.

I told the colonel there were several legal tactics that might work. I was pretty sure we could use the civil rights statutes enacted by Congress after the Civil War to protect blacks and then expanded by the courts to protect others from class-based animosity. I thought the U.S. Constitution and Texas laws might also provide relief.

I thought we might even be able to cite the Sherman Antitrust Act's provisions prohibiting restraint of trade. Trade: Besides outright discrimination this was at the bottom of things in Galveston Bay. The Americans didn't want the Vietnamese shrimpers to compete.

We talked for an hour. The colonel was interested, but he was also worried. The *New York Times* article had only mentioned Beam's boat-burning rally and the March 15 boat ride, not the specifics of the month of terror between the two events. The colonel told me about many other acts of intimidation, then showed me the videotape. This would be good material if we went to court. But Colonel Nam was afraid that if the lawsuit was filed, the Klan's threats of violence would become real.

"I won't lie to you," I said. "That's a possibility. But I think the best way to make sure there isn't any violence is by going to court."

The colonel thought for a moment. "I have to bring this up with the association. It's their decision whether we do something," he said.

"I understand that, sir," I said. "But you need to do it soon. The fishing season's coming up real fast."

I looked one last time over the vast bay before leaving. There was no way the Coast Guard could protect every shrimping boat out on that water. It would be easy for Louis Beam and Gene Fisher to run over the "gooks." They could pull alongside the refugees and toss in a jug of burning gasoline. They could take their AR-15s, kill everyone, and then speed off. In his writing, Beam often bragged about the number of the enemy he had shot and killed from his helicopter in Vietnam. He had to be stopped in Galveston Bay.

On the drive back to town, Hayslip said he thought the meeting had gone well. "I learned a few things myself," he said sincerely. "I never heard of the Sherman Act being used in a civil rights action."

Neither had I. I didn't know if the tactic would work. For that matter, I didn't know if we could successfully use the civil rights statutes. Seabrook was not Decatur—not yet, anyway. No one had been physically harmed, and no evidence linked any particular individuals to the burning of the boats that belonged to the Vietnamese.

To win a preliminary injunction, we'd have to show that the Vietnamese fishermen would suffer irreparable injury if the court didn't act. A judge would decide whether there were grounds to hold a hearing for such an injunction before the fishing season. If the judge didn't think those grounds existed and instead scheduled a hearing for after May 15, we might as well forget it. Most of the Vietnamese fishermen, afraid that Beam and the rest of their antagonists would "fight, fight, fight," would be gone, gone, gone from Galveston Bay.

The Vietnamese Fishermen's Association gave us the green light before week's end. Almost immediately, the Center's Mike Vahala and Randall Williams traveled to Seabrook to assemble the facts necessary for a lawsuit. Hayslip and two Catholic priests (one Vietnamese and one American) worked with Mike and Randall. When reporting instances of harassment on the water, the refugees had not always found the Coast Guard and other law enforcement agencies sympathetic. The Catholic church had been supportive, and the priests had assiduously recorded all reported threats.

Some of those acts occurred while Mike and Randall were in Seabrook. On April 3, two men assumed to be working with the Klan or the American Fishermen's Association drove their red-and-white pickup truck to My's Seafood in Seabrook and pointed a pistol at Miss Do Thi Do, the Vietnamese owner.

The Center has always been blessed with exceptional attorneys. The lawyers backing me up on this case were typical. Steve Ellmann, a thirty-year-old graduate of Harvard Law School, came south to clerk for the Eleventh Circuit of the U.S. Court of Appeals before joining us. The son of Professor Richard Ellmann, the world's foremost scholar on James Joyce, Steve was not only brilliant, but an idealist in his beliefs. Tall and slender, with inquisitive eyes that radiated compassion and warmth, he was a master at taking my gut-reaction legal theories and making sense of them.

While Steve would do virtually all the brief writing on this case, John Carroll, the Center's law director, would also play an important role. An ex-marine who had served in Vietnam, John had graduated at the top of his class at Cumberland Law School in Birmingham. After receiving his master's in Constitutional Law from Harvard, he had joined the Center and became my sounding board for ideas on the nuts and bolts of our cases.

We worked quickly, filing our complaint on April 16, three weeks after my visit. The opening of the fishing season, the day on which Beam's "Grand Dragon's dispensation" expired, was four weeks away.

Before the complaint was even filed, we retained David Berg and Philip Zelikow, two excellent Houston trial lawyers, as local counsel. They kindly agreed to volunteer their services. We always want local counsel in these cases: They can handle emergencies, prep us on local court customs, and show us the best restaurants and pool halls. If properly chosen they can exercise clout and deal with local attorneys or officials who might be suspicious of outsiders. And, in jury trials, they can also show jurors that there's a local connection to the case, that we're not just a bunch of hired guns from out of town fighting a battle that really doesn't affect us.

There would not be a jury in this case. We were seeking injunctive relief, a matter decided solely by the judge. A dozen judges sat in the district court where we filed the suit. When the court's lottery system assigned Judge Gabrielle McDonald to our case, we couldn't have been happier: Judge McDonald was a black woman in her late thirties who had tried civil rights cases as an attorney before her appointment to the bench by Jimmy Carter.

Beam knew the luck of the draw had gone our way. He moved that the judge, whom he described as a negress, remove herself from the case. She refused.

Colonel Nam's statement to the press was an eloquent summary of the lawsuit.

> Today, the Vietnamese Fishermen's Association has filed suit in Federal District Court to protect the rights of its members from intimidation, harassment, threats, violence, and other illegal actions by those who would attempt to illegally obstruct them from fishing in Galveston Bay.
>
> We are asking the court to issue an injunction against the named defendants enjoining them from any acts or conduct that would deprive the association's members of their legal rights to pursue their commercial fishing operations as protected by the laws of the state of Texas and the United States.
>
> I have stated in the past that I and other members of the association would voluntarily leave the Galveston Bay area if this was necessary to prevent our property from being destroyed, to protect the lives of our families, and to be able to carry on a livelihood free from harassment.
>
> While members of the association consider their options of leaving or staying, we have decided to seek the protection of the laws of this nation that were written to protect the free operation of a person's business and that protect a person's life and property from illegal acts.
>
> We Vietnamese came to this country seeking a land of freedom where we could raise our families in peace. Those of us who have settled in the Galveston Bay area have worked hard to be good citizens and to spend our time in productive work. We have come to love our new home and to hope that, for us and for our children, the American dream will become a reality.

Beam's promise of "blood" by May 15 was enough to move us over our first legal hurdle. Judge McDonald scheduled our hearing for a preliminary injunction for May 11. That would give her just enough time to render a decision before the boats took to the water. Whether it would leave enough time to prepare our case was another matter.

It didn't take long for the Klan to let us know what it thought about our lawsuit. On the morning after we filed, David Berg found an unmarked envelope outside his office door. Inside the envelope was a photocopy of the Klan's calling card, warning Berg not to let this "social visit" be followed by a "business call." Two nights later Berg found another envelope and calling card waiting for him at home. He received these threats with a mixture of fear and humor, nervously joking that Beam was facing his worst nightmare: a black judge and a Jewish lawyer.

The next shots in this war of nerves were fired from a camera on April 30, the opening day of depositions, my first face-to-face encounter with Gene Fisher and the armed Louis Beam. We had just arrived at the offices of the defendants' lawyers and settled our clients in the conference room when a young blond man entered and began taking pictures of Colonel Nam and the other plaintiffs. Despite the protests of Randall Williams—I was down the hall with Sam Adamo—the intruder continued firing away, poking his camera right into the faces of the refugees.

Randall asked the photographer his name. When the man mumbled something about being a soldier, Randall fetched me.

I was outraged. "Beam's behind this," I said as we hurried to the conference room.

The man was still clicking away. "Sir, this is a private room. You're going to have to leave," I said.

No response. I thought about picking him up and carrying him out, then figured that wasn't the best way to start the first day of depositions. I summoned Adamo, who, after telling me he thought the man was Beam's photographer, persuaded him to leave.

Exit the photographer, enter Gene Fisher, a scowling, heavyset man with dark hair and a bushy moustache. I couldn't gauge how articulate he was; he took the Fifth Amendment to almost every question I asked. We would have to go to Judge McDonald the next morning to get an order instructing him to answer.

Before terminating Fisher's deposition, I wanted to resolve the mystery of the intruder. His actions were one more example of harassment. Linking him to Beam might strengthen our case. Fortunately, the man had not left Adamo's offices. Instead of making us go through the formal procedure of subpoenaing him for a deposition, Adamo advised the photographer to answer questions limited to his behavior in the conference room.

The man told us his name was Russell Gregory Thatcher. He refused to give his address. I asked him why.

"Hardening the target," he answered. "You minimize the output of information about yourself."

Another nut case, I thought. I pressed him on why he needed to minimize such information.

"It's simple military tactics and procedure." Thatcher's intense blue eyes scanned the room like one of those security cameras in a bank. I had no idea whom he expected to confront.

Despite Thatcher's effort to minimize information output, I established that he was a friend of Louis Beam and that Beam had given him the time and address of the day's depositions. He refused to state whether he had ever trained at Beam's paramilitary camps, first on the grounds that it might incriminate him, then, "because I'm a survivalist, and as a survivalist I minimize my contact with the enemy under such circumstances as this right here."

Q: And who do you perceive to be your enemy here?
A: I perceive you as one of my enemies. . . . You're a tool of the system which I find oppressive to basic human rights, those human rights as founded by the Constitution—not human rights but through civil rights, and as such you're my enemy.

I wasn't sure what he meant, but I knew I'd rather be his enemy than his friend.

I asked him if he was a Nazi, a member of the National Socialist Party.

"Yes," said Thatcher.

Why had he taken the pictures? "This is a historical event," he said. "Any confrontation between the supposed authorities of the country and those that . . . are subverting our land as opposed to a person like Louis Beam, I consider it a historical event, and it should be recorded for posterity."

To some, Thatcher's behavior might seem nothing more than comical. But Thatcher was a Nazi and, probably, a trainee in Beam's paramilitary Texas Emergency Reserve. His eyes danced like those of a zealot. He peppered his language with military phrases. Clearly, he saw the world as us versus them and was willing to do something about it, whether in Greensboro, Seabrook, Chattanooga, or Houston. Today he had only pointed a loaded camera. Next time we might not be so lucky.

We didn't have to wait very long for "next time." A few minutes later, Beam came in for his deposition, raising the stakes in this game of intimidation. Colonel Nam saw the revolver, and we were through for the day.

Did Beam want us to see his gun? Did he plan to use it? We had no desire to find out. By the end of this very first day of discovery, we had filed our first motion for a protective order. We wanted all future depositions held at the federal courthouse with a U.S. marshall present.

Judge McDonald would hear the motion the next day. Before she had a chance, somebody gave us more ammunition. Five hours after we filed the motion, David Berg was driving home when he noticed a red-and-white pickup truck pull out from the curb and start following his car. It was hard not to notice. Either the driver was clumsy at tailing or he had meant for Berg to see him.

Instead of pulling into his driveway, Berg continued past his house. At the first intersection he took a right turn, then stopped his car. The pickup truck took a left, turned around in a driveway, and then headed back toward Berg.

A fit, well-built man in his mid-thirties, Berg was one of the best criminal defense attorneys in Texas, no stranger to the world of danger and violence. The truck reached the intersection. Berg steeled himself for a confrontation. But suddenly, the truck turned right and sped away. Berg gave chase, but couldn't catch up.

When Berg called to tell me what had happened, I remembered that the men who had pointed a gun at Do Thi Do in front of My's Seafood had also driven a red-and-white pickup. We added this latest threat to the catalog when we presented our motion to Judge McDonald the next morning. The judge already seemed sensitive to the situation: The hearing on the motion was held in her chambers instead of open court. Marshalls stood outside the door with hand-held metal detectors to monitor all who entered or waited outside the chambers. Only the lawyers were allowed in. Beam and the defendants waited outside with the press corps that had grown day by day.

Beam carried a tote bag. Reporters asked him what was inside.

"I carry my robe like a soldier carries his uniform," he said. "When I make a public appearance, I put it on. . . . Thank God it's permanent press."

He described me as a "demon possessed" and said he'd kept a holy cross between us during the aborted deposition. "Dees is a wizard," he continued. "He's concocted in his black pot all these fancy words and phrases." Then he accused me of diverting attention away from the real issues in Galveston Bay. "These Alabama lawyers care nothing about the Vietnamese fishermen. I care more than they do, and I'm going to prove it. They're just concerned about getting the Klan," Beam said.

After a short hearing, Judge McDonald ruled in our favor. All depositions would be taken at the Federal Building with U.S. marshalls present. No guns would be allowed. Beam could wear his robe, but no hood. We were relieved. Beam said he was relieved, too. "I appreciate the protection of federal marshalls because a man possessed of a demon is capable of any atrocity," he said.

We took Beam's deposition two days later on Sunday, May 3. As expected, he wrapped himself in the American flag. He argued that he always told his men to refrain from doing anything illegal. While he couldn't remember whether he made some of the inflammatory statements attributed to him by the press after the February 14 boat-burning, he didn't deny most of them. He refused to answer questions about the operation of paramilitary camps because he was under indictment by the federal government for trespassing on federal grasslands while conducting a paramilitary training camp. (He was later found guilty of this misdemeanor, but the conviction was overturned on appeal.) However, he did admit he had invited American fishermen to attend those camps. He said he'd told the fishermen that after training with him, they'd be ready to take on "the Vietcong." (We had previously thought he had said they'd be ready to take on "the Vietnamese." This was a critical difference and would have to be resolved.) At the same time, he said he was a friend of the refugees, had fought for them in Vietnam.

We knew this "friend" of the refugees had scheduled a rally on behalf of the American fishermen for May 9 in Santa Fe and had invited the Nazis. Who would speak? Beam's response was chilling.

Richard Butler was coming from his compound in Hayden Lakes, Idaho. Butler, a sixty-year-old former aerospace engineer, was the patriarch of the militant right, the leader of the Aryan Nations. He had called for the establishment of an all-white nation in America's Northwest. He had popularized the Identity religion among right-wing extremists through his Church of Jesus Christ Christian.

The Identity religion was another vicious effort to use the Bible to justify hate violence. Butler and his followers believed that Jews were the descendants of Satan and white Anglo-Saxons were the true Israelites, God's Chosen People. They also believed in an impending worldwide race war which only whites would survive. Beam was a loyal member of Butler's flock. In his speeches and writing, Butler emphasized the need to take back control of the government from the Jewish conspiracy using blacks, Vietnamese, Hispanics, and other people of color to destroy America.

I asked Beam if Butler belonged to the Nazi party. "There are no Nazis. World War Two is over. We're suffering from paranoia," he responded. He said he didn't like efforts to link the Nazis to his group. "They're National Socialists. I'm a Constitutionalist. God's law is in the Constitution. A National Socialist is fine for Germany; this is Texas. We've got the Constitution."

Another face from the right-wing rogue's gallery was also expected in Santa Fe. Beam acknowledged: "I have invited the Greensboro hero from that Greensboro shooting. You may remember that the Klan lawfully, with the will of God behind them, executed five Communists in Greensboro, North Carolina, and was found innocent of any wrongdoing by a jury of their peers, and I have invited one of them to Texas to tell us why they felt it was necessary to do what they did in Greensboro." I wondered what Colonel Nam was thinking as he heard this.

We thought the deposition had gone well. We thought the whole case was going well. Mike and Randall had found several Vietnamese and Americans who had been threatened or intimidated; most were willing to give us statements. While some, like Margaret Anderwall, had expressed fear of testifying on behalf of the Vietnamese fishermen, we hoped that they would. Their testimony was needed to demonstrate that Beam, Fisher, and their groups were interfering with the refugees' rights to pursue their trade.

Of course, at their depositions Beam and Fisher denied they were making threats or encouraging others to harass the refugees. Each claimed he had nothing to do with the March 15 boat ride. Beam further insisted that any of his comments that might be interpreted as threatening to the refugees had been directed at the Vietcong and North Vietnamese who had settled in Texas, not the loyal Vietnamese. "[The Vietcong] will, if they get the opportunity—and you, Mr. Dees, may provide it to them—they will cause a dispute or trouble between us and these Vietnamese. And I am going to try to stop that."

Any violence, Beam continued, would be the fault of outsiders. "It wouldn't surprise me a bit if a Vietcong or former North Vietnamese agent doesn't toss a firebomb in them boats. I don't believe really that these Vietnamese would burn their own boats, but I think it's a very possible thing that an agent of Hanoi or an agent of Ho Chi Minh City"—Beam paused and spit to indicate his contempt—"sent someone over here to burn those boats."

We needed to demonstrate that the perpetrators here weren't the Vietcong or any other imaginary scapegoats the creative Mr. Beam wanted to blame, but Beam's own men or members of the American Fishermen's Association. Beam and Fisher wouldn't help us make the connections. During their depositions they initially refused to name the members of their organizations. They each admitted destroying membership lists within recent days in anticipation of being asked to reveal allies. And without the lists, each said innocently, they simply couldn't remember names. At one point Fisher insisted he alone was the entire American Fishermen's Association, although he did admit he had collected money from several American fishermen to press his cause.

Undaunted, Mike and Randall assembled photographs of trainees at Beam's camps and of customers at Beam's bookstore. They showed these along with photos of the March 15 boat ride to refugees and other locals to see if they recognized anyone.

The morning after Beam's deposition, Randall, Mike, and I were discussing how pleased we were with the progress of the case when Colonel Nam called. He wanted to meet immediately. He sounded troubled.

"Thank you for coming," the colonel said as we sat down in his living room. Then he let me have it. "The elders of our community have asked me to talk to you, Morris. We want to thank you for representing us, but we have decided to drop our lawsuit."

I was stunned. The climate was certainly frightening. Thatcher's camera and Beam's gun had unnerved all of us, and rumors were floating that the Klan intended to kill Colonel Nam and me. But the hearing was only a week away. If the colonel and his friends could just hang tough . . .

"Colonel, we've got Beam on the ropes now. We've taken all these depositions. We've got a good case here. I think we can win," I said.

"I understand," the colonel said. "But what can a court injunction do? If they want to shoot you in the night, they can."

I explained again that if the court ruled in the refugees' favor and then anyone violated that order, he would go to prison for contempt. Of course, I realized that if a Klansman shot someone, the fact that he might go to prison would provide little consolation to his victim. But I truly believed that with the court looking over their shoulders, the defendants would be less likely to bother, much less shoot, the Vietnamese.

"Morris, this is not my decision alone," said Colonel Nam. "The elders feel there is bad blood. They say if we don't stop now, the Americans will be mad at more than the fishermen, be mad at all of the Vietnamese businessmen." He explained that the Vietnamese business community—owners of restaurants, flower shops, convenience stores, and other establishments—feared economic repercussions if the case went forward and the Vietnamese were portrayed as threatening to the Americans.

As much as I wanted to fight Beam and the Klan here and now, my obligation was to my clients. If they wanted to drop the suit, I'd drop the suit—but not without trying to persuade them that it was in their interest to continue.

"Colonel, I'd like to talk to those people who made the decision. I'd like to meet with the elders."

The colonel looked surprised. He got up from his chair, walked over to the window, and stared out over the channel for a long time. "I'll see what I can do," he said.

I couldn't tell whether his heart was with the elders or with me.

A priest led me down a church corridor to a small meeting room. Forty Vietnamese elders, some dressed in suits and ties, some in traditional Vietnamese clothing, sat in two wide rows of folding chairs. I joined Colonel Nam and an interpreter at a table in front.

"Sometimes lawyers are called counselors," I began. "I'd like to give you my counsel tonight."

I was so excited, I was speaking too fast. The interpreter signaled for me to slow down. I took a deep breath.

"I don't really know what your vision of America was before you came to live in this country, how you thought you'd be treated here. But I'm ashamed at the way you have been treated. In the United States all citizens are supposed to be treated equally, regardless of race, creed, or color. It doesn't matter if you're black or Jewish or Vietnamese, whatever, our Constitution provides for equal treatment under the law.

"Unfortunately, just because something is written down on a piece of paper, even if that paper is the Constitution, doesn't mean that everyone is going to respect it and abide by it. When I was growing up in Alabama, Constitution or not, black folks were second-class citizens. They had to fight for their rights. Dr. Martin Luther King, Jr., and others gave up their lives so their brothers and sisters could have their lawful rights.

"One of the groups that wanted to keep the blacks in their place was the Ku Klux Klan, the same Ku Klux Klan that wants you to pack up your bags and get out of town. I sure hope you don't think these people, people like Louis Beam and others hiding in their hoods, represent America. Because they don't. The Klan is nothing but your basic group of criminals and outlaws.

"I know the Klan, and I know that if your fishermen leave without putting up a fight, Louis Beam and his crew will not stop. You've heard the talk. Some folks are saying the Vietnamese shouldn't even be allowed to live on the coast. It may be the fishermen that feel the heat now, but you can be sure that if they get the fishermen to give up today, then they'll go after the rest of you tomorrow. 'Why should the Seven-Eleven be run by a foreigner? Why aren't there any Americans employed at the flower shop? This is hurting American business.' That's what they'll say.

"You have just as much right to be here as Louis Beam or Gene Fisher. That is what America is really about. That's what the people who came to this country over two centuries ago as immigrants just like you had in mind. That's the vision of America you have to believe in and fight for. You have to—"

A slow, rhythmic clapping had begun. It wasn't terribly loud, but it was steady. I had no idea what it meant. The expression on the faces of the elders hadn't changed. It was just that now they were clapping—slowly, steadily. Were they trying to get me to sit down? Was it meant as a jeer? Were they behind me?

I looked at Colonel Nam. He, too, was clapping, but his face was as impassive as the faces of the elders. I looked at the interpreter, a young Vietnamese-American who was a pilot for Pan Am. He smiled. "They like what you are saying," he said.

Tears came to my eyes. I walked out from behind the table; I wanted the elders to feel my emotions. "It's up to you all," I said. "I just want you to know your lawyers are behind you. In a week this will be all over and then a court of law will show you the America today is not the America of Louis Beam, but an America where the color of your skin or the country you came from doesn't make a difference."

I moved back behind the table. Colonel Nam nodded. "Please wait with the priests while we talk," he said.

I was pacing restlessly in the priests' office when the colonel returned from the meeting room. "We'll continue with the lawsuit," he said. I moved to hug him, but then stopped—that kind of display of emotion would be inappropriate. I bowed. He bowed back, betraying a slight smile.

I couldn't promise Colonel Nam that it would be any safer over the next week. The following day Beam threatened me with his "You die" chant, and then assumed the firing position as Vahala and I left the parking lot. I stayed up late that night drafting our second motion for a protective order and the motion seeking a court-ordered psychiatric examination of Beam.

Judge McDonald set the hearing on the motions for May 8. That gave us two more days without protection. I didn't want to give Beam a chance to harm me or anybody else. My younger brother Leslie had a business in Montgomery supplying firearms and other equipment to law enforcement officers. I asked him to rush bulletproof vests for the entire Center staff working in Texas, and a gun for me. We had them before the day was out.

Beam wasn't happy with our motion. He said if he had to undergo such a test, he wanted me to undergo a religious examination to determine if I were possessed by demons. "Let's find out who is insane," he told the press.

Before the hearing, we discovered just how "insane" Beam was. An anonymous student at Rice University in Houston called David Berg's office and reported that he knew a student who had filmed Beam extensively. It wasn't too long before Randall and Mike were in a dormitory visiting Wayne Derrick, a budding young filmmaker whom Beam had hired to document his rise to power. Derrick said he had videotape of Beam's paramilitary camps; Beam and Fisher's initial meeting; the boat-burning rally and Beam's speech. A gold mine! We secured these tapes with a subpoena.

The hearing took two hours. Judge McDonald told Beam in no uncertain terms that if he harassed us anymore, he would find himself in jail. "I will warn you, Mr. Beam, I will find you in contempt," she said.

I took the witness stand. Under cross-examination Adamo asked me if I really felt threatened. "Yes," I said. "I've studied Mr. Beam's statements. I've looked at over five hundred newspaper accounts, what he said to an undercover investigator, and television tapes of his speeches. His attitude is that he is going to kill those people he doesn't believe in. Quite frankly, I think that he is insane."

The judge refused to provide us special protection, but she enjoined Beam and the other defendants from contacting us and "making threatening and vile remarks, unsolicited hand gestures, and other distracting actions toward the plaintiff's counsel."

Before the hearing we had withdrawn our motion asking the court to order a mental examination of Beam. The judge had indicated she didn't have the power to do so. Besides, we'd accomplished our purpose: showing the world who Louis Beam was and showing Louis Beam who he was up against. We knew we had embarrassed the Grand Dragon in his own backyard. We didn't know we had sown the seeds for a vendetta that would last for years and become more dangerous at every turn.

When I had been on the witness stand, Berg had asked me how I regarded Beam. "I think he's a nut," I said, "but I am not going to turn my back on him." That was Louis Beam. There were elements of the buffoon in his behavior, but nobody—not me, not the Vietnamese fishermen, the state of Texas, or the United States government—could afford to ignore him or pretend that he was just some harmless ideologue.

"I've got the Bible in one hand and a thirty-eight in the other hand," Beam had recently told a Ku Klux Klan convention, "and I know what to do." If that was all there was in his arsenal, he would have been worth watching. But he also possessed the power to move people and had his own army, equipped with semiautomatic assault weapons and U.S. Army surplus vehicles—considerably more firepower than the scriptures and one revolver.

Our legal team spent long hours trying to figure out how to put an end to the Texas Emergency Reserve at the same time we stopped the Klan from bothering the Vietnamese. As the date of the hearing neared and we compiled more and more information about Beam's secret paramilitary operations, we finally hit on a strategy. We amended our original complaint and asked the court to bar Beam from conducting any guerrilla operations in Texas. Among other things, we argued, Beam's camps violated a state law prohibiting private paramilitary training. This was the knockout punch we were looking for. If the court ruled our way on this, for all intents and purposes, Louis Beam would be out of business.

CHAPTER 3

May 1981   Houston, Texas

By the time Judge McDonald ascended to the bench, the courtroom
was full. David Berg, Phillip Zelikow, and I sat at one of the mahogany tables in front of the judge along with Colonel Nam, the three
other plaintiffs from the Vietnamese Fishermen's Association, and our
interpreter. Randall Williams and Mike Vahala were close behind us
with boxes of indexed exhibits. A few feet away sat defendants Beam,
Fisher, Stanfield, and the Collins brothers, and their lawyers, Sam
Adamo and Richard Cobb.

The difference between the tables was dramatic. The refugees wore
suits and ties. Their shirts were neatly pressed, shoes newly shined.
Despite the shabby treatment they had received in America, their
respect for the court was apparent.

The contempt of the defendants for the proceedings, in this land
whose institutions and traditions they constantly invoked, was equally
apparent. Beer-bellied Gene Fisher wore dirty brown slacks and a
work shirt. The Collins brothers, in the typical fishermen's outfit of
blue jeans and blue work shirt, looked as if they had just come out
of a barroom brawl. Jim Stanfield, also wearing blue jeans and an
oil-stained blue work shirt, hadn't even bothered to clean the grease
from his hands. Only Louis Beam wore a coat and tie, having es-
chewed the Klan robe he had threatened to wear.

Security was tight. Federal marshalls sat by the entrance to the
courtroom and by the door leading from the courtroom to the judge's
chambers. Everyone had to pass through special metal detectors.

The press occupied one bench in the gallery, as did the friends and
families of the refugees. Beam's supporters outnumbered them hand-
ily.

Richard Butler, who had come for the weekend rally in Santa Fe (thankfully, an uneventful affair), had stayed for the trial. Dressed in a blue suit and tie, he looked, at first glance, more like an aerospace engineer or grandfather than the keeper of Hitler's flame. Then I noticed the arm band he was wearing: a Nazi swastika and sword. When I caught his eye, he burned a hole through me. Another man, dressed identically, sat next to Butler. Behind them several more Beam loyalists, decked out in black Ku Klux Klan shirts or army-type fatigues, had come to watch. Many sported SS bands on their arms. It was all right with me if they wanted to dress like that. We like to be able to identify the opposition. These folks wouldn't score any points for the defendants by wearing their militancy on their sleeves.

As I set my briefcase on the table, I locked eyes with Beam. It actually took me an instant to realize that victory at the trial wasn't linked to whoever held out longer. I smiled at the Grand Dragon and turned away. He could win this one. I'd wait until I cornered him on the witness stand.

I pulled the witness list from my briefcase, then thought about what we were trying to do. It wasn't that complicated. We were dealing with two types of harm to the Vietnamese fishermen: personal and economic. On the personal level, we wanted to prove that the intimidation and threats of violence violated the refugees' constitutional and civil rights. On the economic level, we wanted to show that our clients were not being permitted to pursue their chosen trade. At the same time as we would make the case to prevent specific acts directed at the Vietnamese, we would also argue for the elimination of Beam's entire paramilitary operation. Here we had to paint for the court a picture of what was going on, demonstrating that the maneuvers actually constituted illegal paramilitary training. We had to show that the Texas Emergency Reserve was more than a group of guys getting together and playing war games or taking target practice.

The two most important witnesses worried us most. The first of these was Margaret Anderwall, the dock owner who had terminated her business relationship with a Vietnamese fisherman as a direct result of the Klan's threats. Her testimony would be crucial, but she had told Randall that she was so afraid of the Klan she didn't want to take the stand.

The second troublesome witness was Beam himself. He was such a loose cannon, we had no idea what he would say or how he would react. We needed to link him and his Klan to the threats and acts of violence, force him to admit his inflammatory statements, and talk about his paramilitary operations.

Defendant Gene Fisher, the disenchanted native who had triggered the chain of events by calling in Beam and the Klan, was our first witness. He described how he had approached Beam, repeating his motivation: that the Klan was the only group with the courage to stand by its convictions. He admitted that Beam had offered military training to the American fishermen and admitted telling the press that fifty to sixty of his fellow fishermen were training at Beam's camps. However, he said that he had been "lying" when he had reported this to the media.

Fisher had made many incendiary remarks over the last six months, some of which he admitted. He did not deny proclaiming that, if requested, his "organization" would put armed men on boats when the season began.

Paul Grey, an agent for the Federal Bureau of Alcohol, Tobacco, and Firearms, followed Fisher. He showed Judge McDonald photographs of the boats burned in the Seabrook area and testified that in his expert opinion the fires were caused by arson.

Dock owners Jim Craig and Ernest Blansfield told of threats they had received from American fishermen and Klansmen for doing business with the Vietnamese and testified that they had taken those threats seriously. Craig noted that Fisher had warned him, "Watch your boats. They're easy to burn." While we couldn't prove who had burned any of the refugees' boats, this testimony strongly suggested who might be responsible.

Do Thi Do, Colonel Nam, and Phuong Pham also testified about the acts of intimidation. Phuong Pham, the thirteen-year-old baby-sitter who had been threatened by the Klansmen on their March 15 boat ride, was still so traumatized that she initially refused to appear. She was terrified that the Klansmen would pay a return visit if she took the stand. Only when Judge McDonald agreed to allow the examination to take place in chambers without the defendants present did Phuong Pham come forward. Her heroism and the heroism of the sympathetic Americans, who risked social and economic ostracism and perhaps physical danger, inspired all of us. And it was essential: We had to show that a pattern of harassment had developed—not just one isolated incident, but a series of incidents pointing to the doorsteps of Beam and Fisher.

A Vietnamese fisherman named Phuoc Dang also provided important testimony about the climate of danger. Mike Vahala had located
him and taken his statement a few weeks earlier. Mr. Dang told Mike
that he had been out on the water in his shrimp boat when an American boat had deliberately and without provocation come dangerously
close to ramming his boat. Then, as the boat passed, one of the
Americans pointed a weapon at him.

As Mr. Dang's time to testify approached, I joined him in the
witness room across the hall from the courtroom. Like the rest of the
refugees, he was wearing a suit and tie. He was a slight man in his
mid-thirties. He was obviously frightened, nervously playing with his
tie, avoiding looking me in the eye.

Mr. Dang spoke little English. He had brought his ten-year-old son
along with him to translate and, I suspected, for moral support. The
boy, Truc Dang, was fresh-scrubbed and eager. He, too, wore a suit.
One of the pant legs had been slit up the side to make room for a cast.
When he stood up, he leaned on a homemade wooden crutch. Truc
explained that he had fallen off a motor scooter and broken his leg.
He also told me he wanted to be a lawyer.

I wanted to review the statement Mr. Dang had given to Mike. We
didn't want any surprises when he took the witness stand. As young
Truc interpreted my questions and his daddy's answers, I realized it
would be wonderful for the boy to interpret in the courtroom, too.
It was important to show that there was a future generation with a
stake in the outcome of this lawsuit.

I told Judge McDonald the witness would be more comfortable if
his son interpreted. The judge said she didn't see any problem as long
as the official court interpreter monitored the testimony. So Mr. Dang
took the witness stand, and his son, the future lawyer, stood up there
with him.

Mr. Dang made a fine witness and Truc a fine interpreter. At one
point, I asked Mr. Dang what had happened after the American boat
crossed in front of his boat. As he answered in Vietnamese, he ges-
tured by holding up his middle finger.

"He say they give him the bad hand, the bad finger," explained
Truc. Many in the courtroom laughed. Truc remained deadly serious.

When Mr. Dang's testimony ended, I asked the judge if Truc could
remain and sit in the empty jury box to observe the proceedings. It
seemed important that he stay and that he sit in that particular spot;
the jury box was on a raised platform and looked down on the tables
at which the plaintiffs and defendants and lawyers sat. Truc Dang was

the symbol of the hopes and dreams of the generation of refugees that had come to America and taken jobs in car washes, in boat yards, and on shrimp boats so the next generation could be lawyers or whatever they wanted to be.

Mr. Dang's testimony and the testimony of the other refugees established the severity of what had happened on the bay and its impact on the psyches of the Vietnamese. We now had to show the economic consequences.

Here we were a little shaky. Dock owners Craig and Blansfield and the Vietnamese had testified that they had received threats. But we had not yet shown that those threats led to the breaking of contracts between the Americans and the Vietnamese, or the elimination or reduction of the Vietnamese fleet. Margaret Anderwall could establish this, providing an important link between the threats and the Klan.

Mr. Anderwall could have testified to exactly what we wanted Mrs. Anderwall to say. There was no indication that he was as intimidated by the Klan as his wife was. Unfortunately, Mr. Anderwall worked as a cook on an offshore oil rig and was currently in the middle of the Gulf of Mexico.

Randall had been dealing with the Anderwalls. When Mr. Anderwall had been ashore, Randall had persuaded the couple to sign a statement about the Klan's intimidation. But under the rules of evidence, the statement could not be admitted in court. On the trial's eve, Randall talked to Mrs. Anderwall. She said she didn't think she had the strength to testify. Unwilling to give up, Randall then called her priest and convinced him to bring Mrs. Anderwall to the courthouse where she could meet me.

After Phuoc Dang testified, Judge McDonald gave us a short recess. Margaret Anderwall was in the witness room with her priest. We had ten minutes to persuade her to help us.

I could tell by looking at her that she was a good woman. She reminded me of my Grandmother Dees, an honest soul with a strong religious background—white-haired with glasses, stout, perhaps sixty years old. She spoke in short bursts, quickly growing breathless.

"Mrs. Anderwall," I said. "I read your statement. Could you kind of tell me what happened over the last year?"

She told me about the threats to her family, the visit from the Klan, and how, despite the fact that she and her husband liked Khang so much, they had asked him to move his boat because they didn't want their house burned.

When she finished, I knelt down on the floor and took her hand, speaking softly. "Mrs. Anderwall, you need to get up on the stand, because I'm trying to get the federal court to stop the Klan from doing this." Her reluctance was understandable. This lawsuit wasn't hers. Some people think that witnesses just naturally want to come forward and tell everything they know, but think for a moment: A lot of folks don't want to get involved in what they really see as other people's business.

"Mrs. Anderwall, you just told me how hardworking and good Khang and the other Vietnamese people are. You know, they're new Americans just like our founding fathers were when they came to this country."

Mrs. Anderwall still looked uncertain. "Ma'am," I continued, "if you would just get up and tell the judge what you know, it won't be as bad as you think. We're shining the bright light of day on the Klan, and everyone is looking—the press, the FBI. They'd arrest them in a minute if they bothered a witness from federal court."

Mrs. Anderwall looked at me sadly. "Mr. Dees, I don't think I can do it. I just can't do it. My heart won't stand it. They're such nice people. They rented a house near us and I was in it and it was spotless. They are really fine people. But I don't think my heart can stand it."

I looked over to her priest. He nodded that she could testify. I held her hand a little tighter. "Mrs. Anderwall, I'm going to go out there and call you as the next witness. I think you'll feel proud of yourself if you go out and do your Christian duty."

"I don't think I can, Mr. Dees."

I walked past the priest and tugged on his sleeve, as if to say "Please help."

The court convened a moment later. I called Margaret Anderwall, turning to the back of the courtroom. In she came, slowly, tentatively. I walked back to her. She was trembling. I escorted her all the way to the witness stand. "This will be all right," I whispered.

When she was sworn in and settled down, I asked her the standard opening questions. What was her name? She told me. Where did she live? She told me. Did she have a pier behind her house? "Yes," she said hesitantly.

Did she know a man named Khang? That simple query opened the floodgates. Margaret Anderwall told her story without waiting for any more questions. How Khang was such a nice man; how a caller had told her he would burn Khang's boat if she and her husband didn't move it; how someone threatened to burn their house if they didn't move Khang's boat; how they had received threatening phone calls from individuals claiming to be in the Klan; how the phone calls told them they would die; how they had received Klan calling cards in their mailbox.

"We didn't want trouble from anyone, and these threats made us afraid and upset," Mrs. Anderwall said. "We didn't want to make Khang move, but we had no choice. We didn't want to hurt his feelings so we said he had to move his boat so we could prepare for our daughter's wedding. His boat had been parked here for two years, and he'd never given us any trouble. But no one wants to have their house burned down or receive threats against their life. We've been ostracized by our neighbors. We just didn't want any more trouble."

As Mrs. Anderwall spoke, she turned to the judge. It must have seemed natural to tell what she knew to the robed authority figure. Judge McDonald nodded. Our witness was moving her. Margaret Anderwall's honesty was obvious; she admitted that she was scared and didn't want to testify. The judge and the gallery and the lawyers and young Truc Dang were all spellbound by her presence—an ordinary American speaking up, telling the truth about the Ku Klux Klan. She stepped down from the witness stand confidently, striding past Beam, her chin held high.

Louis Beam strutted to the witness stand. His message was unmistakable: I am superior to the black judge, the yellow plaintiffs, the Jewish lawyer Berg, the demon Dees. Superior to the rest of you would-be Aryans taken in by the Jewish conspiracy.

My opening questions centered around his involvement in the affairs on Galveston Bay. He insisted that by intervening he was trying to put out a fire, not start one. When I referred to the coalition of American and Vietnamese fishermen that tried to resolve peacefully the problems on the bay, he shook his head. "We can see how successful they've been," he said sarcastically. "It's quite obvious: Until we entered the situation, it was a crisis."

And what was his response to the crisis?

Q: Did you urge these American fishermen to fight the Vietnamese if Vietnamese fishermen appeared to be going to take over Galveston Bay?
A: No.
Q: You didn't say that before you give up your fishing birthright that you should fight?

A: I would have said before you give up your birthright you should
   fight.
Q: Were you referring to the Vietnamese fishermen taking over down
   in that area?
A: I'm referring to giving up a birthright. It could come from a threat
   from Vietnamese, Chinese, or Cubans. It wouldn't matter to me.
   I'm not for giving up anything that our ancestors fought and died
   for. Nothing at all.

We moved to a discussion of the media, with Beam noting, "[The]
media lies all the time. They lied about me being anti-Vietnamese."
This was the opening I was waiting for.

Q: You don't lie to the media?
A: No. I don't need to. Truth resides with our side.
Q: So when you told the reporter about a month and a half ago that
   you had three military camps in operation at that time, that was the
   truth, wasn't it?
A: You bet it is, except that I'll have to define what camps is. We have
   three training locations . . .

There, he had acknowledged the camps. But no sooner had he
admitted their existence than he said that training had stopped since
January when he had been indicted by the U.S. government for trespassing on federal grasslands. He was contesting the charge. "I had
to call everything off until the feds go back to watching the borders
and chasing criminals and stop chasing patriots around the country,"
he explained.

We needed to link Beam's Klansmen to the acts of terror. I asked
for names of his group's members. Beam said any names he could give
me were pseudonyms taken to avoid illegal attempts to secure membership lists, and that in February he had ordered those lists destroyed.
He did identify one Klansman—a heavyset, red-haired, bearded fellow known as Big Al.

I showed Beam a photograph in which Beam was directing several
heavily armed men wearing standard Marine Corps–issue fatigues.
Beam acknowledged Big Al was among the "soldiers." He said Big
Al and these men had also been at the boat-burning rally, and that he
thought Big Al was responsible for getting them there.

I showed Beam a picture taken during the March 15 boat ride.

Q: That's old Big Al?

A: That's him. Couldn't miss him.

John Van Beekum, a photographer with the *Houston Chronicle,* had traveled to Seabrook on an outing with his girlfriend on the morning of March 15. Encountering the Klan boat ride by accident, he snapped numerous photos, providing us with several good color shots. Now, having identified Big Al, we looked at those on board one by one. While Beam professed ignorance about names, he did acknowledge that he had seen many at Klan rallies and that some had even served on his security force. One man appeared to be armed with an Uzi.

"Is that an Israeli-made submachine gun he's holding?" I asked.

"No . . . that would be illegal. As you well know, the Texas Klan doesn't do anything illegal." Beam smiled.

We wanted to link Beam more closely to the boat ride. At his deposition he had said that he received a call about the ride fifteen or twenty minutes before it took place. (Both he and Fisher insisted the ride was spontaneous, but another witness, Emery Waite, testified he had heard about it a week in advance.) Beam said the phone call woke him after a late night spent reading the Roman historian Tacitus. The caller told him that a group wanted to take a ride on the boat. "I said, 'Well, why are you calling me?' He says, 'Well, we want to wear our robes and carry our weapons.' I said, 'Well, that throws a different light on it.' "

Who was the caller? Beam couldn't remember. I pressed him. He finally said that it had been Big Al.

Did Beam approve of the ride? He said he didn't disapprove, but cautioned that the riders be careful not to violate the ninety-day dispensation he had given. "On that basis [to say] I approved the boat ride or did not object to it would be probably correct," he testified.

Q: And your top lieutenant, Big Al, was on board in uniform. Is that correct?

A: I believe that was established just previously in those pictures, wasn't it?

Who was the target of Beam, Big Al, and other Klansmen and fishermen? We played the videotape of the February 14 rally. There was no mistaking the Grand Dragon's words. He told the crowd that when the American fishermen came out of his camps, "you'll be ready for the Vietnamese."

One of Beam's plans for the Vietnamese was, he testified, Klan sea patrols. For the May 15 opening of the fishing season, he had considered "escalating" beyond the March 15 ride, employing "the same techniques that Martin Luther King used." King, he explained, "would go into an area and create tension, and that would force the local community to act."

But Beam's techniques would not be as passive as Dr. King's. He planned to distribute pamphlets explaining how to make citizens' arrests from boats motoring back and forth in the bay. "And we were going to threaten, if necessary actually attempt, although I don't think that would have ever been necessary, to make citizens' arrests when we found people out there violating the law."

We concluded by focusing on Beam's military camps, playing a portion of Wayne Derrick's videotape showing Beam leading his armed men through maneuvers. This was powerful, frightening stuff. At one point, Beam, his face darkened with charcoal, his hands gesturing wildly, explained the purpose of an ambush to his troops: "When you attack, there is only one thing for the enemy to do . . . DIE!"

After playing the tape, I caught a glimpse of the spectators. Several members of the media looked shocked to find out this kind of organized paramilitary activity was taking place in America, that Louis Beam was actually as dangerous as the suit was portraying him.

Beam now testified that active-duty officers were training with him. He explained that these officers were disenchanted with their army training because "the quality of troops is very, very low and they feel by coming around a group of highly motivated white men who . . . have a desire to train to defend this country, they can get better training." The reason the army troops suffered, he implied, was that the black soldiers lacked discipline.

When Beam left the stand, he strutted back to his seat, unaware or at least unwilling to acknowledge that his world was collapsing around him.

We couldn't prove our case against Beam's paramilitary operations by his testimony alone. Derrick's videotape had given the court a look at the paramilitary activity. It was up to our expert, Tom Wilkinson, to suggest that this activity was unlawful.

Wilkinson was an imposing character—tall, broad-shouldered, with the intensity of a former Vietnam combat training officer and Green Beret reserve member. He testified he had watched four hours of Derrick's videotape, observing Beam giving classroom training and conducting field exercises with armed men.

Tom explained that the nature of the training, the organization of command, and the manner in which orders were given had led him to conclude that this was "most emphatically" a sophisticated, viable military operation. Beam smiled as Wilkinson damned him with praise. He was proud of what he had accomplished with the Texas Emergency Reserve. What a shame that he had channeled his considerable skills toward such a repugnant end.

We rested our case. Adamo's cross-examination of our witnesses had been thorough, but he could do little to change the facts. His defense was similarly hampered: The thrust of his case was that the passage of a law by the Texas state legislature on May 12, the second day of the trial, had lessened the American fishermen's concerns about the upcoming season and that violence or threats of intimidation were no longer in the cards. Indeed, the legislature had passed a "limited entry" bill severely limiting the number of persons eligible for shrimping licenses in 1982 and 1983. All the fishermen, Vietnamese as well as American, hailed this as a positive move. But, as I noted in my closing argument, it was unrealistic to suggest that the passage of this bill alone would solve all the problems on the bay. The need for a court order enjoining the Klan and the American fishermen from interfering with the refugees remained essential.

Judge McDonald agreed. On May 14, the eve of the new fishing season, she ruled. Finding violations of the civil rights statutes, the Sherman Antitrust Act, and Texas's common law tort of interference with contractual relationships, she entered a preliminary injunction barring the defendants from engaging in unlawful acts of violence or intimidation against the Vietnamese. This included putting armed persons on boats within view of the refugees, burning crosses in the area where the plaintiffs lived and worked, having gatherings of two or more robed members of the Knights of the Ku Klux Klan or affiliated Klan organizations within view of the plaintiffs, and engaging or inciting others to engage in boat burning, armed boat patrols, assault and battery, or threats of such conduct.

Louis Beam's hands had been slapped and then tied. Colonel Nam and his countrymen could go safely onto the waters when the new shrimping season began in less than twenty-four hours.

Beam was already talking to the press when I left the courtroom. Incredibly, he was proclaiming victory. The legislature's passage of the limited entry bill was a direct result of his February 14 rally and speech, he insisted. Never mind that the bill had been introduced in

January. Never mind that one of the terms of this "victory" mandated that two robed Klansmen couldn't so much as get together in the sight of any of the refugees. And never mind that the very existence of his Texas Emergency Reserve was hanging by a thread.

Judge McDonald had ruled that while there was not enough evidence presented at this hearing to warrant the preliminary injunction barring the Reserve, she would resolve that issue at a full-scale trial at a later date. She also announced that she had been informed that Mark White, Texas's attorney general, planned to intervene in the case. He would be taking our side, arguing that the Reserve violated the state's statute banning private paramilitary organizations. Our chances for delivering that knockout punch to Beam were improving.

The Vietnamese fishermen knew they would have to be up early the next morning for the start of the season, but they insisted on taking us out for dinner to celebrate the court's decision. A Vietnamese restaurant owner prepared a special feast, and we joined the fishermen and the elders for a party. There, the Vietnamese presented each lawyer and Center staffer with a special gift: a wooden plaque in the shape of Vietnam. A fine clock was set into the wood.

The next morning we were up early to watch the fleet take to the waters. The mist still hung over the shore like a net. The same priests who had helped us find witnesses were there, along with several U.S. marshalls, apparently sent by the court to ensure that the injunction was observed. The boats, still a ragtag lot, lined up as if to start a regatta. The Vietnamese fishermen looked more comfortable in work clothes than in suits. Everyone was silent as the priests blessed the fleet, a centuries-old custom. They asked for the safe return of all those who ventured out into the sea to make their living. After a moment of prayer, the crew's busy chatter again filled the air.

The sun was rising now. I looked out over the bay. The mist was lifting. The horizon and the promise of this new day seemed to have no limits. I felt proud to be a lawyer.

The case was not finished. While Louis Beam had agreed that the preliminary injunction that Judge McDonald had entered on May 14 could be made permanent, he was planning to fight the upcoming effort to restrict the Texas Emergency Reserve from engaging in its paramilitary activities. Rather than hold a trial, both sides agreed to submit depositions and briefs to the judge.

We gathered information about Beam's camps over the next months, taking sworn testimony from active participants—most notably Neil Payne, who had conducted training sessions at the camps, and John Place, the chief of the Klan security guard. Since Beam had repeatedly refused to testify about the specific acts of the Texas Emergency Reserve, this was the first time insiders had shed light on the organization's operations. Their testimony confirmed what we had seen in the videotapes.

While we were assembling this powerful material, Beam scrambled. In need of money to continue the defense, he sent a letter to would-be supporters. In it he proclaimed victory at the May hearing where we had won the preliminary injunction. "Armadillos, long-necks, and white victory: nowhere else but Texas," wrote Beam the revisionist historian.

He added: "Of course no victory is obtained without cost and sacrifice. As a result of our newfound power, I have come under attack by the forces of evil . . . Morris Dees, an Antichrist Communist Jew who has founded a con game known as 'The Klan Watch'. . . . The cost to this point of two weeks of court battle in front of a Carter-appointed Negress 'Judge' has been substantial. . . . The terrible pity is that we could purchase now with our money that which will later cost our blood and the blood of our children."

Beam proposed the "Fight and No Surrender 39 and 1 Counter-offensive." He asked his followers to contribute one hour of their forty-hour workweek to labor for the Klan by donating an hour's wages "to race and country"—in other words, to the Louis Beam defense fund.

I don't know how much money Beam raised, but it didn't help. In June of 1982, Judge McDonald ruled that the Texas Emergency Reserve was, in effect, the military arm of a dangerous chapter of the Ku Klux Klan and constituted a real threat to Vietnamese fishermen and others. Through Randall and Mike's investigation, we had established that many of those on board the March 15 boat ride were members of the Reserve. The judge noted that this was "the best illustration" of how the Klan used the Reserve to intimidate.

Citing Tom Wilkinson's testimony and the depositions of Payne and Place, she concluded that the Reserve was a military organization and that its military and training operations fell outside the scope of the

First Amendment, violating the Texas statute barring paramilitary activities. She granted our request for an injunction enjoining the Reserve from carrying out those activities. Louis Beam and the Texas Emergency Reserve were out of business.

Unfortunately, Beam was not out of my life by a long shot.

CHAPTER 4

December 1936   Mount Meigs, Alabama

If it hadn't been for my daddy, Morris Seligman Dees, Sr., I don't think I'd ever have found myself mixed up with Louis Beam and the Knights of the Ku Klux Klan. It was Daddy who insisted I study law. As a teenager, I fancied myself a preacher. Our family had helped build the Pike Road Baptist Church—a red brick structure that sat next to the school about five miles from our house in Mount Meigs—and Reverend Russell, who came out from Montgomery to preach once a month, put the fear of God into me early. His work was complemented by my fifth-grade teacher, Miss Margaret Waugh. Ancient and afflicted with palsy, always outfitted in black dresses with high white collars, her hair pushed into a permanent bun, Miss Waugh made us memorize a different Bible verse every week and warned us of the evils that lay outside God's shrine:

> Tobacco is a filthy weed and from the devil doth proceed.
> It picks your pockets and burns your clothes
> And makes a smokestack of your nose.

I was an impressionable boy (to this day I've never smoked a cigarette), and by the time I was in high school, I could quote many a scripture and was speaking at Baptist summer youth revivals. I seemed to have a knack for swaying a group, so the ministry seemed a logical calling. But Daddy, who could sleep through church services despite the hard pine pew, had his eyes wide open when it came to supporting oneself on the wages of a country preacher. "Bubba," he said, "you can be a preacher anytime. You can do that on Sundays. But you need to do something you can make a living at."

51

Fine, I thought, then I'll be a farmer. That seemed to come as natural as preaching, and I had plenty of experience. From the time I could lift a hoe, I had worked in the cotton fields. In junior high I grew and sold watermelons. In high school I had my own cotton patch and a chicken, pigs, and cattle operation that was netting me five thousand dollars a year by graduation. The Future Farmers of America named me Star Farmer of Alabama and awarded me a scholarship to Auburn University. But, again, Daddy had other ideas. He had been a cotton farmer all his life, and he was convinced it would be even harder for me to make a living off the land than it would be to make a living off the Word. "You be a lawyer, Bubba," he said. "No boll weevil ever ruined a law book."

In my heart I knew that farming wasn't in my stars for a very simple reason: To be a successful farmer in central Alabama, you needed something our family didn't have, had never had—land. What you could do in life, not to mention your place in society, was measured by a simple yardstick in Montgomery County: the number of acres you owned. My classmate Jim Scott's family, which proudly traced itself back to a line of plantation owners from the years before the Civil War, had large land holdings. So did the McLemores, the Handeys, the Doziers, and even old Miss Katie Bowen, the half-black, half-white daughter of a Yankee officer who had carried his carpetbag down South during Reconstruction.

These families had lived on or farmed the same land for generations. But the Dees family, which had migrated from coastal North Carolina to central Alabama after sailing from Scotland early in the eighteenth century, had hopscotched all over Montgomery County without ever owning a piece of property until 1948 when Daddy purchased 110 acres of the old Wigglesworth estate in Mount Meigs and put up a brick house.

When Daddy was born in 1909, my grandfather, Arthur Lee Dees, was living in the south end of the county, only twenty-five miles but a world away from genteel downtown Montgomery—the state capital, the "birthplace of the Confederacy," and a city where having blue blood was almost as important as having white skin. Grandfather Dees, a county road foreman, rented a simple wood frame house on a cotton plantation.

Cotton had been king in Montgomery County for 125 years, but in 1918 an unprecedented boll weevil infestation interrupted that reign. The effect of the insect on the crop was so devastating that the land quickly turned to other uses—peanut farming and raising cattle.

When the boll weevil moved in, the Dees family moved out—north to Mount Meigs, ten miles east of Montgomery, considered a more civilized community with a better-educated group of folks. Cotton was still being farmed in "the Mount," and Grandfather and "Mam Maw" Dees and their brood of eight children rented about a thousand acres on the old Lyle estate down by the Tallapoosa River. That sounds like a lot of land, but most of it was just cypress swamps and oak woods that were suitable only for hunting and timber—and the landowners, not the Dees family, held the timber rights. There were about a hundred acres of good bottomland for cotton farming. Grandfather couldn't grow enough cotton to support the family, so he took a second job as county road foreman in the Mount Meigs area.

Daddy, named after Morris Seligman, a Jewish merchant in Montgomery whom my grandfather admired, farmed and hunted the land around Mount Meigs from the time he was a boy. He was the oldest son, and when he was needed to help support the family, he dropped out of high school and began the hard life of a cotton farmer.

When I was born in 1936, Daddy was working as an overseer on the Jim Pinkston cotton plantation seven miles east of Mount Meigs. Although this was seventy years after the Civil War, things hadn't changed that much as far as the plantation system was concerned. The Pinkston plantation was farmed by fifty to seventy-five field hands, all of them black. (They weren't called blacks then; they were "colored," "negro," "nigra," or "nigger.") There were fifteen or twenty black families living in rent-free squalor on the land.

Until the mechanical cotton picker was perfected in the 1940s, cotton farming demanded field hands willing to do backbreaking work in unbearable heat for shamefully low wages. There weren't too many folks who would stand in line for such a job. Slaves didn't have a choice. Between the time Eli Whitney invented the cotton gin in 1792 and the Civil War, the number of slaves in Alabama and throughout the cotton belt increased dramatically, and it was this pool of exploitable labor that formed the backbone for the South's largely cotton-oriented economy. The Civil War was fought solely to keep the cheap labor, the states' rights argument merely being political propaganda to cause non-slaveholding whites to fight for wealthy plantation owners, cotton merchants, and bankers.

The store-porch talk I heard as a boy and the history lessons in our segregated school would make one think that all white Alabamians rushed to save slavery. The truth was that politicians had to campaign to convince people like the Dees family—those without slaves—that they had a stake in disunion. Folks like my maternal great-grandfather, who served in General Joe Wheeler's Confederate cavalry, were urged to fight for the supremacy of the white race. In 1861, for example, Governor Brown of Georgia argued that slavery was "the poor man's best government. Among us the poor white laborer . . . does not belong to the menial class. . . . He belongs to the only true aristocracy, the race of white men." Still, the war was so unpopular with non-slaveholding farmers that the Confederacy was forced to pass the nation's first conscription act—an act that appealed to slaveholders by allowing exemptions based on the number of slaves owned.

Even when defeat loomed, non-slaveholders were still pressured to fight for the rich planters' way of life on the grounds that only victory would preserve the life-style of all whites. A Union victory would see "the poor man . . . reduced to the level of a nigger," wrote the *Charleston Mercury.* Eighty years later, this was the message I got from the white men in Mount Meigs: that my skin color automatically made me better than the black man.

When the war was over, the labor pool emancipated, and the land in ruins, the plantation system survived, relying on a labor force faced with so few alternatives that it could be exploited. Instead of slaves to plant and chop and pick the cotton, there were now tenant farmers who paid rent to farm a portion of the plantation, or sharecroppers who didn't pay rent but turned over the lion's share of the cotton they grew to the plantation owners, or field hands who worked for pennies a day. These new farmers and hands were black and white, and they operated in an environment succinctly described by one anonymous observer as "a whole miserable panorama of unpainted shacks, rain-gullied fields, straggling fences, rattletrap Fords, dirt, poverty, disease, drudgery, and monotony that stretches for a thousand miles across the cotton belt." These were the people immortalized by Walker Evans when he came to central Alabama with writer James Agee in 1936—the year I was born—and took the haunting photographs for the classic *Let Us Now Praise Famous Men.*

Grandfather Dees died when I was four. About that time Daddy took over farming the Lyle estate, leasing the land for five hundred dollars a year, or fifty cents an acre. As tenant farmers we were entitled to keep all the cotton we grew. Instead of sharing our crop with our landlord, however, we shared it with the Alabama Warehouse, which not only bought our cotton, but loaned us money at the current interest for seed, fertilizer, supplies, and equipment. Mr. Samuels, who owned the Alabama Warehouse, was Daddy's friend. He was also his creditor.

We didn't live on the lowlands of the Lyle estate, but rather rented a series of homes. The first was a small white frame house without indoor plumbing or electricity near Pinkston's land, the second a similar place in Waugh, a small town near Mount Meigs. After a short time there, we moved to Mount Meigs, population 400, where we rented a couple of other houses—again without running water or inside baths.

Daddy wanted to expand his operation, and he soon found another farm to rent about three miles from Mount Meigs. Called the Smith place, it lay in a corner of a large plantation owned by the McLemore family, which held title to several thousand acres in the area. About this time, too, Daddy and two of the wealthy plantation owners he knew, Gene Handey and Gus Dozier, became partners in a cotton gin. They chose Daddy for the venture because he was willing to roll up his sleeves and work. Also, he was well liked by black farmers, and that meant business. When the cotton was picked, he'd leave the farm and run the gin.

We moved onto the Smith place, which included a big old house with a large screened porch and indoor plumbing. It was wonderful. My momma, Annie Ruth Dees, would pour me and my younger sister Carolyn tall glasses of iced tea, get a stack of books, and read to us on the porch from midafternoon until just before six, when I'd run out to join the hands for the daily march back from the fields.

The fields surrounded the house. Come late summer when the cotton bloomed, it felt like we were living in the middle of soft, friendly clouds. And in fall, when the cotton was picked and we were back on earth, we could turn our attention to gathering the pecans from the trees that lined the half-mile dirt trail running from the gravel county road to our front yard. We'd crack the nuts open and eat them on the spot, or salt them and toast them in butter, or give them to Momma so she could bake pecan pie.

Our neighbors were both black and white, rich and poor. Just a few hundred feet from our back door, Lou and Sonny Douglas, a black couple, lived in a four-room shack with their five children, our regular playmates. There were several black families on the Smith place as well: Bozzie Davis, one of Daddy's best hands, and his family had a place down a path through the fields behind our house, as did Nancy Burch, who helped in the house until I was grown. A fifteen-minute walk down the gravel road brought me to where the wealthy white families—my classmates Jim Scott and Lucinda Hall among them—resided in stately homes. Lucinda lived on a once-prosperous plantation called Chantilly in a white-framed antebellum mansion complete with columns and a sweeping veranda.

We weren't in the same league with these folks, who considered their family trees as valuable as any stand of lumber. Our genealogy and our bank account didn't measure up, but if anyone had asked my parents if we were poor, they would have said no. We certainly weren't as poor as many of the people in the county. And we would never have fallen into the class of people described by the horrible term "white trash." But we were *wealthy poor,* and in some ways that's worse than being dirt poor because you deceive yourself that you can keep up with the Joneses, or in our case the McLemores, the Scotts, and the Handeys.

Although Daddy was always anxious to own his farm, we might have stayed on the Smith place forever if the McLemores hadn't terminated our lease and told us we needed to find some other place to earn our livelihood. (It seems another McLemore wanted to farm the Smith place himself.) This wasn't the first time that we had to give up a farm—it had happened at the Lyle estate, too—and it reinforced the lack of control we had over our lives and the difference between us and the plantation owners.

Buying the 110 acres of the old Wigglesworth estate and building the house on it were in many ways a dream come true for Daddy and Momma, a step up; they finally owned some land. Unfortunately, all but forty acres of the soil on that land—a wet sandy lowland called "crawfish"—was much better suited to raising cattle than cotton. But Daddy had been farming cotton for a quarter-century by then, and it was all he knew.

Farming cotton is a hard way to make a living. The cotton is planted in April, but the season begins before that. In February's gray dampness, Daddy and the hands would take the mule-drawn plows (we couldn't afford tractors in the early years) and run the levees, or terraces, to prevent erosion. In early March, with spring finally more than a whisper, they broadcast, or broke, the land. The hands hitched their plows to two mules, then hitched themselves to the plows and turned the soil, opening long aisles of dirt. The furrows were then laid out and the fertilizer put in.

The beginning of April—the willows, oaks, and pecans now green, the skies blue, the sweet smell of honeysuckle wisteria and wild plum

blossoms in the air—signaled time for planting. The springtooth har-
rows smoothed the land open for the planters that followed behind.
James Agee described this planting perfectly, calling it an "iron sexual
act."

Up to this point, everything was "men's work," but when the
cotton plants pushed an inch above the earth, women (and often
children) joined the men in the fields. With days lengthening, the sun
growing hotter, the hands labored with long-handled, eight-inch iron
hoes from 6 A.M. to 6 P.M. (with one hour off for dinner, the midday
meal) chopping nut grass, coffeeweed, and Johnsongrass that threatened to choke the young plants.

To stop the march of armyworms and boll weevils, Daddy and the
rest of the farmers experimented with pesticides. But even if the
poison did its work, the crop was always at the mercy of the elements.
Cotton is ripened by the sun; too much rain can drown your crop and
your dreams.

The same year Daddy built the house, it rained the entire month
of June, keeping us out of the fields until the Johnsongrass strangled
the young cotton plants and our future. To break even, we needed to
harvest a bale of cotton per acre on the two hundred acres we farmed
on our property and another field we leased. Instead we got just fifty
bales. Daddy developed ulcers, which he eventually overcame.

He was, however, still thirty thousand dollars in debt from crop
losses five years later when I told him I wanted to be a farmer. "You
be a lawyer like Charles Pinkston," he told me.

Charles was the successful older brother of Daddy's best friend,
Barney Pinkston. Barney owned a country store near Mount Meigs
at Merry Crossroads. Whenever Daddy had the time, he'd drive his
Studebaker pickup over to Barney's store. There they would sip bottles of Coca-Cola from the cooler, set their caned chairs on the front
porch, and renew the county's longest-running dominoes rivalry.

The two made an interesting-looking pair. Daddy was six feet tall,
slender, fair-haired with deep green eyes. He always wore khaki pants
and a plaid shirt. In summer, he added a businessman's straw hat, in
winter a felt one. Barney was short and stocky with a ruddy face and
prematurely gray hair kept neatly combed for the "prettiest women
in Alabama" whom he claimed frequented his store. His gut hung six
inches over his belt, testament to the few meals he missed and the
quantity of whiskey he drank. He once showed me the three bullet
scars on his abdomen inflicted by my uncle James in a gunfight that
left them both near death. They had shot it out in my grandmother's

front yard. There was a lot of hushed talk about why it occurred. Whatever the reason, it hadn't changed things between Daddy and Barney.

There was nothing I liked more than sitting out front of Pinkston's store with Daddy—unless it was going raccoon hunting in the oak and palmetto swamps along the Tallapoosa by our land with T. J. Hendricks, a black farmer who lived down the road; or riding my bike to Mam Maw's house and being invited to spend the night in her big featherbed; or hiking the mile and a half to Solomon's Pond and fishing for bream with Momma and an old superstitious woman we called "Rat," who claimed her secret for success was that she spit on her hook and worm before she threw in the line attached to her cane pole; or swimming naked with Little Buddy Orum in the hole under the Western Railroad of Alabama trestle; or terrorizing Mount Meigs's spinster postmistress, Miss Theus Raoul, by riding my pinto pony down Pike Road faster than she was driving her 1932 Chevy; or working behind the counter in my uncle Lucien Dees's country store; or listening to Johnny Ford, an aged black hand, play the blues on an old guitar using the neck of a broken Red Dagger wine bottle to slide over the strings; or greeting Big Jim Folsom, our populist governor, when he came out to our house on Sunday afternoons.

The governor liked to escape from favor-seeking politicians. Usually, he and Daddy took a bottle of Jim Beam out to the backyard and swapped tales until the governor was so drunk that his black chauffeur had to load him into a limousine and cart him back to town.

Daddy had come to know the governor through Charles Pinkston, who'd spent a lifetime cultivating political contacts instead of cotton. Daddy knew about being a lawyer from watching Mr. Pinkston: You practiced law for a while, met the right people, got a chunk of state business or got appointed to an office or got elected judge, and had a guaranteed source of income for life. Daddy figured he could help me find cases, and in fact he brought me my first client.

"Bubba," Daddy said one morning at the breakfast table, "I want you to go up to Shorter and see if you can't get Clarence out of the trouble he's in."

I put down my fork. "Well, what kind of trouble is he in?"

"The state trooper stopped him coming from Shorter to Waugh over in Macon County, and they got him for driving while intoxicated and resisting arrest."

I thought I'd heard Daddy wrong. Clarence Williams was a humble black man in his mid-thirties who lived on our land and drove a tractor for us (we had finally graduated to tractors). He had nine children and was not the hard-drinking type. "Clarence? Intoxicated? Resisting arrest?"

"That's what they say. You see what you can do."

After breakfast I went over to Clarence's shack. The eleven people in Clarence's family lived in two rooms, sharing four iron-framed beds, mattresses stuffed with corn shucks. The boards for the shack had come from the run-down plantation home we had demolished when we built our new house. The inside walls were covered by old magazine pages attached with flour paste. They were a feeble attempt to keep out the damp winter winds that snuck through the boards and roared through the open windows. You could see the tin roof above the uncovered pine ceiling beams. There was no running water or electricity. Oil lamps lit the drab interior. Heat was supplied by a single fireplace and a wood cook-stove that sat in a corner of the small, sloped kitchen at the rear.

Clarence's children, dressed in ragged hand-me-downs, played aimlessly in the dirt yard alongside the shack. Clarence, a strong-muscled man with an impassive face, put on his old felt hat and met me at my truck.

"Clarence, tell me what happened."

Clarence usually spoke in a slow drawl. This morning he hurried his words. "Bubba, you know my car ain't nothin' but a piece of car, and I was driving along there and this tire rod came loose and it ran off and hit that concrete median up there on the road and it knocked me dizzy and I was there, dizzy, and the state trooper came along and he opened the door of my car and he pulled me out and he said, 'Nigger, what you doing drunk?' And I said, 'Boss, I ain't drunk.' And I got out and staggered 'round, and next thing I know that state trooper shoved me in the back of the car and hit me upside my head with a blackjack and took me on up to jail in Tuskegee."

It seemed like an open-and-shut case to me. "Shoot, Clarence, we can beat that. You c'mon with me."

We got in my truck and drove a few miles up the road to Shorter where the "Honorable" Judge Metcalf Letcher held his court. Actually, Judge Letcher was a justice of the peace, and his courtroom was the little country store he owned and operated on U.S. 80.

Clarence took his hat off as we opened the screen door and entered the "courtroom." A sloped wood floor ran narrowly from front to back, framed by shelves of packaged and canned goods and household and hardware products: cigarettes, Bruton snuff, King Edward sardines, mule harnesses and plow points.

Judge Letcher stood behind a counter at the back of the store by a big brass cash register. An old Coca-Cola sign was nailed to the wall behind him. The judge was cutting a pound of yellow cheese for a customer while a state trooper drank a bottle of Nehi Orange.

"What you want, son?" the judge asked me.

I looked down at the floor nervously. "Well, I came up here to represent Clarence."

The judge handed his customer the cheese and rang up the transaction on the cash register. He didn't bother to make eye contact with me, but asked, "What about?"

"Well, you know, he's not guilty."

The judge turned to the trooper. "Well, Officer, tell us what he did."

The trooper drained the Nehi Orange and then told his story. He insisted that "the boy" had been drunk and had tried to resist arrest.

When he finished, I spoke up. "Well, Judge, you know that's not right."

The judge was barely paying attention. Another customer squeezed by me, placing a loaf of bread on the counter.

"Clarence," I continued, "tell 'em what you did."

Clarence started talking and the judge kept trading. Shoot, I thought. This is important to Clarence. He makes five dollars a day driving a tractor. He's got nine little ones. He can't afford to lose his driver's license, can't afford to pay a fine.

When Clarence finished, I made a little closing argument summarizing our view of the case. I felt good. The facts were on our side, and besides, I was the son of Morris Dees, Sr. White folks. I ought to be able to come in and vouch for Clarence and get him off.

After I thanked the court for its patience, Judge Letcher hit the counter with his gavel. "Guilty. One-hundred-and-fifty-dollar fine. Bubba, you tell your daddy he can send three dollars a week up here. That'll be all."

I looked at Clarence apologetically. He just shrugged.

When we got back to the farm, I rushed to the tractor shed. "Daddy, you know it just ain't right. I know Clarence, and Clarence is not guilty."

"Did you tell 'em everything, Bubba?"

"Yes, I told 'em everything. Can't you call the judge up there and do something about it?"

Daddy shook his head. "Nope. Judge Letcher's kind of tough. Besides, story is he keeps two sets of books, one for the state and one for himself, and that he makes a pretty penny on these fines."

"Well, that's just not right." I kicked the dirt. "It's not fair."

Daddy smiled. "Well, if you don't like it, why don't you go to law school."

I was sixteen at the time, still in high school. I'd always figured that if you told the truth, you'd receive justice. But that hadn't happened in Shorter. I thought about this for a while, and it occurred to me that maybe telling the truth wasn't enough. Maybe it was *how* you told it. I figured if I was going to be a good lawyer, I'd better know how to tell the truth. I found a book with the speeches of Thomas Jefferson and Abraham Lincoln and memorized them. When I thought I had them down pat, I went out to an empty cotton field, climbed up on an old tractor wagon, and delivered them, my only audience the red-tailed hawk gliding lazily in the blue sky above.

It was just as well that my uncle Lucien, Daddy's younger brother, didn't hear me quoting the Great Emancipator. Lucien, who could pass for Daddy with his quick smile and Bing Crosby good looks, was particularly ornery when it came to blacks—full of hate and superstition.

Working in Daddy's cotton fields, I became friends with plenty of black kids who worked alongside their parents supplementing the family's meager income. These kids idolized Joe Louis, who had beaten a white man, James J. Braddock, to become heavyweight boxing champion of the world. "Just proves colored folks are stronger than whites," they'd brag to me. When we'd knock off from chopping or picking, we'd grapple one-on-one in friendly wrestling matches, trying to get a neck hold and throw each other down.

One time Thump Davis threw me so hard my ribs hurt for a week. When Uncle Lucien found out about this, he took me aside. "Don't ever hold a nigger by the neck, Bubba, and be damn sure you never fight with one," he said sincerely. "It's a scientific fact that niggers got thicker skulls than we do. You can't hurt a nigger hitting him in the head, 'less you do it with an ax handle or a bullet."

Uncle Lucien's small wood-frame country store sat in the Mount, beside U.S. 80, the main highway running across the southern half of the United States at that time. A handful of other stores were bunched along that stretch of the road, as well as the post office, church, and a few houses. Daddy's cotton gin lay only a few hundred yards away.

Directly across the highway was Cadwell Gilder's store. Mr. Gilder treated blacks more kindly than Uncle Lucien did, and as a result most of them traded there. We traded there too, because the store offered much more than Lucien's few shelves for canned goods and foodstuffs, drink box, and candy counter.

Lucien and his friends laughed at Mr. Gilder because they thought the blacks were taking advantage of him. "Those niggers could steal the tires off ol' Cadwell's car right in front of his house and he wouldn't do a goddamn thing," Lucien said. "They don't give a shit that he treats 'em right in his store. They'd just as soon steal from him as anybody."

Uncle Lucien handled everything in his store from behind the counter. Sometimes I would help him wait on customers. Once I asked him why he didn't let people pick out their own goods like they did in the supermarkets in Montgomery.

"Bubba, you know you can't trust them niggers. They'll steal you blind in a week."

Uncle Lucien was no stranger to stealing. In the years after World War II, sugar, still in short supply, became a prized commodity. Lucien would cut a small hole in the bottom of some of his five-pound sugar sacks and drain out a half-cup. Then he'd put clear tape over the bottom. He sold these doctored sacks to his black customers. "The niggers'll never know the difference," he said, laughing.

Like many other store owners, he also featured a dual-price system. There was a "white price" and a "nigger price." Old man Gus Dozier could expect to buy a can of beans or jar of mayonnaise at a price considerably cheaper than T. J. Hendricks or Sonny Douglas would pay.

The store's nickel slot machine offered another way of taking what little money the field hands had. The machine wasn't legal, but no one ever told the Law that Lucien had it out in the back. Come payday the blacks would line up to play, dreaming of the big payoff that might afford some financial relief. Old Johnny Ford sang the blues on Saturday night about easy money:

Well, if I should be lucky, get my hands on a greenback
    dollar bill again.
Yeah, if I should be lucky, baby, get my hands on a dollar
    bill again.
I'm gonna hold that dollar bill, baby, well, Lord, till that
    eagle grin.

Lucien had rigged the machine so that it rarely paid out, and when it did, it was only in small amounts. This was a big joke to him and his white friends.

"Men who are honorable in their dealings with their white neighbors will cheat a negro without a single twinge of their honor; to kill a negro they do not deem murder; to debauch a negro woman they do not think fornication; to take property away from a negro they do not deem robbery. . . . They still have the ingrained feeling that black people at large belong to the whites at large," Col. Samuel Thomas, the director of the Freedman's Bureau in Mississippi, had written in 1865. He might as well have been writing from Mount Meigs in 1945.

Daddy and Lucien didn't see eye-to-eye on too many things. Daddy never used the word "nigger," and he wouldn't tolerate us using it either. I learned that lesson when I was about five. I'd rushed out to meet Daddy and the hands as they headed back to the mule lot after a day of plowing. Riding Dan, his beautiful red saddlehorse, Daddy nodded to Wilson, one of the hands, that it was okay to put me up on one of the mules for the trip home.

Wilson led my mule by a rope. In the lot there were big feeding troughs full of corn and a big hollowed-out log filled with water from a heavy-duty hand pump. By the time we arrived, some of the animals were already drinking.

Wilson, a tall, dark-skinned man of about fifty, reached a long, weathered arm up to help me. "Time to get down, Bubba," he said.

"I ain't through," I said. I didn't see any reason to quit until *I* was ready. I kept kicking the mule.

"You slide on down now, Bubba," Wilson said, his voice tightroping the fine line between genuine irritation and required respect for a white boss's son. I ignored him.

"Bubba," Wilson said.

"You black nigger, you can't tell me what to do."

I didn't know it, but Daddy was standing right behind the mule. In a single motion, he reached up, grabbed me, jerked me to the ground, took off his belt, and gave me the first whipping of my life. (He was not prone to hitting us; I can remember only one other whipping—after I threw a tin can at Carolyn's head.)

Daddy wore me out with that belt, whipped me all over that mule lot, and when he was done he looked me square in the eye and said, "Don't you ever call anybody a 'black nigger.' You mind Wilson. You do what he says."

Daddy used the word *colored,* and so did Momma, who felt *nigger* hurt people's feelings. That was a far cry from her daddy, a hard-drinking tire salesman from Montgomery who belonged to the Ku Klux Klan. Grandfather Frazer never came right out and told Momma and her family he was in the Klan. But when Momma was about six, she was taken to a small rural church where a group of robed Klans-men were gathered.

Momma watched with fascination as the strange, hooded figures spoke in muffled voices. Of course, she wondered who these grown men were. But there was little to give them away. The white-robed figures were as indistinguishable from one another as cotton plants, except, Momma noticed, for the shoes they wore. So she focused on the shoes, and, much to her surprise, the boots of her father were standing near the front door.

The Klan had experienced a dramatic rebirth in the years following World War I, attracting four to five million members by portraying itself as a "benevolent organization." Momma always assumed that her daddy was one of these new recruits, that the boots she had seen were attached to the feet and legs and heart and soul of John Arthur Frazer. Being a good daughter, she never asked.

Momma felt that her Christian faith demanded she act kindly to all God's children. As a result, all the black people in Mount Meigs loved the slight, blond woman they called "Miss Annie Ruth." Often as not, I'd come into the house and find her sitting at the breakfast table with some of the black women from the community, helping them fill out requests for welfare relief. Other times she'd make calls to public officials trying to cut through red tape for some social service benefit. The white wives of plantation owners and even the wives of the smaller farmers and tenant farmers would rarely take the time to do paperwork for black folks, and certainly wouldn't let them sit down at the family table. But Momma, who believed everybody should get along with everybody else, was the white go-between.

I never called anyone a nigger after my whipping, and by the time I was ten, I was working with Wilson and the rest of the hands in the field. I picked cotton, toted water, and sharpened the hoes used for chopping weeds. While none of this was easy, picking was the hardest.

By the time cotton is ready to be picked, the split bolls have become hard, thorny, unforgiving burrs which even the most talented fingers cannot escape. Experienced pickers pinched the cotton between their fingertips at its roots in the burr to bring it out cleanly in one pluck. But the action was repeated too many times to come away unscathed.

Like everyone else in the fields, I hoped my fingers would toughen sooner instead of later.

If the burrs were the only thing to put up with, it would be bad enough. But there's the cramping of the hand, the sharp pain in the back from constantly bending over and dragging the cotton in the increasingly heavy sack slung over the shoulder or the white oak basket held on the arm. And there is the heat, the unrelenting heat that the hands call "the bear" because once it gets hold of you, it doesn't let go. As the old song "Cotton Field Blues" went:

> I work hard every day, I get me plenty o' res',
> Looka here, peoples, I'm gettin' tired of this ol'
> cotton-pickin' mess.

We cherished our break time. At the dinner hour, Momma would send me a quart of iced tea and a big plate of food (didn't matter what it was, just as long as it was big), and after wolfing everything down, tired as I was, I'd take off with the black kids, Little Buddy, Thump, and John Henry, for salvation: one of the creeks that meandered toward the Tallapoosa River from the cool hardwood swamps.

It was a perfect swimming hole, no briars, the banks all stomped down, the water clear, and the bottom sandy. We'd tear off all our clothes and swim until we had to go back and face the bear.

There's no way to speed up the clock when you're working in a cotton field, but the hands tried to make the time go faster by singing religious songs with a feeling only they had.

> I want Jesus to walk with me,
> I want Jesus to walk with me,
> All along my pilgrim journey, Lord,
> I want Jesus to walk with me.

When the hands weren't singing, they talked. Since I was the only white person in the field, I heard the kind of talk most white folks never heard, conversation the blacks would never have dared engage in, even in front of someone as sympathetic as my father.

"We sure have got it hard," Bozzie Davis would say.

"Colored folks ain't got no chance in this world," Jake Orum would agree. "White folks gonna use us 'til us die."

"Don't know how we're gonna live on this little money," Miss Perri Lee would add, quickly dipping some snuff in her cheek before she continued hoeing. "It ain't no diff'rent from slavery."

I don't know how they did live on that money. The going wage in the late 1940s was about $3.00 a day for men and $1.50 for women and children. Maybe that would have been enough if the hands could have earned it all year round, but they were only paid during the season. There was no other farm work to do after the harvest. There wasn't much work of any kind, and since few of the hands could afford even the most dilapidated automobiles, they couldn't travel into town for other work. A handful of the women supplemented their incomes by working as maids, but the wage for domestics was every bit as pitiful as it was for field hands.

This state of affairs forced most field hands to live off the land. To raise as much cotton as possible, the farmers would plant close to the shacks. The hands used the little land left outside their doors to plant vegetable patches, growing greens for the supper table. Meat came from pigs raised on table scraps or squirrels and rabbits shot in the woods.

Daddy recognized the hardship of their lives. They often sent their kids to our back door with barely literate scrawled notes: "Mr. Deeds, I needs to borrow $5 'til Saddity I will pays you bak if it ain't rain," read a typical request. Daddy hardly ever said no, and more often than not he never bothered to collect the debt. (In contrast, Uncle Lucien offered blacks a "five for ten" plan; he'd loan them five dollars on the condition they pay him back ten dollars within one week.)

Daddy also gave black people something that was even scarcer than money—respect. When we finally returned to the fields after the month of rain in 1948, we faced scorching heat. "Can't remember it ever being this hot," said Miss Perri Lee. "Must be a hundred." Not even five feet tall, she was barely visible under faded head rags and several layers of clothing. (The more clothes you wore, the more you sweated and the wetter and cooler you got.) As she spoke, she reached into her pocket for a pinch of snuff. She slipped it into her gums without losing a beat chopping Johnsongrass twice as high as the cotton plants.

I was eleven years old. Perri Lee was in her sixties, and if she said it was the hottest it had ever been, I believed her. I looked out over the field. The heat shimmered off the land, blurring my vision so that it seemed I would fall into one of those dream sequences you see in the movies. All the hands were laboring. Most of them were as old as Perri Lee; the young men and women had all headed north after the war to look for a better way of life.

Daddy had put me in charge of the clock this season. It was my job to tell the hands when they could knock off for dinner and when they could quit for the night. I put down the hoe I was sharpening and looked at my shadow. Ten thirty, I thought. I opened the new pocket watch I'd bought for the job, then smiled. Right again.

"Bubba, Bubba," Jake Orum called. "The bear's done got George."

I followed Jake's voice through the field still muddy from the endless rain. I found Jake and half the other hands standing over George Smiley, one of the older workers, a slender, light-skinned man with the beginnings of a gray beard on his face.

The bear had indeed got George. He was wrapped up in clothes that were soaking wet. But it hadn't helped. He had passed out, hoe still in his hand.

"Let's get him under that shade tree over yonder," I said. And a bunch of us dragged his limp body to the tree. We set him up against the trunk. In a minute or so, he came to.

"Bear done got me good," George sighed.

We should have taken him to a doctor, but we had a month's lost time to make up. "Let's get back to work," I said. We left George under the tree.

Daddy pulled up in his truck about twenty minutes later. He took a handkerchief from his pocket and wiped his forehead. "I think we better knock them off," he told me.

I looked at my watch. "It's only eleven o'clock. We ain't gonna knock 'em off now."

He readjusted his straw hat. "It's too hot to work out there."

I put my watch back in my pocket. We had a crop to save. "Naw, we're gonna work 'til twelve."

He shook his head. "No, son, we gonna knock 'em off. Ya know, they got feelings just like we do."

On another morning later that same summer, he drove up just as I was carrying water to the hands. It was my job to tote a two-gallon bucket from the field and fill it at a pump about a half-mile away. Then I'd take the bucket from one field hand to another so the chopping wouldn't have to stop.

Miss Perri Lee put down her hoe. Daddy picked it up and worked her row as the tiny woman moved to the bucket. There were no paper cups. The hands drank from a gourd with a hole cut into its rounded big end.

Miss Perri Lee took a dipperful of water, moved it to and fro in her mouth and then, having rinsed the snuff from her cheeks and gums, spit it all out. Then she took another dipperful and drank it straight down.

When she was done, Daddy traded Miss Perri Lee her hoe for the dipper and took a long drink.

There is something about this simple scene, something that it says about my father, that even now the memory brings tears to my eyes. The field hands, all of them black, never thought twice about drinking one after another from the dipper until the bucket was empty. And white folks had no qualms about sharing the same bottle of Coca-Cola or something stronger. But how many white men in Montgomery County, in the South, in the entire nation for that matter, would have been color-blind enough to do what my daddy did in 1948—when the Jim Crow laws were at their peak, when there were separate water fountains for white and "colored"?

Uncle Lucien thought there was something wrong with Daddy for acting like this. One afternoon when I was twelve or thirteen I took my bike over to U.S. 80 and started riding back and forth between Uncle Lucien's store and Cadwell Gilder's store. Daddy was over at Gilder's, sitting on a porch bench with some black farmers, talking and eating his favorite store-bought snack: a can of sardines, crackers, a slice of cheese, an onion (which I can still smell), a dill pickle, and a Coke.

I guided my bike back to Lucien's. "Look at Brother," my uncle said. (Brother was what Daddy's family called him.) "He ain't nothin' but a damn nigger lover."

I was suddenly lightheaded. *Nigger lover.* I don't think I'd ever heard that expression before. I wasn't sure what to think. I knew of three white men who lived with black women or had black girlfriends and had never heard anything bad said about them.

I loved Uncle Lucien. He and his wife, Aunt Ruby, were second parents to me. They didn't have any children, so they smothered Carolyn and me with presents. Lucien snuck me firecrackers. He let me work in his store—sometimes on my own while he went to town—and paid me more than he had to. On many Fridays, I'd get off the school bus at his house and stay for the weekend. He and Ruby took me to the circus. In 1948, they took Carolyn and me on our first trip, driving all the way to New Orleans in Lucien's brand-new Kaiser.

Because I was so close to Uncle Lucien, I took his words seriously. And the way he said *nigger lover*—letting the words drag so slowly from his mouth—made me feel for just a moment that Daddy was really doing something wrong.

There's little doubt in my mind that many of the white people in the Mount agreed with Uncle Lucien's assessment of my father. These people had grown up in a system of apartheid, and as long as they were the haves instead of the have-nots, they didn't see any reason to open the door of equal opportunity by fraternizing with blacks or giving them any breaks. How these people treated blacks varied. At one extreme were those who would just as soon throw a rock at a "nigger's" head and leave him or her for dead on a country road. Somewhere in the middle lay most plantation owners. Outwardly, they were very civil to "their" blacks, calling the women "Auntie" and the men "Uncle"; but behind closed doors, they formed White Citizens Councils designed to keep black people in their historical place. My parents occupied the other extreme, according blacks a dignity that was rare in our surroundings. But while they were so different from Lucien and others, one thing must be made clear: Neither Daddy nor Momma was a civil rights activist. They believed black folks were entitled to be treated with respect, that they deserved better social services, that they should have better opportunities for advancement, but they also believed in, or at least did not question, the system of segregation that perpetuated such gross inequities. And so, I confess, did I.

College-educated blacks lived in the Mount. One of them, E. B. Holloway, the director of the Alabama Industrial School for Black Children—a fancy name for the local juvenile prison—visited frequently in our home. (This, of course, infuriated Uncle Lucien.) A solid middle class of black farmers owned their land, property that had been in their families since Reconstruction or had been deeded as part of a program instituted by the Roosevelt administration. But while these blacks may have been treated with greater respect by whites than the powerless field hands, everything in Mount Meigs (as throughout the South) was divided along racial lines.

Most whites used the private back entrance to the post office, and of course the schools were segregated. I never took a class with a black person from the time I entered the first grade in 1942 to the time I graduated from the University of Alabama Law School in 1960.

Working in the fields with black people whom we counted as friends enabled us to deal with them one-on-one, in a way that Uncle Lucien or plantation owners who farmed from their pickup trucks could never have approached. But that did not mean we thought that schools or restaurants or theaters should be integrated. We accepted the system that had dominated until the Civil War and then after 1901 when a new state constitution erased the "unpleasant" effects Yankees had forced on the South.

Truth be told, I was much more concerned about making money than I was about making waves. Watching my daddy, realizing how beholden he was to the people who held title to the land he farmed and the banks and cotton warehouses that held his notes, I refused to repeat his struggle as a tenant farmer. I never wanted to be told by somebody else to pack my bags and get off the land. I didn't like leaving the Smith place, didn't like that it could never be the Dees place. So from a very early age I started doing anything and everything I could to make certain I'd have the financial security my parents never achieved.

Working in the fields for Daddy allowed me to start a bankroll. But that bankroll could not grow fast enough by chopping cotton at $1.50 or $3.00 a day or picking it for two cents a pound. So I looked for other ways. I picked Coke bottles off the side of the road and turned them in at a penny apiece. I delivered newspapers, sold peaches, watermelons, and compost.

At the new house, Daddy gave me a little patch where I could raise my own cotton. Then, using the money I'd saved from Coke bottles and the paper route, I bought my first calf from a black neighbor for fifteen dollars. Daddy let me have the bottom below the house for pasture. I cleared it up and kept it mowed. We mated the calf with one of Daddy's bulls and soon my herd started growing. When I was in high school, I'd take off for the stockyards during my free periods and try to bargain for another head or two. If I could get one, I'd put her into the back of my panel truck, take her home, and then drive back to school.

I started buying pigs from neighbors, too. The going price for young pigs weighing up to 80 pounds was five dollars. I'd fatten 'em up to over 210 pounds and then sell them for forty-five dollars. Most of my feed came from the high-school lunchroom. The manager agreed to supply me four fifty-gallon cans full of scraps if I promised to return them clean the next morning.

Next, I added chickens. I kept them out back of the house, rising every morning at 5:30 to feed them. By my senior year, I was dressing about 250 chickens a week. I iced them down and sold them to three or four country stores for a nice profit.

A few of my high-school classmates laughed at my entrepreneurial ventures. Some of my friends from old wealthy Montgomery families had never worked a day in their lives. They found it comical that Bubba was hauling scraps from the lunchroom for his pigs. I was too busy to worry about what people thought. I was more concerned that someone might beat me to the garbage.

This hustling didn't always sit well with Daddy. He didn't like the idea that I was always selling something. It didn't square with his image of himself in the community. "Don't you be taking those raffle tickets to my friends," he'd tell me as I'd prepare to go into town to raise money for a Future Farmers project.

Those "friends" were among the most prominent people in town. They were doctors, lawyers, plantation owners, merchants. They liked Daddy, and fraternized with him. Although he was every bit their equal intellectually and morally, he wasn't on the same level with them socially because he didn't own land, the mark of wealth in those years. I think he found this difficult to accept and felt it important to maintain the image that he was a landed gentleman farmer, when in reality he scraped by with borrowed money. Appearances were important to him; he bought a new car more often than he could afford. He discouraged me, too, from becoming a "tinkler"—the name given to old Jewish peddlers around the turn of the century who roamed the countryside with rolling carts full of everything for sale.

I don't fault Daddy a bit for this. In the deep South, social status is the rod by which so much is measured. A family's declining estate, with its old furniture, silver and crystal and other relics, gives a perception of wealth, even if little exists. I remember going over to the Handys' thousand-acre plantation for supper when I was about fourteen. I had shot a deer, and the Handys had prepared it and invited Momma and me over. They had a great big rambling, columned house built before the Civil War. The ambitious sons had chosen military careers, leaving Miss Jean, a graying spinster and Momma's bridge partner, her overweight sickly bachelor brother Old Man Stewart, and Miss Nellie, an aged great-aunt, to live out their years from the rents of tenant farmers.

The rotted eaves of the once-splendid mansion were covered with wisteria vines, but the rooms inside retained a regal air of bygone days. Feeling uncomfortable sitting at the formal dining-room table under the huge crystal chandelier, I kept looking to Momma for guidance on when to use what piece of silverware. Miss Jean Handy had a little bell she kept by her place, and when she rang it, Tommy

Owens, a young black teenager, came in with the food. It would have been easier to pass the food around like we did at our house, but this bit of ceremony and servitude must have made the Handys feel important.

I recognized Tommy; I'd played with him in the fields where he wore overalls and an old denim shirt. In the Handys' home, though, he was dressed up in a little butler's suit. Every time Miss Handy wanted something, she rang the bell and in he came. I was glad when supper was over.

The plain truth is that the Handys, the McLemores, the Scotts, and the Doziers had land and money, and we were in debt up to our ears. Those families had trusts and estates. We had a line of credit and our honor. I listened to Daddy and Momma's conversations and knew that some months we borrowed to pay our bills.

If becoming a tinkler meant no Mr. McLemore could ever tell me to move, no Mr. Samuels could hold my notes over my head, then so be it. Deep down inside, Daddy appreciated this. He insisted that practicing law offered the best way to avoid a life of debt. He had me convinced until I met a girl named Beverly Crum.

CHAPTER 5

September 1954   Montgomery, Alabama

She stood by the radiator in the hall next to the school's front door, five feet eight inches tall, black pony tail, hooped blue skirt, and white blouse. Slender and tanned. It was her first day in tenth grade and the beginning of my senior year.

Beverly Crum did not have a lot to say.

"You're not from around Montgomery, are you?" I asked. "I don't remember seeing you before."

"No," she replied. "And I probably won't be here for long. My father's a colonel at the Air War College. We move a lot."

I passed the radiator each morning going to the vocational agricultural department for my first class. I had been valedictorian of Pike Road Junior High, but had opted for the less academic vocational courses in high school. Despite my daddy's urgings to study law, I still really wanted to farm. Beverly wasn't studying agriculture, but she managed somehow to be at the same radiator more frequently after our first meeting.

I learned that her folks were from rural Kentucky where her grandparents had owned a horse farm. Her uncles still lived there, and she visited them often. She loved farm life. We had something in common.

After a few dates, I took her to Mount Meigs. We drove to where the Western Railroad crossed Millie's Creek, the place where Little Buddy and I swam during breaks from picking cotton. We had a picnic and then walked along the creek for a couple of miles to where it flowed into the Tallapoosa River. She told me how tired she was of moving from air base to air base, never having any real roots. She was amazed that my grandfather had worked the same fields we passed and that my father was still farming the same land. I showed her trees with beehives, trees where T. J. and I found raccoons. On the way back to town, I introduced her to Momma and Daddy.

We had dated for six months when she told me that her father was being transferred to Germany. During those six months, we had explored the fields and woods of my boyhood. We had shared more than teenage passion. Beverly was a serious girl with ambitions for college and a career. She listened to my dreams of owning a farm. We talked about sharing that farm one day. We were falling in love, and now it seemed we would be separated forever.

Several of our friends had eloped—some because they were good Baptists and didn't feel they could have sex unless they married; others because they weren't such good Baptists and were expecting babies. Few if any of these classmates would go on to college and law school.

"Let's get married before your father leaves," I said. She agreed.

You don't elope in a panel truck unless you have to. On April 15, 1955, I told Daddy my truck wasn't running well and asked if I could borrow his car to go to a Future Farmers hog-judging contest in Dothan, Alabama, for the weekend. Instead, I went to school and picked up Beverly, who had told her parents that she was spending the night at a girlfriend's house. We drove across the border to Meridian, Mississippi, where they didn't care how old you were; if you wanted to marry, you could. We tied the knot in a small Baptist church, then we had dinner, watched a cowboy movie in the town's only theater, and spent the night in the honeymoon suite at Meridian's nicest hotel.

In the morning, we drove back to Alabama and went to the hog-judging contest. I dropped Beverly at her house that night. We were back in high school on Monday.

Like the other couples we knew who had eloped, we decided to keep our marriage a secret. I searched all over the house for the best place to hide the marriage certificate and finally put it behind a rafter in the barn. I did tell Momma what we'd done, but only after I made her swear not to tell Daddy. She was surprised, but supportive—she loved Beverly dearly—and kept her promise . . . for a while.

Fortunately, I was out of the house when Momma decided to tell Daddy. When I came home for dinner, he had already threatened to fire Nancy, the maid who had been with our family since before I was born, and to throw out Momma's new washing machine, the first she'd ever had. I guess he wanted to make Momma suffer for her silence.

When I walked in the door, Daddy was beside himself. "Bubba, you have ruined your life. You are just like all the other white boys around here who ran off and married. You are going to be broke. I thought you was going to college."

"I'm going to farm," I said. I felt I had thought this thing through. Daddy rolled his eyes. "Shit. Where?"

"Right here." I pointed to where I kept my livestock. "I have everything out in the backyard already."

He shook his head. "You ain't farming this farm. It ain't big enough for two families." Daddy stormed out of the house.

"Then I'll get someplace else," I yelled after him.

But there wasn't "someplace else" available. From fence row to fence row, every farm was taken. I realized I had to do something else.

Daddy came back about two hours later. He had cooled down. "I'll back you up, Bubba," he said quietly. "You want to go to college, I'll help you."

I had five thousand dollars in the bank, fifty head of cattle, and about two hundred hogs on the farm waiting to be sold. And here Daddy was—thirty thousand dollars in debt—offering to help. "Just having your blessing is enough," I said.

The next day I drove over to Tuscaloosa and filled out an application for the University of Alabama's School of Business and Commerce. Law was back in the picture.

When Beverly and I took off for Tuscaloosa in the summer of 1955, the student body at the University of Alabama was still all-white. One year earlier, in the historic *Brown v. Board of Education* decision, the United States Supreme Court had unanimously struck down the "separate but equal" doctrine, ruling that there could be no true equality in the schools as long as they were segregated. But no black student had yet tested the court's decision by trying to enroll at 'Bama.

The court's ruling threw the South into turmoil. Although the court refused to order immediate integration and instead mandated that integration of public schools proceed "with all deliberate speed," blacks were encouraged to see that the times were finally changing. Whites, on the other hand, were outraged. The governors in several states announced they would ignore the decision. Many prominent businessmen formed White Citizens Councils to fight integration.

I hadn't paid any attention to the ruling when it came down in 1954. I was much more worried about my farming operation than about what a court had to say about a school district in Topeka, Kansas. But if the words of the nine justices in Washington, D.C., failed to stir me, the story of one black fourteen-year-old in Money, Mississippi, touched me so deeply that for the first time I seriously examined the Southern way of life.

The black youth's name was Emmett Louis Till, and on August 28, 1955, he was brutally murdered by two white men, Roy Bryant and his half-brother J. W. Milam. Why? Apparently Till, a self-assured teenager who was down from Chicago visiting relatives, had chided his Southern cousins for kowtowing to white folks. Then, on a dare, he had entered Bryant's country store, bought some candy, and said "Bye, baby," to Mrs. Bryant on his way out.

Word spread through Money about Till's uppityness. A few days later Bryant and Milam dragged him from his cousin's home and inflicted the punishment required for such a terrible "crime." In a paid interview Milam later told a journalist that they shot Till in the head, wired a seventy-five-pound cotton gin fan to his neck, and then dumped his body in the Tallahatchie River. "What else could I do?" Milam said. "He thought he was as good as any white man." When the horribly disfigured corpse was found a few days later, Emmett Till's relatives were only able to identify it because of a signet ring that remained on one finger.

Till's mother ordered an open-casket funeral so the world could see what had been done to her son. *Jet* magazine ran a picture of the corpse. Thousands of people viewed the body and attended the funeral. I watched it on television.

Bryant and Milam were charged with murder. Although much of the nation was outraged at the pair's deed, white Mississippians raised ten thousand dollars to pay their legal expenses, and five local lawyers volunteered to defend them. At the trial, the half-brothers admitted they had kidnapped and beaten Emmett Till, but insisted they had left him alive. It took an all-white jury only one hour to return a verdict of not guilty.

At the time of the murder, I had never written to a newspaper. But here was an innocent teenager, no different from my friend Little Buddy, and now he was dead and his momma was crying for the whole world to see. "Maybe we believe in segregation," I wrote the newspaper from the apartment Beverly and I had taken in Tuscaloosa. "But we also believe in justice. If this young man did something illegal, then he ought to be tried and convicted before he is punished, not lynched." The paper published the letter, proving that even thirty-five

years ago there were, on occasion, venues for moderation in the
South.

The University of Alabama was not, in 1956, one of those venues.
That year, a federal court ordered the school to admit Autherine Lucy,
a black student, and all hell broke loose. When Lucy drove onto
campus to enroll, accompanied only by a priest, she was confronted
by a mob of ten thousand angry whites, including scores of Klansmen
who screamed "Nigger, go home" and threw bricks and bottles at her
car. When that didn't cause her to retreat, the mob moved closer and
began to rock the car. Eventually Lucy managed to get out of the car
and move quickly through the hate into a campus building.

We students had been told to stay in our rooms. Some of us dis-
obeyed the order. I was there, not out of sympathy for the cause of
integration, but out of curiosity. I watched events unfold from the
steps of the Student Union Building a hundred yards away. This was
the first time I had ever seen Klansmen in action, the first time I had
ever seen a mob. As it surged, retreated, and surged again like some
monster, I felt frightened and disgusted. Many of these people were
good, rational folks when they didn't have to think about integration,
but once they became part of the crowd, they were swept up in the
frenzy and turned into mean, dangerous aggressors.

I found myself backing up the steps of the building, trying to put
some distance between me and them. I felt sick to my stomach. In
Autherine Lucy's face, I saw the faces of many of the black people I
had known in the Mount—Little Buddy, Miss Perri Lee, Wilson,
Clarence. All my sympathy for the underdog came out at that moment, and in my own way I felt as angry as that crazed mob.

At this moment, I really did question my belief in segregation. Up
to this time, I thought I believed in the system because everyone
believed in it. At Pike Road Baptist Church, Reverend Russell had
preached about all the things you were supposed to do to be a good
Christian. He gave talks about not cheating or stealing or lying. But
he never mentioned that black folks were treated like second-class
citizens, never questioned the morality of segregation.

Religion was still a big part of my life. I still had my heart set on
preaching—part-time, anyway. Beverly and I had joined a Baptist
congregation on campus, where I had been named superintendent of
the Sunday school for married couples. On the Sunday after Autherine Lucy had met the mob, I stood up and addressed the fifty people
gathered at the school assembly.

"I'd like to read from First John," I began. " 'If a man say, I love

God, and hateth his brother, he is a liar: for he who loveth not his brother whom he hath seen, how can he love God whom he hath not seen?' " I put down the Bible. "Something really disturbs me," I said. "How can we profess to be Christians and really hate our brothers?"

The assembly looked perplexed.

"Autherine Lucy tried to get on this campus," I continued. "We don't know her and we might not have been out there opposing her, but I think all of us didn't want her to be there. So how can we be good Christians? Do you remember when Jesus gave the Pharisee woman the 'water of life'? What are we to think of the courthouse here in Tuscaloosa where there's one drinking fountain for white folks and one for colored? Were Jesus here, would he not say to a black woman, as he said to the Pharisee woman, 'Here, drink from the same water'?" And as I said these words, I remembered Daddy drinking out of the same bucket.

None of the assembled spoke up. Later that week I received a visit from our preacher, Reverend Williams. "We're going to make some changes in the Married Students Sunday School," he told me. "We're just growing so fast that we think we need someone with a little more experience than you have to plan the programs. You can be the assistant if you want." He never mentioned my lesson—the real reason for his visit.

Reverend Williams probably had pegged me as some kind of radical rabble-rouser, but the fact that I was occasionally moved by the injustice suffered by a particular individual like Emmett Till or Autherine Lucy didn't, in my eyes, paint me a civil rights activist. Although the birth of the modern civil rights movement took place right in my backyard, I didn't pay much attention to it. The 381-day Montgomery Bus Boycott, triggered when Rosa Parks refused to give up her seat to a white person, passed me by completely.

I was too busy trying to make good grades and good money to consider civil rights. Beverly was finishing high school in Tuscaloosa. Our parents were helping us out financially, but I was also working to support her and our baby son, Morris III, whom we called Scooter.

An idea for making money came in the mail, and it would turn out to be one of the most significant events of my college years. Momma sent me a fruitcake for my birthday. I hadn't returned since leaving in September and was really homesick. So were a lot of other students, and their moms, I suspected, longed to make them feel good on special occasions. Why couldn't I write each student's parents and offer to deliver a freshly baked birthday cake?

'Bama Birthday Cake Service was in business the next school year. The response was terrific. Over 20 percent of the parents ordered our cakes, custom made at a local bakery. I sold 350 cakes a month and netted three dollars for each. But the real bonanza was the education I got in direct mail. Thousands of postal employees delivered my sales message, all at once, all over America. I learned to write sales copy, to design an offer, and to mail at the most opportune time.

A fellow student, Millard Fuller, had joined me in this new business venture, and before graduation we had expanded into selling fund-raising products to clubs and organizations. We did it all by mail, with customers in thirty-two states and sales of nearly half a million dollars. We took some of our profits and bought real estate near the campus.

Millard and I made a good team, probably because of our similar backgrounds. Millard had grown up in the sandy hills of east Alabama, where his daddy ran a country store and farmed. His daddy, like mine, wanted a better life for his son and encouraged him to study law.

Tall and lanky with straight black hair, Millard had arrived at the university driving a 1946 Ford. He was so poor that I lent him the tuition for his first year of law school. We met at a Young Democrats gathering. After the meeting I gave him a ride back to his room, and we stayed up most of the night talking, finding out how much we had in common.

Our conversation that first night, and in the days and years to come when we were almost inseparable, was not limited to business. We shared a passion for politics, too. Each of us was thinking of running for elective office after law school.

My interest in politics dated back to 1946, when Daddy had taken me to Big Jim Folsom's first inauguration. Folsom was a huge man, six feet eight inches tall, even larger than life to Alabamians. A populist, he had won election by campaigning against what he called "the big mules"—the large corporations and the silk-stocking group, who had controlled the state government for years.

The 1901 State Constitution and the creation of the poll tax had disenfranchised thousands of black people across Alabama, but the few who did vote in 1946 supported Big Jim. In his inaugural speech, he proposed the almost revolutionary notion that everyone should have the right to vote and that the poll tax be eliminated, but nothing was done until the civil rights legislation of the mid-1960s.

When I was in college, Folsom saved me from starting down a disastrous path. Just twenty-one, I had qualified to run as a delegate to the state Democratic convention. Alabama was divided between two factions: the loyal Democrats or "yellow dogs" and the States' Rights Democrats. I didn't really know the difference between the two. After I qualified for the ballot, the States' Rights faction asked me if I wanted to run on its ticket, and I agreed.

When Big Jim saw my name in the paper, he called Charles Pinkston, who called Daddy and said, "What the hell is Bubba doing?" It turned out that the States' Rights group was aligned with Strom Thurmond's Dixiecrats who had split with the main branch of the party in 1948. I quickly signed up with the loyal Democrats.

Running on a "segregation forever" platform, the States' Rights slate won my district. I don't think I would have been comfortable taking that position at the time; I'd already been moved by the Autherine Lucy affair. But who knows? I was malleable then. Many of those on the States' Rights ticket went on to hold the big offices in Alabama. Who's to say if I had been in that camp, I wouldn't have been blinded by the prospect of political office and gone along for the ride? Other politicians, in Alabama and elsewhere, have been known to sacrifice ideology for office. Witness George Wallace.

I first met Wallace at Folsom's second inauguration in 1954. A state judge at the time, he had been Big Jim's campaign manager in southern Alabama.

"Bubba, this is Judge Wallace. He's gonna be governor someday," Daddy said prophetically.

In those days, Wallace was a populist in the Folsom mold. He, too, had the support of the few blacks who voted. I followed his career over the years, and when I was in college I wrote him and asked if he could help get some General Motors engines for mechanics classes at the all-black reform school in Mount Meigs. I also invited him to speak at the pre-law society I had formed at the university as an undergraduate.

When he ran for governor in 1958, I helped coordinate youth activities for his campaign until I met MacDonald Gallion, the Democrat candidate for attorney general. Gallion, whom Daddy also knew, offered me greater responsibility in his race. I left Wallace, put off law school for six months, and went to work for him.

Running against John Patterson in 1958, Wallace became the overwhelming choice of black voters. His stance was much closer to that of Big Jim Folsom than Patterson, "the segregation forever" candidate. Patterson won.

United Klans of America's founder, Imperial Wizard Bobby Shelton, supported Patterson, and the lesson of the election wasn't lost on Wallace. After losing, the populist reassessed his political career, vowing never to be "out-segged," or out-segregationed, again. The rest, as they say, is history. He lost my support, but he beat Big Jim the next time out in 1962. At that time Alabama governors could not hold the office for successive terms, and Wallace captured the Patterson constituency by vowing to stand up to federal courts and forced integration. (Interestingly, Patterson greatly tempered his views on race over the years and later provided valuable assistance in one of my cases.)

Shelton did not publicly endorse Wallace, but his Cadillac was a familiar sight in Wallace motorcades. The Klan circulated cartoons showing Adam Clayton Powell sitting on Folsom's knee at the governor's mansion, a reference to a visit the controversial black congressman from Harlem had made at Folsom's invitation in the mid-1950s.

Mac Gallion did win in 1958. By the time of the election, I had worked my way up his organization so that I was functioning like a campaign manager. Despite my position, I didn't feel totally comfortable working on his campaign. Gallion was quite racially extreme compared to George Wallace or even his opponent Richmond Flowers.

After the election, Gallion assured me he would name me his chief assistant attorney general when I graduated from law school. I told him I wasn't interested. I didn't like the back-room dealing and ass kissing I'd seen during the campaign. I didn't like the notion that after working for four years, fickle voters could turn you out. In short, I'd learned firsthand that politics wasn't for me. I wanted to control my own destiny.

By the time Millard and I graduated from law school, our enterprises were generating more money than we could expect to make as young lawyers. We debated whether to stay in Tuscaloosa and be businessmen or return to Montgomery and become attorneys. Daddy lobbied long and hard for the latter. Real estate and selling fund-raising products by mail seemed too risky for his taste.

While business was exciting and profitable, I wanted to try cases. Millard and I finally decided we could do both. We sold our buildings, passed some of our student businesses on to others, and took the fund-raising enterprise with us to Montgomery.

From the sale of the buildings alone, we each netted about twenty thousand dollars. I took the money and bought a new 1960 Ford and a three-bedroom house in Mount Meigs for fourteen thousand dollars cash. We needed the space. Beverly had given birth to our second son, Johnny, in 1958.

In Montgomery, whom you know often is more important than what you know. No one knew Millard, and most people had never heard of me. After we started the law partnership of Dees and Fuller, we started walking into local law firms and introducing ourselves. "If ever a case comes in your office that you can't handle or it's a little bitty nothing, give us a call," we said.

We had planned to visit every firm in town, but we never finished. The phone started ringing with referrals from those we met—mostly little bitty nothing cases, but they added up. In our first year, we earned more than we would have at a big firm—twelve thousand dollars each.

Daddy had some wealthy friends, but they weren't bringing me any major business. If they had a case worth a darn, they took it to the established lawyers in town. If they had a bill they figured they could never collect, then maybe they'd call me. That was the case with Earl Thornton.

Earl, a pale, overweight clerk at Mr. Samuels's Alabama Cotton Warehouse, wanted me to collect ten thousand dollars he had loaned another tenant farmer years earlier. The farmer had never repaid the loan. Earl had sued him and been awarded a judgment, but the farmer had disappeared and Earl had never collected. Now Earl had located twenty bales of cotton belonging to the man and wanted me to seize it in payment of his judgment.

Under Alabama law, when a judgment is more than ten years old, as this one was, there is a presumption that it has been satisfied. I warned Earl that if the farmer refused to pay, we might end up fighting this out in court. Then I tracked down the man and told him Mr. Thornton would forgo the hefty interest that had built up over the years if he paid the money originally owed. The farmer made no mention that the judgment was eleven years old, and to my shock, he agreed to my terms. Proudly I took the ten-thousand-dollar check down to the Alabama Cotton Warehouse.

Earl sat behind a wood counter with a wire grille like a cashier's cage. I handed the check to him through an opening in the grille.

"I want to thank you, Bubba," he said. "You did a good job." He reached into a drawer, pulled out two one-hundred-dollar bills, and stuck them through the window.

I just stared at him. I was planning to send him a bill as any lawyer would. The fee in a collection matter might be anywhere from a third to half of the amount collected, but I would only charge him 25 percent, twenty-five hundred dollars.

Two hundred dollars! Without a word, I took the money and tore it in half. Then I tore it in half again. And again. He looked at me in shock.

"Mr. Thornton," I said, "I don't need your money. You keep it. Because it is worth more to you than me. You never would have gotten that money if I hadn't been so persuasive. A collection attorney would have charged you at least thirty-five hundred dollars. You keep it. I don't want anything." I walked out the door.

Daddy phoned me an hour later. "Earl called me," he said. "What are you, crazy or something? If it wasn't for those people, we wouldn't have been able to eat many a time."

"That's you, and I'm me," I said. "I don't owe him anything. I don't mind being nice or busting my butt for him. But I expect to be paid for it."

Daddy didn't understand. "You're just too smart for your own britches," he said.

What had ticked inside me all those years that made me explode like that? I was offended. Earl Thornton was taking me for granted.

The Earl Thorntons and Alabama Cotton Warehouses of the world had used my dad all those years, just as they had used every white farmer who they made think was their best friend on earth. Daddy was still buying into it after all those years. Here I was, Morris Dees's son, and Earl was just throwing me a coin or two, like throwing a dog a bone off the table.

While I was worried about collection matters and getting our practice off the ground, the civil rights movement was taking flight. I wasn't yet on board. In fact, I was remarkably oblivious considering that Montgomery, as the state capital and Martin Luther King, Jr.'s base of operations until 1960, was often in the center of things. On May 4, 1961, when a group of blacks and whites started a trip through the South to test the Supreme Court's recent rulings outlawing segregation in bus terminals, I didn't pay too much attention. As their journey continued, I did realize that the Freedom Riders, as they called themselves, were encountering hate and violence. Less than two weeks into the trip, they were beaten by a mob in Anniston, Alabama. After that they were attacked in Birmingham, then in Montgomery, where more than a thousand angry whites beat them without police intervention.

While I didn't applaud this brutality, I never raised my voice in protest. Later when Claude Henley, a rural neighbor charged with assaulting a television reporter during the riot, asked me to defend him, I didn't think twice.

Claude, a thirty-five-year-old used-car salesman, was a big old country boy with a potbelly and a fat cigar that seemed permanently attached to his mouth. He was a defendant in two cases—a civil suit filed by the federal government and a criminal proceeding instituted by the city of Montgomery. He had clearly been involved in some of the action. A picture of him kicking a newsman had appeared in *Life* magazine after the riot. The assault charges brought by the city didn't worry Claude as much as the federal government's suit, which also named the city of Montgomery's police department and several other individuals, including Bobby Shelton, as defendants for their roles in the attack on the Freedom Riders.

Sitting in my office, in red-and-blue-checked slacks, a short-sleeved white shirt, and a brown tie, Claude took a puff on his cigar and blew the smoke my way, making me wish he'd heard Miss Margaret Waugh's "filthy weed" lesson. He said that John Blue Hill, a prominent local attorney, had asked for fifteen thousand dollars to represent him. I had been thinking about charging five hundred dollars. "I'll take your case for five thousand dollars," I said. He agreed.

The federal lawsuit took aim at the police department for its failure to protect the marchers after it realized the trouble in Anniston and Birmingham would probably occur in Montgomery as well. Claude was just a small fish. While the picture in *Life* wouldn't help with our assault defense, it would help in federal court. It demonstrated that Claude hadn't been where the marchers were, but instead a block away, beating up a reporter.

The Justice Department had brought in some big guns for the federal case. I sat at the defense table with Shelton, who was dressed in a blue seersucker suit and white socks, and other Klansmen and their lawyers. They were neither penitent nor worried. They just passed the time making racial cracks.

When the Justice Department's John Doar came over to our table, I asked him what he wanted from Claude. He said he just wanted Claude to agree to be enjoined from future disruptions. That was fine with us. We told the judge, Frank M. Johnson, Jr., and we were out of the case.

In the hallway, two young black men, part of the Freedom Riders group, approached me. "How can you represent people like that?"

one of them asked. "Don't you think that black people have rights?"

I was startled. This was the first time a black person had ever confronted me. "Yes, I do," I said sincerely. "I agree with you a hundred percent." Then I walked off.

Claude and I parted on the street. I didn't let him see that I was shaken. My actions, my morality, had been challenged.

Did I deserve to be challenged? I didn't see representing Claude Henley as a racial thing. To make some money, I was taking a case that just happened to be tied up with the Freedom Riders. My God, it wasn't that I was interested in the Klan! I was interested in making five thousand dollars representing a neighbor and keeping him out of trouble.

But looking in the face of my accuser, I felt the anger of a black person for the first time. He saw me as an enemy representing the Klan, just as years later Louis Beam and his compatriots would see me as an enemy opposing the Klan. Here I was feeling that I was friends with blacks, remembering that I had spoken up for Emmett Till and Autherine Lucy, and all of a sudden this young man was doubting me. I vowed then and there that nobody would ever again doubt where I stood. It took me a couple of years to make good on that promise.

CHAPTER 6

September 1963   Birmingham, Alabama

The four little girls were in the basement of Birmingham's Sixteenth Street Baptist Church straightening their fancy white dresses when the dynamite bomb exploded. The church shook. Walls crumbled. Ceilings fell. The people upstairs coming into the holy place for a special Youth Sunday celebration screamed, then raced outside. The girls in the basement didn't even have time to scream; Addie Mae Collins, Cynthia Wesley, and Carole Robertson, all just fourteen years old, and Denise McNair, only eleven, were killed instantly.

This wasn't the first Birmingham bombing. Ministers' homes, a black-owned hotel, and other churches had been destroyed. But there had been nothing as evil as the dynamiting of children during Sunday school. After the bombing, the aptly named white supremacist Connie Lynch told a Klan gathering that the bombers deserved medals. The four little girls who had died "weren't children," he said. "Children are little people, little human beings, and that means white people. . . . They're just little niggers . . . and if there's four less niggers tonight, then I say, 'Good for whoever planted the bomb!' "

Less than three weeks earlier, Dr. King had given his famous "I Have a Dream" speech in Washington, D.C., to the largest civil rights gathering in history. Now he spoke to eight thousand mourners at a joint funeral for three of the victims. "The innocent blood of these little girls may well serve as the redemptive force that will bring new light to this dark city," he said. "Indeed, this tragic event may cause the white South to come to terms with its conscience."

Ninety miles away in Montgomery, I felt the reverberations of the bombs, and as Dr. King prophesied, I came to terms with my conscience.

*   *   *

Beverly and I were still good Baptists. We said our prayers together every night. We belonged to the Pike Road Baptist Church—the church my family had helped build, the church of my parents and grandparents, the church that had given us a Bible with our names in front to commemorate our marriage. When I had returned home from law school, I'd been named superintendent of the Sunday school.

On Sunday, September 22, 1963, I stood before the congregation. Before saying anything, I looked over the assembled: our friends, our neighbors, the parents of the children with whom my boys went to school, the people who owned the stores where we traded, the people to whom I had always been "Bubba."

"Brothers and sisters," I said, "there's another Baptist church that needs our help."

"Tell us, Bubba," someone said.

"It's a church that has had a tragedy."

The congregation, my friends, nodded approvingly. I wasn't surprised. These were goodhearted, charitable people. They weren't the type to turn down fellow God-fearing folk in a time of need.

"Where is the church?" someone asked.

"You've heard of it," I said. "It's the Sixteenth Street Church in Birmingham where those four little girls were killed last Sunday and the church was destroyed."

The blood drained from my friends' faces, the nodding stopped. The members of the Pike Road Baptist Church quickly fell into two camps—those who were angered by the suggestion and those who were too shocked to be angry. I couldn't make out their whispers, but I could read their expressions.

I pulled a check from my pocket. "I'm giving this to help the church rebuild," I said. "I hope you all will either write a check of your own or give what cash you can."

An old woman sitting in the back of the church stood up. "This ain't none of our business, Morris, Jr.," she said. "This ain't nothing we want to get involved in."

The nodding began again.

I felt I had to go on. "I'd like for you all to join me in a little prayer for the girls before we go to our classes," I said.

There was a deathly silence.

"Please, won't you join me in a prayer? We all have children of our own. No matter how you feel about—" My words hit their frozen hearts and fell to the floor. Head bowed, I prayed silently. Soon, I heard a rustling and then some footsteps. I looked up. Beverly stood beside me, and we prayed together.

We stayed up there at the front of the church . . . and stayed, nobody joining us. I prayed and prayed, and when I finally looked up, just the two of us were left in the sanctuary. Everyone else had left for Sunday school.

Years later Beverly would look back on this day and say, "That was the beginning. You knew your life was going to change and you had to go on with it."

More than a quarter of a century after the fact, it seems like such a small gesture. Asking for a contribution, praying for the souls of little girls hardly seems extraordinary, certainly not worthy of self-congratulation. I hadn't gone to Washington, D.C., for Dr. King's march; I'd never marched period. I hadn't stood up to Bull Connor in Birmingham. Just a silent prayer, an act consistent with Christian teachings, praying for the souls of other Christians. *Children.* And yet my good friends and neighbors could not free themselves from the slavery of the Southern tradition and, forgetting about color, do the Christian thing.

It *was* the Christian thing. I remembered one of Reverend Russell's sermons. On Judgment Day, a man consigned to hell had asked God why. God had answered: "When I was hungry, you failed to give me food. When I was without clothes, you didn't give me any. When I was sick, you didn't come to visit me."

Reverend Russell had rightly told us this meant that we had to minister to the sick, to feed and clothe those in need. I'm not one to put words into the Lord's mouth, but the logical extension was: *When I was denied the basic rights for things like education, you did nothing. When I was without the right to participate in government, you denied me the right to vote.* But the white Southern preachers didn't complete that circle. They turned the civil rights movement away from their doors.

On the way home from church, I wondered if Daddy or Momma would have joined Beverly and me if they had been there. Momma would have been torn. She would have prayed silently for the young girls, and, most likely, she would have quietly slipped a check into the mail. But she wouldn't have wanted to make her friends in our church upset. It would have been a hard decision for her.

I figured that if Daddy were still alive, he would not have understood my actions any more than he had understood my tearing Earl Thornton's money. But he was two years dead by then. One Saturday evening in the fall of 1961, he was out making his social calls on his drinking and boasting buddies. Driving his new Mercury, he had veered off U.S. 80 and hit a tree. He was killed instantly.

When Beverly and I got the message that something had happened to Daddy, we raced to Momma's house. Momma met me at the door and told me he was dead. I kissed her, ran into the field behind the house, and sat down and cried—as much for myself, I think, as for Daddy. The most influential man in my life was gone.

After I spoke up for the four little girls from Birmingham, I didn't start trying cases that challenged segregation. I might have if somebody had come to me, but nobody did. Why would they? I wasn't known in the movement—for good reason: I wasn't part of it. I wasn't even practicing law at the time.

Just after Millard and I had started our firm, a high-school girl walked into our office selling a "favorite recipes" cookbook as a fund-raiser for the local Future Homemakers of America club. It struck me that the concept had incredible possibilities.

Within three months we had collected recipes from across the country and put together our own book, *Favorite Recipes of Home Economics Teachers*. We sent a free copy to all nineteen thousand home economics teachers in the country along with instructions on how their Future Homemakers of America clubs could earn one dollar a book without risking anything. Our profit would also be one dollar a book. Within another three months, we had sold 250,000 copies. The new publishing and direct-mail business was so profitable we shut down the law office.

In the months after Birmingham, I thought a lot more about civil rights and justice, trying to square what was happening in the streets with what I had been brought up to believe in church. Millard, raised a Congregationalist, was going through the same soul-searching. We spent long hours sorting out our own feelings. There was a lot of baggage that had to be dumped, a lifetime of indoctrination that said giving black people their rights would destroy our cherished way of life. But the events surrounding us made us realize our way of life had to change: the election of George Wallace, who had made good on his promise not to be out-segged, and his dramatic defiance of attempts to integrate; the riots over James Meredith's attempts to break the color barrier and enroll at Ole Miss; the murders of Medgar Evers and several other blacks and whites committed to the struggle for equality; the disappearance of the three civil rights workers—Schwerner, Chaney, and Goodman—in Mississippi.

Our business, which was growing dramatically, was one place where we could change things. In December of 1964, we rented the ballroom of the Jefferson Davis Hotel, one of the city's finest, for our Christmas party. The hotel wasn't integrated—there were no integrated eating or sleeping establishments in Montgomery at that time—but that didn't stop us from inviting our black employees, who made up about one quarter of our work force and held some positions traditionally reserved for whites. We hadn't told the Jefferson Davis that our group would include blacks, and when we showed up, there were more than a few surprised and distressed looks on the faces of the hotel staff, but no one said a word to us.

Our white employees had worked with blacks every day, but most of their spouses had not. For almost everyone, it was the first time they had been in a room where at the same time blacks were dancing with blacks and whites with whites. That in itself was an eye-opener, and when Millard and I each danced with some of the black women who worked for us, an amazed silence fell over the place.

That silence did not extend beyond the hotel. Montgomery is a small town. Word spread about the integrated party at the Jefferson Davis, embellished with each telling, spawning numerous rumors about our business. A few days after Christmas one of our employees, a white woman named Marilyn Black, overheard another woman mention our company. "That's the place where they print Communist literature for all these niggers and their marches," the woman said. "You can tell when those people come at night with their briefcases and they leave with boxes of things." We did print in-house, but those boxes leaving in the middle of the night were full of books like *Favorite Recipes of the Republican Women,* not civil rights pamphlets.

Two years after the Birmingham bombings, I took part in my first civil rights event. In March of 1965, Millard and I drove a number of people to Selma for what became the historic forty-nine-mile march led by Dr. King from that city to Montgomery in support of the Voting Rights Act of 1965.

Volunteering to drive hadn't seemed like a big deal, but by the time we got to Selma, I realized the implications. State troopers lined the main avenues, directing cars like ours to a central parking area. Two weeks earlier, the first demonstrators attempting to march from Selma to Montgomery had been brutally beaten by troopers, whose battle plan had been discussed in advance with Governor Wallace. After that Dr. King had gone to federal court to get an order permitting the march. This time the troopers were under court order to protect the marchers, not assault them.

I knew some of these troopers. Not one to forget an old political debt—Daddy's support in 1958—George Wallace had made my newly widowed momma a justice of the peace after his election as governor in 1962. The troopers were always at her house. They were generally friendly to me, but on this day, the ones who recognized me shook their heads sadly. The ones who didn't know me jotted down my license number. No doubt some of these were the same men who had used their clubs on the marchers less than two weeks earlier.

There must have been a thousand people in the square outside the AME Church, headquarters for the march. A man with a megaphone stood on the church steps and announced, "Let's all get down and pray."

My days of kneeling and praying had lessened considerably since the Birmingham bombing. I had begun to question the white church's role, or lack of one, in speaking up for justice. Millard knelt right away. So did almost everybody else. I resisted.

Looking around, I saw a thousand black and white men, women, and children on the ground, and scores of policemen and troopers, some plainclothes, some in full dress, standing. Police vans ringed the square. More troopers stood on the vans, some armed with guns, some armed with cameras. My heart beat with those in prayer, not in a state of war. I knelt, too.

Millard and I didn't march to Montgomery. We waited until the journey was just about over, then hurried downtown to watch the committed arrive and make their speeches. The word had gone out for the white people of Montgomery to stay out of downtown. City and state officials didn't want it to look like anyone was interested in what the blacks were doing. But Millard and I were interested and sympathetic.

The normally tranquil capitol grounds had become a war zone. Police lines prevented access to the area where the tired marchers would make their speeches. Army, National Guard, and state troopers patrolled the ground, stood guard on top of buildings, hovered in helicopters. Unless you were part of the march, you weren't supposed to get anywhere close to the capitol, but we knew some deputy sheriffs and they let us pass through the lines. We walked in front of the capitol and the State Troopers building and sat down by ourselves on a grassy knoll where we could see the speaker's rostrum, a vast raised wooden platform. About two dozen black leaders were sitting up there—Dr. King, James Farmer, John Lewis, Ralph Abernathy. I thought how much this must bother Governor Wallace and the rest of the state and city leaders. While the state flag and the Confederate flag waved in the spring breeze, a group of black citizens who had refused to be beaten back by the white state army—the troopers— were making speeches challenging the Southern way of life, asking for the right to vote.

Not too long after the speeches started, I spotted my uncle, James Dees. He was standing by himself under a tree not more than a dozen yards from us. He saw me and headed my way. James was fifty-two, with a red-freckled face, not handsome like my daddy and Uncle Lucien. He had a temper and could drink pretty well. Like Uncle Lucien, he loved me as a son, but the stories of my recent civil rights activities had not sat well with him. He looked at me and Millard coldly. "I know all about you," he snarled. "You're nothing but a bunch of nigger lovers."

He opened his coat. In his belt was a .38 pistol. "I oughta take this gun and kill you both here on the spot," he said.

"C'mon, Millard," I said, motioning for us to leave. This was not the time for a confrontation.

God only knows what was in James's mind. He might have shot Martin Luther King if he could have gotten close enough. More likely, in these changing times, he probably just wanted to take a stand for his way of life, the old Southern way of doing things. It was more than he could stomach to see those black people so close to the seat of power in Montgomery.

Uncle James wasn't the only one who thought Millard and I were "nigger lovers." The state troopers asked our sheriff what I'd been doing in Selma. And Beverly's friends asked her.

This was the beginning of hard times for our family. My public acts, so small in the scheme of things, were magnified in Montgomery's fishbowl society. Unfortunately, more often than not, Beverly and the boys paid for my acts. They were the ones whose friends and class-mates stayed away or cursed them. Beverly could understand this, and as her heart beat as one with mine on these issues, she accepted the consequences of my actions. The boys, ages nine and seven at the time, didn't fully understand. They just knew that many kids wouldn't sit with them on the school bus or invite them to birthday parties because of something I had done.

I wasn't as sensitive to this ostracism as I should have been. As a result I was usually ignorant of the scorn of my neighbors or simply ignored it. I think this was because I had never given a lick about being part of Montgomery society, never desired to be part of the blueblood plantation scene with its small talk and pettiness.

When I had returned to Montgomery after law school, Daddy had told me I should join the exclusive Montgomery Country Club. I knew I'd feel as uncomfortable there as I had in the great dining hall at the Handy plantation more than a decade earlier. If I had spare time, I told Daddy, I'd rather hunt than play golf; I'd rather swim in a creek than a pool; and I'd rather eat dinner with the folks I knew, like T. J., than the people I *should* know.

Besides, I had a new passion. When I had bought my first calf, I had practiced roping her until I had the catch down to fifteen seconds. I had dreamed of owning a cattle ranch with quarter horses and Herefords. That dream had come true. After purchasing Rolling Hills Ranch with cookbook profits, I bought the best roping horse money could buy and hit the rodeo circuit. Weekends I'd trailer my horse to the nearest rodeo, and afterward would shoot pool with the other riders until daylight. They didn't care who you were or what you did for a living.

The reputation I was developing in Montgomery as a "nigger lover" soon made country club membership moot. Not too long after the Selma march, we were at a party at the home of one of Beverly's friends, one of the country club set. Our host came up to me, drink in hand. He was a colonel at Maxwell Field, just as Beverly's father had been, and apparently for this reason he felt protective of her. "Morris," he said, taking a long sip on his cocktail, "you know you ain't never gonna get anywhere the way you're going. You ought to leave this nigger thing alone. It's gonna hurt your wife's reputation." There was more than gin in his voice. There was anger.

I didn't return that anger. "Colonel," I said quietly, "I don't want to cause a problem. I do what I think is right, just like I'm sure you do what you think is right. I've got no personal bad feelings against you, but I don't really care what Montgomery thinks."

"You mean you don't care what people think about you?" He was genuinely surprised.

I shook my head.

That ended that, and, for the most part, ended our invitations to the parties hosted by Montgomery's in crowd. It didn't bother me, and if it bothered Beverly, she never told me.

We started spending our time with a more thoughtful crowd—the people of Montgomery's small, newly formed Unitarian Fellowship. Because I couldn't reconcile the moral stance of our church with the events of the day, we had been spending less and less time at Pike Road Baptist Church. The Unitarians appealed to us because they not only preached "justice for all," they practiced it. I had also begun to question the Baptist tenets and dogma and found the Unitarian philosophy refreshing.

Some of the Unitarians were active in the local chapter of the American Civil Liberties Union, and eventually I became involved. I was still a full-time businessman, but I did agree to work on ACLU cases when I had the time. In August of 1967, I filed a lawsuit in federal court on behalf of Gary Dickey against the Alabama State Board of Education. Gary, a white Vietnam veteran who was student editor of the newspaper at Troy State University, had been suspended for writing an editorial critical of Governor Wallace. In explaining the action, Troy State's president, Ralph Adams, a good friend of the governor, explained that the *Birmingham News,* owned by Jews, never published material critical of Jewish people, and therefore the school paper, which received state funds, should not be critical of the legislature or governor. Judge Johnson saw it as we did—as a question of freedom of speech. "A state cannot force a college student to forfeit his constitutionally protected right of freedom of expression as a condition to his attending a state-supported institution," the judge ruled. He ordered that Gary be readmitted to the college.

My business responsibilities made it difficult to commit too much time to the ACLU. Millard, who had reevaluated his life and decided, in his words, "to serve God," had left the business a few years earlier to form what would later become Habitat for Humanity, a dynamic not-for-profit organization devoted to providing livable, affordable housing for the poor, whose participants include former president Jimmy Carter. I missed Millard's friendship and business sense. He was a superb financial manager who provided a watchful eye over the bottom line while I was busy coming up with new product ideas and marketing plans. But despite the gap left by his departure, the company was still moving forward. We were the leading cookbook publisher in the United States, selling 750,000 books a year in the Home Economics series and another 2.5 million cookbooks to women's clubs and church groups. These sales along with the sales of our other fund-raising products totalled about $6.5 million in 1967. That same year, along with consumer activist Ralph Nader and attorney Joseph

Califano, I was named one of the Jaycees' ten "Outstanding Young Men in America."

With a million dollars in cookbook profits and a line of credit at Montgomery's First National Bank, I was in the process of creating a trade book publishing company that I hoped would move me into the big leagues. I had initially wanted to start the new company with a sex-education library for teenagers. But sex education was a controversial issue in 1967, and Wally Black, a publishing friend and retired Air Force officer, persuaded me to begin with *Above and Beyond,* an aerospace encyclopedia capitalizing on the late sixties' space craze. Our base of operations for the encyclopedia was in Wally's hometown, Chicago, more fertile ground than Montgomery for finding editors. As a result I was spending a good deal of my time up north.

Things were not going well. The project was behind schedule almost from the moment it was launched, and costs were skyrocketing because of money wasted on high-priced writers and padded expense accounts. I was on my way to Chicago in February of 1968 to try to straighten things out when a snowstorm closed O'Hare Airport, forcing us to land in Cincinnati.

When I learned that O'Hare was snowed in until morning and I would be spending the night on a hard chair in Cincinnati's airport, I cursed Wally Black, who, I imagined, was out wining and dining a beautiful blonde—at my expense! I stopped at the airport's snack bar, picked up a hot dog and Coke, and then browsed the newsstand. One book, *The Story of My Life* by Clarence Darrow, caught my eye. I flipped through the table of contents. It read like the literature of our Unitarian church:

THE EVOLUTION CASE: Mr. William Jennings Bryan made it clear that he was not so much interested in the Age of Rocks, as in the Rock of Ages. . . .

WHY CAPITAL PUNISHMENT: When judges add to the death sentence, "And may God have mercy on your soul," they have their fingers crossed.

I bought the paperback, a reprint of the 1934 original, and found a seat to eat my supper.

Before daylight I finished Darrow's story of his life. It changed mine forever. I was reading my own thoughts and feelings. Darrow wrote that as a young boy, "not only could I put myself in the other person's place, but I could not avoid doing so. My sympathies always went out to the weak, the suffering, and the poor. Realizing their sorrows, I tried to relieve them in order that I might be relieved. I had a thoroughly independent, perhaps individual, way of looking at things, and was never influenced by the views of others unless I could be convinced that they were nearly right. I had little respect for the opinion of the crowd. My instinct was to doubt the majority view."

I remembered being mocked for writing the letter to the newspaper after Emmett Till had been thrown into the Tallahatchie River. I remembered the blank looks on the faces of the Sunday school assembly in Tuscaloosa and the follow-up demotion contrived by Reverend Williams after I talked about Autherine Lucy. And I remembered asking the Pike Road Baptist Church to pray with me after the Sixteenth Street Baptist Church bombing.

I read on. When the American Railway Union's members went on strike in 1894, Darrow was counsel for the Chicago and Northwestern Railroad Company. It was a high-paying job with a bright future. The bitter, violent strike directed by the socialist Eugene V. Debs had grown out of a demand for higher wages and safer working conditions. Darrow said he sympathized with the workers and agreed with their demands. He was angered that a rival railroad had obtained a federal court injunction ordering the strikers to return to work or face criminal contempt charges. He resigned his railroad position to represent the workers.

Once freed from the restraints of the corporate world and able to follow his conscience, Darrow undertook cases that made legal history in the fight for human dignity and justice for the powerless. I read about those cases all night. I could relate to his dilemma of leaving the safe, accepted, business-as-usual world.

I hadn't done enough since Justice of the Peace Letcher had shown me Southern justice by waiting on the customers in his country store while fining Clarence Williams for being poor and black. When Dr. King led the twenty-five thousand marchers from Selma up Dexter Avenue to the capitol, part of me had wanted to take that step into the street and join them, but I hadn't. When Uncle James Dees had called me a "nigger lover," I should have called him on it, pistol or not. Daddy had often told me that a coward dies a thousand times, but a brave man only once. I had never backed away from a fight before I meekly retreated from Uncle James. But as I listened to Dr. King make his speech that day, I had realized the fight was with myself, and I wasn't quite ready for the risk it entailed.

*   *   *

On the flight to Chicago the next morning, I thought a lot about Clarence Darrow. I also thought about a sermon Reverend Russell had given when I was a teenager, one that caught my attention because I thought he was going to talk about farming:

"To every thing there is a season, and a time to every purpose under the heavens," Reverend Russell read from Ecclesiastes. There is, he continued, "a time to keep silent and a time to speak."

When my plane landed in Chicago, I was ready to take that step, to speak out for my black friends who were still "disenfranchised" even after the Voting Rights Act of 1965. Little had changed in the South. Whites held the power and had no intention of voluntarily sharing it. Blacks were excluded from good jobs, decent housing, elective office, good educations, jury service, and a host of other aspects of the community enjoyed by whites.

The bitterness caused by the Civil Rights Act of 1964 and the intrusion of federal agents hardened the South's will to resist. When the army of Justice Department lawyers began to return north after Congress passed the Voting Rights Act, Deep South officials and private groups closed ranks to limit black gains.

It would take lawsuits to achieve these gains. There were few black lawyers around and hardly any white ones who would touch controversial cases. I was a good lawyer wasting my time trying to make a few more million dollars.

I had made up my mind. I would sell the company as soon as possible and specialize in civil rights law. All the things in my life that had brought me to this point, all the pulls and tugs of my conscience, found a singular peace. It did not matter what my neighbors would think, or the judges, the bankers, or even my relatives. I only wished my daddy had been alive to share my decision. "To everything there is a season." For me, it was going to be a season for justice.

When I returned from Chicago, two important messages were waiting for me. A writer for *The Reporter of Direct Mail Advertising,* the major trade publication of the mail sales industry, had called to say the magazine wanted to do a cover story on my business. That's like a rock star being on the cover of *Rolling Stone.* A favorable article might put a bee in the bonnet of a prospective buyer.

The second call was from Fred Gray, one of the most prominent lawyers of the civil rights era, a black Alabamian who had represented Dr. King during the Montgomery bus boycott. Several weeks earlier Fred had asked if I would help him represent the Alabama State

Teachers Association, an all-black organization, if it filed suit to stop the building of Auburn University in Montgomery. It had seemed clear to me that bringing Auburn to town would only perpetuate the separate but unequal dual education system in Alabama. Whites who wanted to go to college in Montgomery would now go to the new Auburn branch instead of considering Alabama State, an all-black college that could have used the money to offer the same classes as Auburn. I had told Fred that if I had the time I would get involved. Now he had called to tell me he was ready to file a lawsuit. I said to count me in.

Taking one of the first depositions, I learned that one of the leaders behind the Auburn effort was Frank Plummer, the president of the First National Bank. This would have been fine but for the fact that my business owed the bank about $2 million in loans and our collateral was weak as wellwater. Mr. Plummer didn't need an excuse to call in the loan, and calling in the loan could break me and shatter any hopes of selling my company at anything except a bankruptcy auction.

I called on Mr. Plummer at the bank, not to plead for mercy—I had no intention of dropping out of the case—but to let him know that I was involved in a lawsuit that I believed in. He seemed to understand. "You do what you have to do, Morris. This won't affect our business relationship. Your loan will be judged on its merit."

I spent the early part of 1968 shifting gears, trying to keep Auburn out of Montgomery and *Above and Beyond* beyond the creditors. Neither was easy. In the Auburn case, I interviewed almost every high-school principal in the area. The principals at the thirty-five predominantly white schools told me that their students were actively recruited by Auburn-Montgomery officials who held meetings at the schools. The principals at the predominantly black schools said no one from the university had ever contacted them. This seemed to bolster our case, but in July a three-judge panel including Judge Johnson ruled against us, finding that a state could build new colleges as long as its doors were open to all.

While all this was going on, the cover story on my business appeared. As I had hoped, it attracted the attention of two giants, Times Mirror Corporation, owner of the *Los Angeles Times* and a dozen specialty publishing companies, and CBS Marketing. After talking with Times Mirror's president, Al Casey, I knew he was my man.

The preliminary negotiations took several months, as accountants pored over the books. In the meantime, I pushed Wally Black to start the Life Cycle Library, the sex-education encyclopedia. Most of our

fund-raising products and books were sold through direct-mail solici-
tations that I had written. Now I wrote a mailer that could be used
by World Book to test-market this new project to its list of six million
customers. Fortunately, Casey liked the idea of the encyclopedia.

As this chapter of my life as a businessman appeared to be ending,
so, unfortunately, was my life with Beverly. Only kids when we married, we now had grown apart. We had two terrific sons and a fine
home, but the tensions of business and, more important, the turmoil
caused by my restless soul took a heavy toll. We divorced.

Beverly always stuck by me in the face of community rejection. We
never doubted our love for each other, a love that remains to this day.
A teacher in Washington, D.C., now, she calls the Morris Dees that
she lived with her "magnificent obsession." In the years since we
separated, we've laughed that we were more like brother and sister,
raising our children when we were only children ourselves. Our
oldest, Morris III, is now in medical school after several entrepreneurial successes, and our youngest, Johnny, is a builder.

Not too long after Beverly and I divorced, just as talks with Times
Mirror began, I married Maureene Buck. We had known each other
for years. She was an editor at my company, and we served together
on the Montgomery Little Theatre Board of Directors. A beauty
queen and actress, Maureene had won Miss Maid of Cotton and about
every other pageant in Georgia and then joined Delta Airlines as a
flight attendant before coming to our publishing company.

Beverly moved to Louisville after we split up. The boys continued
to live with me on Rolling Hills Ranch. Maureene had a five-year-old
daughter, Holly, and a three-year-old son, Blakely. As merger talks
with Times Mirror moved forward, we merged our families.

The talks continued into 1969, and I stayed at the company, still
taking on the occasional ACLU case. In early February, the Auburn
University administration refused to allow Yale's Reverend William
Sloane Coffin to speak to a student group. This wasn't surprising: The
movement against the war in Vietnam boiled most Alabamians' blood
every bit as hot as the civil rights movement did, and no Ivy League
intellectual, even if he was a chaplain, would receive a forum. I had
gradually decided we had no business in Southeast Asia, but even if
I had favored the war I would have fought for Reverend Coffin's right
to air his views. On behalf of the students, I sued to permit Reverend
Coffin to speak. Judge Johnson, as in *Dickey,* saw this as a case in which
the First Amendment right to freedom of speech was paramount and
ruled in our favor. Coffin, protected by Alabama troopers, finally

made his speech, creating huge headlines throughout the state.

When I arrived at my office the morning after Reverend Coffin spoke, I found that a new addition to the building had been vandalized. There was no mistaking who had done it. "KKK" was slashed into the newly plastered walls of an unlocked area with an axe and written all over the walls. A water hose had been turned on under the front door, flooding our computer room.

I was furious. Earlier in the week, I had received a threatening letter and we had spotted some people in the parking lot watching our building, but this went beyond threats. I telephoned my old neighbor and former client Claude Henley and asked him to come down to the building.

"Friend," I said when he arrived, "I helped you out with that Freedom Riders thing. I got you out of that case. And now the Klan's messing with me."

"How do you know it's the Klan, Bubba?" he asked, puffing on his cigar. "Maybe someone just put those letters up there to make it look like the Klan."

I told him that we had taken down the license plate number of the car that had been in our lot earlier, and that we had traced it to one of the United Klan members who had been arrested several years earlier for bombing buses in Montgomery. The United Klan was, of course, Bobby Shelton's faction, the group that had beaten the Freedom Riders, the group suspected of the Sixteenth Street Baptist Church bombing and the murder of Viola Liuzzo during the 1965 Selma-to-Montgomery march for voting rights.

"Claude," I continued, "let's get old Bobby on the phone right now." I dialed Shelton's number at the Klan's headquarters in Tuscaloosa and turned on my speakerphone.

This wouldn't be my first conversation with Shelton. A year or two after the Freedom Riders case, he had called and asked if we could meet. Out of curiosity, I agreed. When he pulled up in the big Cadillac he'd driven in the Wallace for Governor campaign, I climbed in. As the Imperial Wizard and I cruised Montgomery, he made me a proposition. He knew I was in publishing. Would I be interested in printing the *Fiery Cross,* the official newspaper of the United Klans of America?

I'd swallowed my laughter and then refused. I told him we didn't print newspapers: I didn't tell him that even if we did, I wouldn't spread his message across the country. Our different views about politics and race never came up.

This phone call with Claude in my office would not be as polite.

When Shelton answered, I told him what the Klan had done to my building. Reaching behind the drapes in my office I pulled out the Browning automatic shotgun I'd bought after receiving the threatening letter. I aimed it at Claude. "Tell Bobby what I'm doing, Claude," I said.

Claude's cigar was shaking. So were his knees. He described the shotgun to Bobby in vivid detail.

I put a shell in the chamber. "Now tell him what I'm doing, Claude," I ordered.

Claude again obliged.

"Bobby," I said, "I'm going to blow this son of a bitch's head right off of his goddamn neck. You don't fuck with me now."

I looked up at Claude. "You think I'd shoot you, Claude?"

"Yes, yes. I think you'd do it."

Bobby interrupted. "Claude," he said, "if you can talk to somebody down there and find out what's going on, you tell him to let Morris alone. Just leave him alone."

I smiled at Claude. "Okay, Bobby," I said into the speakerphone. "That's it."

I put down the gun. The color came back into Claude's cigar.

The building had been repaired by the time I flew out to New York a few months later to meet with the Times Mirror's Al Casey and Martin Levin, president of Times Mirror's New American Library subsidiary. On the flight my lawyer, Leon Capuano, and I discussed what I should ask for the business. Up to this point, no one had mentioned money.

We were projecting 1969 sales of over $9 million, and after-tax profits of $500,000. Profits should have been over $1 million, but were reduced by start-up costs in Chicago and debt-service on our loans. Those loans now included another creditor. After my visit with Frank Plummer, the First National Bank had not immediately called my loan, but later that summer I was informed that the bank could not stay on the loan without participation from another lender. I'll never know Plummer's reason for this change of heart.

This gap was filled by Mercantile Financial Corporation of Chicago, a firm that lent on receivables. Times Mirror's auditors could see Mercantile's stamp on all our customer invoices. There was no hiding our need for capital. They also saw that this new credit arrangement cost double what First National had charged.

I had two choices: raise money by selling some of my stock soon, or sell the company. I didn't want to sell stock and answer to minority stockholders. That would also mean I would have to run the company for a few more years until a positive cash flow wiped out debts and a competent CEO was installed. If Times Mirror would pay me $3 million, I told Leon, it could own my company. I was thinking 8 percent times the $2 million left after taxes. My expanded family and I could certainly get by on $160,000 a year, and I would be able to practice law like I wanted. Leon thought $3 million was too high a price tag to put on the company. It seemed like a lot to me, too. I never had any cash to speak of. Everything I earned since I owned my first cow in junior high school I had plowed back into business or, in recent years, leveraged into the purchase of farmland outside Montgomery. Still, it was worth a try to ask for that much for the business—if not more.

Al Casey was the model CEO of a Fortune 500 company. Irish to the core, his quick smile and reassuring manner suggested he, not I, was selling something. As he opened his thin leather folder, I could see the edge of a document entitled "Contract for Sale." I read as much of it as I could without appearing obvious. It was clear he had come to do business. I waited for him to say something.

"Morris," he said, "I looked over the numbers. Your company has some problems."

"Mr. Casey," I replied, "I agree with you, and that's why I don't think now is the best time for me to sell. Before I started the Chicago division, we had cash to burn and made over a million a year. The initial test mailings on the Life Cycle Library exceeded our expectations and we're forecasting sales of three to four million sets. I guess I was premature coming way up here to talk to y'all."

I folded my papers, then began to rise. By the way he leaned forward, he unknowingly signalled me to sit back down. I had seen this many times, when a housewife said no and at the same time opened the door wider for me to come in with my wares. Mr. Casey was not aware of it, but he had just upped the price.

"What do you want for your company, Morris?" Casey asked.

"Six million, Mr. Casey," I said. "And I'm probably selling cheap because Times Mirror stock is priced at twenty times earnings. That would make our five hundred thousand after taxes worth ten million to you." I was glad Leon was out of Casey's view.

"You got a deal," said Casey.

It had happened as simply as selling a load of watermelons to

Barney Pinkston for a quarter apiece after he had insisted he would only pay me fifteen cents. Again, I wished Daddy could be around to celebrate. Now I was going back to what he had wanted me to do—practice law.

The high of achieving financial security lasted only until I plunged into my new career as a civil rights lawyer. In June, a member of our Unitarian church asked if I would represent two black youths refused admittance to the Montgomery YMCA's summer camp. Suing the Y would not only rock Montgomery, it might break new ground. The YMCA was a private organization that received no public funds.

I knew a lawsuit against the Y would not sit well with most of the white folks in Montgomery, but I hadn't reckoned just how it would anger the country club set, the leading businessmen, and big landowners, many of whom sat on the YMCA's board. The case wasn't even three weeks old when these movers and shakers started moving and shaking. And when they did, they quickly proved they could be just as dangerous and destructive as the Ku Klux Klan when they targeted an enemy. In the summer of 1969, that enemy was me.

CHAPTER 7

July 1969   **Rolling Hills Ranch**

Beverly called in the middle of dinner. I wasn't surprised to hear her voice—despite the divorce, we still cared for each other and talked often—but our conversations almost always took place later in the evening, just before the boys got ready for bed.

"Bubba?" She sounded too tentative, hushed, as if she were afraid someone was listening.

"What's wrong, Beverly?" I asked.

She continued to whisper. "I just got a very strange phone call."

"From who?"

"I don't know. Some man who wanted to know if you'd ever brought home cash, whether you acted unethically as an attorney."

"Now, why the hell . . . ?" I stopped and thought for a moment. Just three weeks earlier, I had filed a lawsuit to integrate the Y, which had been segregated since it opened in 1869. The headline-making suit had angered most white folks in town, including several on the Y's board, which numbered many of Montgomery's top business leaders and landowners.

Only a few hours before Beverly called, I had taken the deposition of Bill Chandler, the Y's executive director. While I had known Chandler a long time and had always liked him, my questions were tough and the session tense. During a break in the deposition, I found two documents that dramatically strengthened our case. I thought I'd been careful to hide my excitement and not let Chandler and his lawyers see I recognized the importance of my find.

"I wonder if the call has something to do with the case," I said to Beverly.

"What do you mean?"

"I mean I wonder if some people are trying to destroy me so they can destroy my case."

"Would they sink that low?" Beverly asked.

A few minutes later, I could answer her. After talking to a friend, I concluded that the caller had been Cliff Tisdale, who came from one of Montgomery's most prominent families and now owned a big company in town. Beverly and I had gone to high school with Tisdale, but we had never been friends and our paths had rarely crossed during the past several years. I did know, however, that Tisdale was a strong supporter of the YMCA and sat on one of its boards.

It might sound strange that in July of 1969—fifteen years after *Brown v. Board of Education,* thirteen years after the Montgomery bus boycott, five years after the passage of the Civil Rights Act, four years after the Voting Rights Act, one year after the death of Martin Luther King, Jr., and just two weeks before a man would walk on the moon—the powers that be in a city, even a city in the heart of the South, would be so disturbed by an effort to integrate the Young Men's Christian Association that they might start a witch-hunt against the lawyer who brought the suit. But from the moment it was filed, *Smith v. Montgomery YMCA* struck a raw nerve.

The Montgomery Y was an important symbol, an impenetrable fortress in the battle to hold on to the old, cherished Southern way; an educational, recreational, and most important, a social institution that had managed to maintain segregation while many other institutions had been forcibly integrated by Congress or the courts. Most whites reasoned that if the federal government could dictate how the Y—a private organization—operated, then the troops might as well surrender. If the Y fell, they believed, there would be no safe haven but the costly Montgomery Country Club and a handful of private dining clubs, and maybe those would fall next.

Along with the symbolic effect that integrating this last bastion of segregation presented, another implication conjured the darkest fears about commingling of the races. Despite the last fifteen years of court orders and federal laws barring racial discrimination, whites could still avoid mixing with blacks. Blacks might sit anywhere on a bus or in a restaurant now, but that didn't mean a white person had to share a seat or a table. It might be easier for blacks to vote, but whites still held political power. While blacks could even attend the same public schools as whites, the majority of wealthy whites in Montgomery opted for private school. But avoiding contact with blacks would be more difficult in the YMCA's recreational programs. The YMCA operated eight swimming pools in Montgomery; the city didn't have any public pools. Integrating the Y would allow blacks in the same pools with whites. There was no practical way to keep the colors from running together in water, short of staying out of the water—an unpleasant alternative considering the torrid Montgomery summers.

The idea of white children and black children in the same water at the same time, particularly half-naked black boys and white girls, stirred long-standing sexual taboos and was more terrifying to white folks than any mixing that might take place fully clothed. The Klan had long played on this fear. Integration led to interracial sex which led to nonwhite children which eventually would lead to the "ruination" of the entire white race, went the KKK's standard parade of horrors, hardly a new theme. In 1860, an Alabama newspaper had declared that the election of Abraham Lincoln "shows that the North [intends] to free the negroes and force amalgamation between them and the children of the poor [white] men of the South." At the same time, South Carolina's Baptist clergyman James Furman warned: "Abolition preachers will be at hand to consummate the marriage of your daughters to black husbands. . . . Submit to have our wives and daughters choose between death and gratifying the hellish lust of the negro! . . . Better ten thousand deaths than submission."

Almost one century after those words had been used to encourage secession and the continued subjugation of blacks, the city of Montgomery had demonstrated how little the Southern psyche had changed. In June of 1957, the city had passed an ordinance entitled "Segregation" that made it a crime for blacks to use a "white" park or "white" swimming pool. In August of 1958, blacks had petitioned the city to integrate the fourteen parks containing swimming pools, tennis courts, and other facilities. The city commissioners quickly denied the request, proclaiming, "The Commission will not operate integrated parks." In December 1958, black leaders filed suit to integrate the parks and have the city ordinance declared unconstitutional, and, true to their word, without even waiting for the U.S. District Court to decide, the city commissioners closed all of Montgomery's parks to blacks and whites alike. Nine months later, in the case of *Gilmore v. City of Montgomery,* Judge Johnson ruled that the practice of operating segregated parks was illegal, and he enjoined the city from doing so when and if the parks were reopened.

To avoid the handwriting on the wall, the city tore down the wall. The public parks, pools, tennis courts, and other recreational facilities were permanently closed. In this battle against forced integration, bulldozers rolled in and filled the pools with dirt; an army of city workers fenced in those parks that weren't sold off or given away.

Such digging in at the heels was not new to Montgomery. In 1958, when the public library had been ordered to open its doors to people of all colors, the city had devised an ingenious solution to the "danger" of integration. All the chairs were taken out of the library reading rooms and public areas to eliminate any possibility that blacks and whites might mix too closely.

The city had been even more intransigent during the Montgomery bus boycott. While the boycott eventually led to the elimination of segregation on buses, the boycotters initially demanded far less. After Rosa Parks's arrest, Dr. King and his followers were still willing to accept bus seating by race—blacks taking seats from the back and whites taking seats from the front. The boycotters merely wanted to eliminate the reserved section for whites, a compromise within the principles of segregation. The demand was so moderate that some civil rights groups, including the National Association for the Advancement of Colored People (NAACP), criticized Dr. King's group for not pushing for full integration, and the white editor of the *Montgomery Advertiser* advised white Montgomery to accept the proposal.

Instead the city had fought and not always fairly. As the boycott gained momentum, its leaders were arrested under a rarely used 1921 statute prohibiting boycotts "without just cause or legal excuse." At the same time, the attorney representing the boycotters was subjected to all sorts of pressures: The local draft board revoked his ministerial deferment, and the city arrested him on the seldom-invoked charge of barratry, the act of stirring up or inciting quarrels or lawsuits. This frivolous charge had only one purpose: to intimidate the boycotters.

The harassed attorney had been none other than Fred Gray, who had asked me to assist him in the suit to block the Auburn University branch in Montgomery. When presented with the YMCA case, I returned the favor, asking Fred to help. If my instincts about Tisdale's call to Beverly were correct, I was getting the same treatment Fred had received thirteen years earlier. The color of my skin, Daddy's friendship with the important folks in town, my own business success and accumulation of land didn't mean a lick. The split that had been growing for years between me and the white establishment in Montgomery was now complete. War had broken out. It remained to be seen how civil it would be.

*   *   *

I had fired the first shot by filing *Smith v. YMCA*. Vincent and Edward Smith were seven-year-old cousins who simply wanted to go to the Y's two-week summer camp. Traditionally, the camp was open to anyone who filled out an application and paid the twelve-dollar enrollment fee—with one major exception.

Accompanied by their mothers and two members of the Montgomery Human Relations Council who foresaw difficulty, Vincent and Edward went to the Central branch of the Montgomery Y on June 3 to turn in their applications. Vincent's mother, Annie Ruth, later testified that she and Edward's mother, Mary Louise, gave Executive Director Chandler completed, signed applications, and "he said that he could not accept our children because it was an all-white camp."

At his pretrial deposition six weeks later, the same day Tisdale telephoned Beverly, Chandler first insisted that the Smiths never offered applications, then backpedaled:

Q: Now why couldn't you accept the applications?
A: Well, of, course, no applications were offered, first of all. They were not offered in good faith. They were offered for a purpose contrary to participation in [camp]. They were offered for the purpose . . . of bringing about integration.

Yes, the Smiths wanted to integrate the YMCA summer camp. During this period black individuals in conjunction with organizations like the Human Relations Council and the newly formed National Democratic Party of Alabama were trying to integrate those institutions untouched by the times. As its behavior made clear, the YMCA wasn't about to integrate voluntarily. And the city commission and state legislature certainly weren't going to eliminate segregation.

Chandler, who as executive director had no trouble making big decisions and no trouble accepting white children for the camp, told the Smiths he had no authority to accept applications from Negroes, and would have to refer the matter to the Y's board of directors. As the boys waited in the corridor outside his office, he told their mothers they could expect a decision within ten days.

When the Human Relation Council's Bill Schutz, whom I knew from the Unitarian Fellowship, called the next day to ask me to bring a class action suit stopping racial discrimination at the Montgomery YMCA, I told him the odds would be against us. "The Y is a private organization, just like the Montgomery Country Club," I explained. "The civil rights laws don't generally apply to these kinds of places."

Still, I asked him to bring the Smiths over to my offices.

Soft-spoken Annie Ruth Smith and Mary Louise Smith didn't have to speak loudly to persuade me of their integrity and strength. They both worked as maids at the Royal Inn Hotel, and in their faces I saw the faces of so many of the women I had worked with in the cotton fields—women who, once the harvest was over, journeyed from Mount Meigs to Montgomery to take similar jobs in hotels or the homes of white folks to earn much-needed money. Women like this, I now knew, had been the foot soldiers in the Montgomery bus boycott, risking their livelihoods by giving up their only form of transportation to take a stand. Years later I would learn that in October of 1955, two months before Rosa Parks set the bus boycott in motion, Mary Louise Smith, then eighteen, had refused to give up her seat on the bus and had been arrested, convicted, and fined nine dollars under the segregation law. At this point black activists considered taking action, but stopped because they thought her background—her father was an alcoholic and she lived in a shack out in the country—did not make her a suitable figure to rally around.

If the Smith sisters reminded me of the women from the fields, their boys reminded me of all the black kids I had worked and played with, particularly my best friend and swimming pal Little Buddy Orum. My mind raced back twenty years. I had gone to the YMCA summer camp, and remembered how good it felt to jump off the pier into Lake Jordan. I remembered, too, wishing that Little Buddy could be there because we were both strong swimmers and could surely outrace the city boys.

I don't choose my cases because of the memories revived by the faces of potential clients, but the resolve of the Smiths along with the possibility that this lawsuit might change things for the better in Montgomery persuaded me to take on the Y.

Our complaint charged that the YMCA had refused to accept the Smith cousins' applications because of race. We asserted that the YMCA's recreational programs constituted public accommodations and that by engaging in racial discrimination, the Y was violating the Civil Rights Act of 1964. We also argued that the public services performed by the YMCA and the benefits the Y received from the government made it, in effect, a quasi-governmental agency and required it to comply with the standards embodied in the Equal Protection Clause of the Fourteenth Amendment.

As I had told Bill Schutz, I wasn't terribly confident about our chances for victory. We might be able to show that the Y had a policy of segregation. It would be more difficult to prove that the organization's programs fell under the heading of "public accommodations"—the Y no longer rented out rooms—and almost impossible to demonstrate that the Y was a quasi-governmental agency. At this time no court had ever ordered a private group to integrate unless there was proof of substantial governmental involvement.

My first job was to find out as much as I could about the YMCA's operations. If I were trying a case like this today, with the resources of the Southern Poverty Law Center behind me, I would have sent out an investigator to do much of this preliminary legwork. But my only resource was my company, where I had agreed to work for at least one more year as part of the buy-out deal with Times Mirror Corporation. Although skilled at tracking down recipes, our people didn't have too much experience finding the ingredients for lawsuits. I was on my own.

I already knew a little about the YMCA. One beautiful day in 1964, our company had held its summer picnic at the Y campground on Lake Jordan, about twenty miles from town. Although we realized the Y was segregated, we brought our racially mixed group of employees without advising anyone in the organization, just as we would later do at the Jefferson Davis Hotel.

While we expected to share the Y's large lakefront facilities with other groups and individuals, nobody else ever showed up. Not until I saw a sign hastily posted by the Y did it become clear why we had the lake to ourselves: *Private Party.* Rather than subject any of the white folks to sharing the water with blacks, the Y had "segregated" us from the outside world.

More recently I had dealt with the Y in my capacity as president of the Unitarian Fellowship. Our group rented space in a meeting room of the South Montgomery Y branch until the Fellowship's public stances on civil rights and the war in Vietnam, and the presence of two black individuals at our services, apparently rubbed the Y's board the wrong way. A director told us we would have to leave because "Unitarians don't believe in Jesus." When I countered that the Y's tolerance of those who didn't believe in Jesus extended all the way to its own Jewish president, we were allowed to stay, although the relationship remained tense.

These experiences gave me insight into what I was facing, but I needed more facts about YMCA practice and policy. After talking with the Smiths and before filing suit, I wandered over to the YMCA's

Central branch to visit my cousin Sarah Griggs, who worked as an administrator in the office. Like most of my relatives, Sarah, a pleasant, middle-aged woman, probably didn't approve of my politics, but she was from the blood-is-thicker-than-water school and we got on just fine. I asked Sarah a few questions about how the Y operated—if it still rented rooms, for example—and then asked her for some literature.

While this material provided a little more background, it wasn't until after I filed suit on June 11 and subpoenaed documents and took depositions that I had a clear picture of how the organization worked.

The YMCA and Bill Chandler, whom we had sued individually as well, took our suit seriously. They retained Oakley Melton and Merton Roland Nachman, two of Montgomery's most distinguished, sharpest, most politically connected attorneys. Oakley, forty-two, short, and athletic, was a past president of the Alabama Bar Association, active on the Y's board, and honored as one of the "Men of Montgomery" by the Y for his many community activities. His successful private practice represented a number of associations and corporate clients like Coca-Cola Bottling. I had known and liked him since high school when I was a page in the Alabama House of Representatives and he was the reading clerk. With his prematurely gray hair, his warm smile, sincere manner, and slightly rumpled gray seersucker suits, he might at first seem avuncular, but he was an astute politician as well.

M. R. "Rod" Nachman was a native Alabamian who had gone north to Harvard Law School and now practiced at Steiner, Crum and Baker, one of Montgomery's most prestigious insurance defense firms. In 1960, Nachman represented the popular, prosegregation Montgomery police commissioner L. B. Sullivan in the landmark libel case *Sullivan v. New York Times,* in which the United States Supreme Court eventually fashioned a special rule to prevent the racist Alabama judicial system from imposing a devastating penalty against the newspaper and a group of black preachers.

I liked Bill Chandler. Chandler was a good Christian; I knew that firsthand. When I was in high school, I heard him pray to Jesus for us boys and girls to live good lives. Apparently unwilling to leave matters entirely in the Lord's hands, Chandler himself had later suspended me from a YMCA program called Poet Hi-Y because he overheard me using a cussword at a meeting.

Chandler, forty-three, stood over six feet tall, was strong and athletic, with piercing grayish eyes, slightly hollow cheeks, and a constant smile. He had come to the not-for-profit, tax-exempt YMCA in 1946 when it was a small-potatoes operation providing inexpensive rooms for transients. By 1969, he had steered the Y out of the rooming-house business and into other programming that attracted a broader spectrum of the community, generated more dollars, and facilitated fund-raising. The organization's all-white City-Wide Board of Directors became a Who's Who of Montgomery's "finest."

Under the leadership of Chandler's board, new branches were built, membership soared from one thousand to almost eighteen thousand. The YMCA became the major provider of recreation in the city, operating five branches in the Montgomery area, running everything from youth football leagues to swimming pools. And, much to the pleasure of the white establishment, the Y's programs and facilities remained segregated.

The East and South branches served predominantly white neighborhoods, with a total of eight thousand members, none black. There were no black staff and no blacks on the Board of Managers. Although located in a racially mixed section of the city, the Central branch also had an all-white membership. None of these branches had ever solicited blacks for membership. The same was true at the all-white three-thousand-member Prattville branch operating in a nearby community. Only the Cleveland Avenue branch, which served a predominantly black area and had a predominantly black staff, courted blacks. Of its two thousand members, all but fifteen were black. The few white members were honorary—mostly businessmen who donated money. Henry Spears, the black executive director of the Cleveland Avenue branch, had never even seen the Y's whites-only summer camp.

In addition to soliciting membership at large, the Y recruited extensively for its recreational programs—football, swimming, youth clubs, camps—from Montgomery's public schools. Every predominantly white school was assigned to one of the all-white branches, even if the school happened to be closer to the Cleveland Avenue branch. And every predominantly black school was, regardless of its location, assigned to the Cleveland Avenue branch. Blacks who attended recently integrated, predominantly white schools were permitted to join only the Cleveland Avenue Y. Even dual city-wide football leagues were segregated; there was one league for the white branches and one for the Cleveland Avenue branch. Of the Y's eight swimming pools, only one served blacks. While the Cleveland Avenue branch had its own pool, it was excluded from city-wide swim meets held at white branches.

When I asked Chandler about the Y's segregation, he was less than forthcoming. Had the Y maintained a policy of segregation over the last ten years? Chandler responded that there was no set policy, but acknowledged that in practice the Y was segregated. Then he began dancing.

Q: Now what if anything have you done as executive director of the YMCA program to eliminate this segregated practice?
A: I have tried to work on one main point . . . serving people in an effective program that would enable us to make our program as attractive to them as possible where they would voluntarily want to come in and participate

  Specifically as to take your question, we have tried to get the program as is necessary to meet the conditions of the city of Montgomery, to serve people where they are and as they are. For example, we could not go into a room of Negro and white children without serving all that were there, nor would we want to put a child into a program where he would be ill at ease and unaccepted and put under conditions that would be difficult for him to operate without complete acceptance and complete benefit from the program involved.

I should have expected this bureaucratic bull. I think it's only a slight exaggeration to say that in 1969, the message delivered by many of the white men who wore suits and ties in Montgomery wasn't that different from the message from those who wore robes and hoods. It's just that it was delivered differently: not secretly by night, but openly by day; not hacked into walls by social misfits, but written into bylaws and then explained by pillars of society like Chandler and defended by the best legal minds.

In Chandler's eyes, as in the eyes of almost all of the distinguished YMCA directors, segregation was not a cancer to be eliminated, more a birthmark that you lived with and became quite comfortable about. This harked back to the mentality of the nineteenth-century plantation owners who had argued against emancipation because freed slaves would be unable to take care of themselves or make their own decisions. Chandler sounded as if he were doing a favor to black persons by keeping them out of the Y's all-white programs.

But was he really worried about making two seven-year-old black children "ill at ease"? Vincent and Edward Smith and their mothers were fully aware that the camp was all-white. They had decided that the benefits of the program—the opportunity to enjoy the camping experience—outweighed the risk of not being fully accepted by other campers. The real problem was that the integration of the camp or other Y programs might make *white members* ill at ease.

At the deposition Chandler downplayed the fact that prior to the suit, no black person had ever attended YMCA camp. He explained that on special weekends blacks visited the camp, and that plans were under way to build a separate black camp. When he looked at me and explained the "tremendous need for a predominantly Negro camp" in this year of our Lord, 1969, I thought: Bill, what happened to the YMCA's Christian principles?

Despite all this evidence of separate and clearly unequal facilities, the YMCA's executive director was telling me that the Y might be segregated in practice, but no official policy of segregation existed. As Chandler spoke, I was confident that Judge Johnson would find the Y's arguments as pathetic and disingenuous as I did. But that was only the first step toward victory: We still needed to take the Y out of the "private group" category and show it was subject to the Civil Rights Act or Constitution.

I spent a fair amount of time at Chandler's deposition trying to establish that snack bars operated by the Y constituted public accommodations, but didn't get very far. I did force him to acknowledge that the city provided the Y several benefits free of charge—water for the swimming pools, the paving of a parking lot—but I doubted whether this would persuade Judge Johnson to mandate a change in the organization's racial policies—particularly in light of the Y's actions since the suit had been filed.

On June 24, two weeks before Chandler's deposition and two weeks after we filed suit, Annie Ruth and Mary Louise Smith had each received letters informing them that their sons had been accepted to Camp Belser. During this same period, we found out, the Y had selectively phoned and sent camp applications to certain other blacks. That the YMCA had suddenly found religion didn't fool us, nor, we hoped, moot the lawsuit. Case law suggested that post-suit changes of heart were "equivocal in purpose, motive, and permanence."

Vincent, Edward, Annie Ruth, and Mary Louise Smith wanted to change YMCA policy once and for all. They didn't even nibble at the bone the Y now threw them. Try as he might, Rod Nachman could not break Mary Louise at her deposition.

Q. Have you decided to send your son to Camp Belser?

A. If he be able to go and providing regardless of race, color, or creed any other child being able to go and enjoying all the facilities that is offered them, I will be more than glad to send my child.

Q. What damages have you suffered . . . ?

A. Damages—just to discriminate, that is damage by itself, to discriminate a person. And I feel that my child has been discriminated.

Q. Even though his application has been accepted?

A. Well, he may be accepted on conditions that he may go and just, you know, go there and maybe another neighbor's child wouldn't be able to go, you know. Just because we have went there and they might accept our child, and maybe my neighbor wants to send their child and they won't accept them. That is the way I look at it.

Q. I see. Then this is what you state are the damages you have suffered?

A. Discrimination.

Few witnesses ever spoke more succinctly. Bill Chandler could have learned a lesson from Mary Louise Smith. Of course, it's easier to speak so directly and truthfully when you don't have anything to cover up.

To end the discrimination Mary Louise wanted ended, I needed more than the transparent excuses of the YMCA officials and the routine business documents they had produced. I needed a smoking gun, something that would shoot down the Y's primary defense that it was a private organization which could not be touched by the public law. I found it by pure accident.

I had subpoenaed YMCA records for the last ten years, and Chandler and his lawyers had brought along about a half-dozen big file boxes to the deposition. Wanting to make sure everything I had asked for had been produced, I announced at the outset that I'd like to go through the list item by item. I didn't want to examine each document at this time; I just wanted to make sure the records were there.

When it was time to break for lunch, I was more interested in looking at the documents than going out to eat. "Mind if I stay here and look through the minutes?" I asked Oakley.

"No problem." Oakley and everyone else departed.

At first I didn't find anything too damaging. Then I came upon a bunch of unfiled papers, three inches thick, sitting at the back of one of the boxes. My ears perked. I don't offer documents that harm my case on a silver platter, but neither I nor other ethical lawyers like Nachman or Melton fail to produce documents known to exist that come within the purview of a subpoena. Maybe this unmarked file . . .

Mimeograph paper, stencils, more mimeograph paper, and then— Bang! The smoking gun: a 1958 document describing the "City Rec- reation–YMCA Coordinating Committee," a committee no one out- side a few trusted YMCA and city officials had ever heard of. According to the document, "The objective of the coordinating com- mittee will be to coordinate the programs of the City Recreation Department and YMCA to provide the maximum program of recrea- tion and character building to the maximum people with the minimum overlapping." This included athletics, club programs, and informal education like ceramics, art, and bridge.

I turned the page to see how athletic programs were to be coor- dinated. "Swimming—This is the YMCA's responsibility."

I shivered. It was as clear as the Confederate flag still flying over Alabama's capitol: At the same time that the city had responded to the *Gilmore* suit by shutting down the swimming pools and parks, it had surreptitiously drafted an agreement with the YMCA for the Y to provide those terminated recreational activities. Why? Because the YMCA, a supposedly private organization, could continue to operate those activities in a segregated fashion out of the reach of the federal courts.

I had to give credit to Chandler and his City-Wide Board for creativity if not morality. Little wonder that the YMCA had grown so dramatically over the last ten years. The empire was built on a clever agreement that allowed the city powers to quench their most insatia- ble thirst—the thirst for segregation.

In the box, I found an even more damaging document that obvi- ously reflected the motive behind the creation of the Coordinating Committee in 1958. In a 1965 letter to city staffers and YMCA personnel and directors, the Honorable Earl D. James, the mayor of Montgomery, had called a meeting to discuss the coordination of services. The mayor's final sentence was most revealing: "I suggest that we do not include the Negro staff members or board members."

I quickly copied the letter and the Coordinating Committee agreement and put them back in the box. I could have grilled Chandler on them after lunch, but I didn't want to tip my hand. It would be much more effective to hit him with this at the trial. After the deposition ended I would chronicle how the YMCA stepped into the city's shoes to provide a whole range of segregated activities to the city—to prove that the YMCA had become a quasi-governmental agency.

When I left the office that evening, I felt a hell of a lot more confident about our case than when the day had begun. Then Beverly called. Suddenly *Smith v. YMCA* had become YMCA versus Dees.

Cliff Tisdale must have figured that since Beverly and I were divorced she'd be happy to spill the beans on me. He was dead wrong. There were no hard feelings, no beans to spill. My actions as an attorney and businessman had always been aboveboard. I wouldn't lose any sleep wondering if this fellow or anyone else could get the goods on me. But I would stay up most of the night fuming that somebody was trying to smear my reputation, to discredit me as an attorney, to shut me up, professionally at least, for good.

I doubted very much that Tisdale had acted on his own, without the knowledge or the approval of at least some other YMCA heavy-weights. Almost every important civic leader in Montgomery was on the Y's board, including the mayor. It didn't make sense that one of their number would act unilaterally.

Were the stakes of this case so high that a small group from this body had made the conscious decision to destroy me? I didn't want to believe that such distinguished, law-abiding citizens would, in Beverly's words, stoop so low. But by the time I finally fell asleep, I was certain that was the case.

I woke before dawn, slipped into my blue jeans quietly so as not to wake Maureene, and went out to clear some brush in the southeast corner of the farm. It wasn't really the brush I wanted to clear so much as my mind. Learning that someone was checking up on me was like arriving at the office and finding KKK on the walls or coming home and finding I'd been burglarized, that someone went through my drawers, my papers. This invasion of privacy made me feel dirty. I couldn't help but feel that the rich bluebloods who years earlier had told our family to move were now trying to reach my secure sanctum and once again put me on the street.

There's a keep-your-hands-off-me attitude peculiar to the South. Being a Dees, I come by it naturally. By the time the sun dissolved the morning fog, I had cleared the brush and formed my plan. I would show my antagonists that they had picked on the wrong boy. They had made this fight personal.

In the days since I had filed the suit, we had engaged in settlement negotiations, but there had been no progress. The Y said it would agree to an open-door policy in the future, but wanted no court order to control that promise. "Unacceptable," I had said. Without a consent decree enforceable through the contempt power of the court, the new bylaw passed by the Y would mean nothing. We wanted a signed settlement agreement opening all YMCA programs to blacks, with schools assigned to the closest Y branch without regard to race.

I thought there was a good chance that if I pretended to Oakley and Nachman I was worried about the investigation, they would pass that information on to the Y board. Someone then might offer to drop the investigation if I would soften my demands and agree to a quick settlement favorable to the Y. In return for agreeing to that settlement, I could ask for a letter acknowledging that the Y board was investigating me and an additional letter from the Y's lawyers personally guaranteeing that once I settled the case I would be free from the investigation. When I received those letters, I would tell the Y to take the proposed settlement and shove it you-know-where, and then use the documents to expose the sleazy behavior.

There was a dangerous downside to this gambit. It is a grave ethical violation to settle a class action suit by selling out the class for personal (and undisclosed to the court) gain. I had no intention of actually settling, but if the Y's lawyers revealed my actions to the court before I could carry the plan to its conclusion, I'd be in deep trouble. Would Oakley or Nachman blow the whistle on me? I sensed that they might be more interested in getting rid of the case than in taking the risk that Judge Johnson appoint another lawyer for the class. On the other hand, if they did expose my willingness to settle for apparently personal reasons, they might win favor with the court. This could work to their advantage in future settlement efforts.

It occurred to me, too, that they might even bolster their case against me by filing a trumped-up ethics charge based on my obtaining information from my cousin Sarah. They could argue that getting facts before filing the suit was deception or—that catchall used to nail unpopular lawyers—conduct unbecoming an attorney. While I didn't think I'd done anything wrong by soliciting public documents from Sarah, that might not matter. The local Bar Association's grievance committee was certainly friendlier to the Y and its esteemed counsel than to a troublemaker like me.

I know that if I'd have presented my plan to friends and lawyers whom I trusted and respected the most, they would have told me to let things take their course, not to play such a high-risk game, but just try the case and win it and let the verdict be the just desserts for the Y board. That, however, is not my style.

Once at my office, I called Bill Oldacre, the proctor of the Montgomery Bar Association. I asked him if any complaints had been filed against me or if the bar was conducting any investigation of my activities. He said no. I got the same answer from John Scott, my neighbor and proctor of the Alabama State Bar Association. I had expected these answers but had to be certain no official effort was under way to investigate me, and that Tisdale's call wasn't linked to either of the only two organizations which could conduct such an investigation. Now I could make another phone call—to Oakley Melton.

"Oakley," I said, "I've been thinking some more about that settlement proposal you made."

I told him I'd heard rumors that someone was checking up on me, and that while I didn't know if that had anything to do with the Y case, there was no reason to bring up things from my past best left alone. "You understand, Oakley, nobody's been perfect," I said.

Oakley just listened. I asked him to come to my office so we could talk settlement.

It took a day for everything to fall in place. Early the next morning, July 10, Oakley called to tell me he thought the case could be settled, agreeing to come to my office for discussion.

After I got off the phone with Oakley, I called my lawyer Leon Capouano. Up to this point, Leon had not been involved in the case and knew none of the lawsuit's details. He was a corporate lawyer, not a "Commie lawyer," as I was perceived by many.

I brought Leon up to speed, told him that I felt someone connected with the Y case was trying to frame me with a bar charge or worse, and that I needed his help. I did not let him in on my plan. I wanted him to be an impartial witness to my meeting with Oakley, not an advocate.

Oakley Melton and Rod Nachman arrived a little before noon. I repeated that I'd heard of an investigation and that it would be best for me if my past remained unexamined. Neither lawyer commented on this. I acted as if my fears and my interest in suddenly settling the case were related. They acted as if they hadn't heard anything I'd said about the investigation. It didn't matter: They were willing to settle, probably thinking I wanted to save my ass.

Oakley gave me a proposed statement: "Be it resolved, that it is the policy of the Montgomery YMCA, Inc., that eligibility for membership or participation in its programs shall be determined without any discrimination on the basis of race, color, or national origin." Oakley also presented me with a document to be filed with the court, stating that the parties agreed to dismiss the suit based on a private settlement that would not be part of the court records.

Of course I didn't tell Oakley, but this was no more acceptable than anything the Y had offered previously. Hell, I thought, Bill Chandler had testified at his deposition that the Y didn't have a policy of discrimination. Moreover, there was still no enforcement mechanism. If the Y didn't live up to the agreement, we'd have to start from scratch and file a lawsuit all over again.

Oakley told me the settlement could be approved at a special Y board meeting that night. I had to buy a little time; I needed one more meeting where I could get something in writing exposing the plot against me. This would serve two purposes: It would let the court know the snakes I was facing, and it would compromise the Y board—in the open. I told Oakley I'd have to discuss the settlement with Fred Gray and would be back in touch later in the day.

I didn't call Fred, of course. I had no intention of settling the case.

I did talk with Oakley later that afternoon. "I've got some minor problems with this agreement," I told him. "Why don't I come over to your office and we can talk."

"Oakley," I said once Leon and I were seated, "I really don't have any problem with this settlement. It doesn't have to be part of the court order. But I want to know more about this investigation of me." I told him I wanted to know who was behind the inquiry and I needed some assurances that if I settled the case, the information gathered would not be used against me.

Oakley said that I was under investigation, that he had no control over the inquiry, but that he thought it would stop once the lawsuit was settled. He added that it was essential to reach an agreement prior to the board's evening meeting. He explained that some members of the board initiated the investigation, feeling that the lawsuit would cripple the YMCA program. Oakley said these board members felt my lawsuit was going to destroy the YMCA.

"What has this investigation turned up so far, Oakley?" I asked.

Oakley mentioned the incident with Cousin Sarah.

"Well, can I stop this?" I asked.

Oakley said he felt a settlement would put an end to it.

I told Oakley that I trusted him as a friend and believed him when he said that he and Rod had nothing to do with the investigation, and that it would stop once the case was settled. But I added that I needed something in writing that acknowledged I was settling this suit with the understanding that the investigation would stop and no action would be taken. I acted as worried about the investigation as I could and didn't even mention the settlement terms. I wanted Oakley to think I had abandoned my clients' interests and would take the Y's noncourt settlement just to cover myself. Fearing that Oakley wouldn't write the agreement if he felt I'd make it public, I added that I didn't need a copy; I'd trust Oakley to keep a copy safely in his office. The language would be strongest if Oakley thought he'd have all the copies.

Oakley dictated the agreement to his secretary, to be signed by the Y board. The first paragraph of the first draft read:

> . . . [We] agree that in consideration of the settlement of the pending lawsuit . . . that we will not in any way disclose, discuss, reveal, advocate or in any way divulge information which we may have regarding the . . . activities of Morris Dees in connection with the preparation, investigation, filing or prosecuting of said lawsuit.

I asked Oakley to add: "or any information which we may have obtained through investigation of conduct unrelated to this case but from prior conduct as an attorney." I wanted him to believe I feared more than just the Cousin Sarah incident. He agreed to the addition.

There it was in black and white, the acknowledgment of an actual investigation. The final paragraph read: ". . . Upon the settlement of the case all such matters shall be fully and finally closed and forgotten."

While Oakley's secretary typed the agreement, I asked him for a letter on his stationery to me that would personally guarantee that the terms of the agreement would be fulfilled. Again, I said he could keep the copies in his files. He asked me to write out what I wanted him to sign. I scrawled a draft and took it out to his secretary.

Dear Morris:

I promise you that when the agreement I drafted today is signed, and the YMCA case is settled, I will personally guarantee that the terms of the agreement will be fulfilled.

Yours very truly,
Oakley Melton, Jr.

Although I had said I didn't need copies of the agreement or the letter, there was no way I was going to leave without them. But how could I get them?

Oakley's secretary solved the problem for me. When she brought in the copies of the agreement and the letter, I noticed a misspelled word in the letter. I suggested it be corrected and was up and to the door quickly so that Oakley couldn't call in the secretary and forever put the documents out of my reach.

I closed the door behind me, and asked the secretary to correct the error. After she did I nonchalantly went to a copier adjacent to her desk and Xeroxed the letter, which Oakley had already signed, and the draft agreement. The agreement wasn't signed, but I didn't have the luxury of waiting for the evening board meeting; too much could go wrong in the meantime. After folding my copies, I reentered the office and gave Oakley the originals. Then I told him I'd see him in court the next morning so we could tell Judge Johnson we had settled the case.

Back at Leon's office, I called Oakley. Looking back, I realize this was a foolish thing to do, but I wanted Oakley to know that the Y had picked on the wrong man and I would not take the attack sitting down. Also, I felt slimy acting as if I had something to hide when I didn't.

"Oakley, this is Morris," I began. "You can tell the Y board tonight that I have no intention of settling the case. I have nothing to hide or fear from any investigation. I just pretended to be afraid so I could find out who was behind this sorry scheme. I made myself a copy of the letter you just signed and the draft agreement, too, and I intend to present them to Judge Johnson."

I did not wait for a response, slamming down the receiver.

I went straight to Judge Johnson's house and knocked on his door. That's not proper behavior, but I was so incensed I couldn't help myself.

Judge Johnson had every right to be angry with me for appearing *ex parte* (without the other party) on his doorstep. Instead, after I showed him Oakley's letter and the unsigned agreement, he calmly told me that he could consider the matter properly only in court.

Fine. The next day I filed an amended complaint summarizing the events of the past three days and charging "the effort of . . . this unnamed group of YMCA board members constituted a direct violation of the constitutional rights of the plaintiffs." In the heat of battle, I also moved that Melton be added as a codefendant and I included a copy of the letter and draft agreement. The YMCA immediately moved to strike the new pleading, terming it "impertinent, scandalous, immaterial, and highly prejudicial."

By the time this motion came before Judge Johnson, I had cooled down. Neither Melton nor Nachman had engaged in improper conduct, and neither of them should be a named defendant. I dropped the count against Melton, and when Judge Johnson hinted that he did not find that the remainder of the amended complaint stated a cause of action, I moved to strike it. My purpose had been served. The YMCA's attempt to discredit me had been brought before the court in proper fashion.

Nothing happened beyond this. And perhaps more important, despite the increased tension that resulted from the incident, no one ever filed a single complaint against me for unethical conduct with respect to the *Smith* case or any of my previous activities. Since I had exposed their seamy effort, a complaint over the harmless and perfectly legal Sarah Griggs incident would have looked like sour grapes. A few Y board members, not their counsel, were guilty. I suspect Melton and Nachman told them to leave well enough alone.

If I hadn't found the secret City Recreation–YMCA Coordinating Committee agreement, I might actually have considered the meager settlement that Oakley offered. But I was certain that we could now put together a strong case, certain that Judge Johnson would give it a fair hearing. In almost any other district court in the South, I wouldn't have felt so confident. Many federal judges below the Mason-Dixon line, particularly those appointed by President John F. Kennedy to appease segregationist Democrats threatening to bolt the party, were not necessarily disposed to give an unbiased hearing to those seeking to eliminate bias. Judge Frank M. Johnson, Jr., was.

Some years after the YMCA case, *Time* magazine would call me the "second most hated man in Alabama," a title I was not ashamed to wear; you've got to be doing something good to get so many folks so

mad at you. The honor of "most hated man" in the state deservedly
went to Judge Johnson.

In 1954, the same critical year in which the Supreme Court had
handed down *Brown v. Board of Education,* President Dwight Eisen-
hower appointed the tall, rugged, serious thirty-seven-year-old Johnson the youngest federal judge in the country. At the time he heard
Smith v. YMCA in late September of 1969, Judge Johnson had interpreted the Constitution and other federal statutes in Montgomery for
fifteen of the most challenging years in history. In 1956, in his first
high-profile case, Johnson ruled in favor of those staging the Montgomery bus boycott. In 1961, he enjoined the city and the Ku Klux
Klan from future wrongs against the Freedom Riders. And in 1965
he ruled that Dr. King and his group could march legitimately from
Selma to Montgomery.

I remembered the judge's moving words. After acknowledging that
the particular plan for the march to block two lanes of public highway
for several days reached "the outer limits of what is constitutionally
allowed," he added that "the wrongs and injustices inflicted upon
these plaintiffs . . . clearly exceeded—and continue to exceed—the
outer limits of what is constitutionally permissible." The relief he was
granting might be considered enormous by some, he wrote, but it was
"commensurate with the enormity of the wrongs being protested."

Guided by the philosophy that the Constitution was a "living and
flexible document," the judge did not always rule in favor of civil
rights activists. He refused, for example, to authorize busing in Montgomery to desegregate the schools. But since the Constitution was
usually on the side of the activists and Judge Johnson was a courageous
jurist, he usually ruled for the prointegration forces. Thus it wasn't too
great a shock when in 1967 somebody looking to send the judge a
message bombed his mother's home.

I had been before the judge on only a handful of cases. *Smith v.
YMCA* was more complicated than any of those. To win we must
persuade Judge Johnson that the Y had put that secret coordinating
agreement into practice and could no longer claim it was a private
organization.

By the time we went to trial, a few black children—selectively
solicited after the lawsuit was filed—had actually attended Camp
Belser. The Y offered this as proof that a leopard can change its spots
and argued that the case was moot. Judge Johnson didn't buy that, nor
much of anything else the YMCA lawyers argued. Chandler took the
stand and dismissed the importance of the coordinating agreement.

But the evidence proved overwhelming: In 1957, the YMCA had operated only one branch, a dilapidated building in downtown Montgomery, and counted only one thousand members. By 1960, two years after the Coordinating Committee had been established, the Y had five branches with five swimming pools. Now there were eight pools and eighteen thousand members.

I also uncovered a 1961 ordinance in which the city had deeded the Perry Street Recreation Park to the Y for the ridiculously low sum of eighteen thousand dollars, reserving the right to repurchase the land for the original sale price if after three years the YMCA failed to construct a facility for "athletic, health, recreational, and religious purposes" at a cost of at least one hundred thousand dollars. Since the Y's Central branch was built on the site within the three years, the repurchase option was never exercised. "The YMCA merely exchanged places with the city as provider of recreation for the neighborhood," Judge Johnson wrote in his opinion. He added that by coordinating its programs with and delegating the operation of others to the YMCA, the city had invested the Y with "a municipal character." He concluded that "the defendants' discriminatory conduct has become so entwined with governmental policies [and] so impregnated with a governmental character as to become subject to the constitutional limitations placed upon state action."

The judge's order granted us almost everything we asked, enjoining the YMCA from (1) denying blacks membership in any branches or excluding them from any programs; (2) building new branches or extensions if the site selected perpetuated past policies and practices of segregation; (3) recruiting at predominantly white schools without also recruiting at predominantly black schools; and (4) excluding blacks from the City-Wide Board of Directors and any other governing bodies. In addition the Y must publicize its new policy of desegregation, providing the court with a plan on how it was going to eliminate segregated memberships and activities. At a minimum, Judge Johnson ordered, that plan had to include the reassignment of Montgomery schools to different Y branches; the reassignment of approximately one thousand "deserving" members without regard to race; and a means for ensuring representation of blacks on the City-Wide Board of Directors and other governing bodies.

As expected, the YMCA appealed the sweeping decision. The Fifth Circuit Court of Appeals affirmed Judge Johnson on all but one point: It would not permit affirmative action to ensure representation of blacks on the board.

Vincent, Edward, Annie Ruth, and Mary Louise Smith were ecstatic. After one hundred years, the discrimination that Mary Louise found so damaging and that the YMCA and city had gone to such lengths to perpetuate had finally ended.

Judge Johnson ordered the defendants to pay Fred Gray and me twenty-five thousand dollars in attorneys' fees. We agreed to forgo that money if the Y would use it to give Y memberships to poor children regardless of race. To its credit, it did.

I had examined Bill Chandler mercilessly at the trial, making him look bad. At the time he deserved it. Still, I bled for him inside. I wanted to stop the proceeding and say, "Bill, let's open up that Bible you brought to the Y meetings and turn to some of the scripture you read. Your Jesus would have let those little boys go to camp. He would not make up an excuse like, 'We are building a Negro camp soon.'"

After the verdict I'm sure Bill thought the YMCA and his career were doomed. But the world didn't end when the Montgomery YMCA was integrated. Contributions didn't stop. No black boys attacked white girls in the newly integrated swimming pools. For the first time many white kids could meet black kids one on one, as I had.

About five years after Judge Johnson's ruling, Bill called and asked that I meet with him about the YMCA South branch. Under the court order, the Y filed quarterly reports on its progress, and could not add a new facility or close an old one without coming to us and the court. Bill explained to me that membership was down and the Y wanted to sell the South branch to the city for use as a rehabilitation center.

I told Bill that he had done a good job running the Y since *Smith,* and that I trusted him and his board—now racially mixed, but still controlled by whites—to make the right decision. I said I would go to court and file a motion to terminate the court's oversight of the YMCA. I drafted the order and two days later it was over.

I never asked about the South branch Y, figuring I could reopen the suit if someone complained. I wanted Bill and the Y to do something on their own for once.

Not too long ago, Bill Chandler actually thanked me for filing *Smith v. YMCA.* "Morris, I couldn't have integrated the Y without the lawsuit," he said. "My board and supporters would not have accepted it."

I was tempted to say that if in 1969 he truly believed that the Y's policies were wrong, he should have stood up to the board. But I held my tongue. It had taken me a long time to stand up in the community and say segregation was wrong. It might have taken Bill and some others even longer, but the important thing was that they, too, had eventually done the right thing.

CHAPTER 8

August 1969 **Montgomery, Alabama**

If the renowned trial lawyer F. Lee Bailey hadn't charged so much for his services, the strange partnership that led to the Southern Poverty Law Center might never have begun. Bailey was Alabama State Senator Mac McCarley's first choice to defend him for allegedly soliciting a bribe from the Fraternal Order of Police, but the attorney from Boston wanted twenty-five thousand dollars plus expenses. That was too much for McCarley, who then approached me on the recommendation of a mutual friend, Birmingham lawyer Cliff Fulford. Cliff, who knew I'd sold my business and was anxious to return to court, had been impressed by my work on the *Dickey* and *Coffin* freedom of speech cases.

This was not a free speech or civil rights case, but it appealed to me for several reasons. McCarley was an underdog. After uncovering the story, the *Montgomery Advertiser* had already tried and convicted the senator with a series of front-page articles. Almost everybody in Montgomery agreed with the *Advertiser*'s "verdict," including Mac's fellow senators, who had expelled him without so much as a hearing. The case was also apparently seen by the district attorney in Montgomery County as a springboard to a judgeship and by the judge as a springboard to the governor's mansion. They were hoping for a conviction so they could please the powers that be.

Plenty of slick, clout-wielding, influence-peddling Alabama politicians supplemented their senate salaries with under-the-table deals. After meeting with Mac, a first-term political neophyte who toed the ultraconservative line laid out by Governor Wallace, I could tell he wasn't one of them. His side of the story persuaded me that with a lot of legwork we might be able to persuade a jury that however

128

foolish his actions, he was no criminal. I signed on—for considerably less than Lee Bailey. Then I called Joe Levin.

At first glance, Joe Levin, Jr., and I made an odd couple: a Baptist cotton farmer's son who rarely went to bars, had never been on an airplane or more than one state away from Alabama until a year after law school, and a Jewish lawyer's son who liked to close out the workday with a scotch and soda or two and had lived in New York City during his army enlistment.* Joe, good-looking with a permanent tan and straight black hair cut modish for the day, loved the city, and I loved the country. Small-town Montgomery did not suit him after his return from Manhattan and its twelve thousand restaurants and as many bars. He longed for a city that never slept.

At twenty-six, Joe had satisfied his parents' lifelong expectations by joining his father's law firm and the assured security of an established commercial practice. Joe Levin, Sr., was a debt collection specialist par excellence, and his son marched to court each day with a stack of files and easy victories. But Joe, Jr., did not like what he was doing. After the *Dickey* decision, he told my younger brother Allen, whom he'd known in college, that I should call if I ever wanted help on a case. When I did call, he mentioned he had been reading news reports of the YMCA case, cheering me from the privacy of his office.

Joe and I worked the hell out of the McCarley case, going on the offensive right away. At the same time we were preparing Mac's defense in the criminal case, we filed suit in federal court to reclaim his senate seat. Expulsion without a hearing, we argued, constituted a denial of due process.

Since under the buy-out agreement, I had to be at my old company during the day, Joe and I would meet around 5 P.M. and work until midnight. I promised him he could take time off for a drink as soon as the trial was over.

We bore down for a solid month. Joe had never worked a case requiring this kind of preparation. In most of his earlier cases, he had picked up a file and talked to his witnesses on the way to court. But he was tireless and bright, a much better writer and researcher than I. I recognized a natural born trial lawyer.

---

*In the army, Joe had spied on Columbia University students engaged in antiwar protests, something he grew to regret. Later, he would testify before a Congressional committee investigating the domestic invasion of civil rights and incur the wrath of many older local veterans, who saw him as a traitor.

When the McCarley jury returned its not guilty verdict after midnight, the bars were closed. Joe had earned his drink. Maureene and I went to his house to celebrate. In my thirty-three years, I had never drunk alcohol—not because of religious beliefs; I had simply seen too many drunks in Mount Meigs. Now, in the afterglow of victory, I gave in to Joe's insistence that orange juice and vodka would taste delicious and that a little liquor wouldn't hurt me.

Joe and Maureene toasted our victory with Scotch, leaving the new bottle of vodka for me. I hadn't eaten much during the three-day trial. The first drink did taste good. I remember asking how much vodka I should mix with the orange juice. The next thing I remember was the sound of the empty bottle falling from the table and somebody removing my shoes.

By the time the Associated Press had named *State v. McCarley* Alabama's news story of the year, Mac had been reinstated in the senate with back pay and Joe and I had decided to start the law firm that would eventually evolve into the Southern Poverty Law Center. We worked well together and wanted the same thing from the practice—a blend of exciting and socially significant cases. I severed my ties with Times Mirror Corporation.

Joe and I signed a partnership agreement stating that our firm would charge people who could afford it and offer our services for free to those who couldn't pay. We planned to support this *pro bono* work with fees we made from our paying cases.

Our plan worked. The large contingent fee we earned representing a black woman taken advantage of by a white developer supported a number of early *pro bono* civil rights cases.

In *Parducci v. Rutland,* we represented an English teacher dismissed from Montgomery's Jefferson Davis High School for teaching the Kurt Vonnegut short story, "Welcome to the Monkey House." The court ruled that the school had violated Ms. Parducci's First Amendment right to academic freedom and ordered her reinstated.

In *Frontiero v. Laird,* a case Joe argued in the U.S. Supreme Court, we represented a servicewoman who had been denied equal pay, equal access to housing, and other benefits received by her male counterparts in the military. The Court required the Department of Defense to change its discriminatory regulations that gave servicemen more benefits than servicewomen.

In *Cook v. Advertiser Company,* we finally alleviated a shameful practice that I had known about since my days as a paperboy in Mount

Meigs. This class action suit arose out of the *Montgomery Advertiser's* refusal, in 1969, to print the photo and wedding announcement of a black couple on the Sunday society page instead of the Thursday "Negro news" page. This "separate but equal" Sunday/Thursday scheme had replaced the old system of having special "Negro editions" marked by black stars, but was no more equitable.

The lawsuit embarrassed the *Advertiser's* editorial staff, which had won a Pulitzer Prize for attacking George Wallace and segregation. The national wire services picked up the story, and the paper's defense that it had the First Amendment right to print what it wanted won few progressives to its side. By the time the court ruled against us—finding the civil rights statutes did not cover this type of discrimination—the newspaper had changed its policy.

Taking cases like these and *Smith v. YMCA* made me very unpopular with most whites in town, especially Daddy's brothers Lucien and Arthur. At one point they came to my office, chided me for my "nigger loving ways," and told me that if Daddy were alive he'd be ashamed at the dishonor I had brought to the Dees family. "If you intend to keep doing this," they said, "change your name."

I told Uncle Lucien to close the door and asked them to sit down. I knew my daddy had not been close to his brothers. Some people in the Mount said my uncles were jealous of Daddy's moderate success. Still, I knew he loved them. Once, one of our close relatives had embezzled money from an employer and had been facing arrest if the funds weren't repaid. I quietly reminded them that Daddy had provided most of the money to save the family name from disgrace. I also reminded Lucien that when I was a small boy, he had told me that my daddy was a "nigger lover." I told them that they never really knew my daddy and had no idea what he would say to me today. I excused myself for an urgent call, and when I returned, they were gone.

Both Joe and I felt that our work on such cases as *Parducci, Frontiero,* and *Cook,* as well as my efforts on the *YMCA* case, was more exciting and rewarding than our profit-generating cases. We also agreed that issues such as freedom of speech, women's rights, and the rights of minorities could keep us busy, offering the opportunity to set important legal precedents.

We decided to establish a nonprofit law center. I could volunteer my time. Joe would need a salary, and we both needed money for expenses. I felt confident that my selling skills, particularly my direct-mail skills, could raise enough funds for the venture.

Thus Levin & Dees evolved into the Southern Poverty Law Center. We chose our name to convey where we were and what we did. Our primary goal was to fight the effects of poverty with innovative lawsuits and education programs. We would target customs, practices, and laws that were used to keep low-income blacks and whites powerless. With this focus we were staking out somewhat different territory than other bodies, such as the American Civil Liberties Union (ACLU) and the NAACP Legal Defense Fund. The Levin & Dees cases already in progress would prove typical for the Center. In *Nixon v. Brewer,* we were attempting to restructure the Alabama State Legislature into single-member districts, giving poor blacks and whites a greater voice in the electoral process. And in *State v. Jimmy Lee McCloud,* we were representing an indigent black man facing the death penalty after being indicted for murder on circumstantial evidence by an all-white, high-income Montgomery County grand jury.

Leon Capouano's office incorporated us for no charge early in 1971. The Center was (and still is) described as a not-for-profit legal and educational foundation. There was little if any publicity. Most people in town still viewed us as Levin & Dees, the firm with the businessman and the collection lawyer that had achieved a few fluke victories against the big boys in some gadfly cases.

We quickly hired a small staff. Howard Mandell, a Rhode Islander fresh from a clerkship with Judge Johnson, joined Joe and me in handling cases. We appointed Mike Fidlow, who had worked in direct mail at Doubleday Books and at my old company, fund-raising director.

Before we could ask for money, we had to establish credibility. We needed a prominent figure whose presence would announce the Center's values and promise. Julian Bond seemed the perfect choice. Born in Nashville and educated at Atlanta's Morehouse College, Julian had helped found SNCC, the Student Nonviolent Coordinating Committee, in the early sixties. By the time he was twenty-five, he had been elected to the Georgia state legislature. But the legislature had refused to seat him in 1965 because of his opposition to the Vietnam War. I had been impressed by Julian's refusal to give in to the powers that be. He had gone to court, and eventually won in the U.S. Supreme Court. I had also been moved, as so many had been, by his powerful, eloquent speech at the Democratic National Convention in 1968 after his name was put in nomination for vice president. At that convention, Julian led the group that successfully challenged the official Georgia delegation appointed by the racist Governor Lester Maddox. To me,

Bond represented the promise of the New South.

I had never met Julian Bond. My friend Chuck Morgan, an Alabama expatriate working for the ACLU in Washington, D.C., knew him and arranged a meeting in Atlanta. Julian was familiar with some of our cases, and when I told him about our hopes and plans, he agreed to serve as president of the Law Center, a largely honorary position. We then established a President's Advisory Council with such prominent civil rights activists as Lucius Amerson, the first black sheriff in Alabama since Reconstruction; legal scholar Tony Amsterdam; Hodding Carter III, the progressive newspaper editor from Greenville, Mississippi, who would later serve in the Carter administration; Charles Evers, the activist brother of the murdered leader, Medgar Evers; Mississippi's Fannie Lou Hamer, whose speech had electrified the 1964 Democratic National Convention; SNCC's John Lewis, later a congressman; and Chuck Morgan.

With this impressive council in place, we sent out our appeal. The mailing focused on the saga of Jimmy Lee McCloud. In denying bond, the judge indicated, *before the trial,* that he believed McCloud would get the death penalty. This statement made the newspapers, and we put the outrageous headline in a direct-mail piece stating Jimmy Lee needed us to make sure he got a fair trial and stayed out of the electric chair. Fidlow secured names of prospective contributors from mailing list brokers, and I got names from people I knew at the ACLU and other progressive groups. Over Julian's signature, we sent out twenty-five thousand letters asking people to contribute to the defense of McCloud and the Center's other work.

The mailing was a great success, drawing contributions from about 2.5 percent of those who received it—considerably higher than the 1 percent we were hoping for. We now had over five hundred donors. The Center was off and running.

Jimmy McCloud and George McGovern were worlds apart, but for the next several months I worked for both. I met Senator McGovern while working on the Nixon case—that's E. D. Nixon, a well-known black activist, not R. M., the president. E. D., who had helped orchestrate the Montgomery bus boycott, was the named plaintiff in our suit to achieve single-member legislative districts in Alabama. The state had been gerrymandered into large, white-majority, multi-member districts to prevent blacks from getting elected. As a result, at the beginning of the 1970s, about one-fourth of the state's citizens were black, but none served in the Alabama legislature.

The attorney in Marion County, Indiana, who had attempted but failed in a suit similar to *Nixon v. Brewer* also happened to be chairman of the Marion County Democratic Party. When Joe and I went up north to find out where he went wrong in his lawsuit, we met another visitor of his—McGovern. Hubert Humphrey and Edmund Muskie were the early favorites for the 1972 Democratic presidential nomination. McGovern, the antiwar senator from South Dakota, had not officially declared his candidacy, but he was already stumping. The polls showed him with about 1 percent support.

Joe and I were invited to hear McGovern speak to the Indiana locals. I liked what I heard. His explanation of his opposition to the Vietnam War was simple yet well reasoned. Joe cracked a few cynical jokes about McGovern's charisma, but later admitted feeling a pang of guilt about his dirty work for U.S. Army Intelligence. After the gathering broke up, I introduced myself to the senator. He asked me what I did and wrote my name down on a card.

I never expected to see the senator again, but a few weeks later, when Fred Gray asked if I would help raise funds for his run to be the first black in the Alabama legislature, I contacted the offices of McGovern and all the Democratic presidential hopefuls. It seemed to me that these would-be candidates (no one had officially declared) needed the black vote to win, and might demonstrate their concern for blacks by contributing a little money to Fred's campaign. Gary Hart, who was running McGovern's barebones precampaign operation, invited us to Washington, and the next thing I knew I was sitting in the Senate Dining Room with McGovern and Hart, eating the famous navy bean soup and explaining the fund-raising letters I wrote for Fred—heady stuff for an Alabama boy like me. McGovern gave us one thousand dollars, a sizable donation to a black candidate for state representative.

A few months later Hart called and asked me to come up to Washington. He explained that McGovern wanted to announce his candidacy officially by sending a letter to newspapers and targeted supporters.

"Are you going to solicit money?" I asked.

"No," said Hart. "We're just going to make the announcement. We were wondering if you could help us with the mechanics of getting it printed and mailed."

I thought about the first letter I'd sent announcing the 'Bama Cake Service. It would have been a waste just to say we would deliver cakes to students and not include an order form. "Why don't you tell the whole story about why the senator is running and ask for money," I said.

Hart explained that the McGovern advisers feared that a solicitation coupled with the announcement wouldn't be dignified.

"Why don't you give me the letter, some material you have about the senator, and some of his speeches, and let me play around with it," I said. I worked on the letter that night, then flew to New York, where Tom Collins, a direct-mail writer I knew, polished what I'd written.

"Morris," one of McGovern's aides told me, "we just can't mail your letter. We'd be the laughingstock of the country. It's too long. No one will read it."

I shook my head. I had reduced the physical size of the letter to personal-, rather than business- (or Senate-) sized stationery, to give it an intimate touch. It began "My Dear Friend" and would be mailed in a personal-sized envelope embossed with the senator's name and the Senate seal in the upper left-hand corner. While a common procedure now, this was considered radical in 1970. Even more radical was the letter's length. It ran about seven pages—six pages longer than what the conventional wisdom dictated.

McGovern had apparently read the letter and passed it on to Richard Wade, a former speechwriter for Jack Kennedy. Wade and others in the brain trust had reduced the letter to one page. The text read basically the same as the draft Hart had originally given me, although they did agree to leave in an appeal for funds. "Just mail this out," one of the advisers told me.

I knew these political experts were wrong. I had tested one-page and four-page letters selling books, and four pages always beat one. Yes, some people buy after the first paragraph or first page, but that doesn't mean they're mad at you for sending them four pages. And others aren't sold so quickly; some people have to look under the hood a dozen times, kick the tires, read the service manual, take two test drives before they buy.

McGovern's experts had made some valuable revisions to my copy, but I still believed a longer letter more effective. I incorporated those revisions into the longer draft I'd submitted. Now it was seven pages again.

I started with a direct personal message: "You are one of a number of people whose help I am asking in the most important effort any American can ever undertake." I wrote about the despair our nation felt over the Vietnam War, noting that "this despair stems from the fact that our great and powerful nation has wandered so far from our ideals that it has almost lost its way." I closed with the ancient wisdom of Ecclesiastes that Reverend Russell had preached to us at Pike Road Baptist, the same "there is a season" verse Darrow's book had brought to mind.

Like the evangelist who came to our summer revivals, I asked in McGovern's name for the reader to "join hands with me now. . . . I believe this is a time to heal. A time to build up. A time to cast away stones of war, and gather together stones for building. A time to speak. A time for love not hate. A time for peace."

I printed Senator McGovern's signature on the bottom of the new effort and shipped out three hundred thousand letters, with six-cent first-class stamps purchased at my own expense. I didn't tell the McGovern people a thing.

Not only was the letter contrary to what the McGovern people wanted, I had tripled the mailing list. McGovern had merely wanted to send one hundred thousand letters to supporters back home and people who had written him in support of the McGovern-Hatfield Amendment to end the Vietnam War. I thought the South Dakota list would be worthless for fund-raising so I added a long list of names from the Americans for Democratic Action, the ACLU, and other liberal lists.

Why did I do it? I'm not sure. Maybe it was because everyone I had seen in Washington was so timid around politicians, acting as if senators were gods. Maybe I just wanted to prove the Beltway crowd wrong.

Pat Donovan, McGovern's secretary, called a few days later. "The senator would like to see you," she said.

"What about?" I asked innocently, as if I didn't know.

"He's very upset that you used the wrong letter."

I told Pat I was busy and couldn't make it to Washington right away. "Let's just wait a few days and see what happens," I said.

McGovern might have been troubled by a letter he had received from a Madison Avenue advertising executive stating that the appeal was "so amateurish, so bald, so badly conceived, so incompetent, that it turned me off entirely." He predicted it would be a "bomb." It was, he wrote, "at the very least ineffectual and it may be more damaging than that." He advised that "an appeal for funds requires great expertise, particularly when done through the mails."

*   *   *

The senator called at the end of the week. "You know, Morris, that mailing had me a little concerned, but it really seems to be working well." He told me about a woman who had sent him the ten thousand dollars insurance money she had received after her son was killed in Vietnam. "She wrote that she didn't want the government's blood money," McGovern told me, his voice cracking with emotion. Older people were sending their Social Security checks, he continued, telling him they remembered the New Deal and hoped he would turn out like FDR.

"Come back up here, Morris," McGovern said. "We have to talk."

The letter would eventually draw a phenomenal 15 percent response rate. The *New York Times* did a feature story about the mailing, and renowned conservative fund-raising expert Richard Viguerie told the press that someone in the McGovern camp knew what he was doing. I flew with McGovern on a private jet to South Dakota, where he announced his candidacy. In his speech, he used the words from the last paragraph of the letter. When we returned to Washington there were boxes and boxes of contributions.

There was also a letter from my uncle Arthur. He said he was following me in the news and was proud to be my uncle. He wrote that he had rethought many of his old beliefs and wanted to apologize for the time he had asked me to change my name. I was proud of him.

McGovern was still trying to organize his campaign. Gary Hart had been serving as campaign manager, but McGovern thought Gary's greatest strength lay in coordinating the political field work while my business background would serve me well as manager.

I called Maureene and said, "Let's do it." I told Joe I'd have to take a leave from the Center, then bought a few wool suits—which was a few more than I had.

The suits fit, but the Washington life didn't. I missed Montgomery. After a month, I told the senator that Gary Hart should be the campaign manager and that I'd be happy to coordinate fund-raising if I could commute from Montgomery. He said that would be fine.

Many of the ideas our group came up with revolutionized political fund-raising. The work was demanding, but fun. I met supporters like Candice Bergen and Warren Beatty, who became a good friend. There was talk that if McGovern won, he would put me in his cabinet. I *would* have moved to Washington if I could have been attorney general. That position offered such an opportunity to balance the scales of justice. Alas, Nixon versus McGovern proved no contest, so I returned to the Center and *Nixon v. Brewer, State v. McCloud,* and a docketful of other cases, including a case to integrate the Alabama State Troopers.

I did not go home empty-handed, however. McGovern, a warm, thoughtful, and sincerely humble man with a keen sense of both the larger world and the smaller workings of his dedicated staff, visited my office often during the campaign to thank me for helping. He told me he had read in the *New York Times* about my suit to integrate the state troopers and about the new Center Joe and I had started. When the campaign was over, he gave me the list of his nearly seven hundred thousand donors and offered to write a letter urging them to help. Over one hundred thousand of these people eventually became Center supporters.

These McGovern donors had made political fund-raising history by giving over twenty-four million dollars and leaving the campaign with a surplus. This success and Nixon's abuse of secret cash gifts from rich special interests caused Congress to pass the campaign spending law prior to the next election, limiting gifts to one thousand dollars per person.

The Montgomery judge who predicted that Jimmy Lee McCloud would get the death penalty spoke intemperately, but accurately. McCloud, an uneducated young black man, had killed an attractive, young white schoolteacher after she happened on him while he was robbing her home. There was little doubt a local jury would sentence him to death.

What McCloud had done was indefensible, but he still deserved to be defended, particularly in a climate where a fair trial seemed out of the question. McCloud's mother had come to Levin & Dees shortly before Joe and I founded the Center. The family was indigent. He was facing the death penalty. And whether you believe in that punishment or not (and in 1973 I was having trouble reaching an absolute conclusion), the fact of the matter is that in Alabama, as about everywhere else, the death penalty has been disproportionately and unfairly applied to blacks and poor whites. We took the case to try to save his life, and we did. We obtained a change of venue based on the judge's pretrial comments and raised enough doubt in a Birmingham jury's mind for them to render a second-degree murder verdict. McCloud received a ten-year sentence.

On its face, this was just another criminal case, but like other cases that came into the Center, it turned into much more. The grand jury that had indicted McCloud had been typical of Montgomery County juries: all-white, almost all-male, and mostly high-income. We decided that once the 1970 census figures were compiled, we would try to challenge the racial, sexual, and income discrimination of the Montgomery County Jury Commission's selection process. It seemed only fair that blacks, women, and poorer folks should have the opportunity to be tried by juries of their peers and that juries in civil cases, too, should reflect the makeup of the community. The commission had systematically institutionalized power in the hands of well-to-do white males.

Our analysis of the census showed that while 54 percent of the people in Montgomery eligible for jury duty were women, only 16 percent of those on jury rolls were female. Similarly, 31 percent of those eligible were black, but only 12 percent on the rolls were black. The roll of potential jurors created by the commission looked nothing like the demographics of the county.

The defense team argued—without any factual basis—that the figures we presented were skewed because they failed to take into account that a large percentage of blacks were illiterate and, therefore, not eligible. Saying the court would not engage in "rank speculation," Judge Johnson found there was indeed racial and sexual discrimination and ordered the commission to devise a new, more equitable plan.

In cases like this, the Center could make its mark. We won *Nixon v. Brewer,* too, and gradually more black faces appeared not only in the jury box but in the state legislature. Where else was power institutionalized? In the state's police power. The case to integrate the Alabama State Troopers arose when an old friend of mine told me he felt he had been denied the opportunity to join the troopers because he was black. In its thirty-seven years, the agency had never had one black trooper. The all-white force was a symbol of the brutal racism that had gripped Alabama for so long. This was the first case where the Center received national attention, and we again won (although the state dragged its feet an unbelievable fifteen years until the U.S. Supreme Court settled the matter in 1987).

While the Center deserved its reputation as a force for integration, we considered ourselves a force for justice, blind to color. To the chagrin of many of our friends in the black community and many of our increasing number of supporters, we filed one of the nation's first reverse discrimination cases in 1971.

Our white clients had been dismissed by their employer, the Macon County Board of Education, because they sent their children to segregated private schools. Macon County, just to the east of Montgomery County, had an 85 percent black population and an all-black Board of Education. This board had instituted a policy requiring employees to send their children to public schools. Of course, we didn't condone the segregated academies that had grown up after *Brown v. Board of Education,* but we believed it was unconstitutional to restrict public employees as a condition of their employment. A federal judge agreed and ordered our clients reinstated.

During these early years, no victory meant more to me than *Callahan v. Sanders.* When my friend Eddie Callahan complained to me that justices of the peace received a fee from the state only if they found a defendant guilty, I couldn't help but think of my very first case. No wonder Judge Letcher had convicted Clarence Williams. We filed a class action suit with Eddie as the named plaintiff. The result: A panel of federal judges issued an injunction stopping the practice.

After the court ruled, I drove out to Clarence's house. The location was different, but the dwelling looked the same. In the twenty years since I had gone to argue Clarence's cause, his life-style had changed little. I found him on the front porch with some of his children and grandchildren. When I told him about the case, he smiled. "Things are changing," he said. He pointed to his grandchildren. "It will be better for them."

Things *were* changing for the better. I started to feel optimistic.

It didn't take too long for that feeling to change. After the McGovern campaign ended, I became involved in two death penalty cases. In one, dubbed the "Tarboro Three" case by the press, three young black men convicted of raping a white woman sat on North Carolina's death row for a crime they insisted they hadn't committed. In the other, a young black woman faced the death penalty for killing the jailer whom she claimed had forced her to have sex.

CHAPTER 9

August 1973   **Tarboro, North Carolina**

The chain of events that put the three black men and the young white woman on their fatal collision course began at about midnight. The men left a party at the Tarboro Inn and swung their green Chevelle onto the Highway 64 bypass. At the same time, the young woman decided to walk home by herself from a friend's house after arguing with her boyfriend. When Vernon Brown, the Chevelle's driver, saw her across the road, he slowed down and yelled, "Where are you going?"

"Who are you?" she asked.

"Wait a minute," said Brown. He made a U-turn and pulled alongside the young woman.

Jesse Lee Walston, Brown's passenger in the front seat, rolled down his window. "Do you want to go with us?" he asked.

Walston opened his door, and the young woman climbed into the back, where Bobby Hines was sitting. Hines asked her name.

"Mary Ann Womack, sugar," she said.

About an hour later, Vernon Brown, Jesse Lee Walston, and Bobby Hines dropped off Mary Ann Womack near a popular late-night hangout in Tarboro. When she saw three boys she knew, she started to cry. "What's wrong?" they asked her.

"I've been raped by three niggers," she allegedly told a friend.

North Carolina's Central Prison sits in the middle of downtown Raleigh, only a stone's throw or an inmate's call from the state capitol. Stark and faceless, the gray stone complex recalls the nineteenth-century prisons described by Charles Dickens. I parked my rental car, then reread the letter the prisoners known as the Tarboro Three had sent to Chuck Abernathy, a Center lawyer, after he had contacted them at my request.

Raleigh, North Carolina, January 1, 1974

Dear Mr. Abernathy:

We are the defendants in the accused case of rape last August the 5th. We were tried on December the 3rd in Tarboro's Superior Court. We were convicted December the 9th, and the death penalty was pronounced against us. . . .

We now face the death penalty because of injustice and prejudice. Also because we turned down a plea of guilty with intent to commit rape which our attorney insisted we take. We told him that we were not guilty of the crime rape.

We will fight right down to the very end. We feel the battle can be won and the truth of the matter can be revealed with the right defense attorneys. . . .

Cordially yours,
Mr. Jesse L. Walston
Mr. Vernon L. Brown
Mr. Bobby R. Hines

I put the letter down and headed for death row.

I'd read an article about the case shortly after the three men received the death penalty. I had asked Abernathy and Levin to contact them and their lawyer Grover Prevatte Hopkins to offer our help. Now I was sitting in a cramped, dirty holding cell with them less than thirty feet away from the gas chamber where they would be executed.

Opponents of the death penalty had thought that this gas chamber, along with gas chambers and electric chairs across the country, might never operate again after the Supreme Court's 1972 decision in *Furman v. Georgia*. That decision had, in effect, outlawed capital punishment as a cruel and unusual punishment because juries were typically given unfettered discretion to impose life imprisonment or execution. But the abolitionists' exaltation had died quickly. A number of states had enacted new death penalty statutes to get around the *Furman* restrictions, and the courts in other states, including North Carolina, had construed the ruling to allow capital punishment under the old statutes as long as jury discretion was removed and the death penalty was made mandatory.

At the time of the Tarboro Three's arrest, North Carolina defendants convicted of murder, rape, or first-degree burglary automatically
received death sentences. The result had been, in the words of the
respected law journal, *Juris Doctor,* "an uncomfortable resemblance
to old-time racial justice in the South." Just down the corridor from
our holding cell sat Samuel Poole, a black man discovered breaking
into a home by its occupant, a white woman. Poole hadn't stolen
anything, nor had he threatened the woman, but when she saw him,
she jumped out of the window and then, unharmed, rushed to the
police. Poole had been arrested, convicted, and sentenced to death for
burglary with intent to rape.

The old-time, pre-*Furman* racial injustice that *Juris Doctor* cited was
no myth. North Carolina was typical of most Southern states. Its
population was approximately 75 percent white and 25 percent nonwhite. Between 1930 and 1970, whites were convicted of capital
offenses in the state by a six-to-five ratio over blacks. Yet blacks
received the death penalty in capital cases four times more frequently
than whites and were executed ten times more frequently than whites
in rape cases.

Now that the death penalty was mandatory for rape, those convicted—be they black or white—would receive the same sentence.
But this didn't mean an end to discrimination. Police could still use
discretion in deciding whether initially to charge an individual with
rape or a lesser, noncapital offense; prosecutors could use the same
discretion in seeking indictments; judges could use discretion in pretrial rulings; and juries could use their discretion by acquitting the
accused because the punishment seemed too harsh for the crime or by
finding the accused guilty of a lesser offense. Since the vast majority
of police, prosecutors, and jury members in North Carolina were
white, the system still put blacks accused of capital crimes at a severe
disadvantage. Almost 60 percent of post-*Furman* death row inmates
were black.

Rape is heinous, but execution for that crime is, to me, cruel and
unusual punishment. Sitting across the table from Walston, Brown,
and Hines, I did not know whether they were guilty, but I did not
believe they should die. (In 1977, too late for the Tarboro Three, the
United States Supreme Court agreed. "A sentence of death is grossly
disproportionate and excessive punishment for the crime of rape," the
Court wrote.)

I wondered if the men had received a fair trial. Tarboro, population
9,425, sat on the small, winding Tar River in the tobacco and cotton

country of eastern North Carolina—the territory of ultraconservative Senator Jesse Helms. About 50 percent of the residents were black, but the jury that had convicted Walston, Brown, and Hines was composed of eleven whites and one black. The jury system, I suspected, was every bit as antiquated as that in Montgomery County, and it was a good bet that many of the local judges were equally biased.

Walston, Brown, and Hines wore the standard prison issue: loose-fitting cotton pants, T-shirts, and tennis shoes. I was first struck at how young they were—each was in his early twenties—and how gray they looked. It doesn't seem to matter what color your skin is; black or white, after doing time, you begin to match the walls of the institution. Although the three had been convicted in December, they had lived behind bars since the week in August when Mary Ann Womack had climbed into their Chevelle.

All three came from Edgecombe County, which included Tarboro, several small farming communities including the all-black Princeville, and Rocky Mount, a moderately progressive town of over forty thousand with a number of small industrial companies. Vernon Brown had grown up on Cotton Valley Farm, where his parents labored in the fields. After graduating from high school, he had worked in a local mill and then entered the army. He received an honorable discharge, returned, and started attending Edgecombe Tech during the day and doing carpentry at night. A tall, good-looking young man with a thin moustache and closely cropped hair, he had no prior police record save a traffic ticket.

Bobby Hines, short and stocky, was employed as a tow motor operator at a tobacco plant in Farmville earning $1.45 an hour. He lived with his mother in Princeville and had no previous arrest record. He was the least talkative of the three.

Jesse Walston, tall and thin, had graduated with Brown from high school, then married and moved to Washington, D.C., where he lived with his wife and two children. He had worked as a tractor-trailer driver for the Hecht Department Store for the last three years. An active member of the Refreshing Springs Church of God and Christ, he was upset that he hadn't been allowed to attend chapel in the prison. He had never before been arrested. When the police called his home to tell him he was charged with rape, he was so certain it was a misunderstanding that he voluntarily returned to Tarboro to clear things up. He hadn't been home since. He did most of the talking, with Brown and Hines adding important details.

Walston told me he had come to Tarboro for a vacation with his family on Friday, August 3. The next night, he and longtime friend Brown had gone to a surprise birthday party at the Tarboro Inn. At about 11:30 P.M., they were getting ready to leave when Hines had asked for a ride. None of them were drunk.

They were heading east on the bypass toward Hines's home when Brown saw a "lone woman" on the other side of the road. When Walston opened the door of the car, the dome light went on. Brown asked Mary Ann Womack what she was doing walking by herself at this time of night. She told him she and her boyfriend had argued because he wanted to drink, but didn't want her to drink, and that she didn't "have to take that kind of shit from him."

Walston added, "She looked like she had been crying, and I could smell alcohol on her breath before she even got in."

According to Walston, Womack told the men that she lived near Edgecombe County Hospital. Brown drove in that direction, but he soon became nervous. "Somebody's following me," he said.

"What's that supposed to mean, sugar?" asked Womack.

"Nothing. I just don't like for somebody to follow me that close." Brown took a sharp left, swinging back to Highway 64.

He then asked Womack if she wanted to get a beer. She said she didn't. A little later Hines, feeling bold because she had called him "Sugar," stretched his arm around her. Apparently there were stories of thrill-seeking white women from Tarboro hitchhiking into Princeville, hoping to be picked up by blacks.

Hines told me he asked Womack if she would have sex, and "she said, 'I'll do anything as long as you all take me home.' " He then asked her where the zipper was on her jumpsuit, and she showed him. "She helped me get her clothes off, and we started to have sex," he said.

"Did she object or fight you?" I asked.

"No, sir," said Hines. "She never objected to anything. She didn't resist. She participated."

Because the tape player in the Chevelle was loud, Brown and Walston didn't hear the conversation in the backseat, but they did glance back and see the couple engaged in intercourse. Brown pulled the car off to the side of a deserted dirt road, and he and Walston got out. Hines and Womack finished—he told me he didn't climax, but thought she did—and then Hines got out of the car.

"Then she told me to 'come on,' " Walston said. "So I climbed in and we had intercourse, too."

"How did she respond?" I asked.

"She cooperated. She was moving her body."

When Walston finished, Brown had sex with Womack, and again, according to him, she did not resist or indicate she didn't want to participate.

After Brown and Womack were finished, Walston and Hines got back into the car, and the foursome drove back toward town. Hines and Womack had sex once again. When they finished, according to Hines, they laughed and talked.

Hines then told Brown that Womack wanted to go home. Brown said he couldn't take her all the way home, but would let her out by the Hollywood Drive-In, a popular night spot. "She said that would be all right," said Brown. He stopped about fifty yards from the drive-in.

Three days later the men were charged with rape.

Walston, Brown, and Hines recounted the story sincerely, and there were no contradictions in their personal accounts. I didn't condone their behavior, but if what they were telling me was true, they didn't deserve to be in jail, much less on death row. If their version was accurate, Mary Ann Womack had voluntarily consented to have sex. Maybe she was vulnerable because she had been drinking or was angry at her boyfriend, but there was no indication of intent to rape, no evidence that she was forced or threatened.

Womack told a different story, insisting that she had not consented, that she had been raped. Why would she make up a tale? Perhaps she had wanted to save face with her white friends after getting dropped off in a state of disarray by three black men.

I knew I would have to read the trial record before deciding whose story was the most convincing, but the fact that the Tarboro Three had dropped her off in plain sight of the drive-in suggested to me they were not rapists. Three black men would be unlikely to rape a white woman in a small town in the tobacco belt of eastern North Carolina and then deposit her in front of a public place.

Why hadn't the jury realized this? The racial climate in this part of the country was not exactly moderate. As someone in Tarboro later told me, all the folks at the courthouse had laughed at the defense of voluntary consent because it was assumed, as a matter of law, that a white woman would never consent to sex with a black man.

When I entered the holding cell, I told Walston, Brown, and Hines that I wasn't going to take over the case but would assist their lawyer in appealing for a new trial or at least in trying to save their lives. When I left the prison, I wanted to do more.

After leaving Raleigh, I drove seventy miles to Tarboro to meet Grover Prevatte Hopkins, the Tarboro Three's lawyer, whom everyone called Jack. He was an odd-looking character of about forty, with an unusually long forehead, a dark, heavy, waxed moustache, and prematurely gray hair combed straight back.

Although a kind, pleasant man, Jack had little experience trying major criminal cases, and this was his first capital case. One of the young men's mothers had been referred to him, and he accepted the case for five thousand dollars, a fairly large fee for Tarboro in 1973, but significantly less than what many criminal attorneys in large cities charged for capital cases. Hines's mother had given him a mortgage on her home. Mrs. Walston and Mrs. Brown paid him in monthly installments.

Jack told me he thought it unfortunate that Walston, Hines, and Brown refused the deal the state had offered right before the trial— twelve years in prison for a plea of guilty to a lesser offense. With time off for good behavior, "the boys," as he called the three young men, would have been eligible for parole in seven years.

I told Hopkins that the young men insisted they were innocent and didn't trust the state to parole them before a sentence ran its full course. Then I asked him if there were any errors in the record on which we could base an appeal for a new trial. He said the judge refused to allow him to examine Womack's jumpsuit—a possible error. When I asked if he would like our help, he seemed relieved.

Before heading back to Raleigh, I visited the mothers of Brown and Walston. Each woman lived down a dirt road in a house reminiscent of Clarence Williams's house. When I told Mrs. Walston and Mrs. Brown that the Center would try to help their sons, they thanked me. Each insisted her son was innocent.

Back in Montgomery, I ordered the record of *State of North Carolina v. Hines, Walston, and Brown.* When the record arrived, I set to work with Abernathy, who had originally come to Montgomery to clerk for Judge Johnson, and Mary Herod, a summer clerk from Washington University Law School in Saint Louis.

Our purpose at this stage was not to retry the case in the appeal, but to find errors that would require the North Carolina Supreme Court to order a new trial. If that was successful, we'd begin an investigation that we hoped would result in a not guilty verdict the second time around. If we couldn't get a new trial, then we'd shift our attention to reducing the death sentence. The injustice of the sentence seemed even more remarkable since just weeks after the conviction, the North Carolina state legislature had eliminated the death penalty in rape and burglary cases. Unfortunately, the legislature had specifically refused to apply the new law to cases tried before its enactment, cases such as *State v. Hines, Walston, and Brown.*

The trial transcript now in hand, I immediately turned to Womack's testimony. I wanted to compare her side of the story with the Tarboro Three's version. Womack said she stood five feet three inches tall and weighed 103 pounds at the time of the incident. After graduating from high school, she had attended business school in Raleigh but had dropped out and started working in a hospital in Tarboro.

According to Womack, on the night in question, she and her boyfriend, Ricky Sanderson, had been out to dinner with another couple, Danny and Connie Vick, and had then returned to the home of Connie's mother. There, Womack became nauseated from drinking a mixed drink and two beers. She told Sanderson she wanted to go home, but he refused to take her. She testified that although sick, she was not drunk.

Womack said she entered Brown's car voluntarily, but it wasn't until she sat in the backseat with Hines that she realized all three occupants were young black males. Because the Chevelle was a two-door with bucket seats, the front seat had to move forward so that someone could climb in or out of the backseat. Womack testified that she realized she couldn't get out of the car, so she relied on the men's promise that they would take her home. When Brown changed routes because a car was following them, she told the defendants they missed the turn to her house. They ignored her, she said. Failing to find a door handle or window handle, she became frightened.

Womack testified that at this point Hines grabbed her breasts, an act that "totally shocked" her. She was initially successful in removing his hands, but Hines pushed her down on the seat and removed her clothes. She tried to push him away, but realizing his superior strength, decided that resistance would be futile. She said she had thought of a conversation with her mother and sister: "In a situation where you couldn't handle, or the odds were really against you, we decided it was better to take it the best we could, whatever the situation was, rather than to be harmed or killed." She added that she had cried during all of the sexual activity, had also told Walston and

Brown to leave her alone, and that at some point her jumpsuit was torn.

Throughout her testimony, Womack insisted she resisted the three men's advances. "I did not give any one of them permission to have sexual relations with me. It definitely was done against my will," she said.

Her testimony seemed to contradict the doctor whom she had seen in the emergency room at Edgecombe County Hospital later that night. In the presence of her mother, Womack had, according to Dr. John Whaley, "informed me she had been raped by three Negro men. She said that she did not put up any resistance because she was afraid that she would be killed." Mrs. Womack also testified she had told her daughter not to fight if ever confronted with such a situation.

Mary Ann Womack testified that it was one or two minutes between the time Hines got out of the car and Walston got in, yet during that time, she hadn't attempted to get dressed, run, lock the car doors, or find the car keys. She said she was too afraid.

Rape is defined in North Carolina as "the carnal knowledge of a female by force and against her will." The force need not be physical. Fear, fright, or coercion may also be construed as force if a reasonable person would believe she was in danger of serious bodily harm if she resisted.

I find it abhorrent that in rape cases the victim often ends up being put on trial, but after reading the transcript, I tended to agree with Walston's brother Leroy, a Metro bus driver in Washington, D.C. He had told the *Washington Post,* "They were convicted because that girl had to protect her reputation and she's willing to pay these men's lives to do it. He [Jesse] did wrong, he had sex with her, but he shouldn't die for it."

Reading the record, I saw several areas Hopkins could have explored, areas that an experienced trial lawyer with adequate funds would have explored. But Jack, who had received only a few hundred dollars up to that point from the families, didn't have the resources to investigate extensively or hire experts. One of the shameful elements of our criminal justice system is that practicing attorneys who must clear seventy-five dollars an hour just to cover expenses are expected to pay the high cost of defending a capital case. At the same time, the district attorney prosecuting the case has almost unlimited funds and numerous assistant district attorneys and investigators. If justice is the state's ultimate concern, why are the scales tipped so heavily against the accused, particularly the indigent accused? Alabama, for example, pays a court-appointed lawyer a paltry forty dollars an hour for time spent in court, and only twenty dollars an hour for out of court time, with a thousand-dollar limit (since about 85 percent of a good defense lawyer's time is spent out of court, this unreasonable limit deters pretrial preparation). No money is provided for expenses or for experts (with a rare exception). A few states, such as California and Florida, do adequately compensate defense lawyers, but in the vast majority that don't, where is the incentive to inspire an attorney (who may be reluctant to start with) to give his or her all to defending the accused? The sad answer is that you hope the professionalism and conscience of the attorney will make up for the shabby compensation.

The state called Womack's boyfriend as a witness. He corroborated her testimony that she wasn't drunk. But Jack had not interviewed Connie and Danny Vick for their accounts. If we could demonstrate that Womack had been drunk or high during the unfortunate incident, we'd have a much better chance. I wanted to know more about Mary Ann Womack from her fellow workers and friends: Had she told them anything? I wanted to talk to the people she saw at the Hollywood Drive-In. Hopkins hadn't interviewed any of these folks either.

I was anxious to start, but first we had to put together a successful appeal.

By the time we filed the appeal in June, we had found eighteen separate groups of errors in the record which, we argued, warranted a new trial for the Tarboro Three. Some, of course, were stronger than others. My strategy on appeal is to list all reasonable errors, preserving them for further appeal, but to concentrate on one or two surefire ones that could have made a difference in the outcome. The court's failure to allow Hopkins to examine Womack's jumpsuit before the trial to determine if it was ripped or stained was, as Hopkins had suggested, one strong point. But we had found something even stronger: the court's failure to stop the trial after a prejudicial comment by the prosecutor had tainted the jury deliberations on the death penalty.

During the selection process, a prospective juror had indicated discomfort in sentencing someone to death. Prosecutor Roy Holdford had replied: "Well, everybody feels that way, but this is the punishment that is provided at this point. *And to ease your feeling, I might say to you that no one has been put to death in North Carolina since 1961.*"

The statement was accurate, but misleading. The death penalty had not been carried out in the United States for several years preceding

Furman v. Georgia, but now death rows were filling up again, executions scheduled. Nineteen other men sat on death row in North Carolina in addition to my clients.

"[Holdford's] remark served to soothe the objections the jurors might have had to a guilty verdict. This statement could have served only to convict the defendants, in a close case such as this, based on a belief that they would not be likely to suffer the death penalty," we wrote in our appeal, citing several cases in which the North Carolina Supreme Court itself had ordered new trials due to similar prejudicial remarks. (It is always best in state court to use state law, since Southern state appellate courts often resent having to reverse on federal grounds. The error regarding the jumpsuit was, arguably, weaker because it would involve the state court's interpretation of federal court rulings and because the court might say, "Yes, it was error, but it was harmless error that had no impact on the jury's verdict.")

In December we appeared before the North Carolina Supreme Court, and on January 31, more than a year after I had first visited Walston, Brown, and Hines on death row, the court rendered its decision. The clerk of the court called Hopkins, who then called me.

"We won! The court ordered a new trial," I told Jesse Lee Walston. The court had agreed that District Attorney Holdford's remark to soothe the jurors was prejudicial. Finding that particular error, the court said it did not have to pass judgment on the other errors we had noted. The court did indicate, however, that interpreted in its most favorable light—the standard applied in appellate review—the evidence had supported the jury's verdict. That showed our work was cut out for us. We simply had to turn up new evidence before the new trial, scheduled for May. I was just about to start my investigation when I was asked to assist on another case in nearby Washington, North Carolina. It, too, concerned an alleged sexual assault and the death penalty. Soon the Center had a new client—Joan Little. Her name was the only thing "little" about this affair, which would become one of the most celebrated and controversial criminal cases of the 1970s, a case that once again would almost cost me my career and good name.

CHAPTER 10

August 1974   Beaufort County, North Carolina

The *New York Times* article written by reporter Wayne King that brought the Joan Little case to national attention began with a classic lead paragraph:

> The ice pick slaying of Clarence Alligood, the 62-year-old night jailer at the Beaufort County Jail, might have appeared a simple case of murder and escape by a woman inmate except for what one law enforcement official termed "the peculiarities in the way he was dressed." (*New York Times*, December 1, 1974.)

Undressed might have been more accurate. Slumped over near the foot of inmate Little's cell cot, Alligood had been stabbed eleven times with an ice pick he kept in his desk drawer. According to the autopsy report, "His shoes were in the corridor, his socks on his feet. He was otherwise naked from the waist down." In one hand he held his trousers. In the other, he clutched the ice pick. Beneath his body was a woman's kerchief. A nightgown lay crumpled on the cell floor, and a night jacket hung on the cell door. The medical examiner reported clear evidence of recent sexual activity—semen on the jailer's leg.

Held in the jail for three months pending the appeal of her conviction on a burglary charge, Little hadn't waited around for the medical examiner's report. After stabbing Alligood, she fled. Then, after hiding for one week, she turned herself in to the director of the State Bureau of Investigation. She claimed she had killed Alligood in self-defense after he sexually assaulted her while brandishing the ice pick.

If Mary Ann Womack had done the same thing to Bobby Hines when he had allegedly fondled her, I don't think she would have been arrested for murder. But the situation in Beaufort County, thirty-five miles from Tarboro, was different. Joan Little was poor and black. Clarence Alligood was white. As a result, at the same time my three black male clients faced the death penalty for allegedly attacking a white woman, this black woman faced murder one charges and the death penalty for apparently defending herself against her white aggressor.

Joan had retained Jerry Paul, a flamboyant movement lawyer with offices in Durham. After calling Paul, I entered as one of her attorneys and began to play an active role. The trial was set for July.

With the Little trial some months away, I devoted myself to the investigation necessary to put together a strong defense for the Tarboro Three. By the time I had settled into the Tarboro Inn, Jack Hopkins had bowed out of the case gracefully. I hired Vinson Bridgers and Larry Diedrick, prominent progressive lawyers from different firms in the area, to join me in the defense.

We needed new witnesses, new physical evidence, and new testimony from old witnesses. We made a list of people who had to be interviewed before the new trial, some twenty-three names.

Although Wanda Sue McLemore had been Mary Ann Womack's roommate at the time of the incident, Hopkins had not interviewed her. I located her in an apartment in Tarboro. A pleasant woman in her early twenties, she told me Womack had said that fear compelled her to give in to the defendants. "You'll do a lot of things to keep from being hurt," Womack reportedly explained.

McLemore also described Womack as a nervous person unable to cope with her own problems. She mentioned that Womack had consulted a psychiatrist and had been taking tranquilizers. I knew about the psychiatrist, Dr. Thompson. At the trial, Womack testified she called out his name during intercourse with one of the defendants. She went on to explain she had only seen him twice, and not since 1971.

I did not know about the tranquilizers. If Womack had been drinking and taking pills on the night in question, her fear may have been the result of something in her head rather than something one of the defendants had done, or she may have voluntarily participated in something she wouldn't have participated in under other, more sober circumstances.

This seemed the strongest theory for our defense—if I could prove it. I talked to others who had testified about her condition. Ricky Sanderson, Womack's boyfriend at the time, was uncooperative.

Speaking to me briefly, he stood by his courtroom testimony that she had not been intoxicated.

Michael Baker, the first person to see Womack at the Hollywood Drive-In, proved more helpful. I found him in the Johnson Youth Center, a juvenile correction facility about sixty miles from Tarboro. The slight, dark-haired sixteen-year-old was serving a three-year sentence for forgery.

At the trial Baker had testified that Womack had approached him shortly after getting out of Brown's car. She was crying and upset and said she had been raped "by three Negroes." Baker had told the jury that he hadn't smelled alcohol on Womack's breath and that she had not appeared intoxicated in any way. His testimony had damaged the defense.

Now he told me a different story: He had seen the Chevelle pull up, but hadn't paid much attention. "Then," he continued, "I heard what sounded like a girl laughing coming up behind me from toward where the car was parked." He turned around toward Womack and then heard her say, "I've been raped by three niggers."

"Are you sure it really sounded like she was laughing?" I asked.

"Yes," he said.

The laughter suggested to me that Womack might have been under the influence of alcohol or drugs. Baker retreated from his trial testimony that Womack wasn't drunk. Now he told me he wasn't sure. "She wasn't staggering, but did not act completely normal," he said. "She could have been high."

I made sure Baker signed a statement, figuring he would be a witness again. He was a friend of Womack and her brother, and I wanted to hold him to these remarks.

Maureene and Ellie came to visit a few days later. We drove out into the countryside and found a peaceful spot for a picnic supper. Ellie, who had been born two years after we married and was now almost five, romped freely, innocently. *If anyone ever lays a hand on her,* I thought . . . .

Was I being too hard on Womack, too easy on Walston, Brown, and Hines? Had I forgotten that civil rights meant women's rights, too, and that "women are a minority that have been victimized historically just as blacks have," as one previously loyal supporter of the Center had chided me in a letter saying she would never again contribute?

After dinner, Ellie fell asleep, and as the stars rose, Maureene and I made love under the cloudless sky. On the drive back to town, we passed the dirt road where Vernon Brown had pulled off and parked. Womack's interlude under the stars wasn't like the one Maureene and I had just enjoyed, not an evening of passion with her lover, but quick sex with total strangers in a car in a corn field. I doubted very much that she had enjoyed any part of it.

Was I victimizing the victim? No, I said to myself. The Tarboro Three were victims, too. "If three white guys had picked up Mary Ann that night and the same thing had happened, no jury would have convicted them of a capital offense," I told Maureene. "In fact no grand jury would have indicted them."

"Mary Ann Womack had been under the influence of alcohol or drugs or both when she climbed into Vernon Brown's Chevelle and as a result she either willingly participated in sexual activity or her view of reality was so altered that she failed to convey to the three men that she did not want to participate." I looked at the sentence I had written. This is what I would tell a jury in my opening statement, but how could I prove it? Michael Baker's ambiguous testimony would not be enough, nor would the testimony of Walston and Hines that they had smelled alcohol on Womack's breath; it was in their interest to say that. Wanda Sue McLemore's testimony that Womack had been taking tranquilizers was not conclusive and might not even be allowed by the judge. I needed more.

The next day, I learned through confidential sources that Womack had picked up a prescription for the tranquilizer Librium from a local pharmacy shortly before the incident. Now we were getting somewhere. Alcohol and Librium don't mix. I could find an expert to testify to that.

But had Womack mixed the two that night? Is that why she got sick? Had anyone seen her take the pills that evening? What was her condition when she climbed into the Chevelle? I decided to visit Connie and Danny Vick to try to find some answers.

After driving sixty-five miles southeast from Tarboro to New Bern, the picturesque small town on the Neuse River where the Vicks lived, I knocked on the door of their house trailer. Connie answered, an attractive woman in her early twenties neatly outfitted in a blue sundress.

"Mrs. Vick," I began, "my name is Morris Dees. I represent Jesse Walston, Vernon Brown, and Bobby Hines, the three young black men that got the death penalty in the case of Mary Ann Womack."

I wanted to be upfront with Connie Vick. When you're confronting witnesses with a probable allegiance to the other side, witnesses who could be hostile, you never know what they might do. Play them the wrong way and later on they might say, "This guy came in here and told me that if I didn't testify, I'd be forced to go before the grand jury." Then they can turn around and say that all the good information they supplied was given under duress.

The young woman began talking before I had even finished my introduction, looking as if she were about to cry. She clasped her hands together and said, "Oh, Mr. Dees, I am so glad you came to see me. I have been living with this thing on my conscience ever since it happened."

"Well, let's sit down and talk," I said.

She showed me to a little couch in the trailer. As a salesman I learned you could tell a lot about a person by the way his or her home looked. This was a modest place, but Connie Vick obviously took a lot of pride in it. There were plastic flowers and clean white doilies on a small coffee table. On the wall a handstitched sampler framed in wood announced, "God is the head of this household." On another table sat a big white Bible—the kind door-to-door salesmen get fifty or seventy-five dollars for. I figured Connie would tell me the truth.

"What's been bothering you about this case, Connie?" I asked.

"I don't think they raped Mary Ann," she said.

I was both puzzled and hopeful. Why was she so certain? "Did you see it?"

"No, sir, but I just know what must have happened."

The story Connie Vick had kept bottled inside poured out. She and her husband had met Mary Ann Womack and Ricky Sanderson at her mother's house about 7:30 or 8:00 in the evening. Both of the men had had a mixed drink. Connie couldn't remember if Mary Ann did. Then the four drove over to Rocky Mount for dinner at Lum's Restaurant. Everyone ate, except for Mary Ann, whom Connie said drank "a lot of beer, at least three or four glasses. I was surprised how much she had drunk."

"How big were the mugs, Connie?" I asked

She moved her hands several inches above the coffee table. "They were the tall ones," she said.

After spending about two hours at the restaurant, the couples had headed back to Connie's mother's house, where they hoped they could sober Mary Ann up before she went home. Ricky didn't want her parents to see her in her present condition. The Womacks were very strict, said Connie. This squared with what I had heard around town. When Mary Ann had gone off to business college in Raleigh, her parents checked up on her regularly. Troubled by her behavior, they had ordered her to see a psychiatrist.

"Do you know if Mary Ann was taking tranquilizers or pills?" I asked.

"No, sir, I don't know anything about that," Connie Vick said, then continued the narrative.

After returning to her mother's house, Connie had gone inside to make coffee, leaving Danny, Ricky, and Mary Ann by the car. Mary Ann was leaning against the car, apparently sick. "After I went into the house, Mary Ann walked away while the men weren't looking," Connie said. "We walked down the street looking for her, but she must have gone the opposite direction because we couldn't find her." The next day Connie had gone to the courthouse for questioning.

"Did you ever talk to the lawyer prosecuting the case?" I asked.

"Yes, sir. He called me on the telephone."

The lawyer was Cameron Weeks, a local practitioner hired by Mary Ann Womack's parents to serve as a special prosecutor on the case.

"Did you tell him that she was drunk?"

"Yes, sir. And I told him I didn't think they were guilty of raping her."

"Well, what did he tell you to do?"

"He just said to stay in New Bern and not to come to the trial."

This was important information. The state had suppressed a critical witness, one who would testify favorably for us. For the first time I felt positive about winning.

Connie Vick felt just as thankful to tell me her story as I was to hear it. For eighteen long months she had held this in. She said she would testify at the trial this time if I called her. The next day she signed a statement reiterating what she had told me. Later I talked to her husband, and he, too, signed a statement, his version the same as Connie's. "Mary Ann had gotten drunk from drinking so much," he wrote.

Unfortunately too many legitimate rape cases are never tried because the victim cannot face the ordeal of a trial. Aware of this, defense lawyers make it painfully clear to the victim before the trial that she will have to share intimate, private details with a jury and courtroom full of strangers. I don't like that. At the same time, I don't like to see three men facing the death penalty or a long prison sentence for a crime they did not commit, because they are black.

The trial date was approaching—time to let the state and Mary Ann Womack know that they were facing a fight. I subpoenaed Connie Vick well in advance of the deadline, just to let the other side know I would call her as a witness. That would give District Attorney Holdford plenty of time to try to find out how she would testify. To make sure he wouldn't have any trouble, I left Connie a copy of her signed statement. I hardly ever do this, but I wanted her to show it when the state came sniffing around. I wanted Holdford to know that the state apparently had suppressed this witness, and I wanted all the Womacks to know that a good friend was going to testify that Mary Ann had been very drunk. I wanted them to think about it every day until the trial started.

To keep Holdford thinking, I filed a motion seeking any statements the prosecutors might have in their files. If I found Connie Vick's statement, I'd have a good case for showing the state had indeed suppressed critical evidence. Although the appeal was over, it would tarnish the prosecution.

Now it was time to let them know I knew about the pills. I subpoenaed the records of Mary Ann Womack's pharmacy. I also filed a motion to have a psychologist examine her to determine her mental condition at the time of the incident: This would indicate whether she was in any condition to perceive fear or was too detached from reality to make a reasonable judgment in Brown's car. Now the Womacks knew her psychiatric history and drug history could be an issue at the trial.

Of course, I wasn't tipping my whole hand. I only wanted the state and the Womacks to know a few choice things about the case we were building. They didn't know we had an expert lined up to testify on the effects of alcohol and drugs on a person's ability to react rationally, remember details, and distort reality. They didn't know that we had ordered aerial pictures of the site where Brown had let Womack out of the car, pictures that would dramatically show how busy the area was and support our theory that Womack made up her story when she thought her white friends had seen her dropped off by the black men.

When my co-counsel Larry Diedrick saw the four-hundred-dollar invoice for the photographs, he told me, "This case proves one thing, a poor person doesn't have a chance." Fortunately the Center's contributors permitted us to undertake the defense—hire superb local attorneys, pay for exhibits, secure experts. Indigent as they were, the

Tarboro Three would otherwise have gone through another trial with an inexperienced, underfunded lawyer.

Larry Diedrick and Vinson Bridgers and another local attorney, Ray Joyner, were first-rate. They investigated prospective jurors so we could know as much information as legally possible about the men and women who might decide our clients' fates; they prepared character witnesses; they organized trial witnesses; they briefed points of North Carolina law related to our motions; they helped prepare the defendants for their testimony. As the trial grew closer and closer, we all worked long into the night at Bridgers's offices spurred by a growing confidence that we could actually win. Unfortunately, the judge assigned to hear the pretrial motions for the case did not seem disposed to give us a fair chance of prevailing.

We had subpoenaed Mary Ann Womack to testify at a hearing on our motions concerning her pharmacy records and psychological history. Her parents brought her. She was slight, with long, wispy brown hair: nothing remarkable about this young woman entangled in such a remarkable series of events.

Holdford objected to every question I asked Womack, and the judge sustained every objection. The judge then ruled against us on almost every motion: The use of tranquilizers was irrelevant to the case, he said, refusing to give us the multi-page listing brought to court by Womack's pharmacist; our psychologist could not examine her; established case law to the contrary, we did not have a right to examine the witness statements the prosecutor might have.

Although the judge wasn't helping us any, the prosecutor and the Womacks knew we could make their lives difficult. Connie Vick was still going to testify. Jury selection was about to begin. It was no secret that I'd make sure there was more than one black person seated on the jury this time. One person can be intimidated by eleven; several blacks in the jury room might not be easily cowed. If I could raise a reasonable doubt here, at least some of the blacks on the jury would hold out for an acquittal and the worst result would be a hung jury. That would force Holdford to decide whether he wanted to take the time and go to the expense of trying the case a third time.

Not long after the court had ordered a new trial, Holdford had said he would offer a twelve-year sentence in return for a guilty plea. My clients turned him down, explaining they were not guilty and wanted a new trial. As jury selection began, Holdford again approached with an offer. The Womacks didn't want to go through with the trial, he said. The state was now willing to offer a six-year sentence in return for a plea of guilty of assault with intent to rape. Counting the time already served, the Tarboro Three could be paroled within a year, the prosecutor said. The judge suspended jury selection while we considered the offer.

I had spent a good deal of time with Walston, Brown, and Hines, who had been moved off death row to the local jail after their new trial was ordered. The rules at the Edgecombe County jail were less stringent than the rules at Central State Prison, and the jailers, white as well as black, were almost all sympathetic to our case. I visited almost every night, bringing pizza, then sitting down to talk about the case.

They asked me what I thought about the state's new offer. "I can't tell you what's going to happen or what to do," I said. "There's a chance if we go to trial, you might get death or a long prison sentence. It's a big roll of the dice and you know what it's like to look down the hall and see that gas chamber. What do you guys think?"

Walston had become their spokesman. "We're not guilty."

"Well," I said, "with some blacks on the panel, I think we'll end up with a hung jury at the worst. I'd say we have a good chance of getting a not guilty verdict, but I'm afraid some of the whites might go against you no matter what the evidence."

The three conferred, then Walston said, "We don't want any settlement that means pleading guilty or going back to prison. Why should we trust the folks who run the prison and parole board? We've been here almost two years for something we didn't do."

I went back out to Bridgers and Diedrick. I had asked them to handle the direct negotiations with Holdford. As an out-of-towner, I felt my presence would only antagonize the prosecutor.

Bridgers thought our case was strong, but he was shocked that our clients had refused the state's offer. "Man, this is a death penalty case," he said. "They should take the six years."

"Go in there and see if Holdford will except a plea of *nolo contendere* to a six-year sentence for assault with intent to rape on the condition they can be released immediately," I said. This plea is not an admission of guilt, only an agreement that the charges will not be contested. Walston, Brown, and Hines had told me they would make such a deal if they could get out of jail immediately.

Bridgers and Diedrick met briefly with Holdford. Then Holdford huddled with the Womacks. Mary Ann Womack and her parents said they would agree to the plea if the defendants would serve another ninety days. Three months would give Womack time to leave town, Holdford explained.

We brought our three clients into the closed-off courtroom so they could talk with their families. The three mothers wept and urged their sons to accept the deal. Jesse Walston came over to me and nodded. I felt a release of the tension that had built since becoming responsible for the freedom of the young men, and I felt happy to reunite the three families.

Twenty-one months ago these three men had lived thirty feet from the gas chamber. The Center had entered the case, hoping to make sure they never got any closer. If someone had told me that the Tarboro Three would not only escape death row but leave prison altogether—*free men*—I'd have said, "Man, what you been drinking?"

Everything we did to defend the three young men may in retrospect seem obvious to good trial lawyers, but it is important to remember that the Tarboro Three had already been convicted and were sitting on death row when we became involved. If what we did was obvious, the story is even more frightening. It suggests other innocent people sit on death row, the victims of inadequate legal representation. How many have died?

After the deal was struck, Jesse Walston sent me a letter:

> Words could never express how very appreciative we are for all you have done for us. It is a debt we could never repay. We can now look forward to a new life and future with our families.

I wrote back inviting all three men to the Joan Little trial. They didn't come to the trial, but they did come to Montgomery. They visited the Center and stayed out at the farm for a few days.

Jesse Walston's wife and children were ecstatic to have him home, and his employers at the Hecht Company welcomed him back warmly to his old job. Vernon Brown, whose son had been born while he was in prison, went back to classes at Edgecombe Tech. Bobby Hines moved out of town.

And what about Mary Ann Womack? Her family had wanted the Tarboro Three to stay in jail an extra ninety days so she could leave town. But Mary Ann Womack never left Tarboro. I later heard she was married and doing well.

CHAPTER II

August 1974   Beaufort County, North Carolina

Only two people knew for sure what happened in the Beaufort County Jail's cell number two in the early hours of August 27, 1974— the inmate and the night jailer. The jailer, Clarence Alligood, did not survive to tell his story. The inmate, Joan Little, did.

Little said that during the three months she had been incarcerated, Alligood had done several small favors for her—brought her sandwiches after hours, given her cigarettes—and that he would sometimes come back to her cell and talk. On the morning in question, she said, he showed up outside her locked cell at about 3:30 A.M. and "told me he had been nice to me and that it was time that I be nice to him, and that he wanted . . . wanted me to give him some pussy."

Joan Little said she refused, but Alligood took off his shoes, unlocked her cell, and entered. He started feeling her breasts, then put his hands between her legs. She began to cry. Alligood slipped off her nightgown, then took his pants off.

"He tried to force me toward him," Little said. "I tried to get away. . . . And at that point I noticed that he had an ice pick in his hand."

Alligood, who stood over six feet and weighed more than two hundred pounds, then grabbed the five-foot-three-inch, one-hundred-pound Little, and, she said, forced her to perform oral sex on him. As she finished, in her words, "sucking him," he loosened his grip on the ice pick and it fell to the floor. She reached for it. He tried to stop her, but she lifted it up. The two struggled. Little hit him with the ice pick and he fell back. The ice pick dropped, and he grabbed it.

Frightened, she took some clothing and fled, leaving Alligood bleeding, but alive. "If I'd have known he was going to die, I wouldn't

162

have left him like that," she said. A policeman bringing in a drunk missed her escape by ten seconds.

Little found refuge in the nearby shanty of a stranger, Ernest Barnes. Police and sheriff's deputies checked the shanty four times. During one search, Little almost suffocated when an officer sat on the feather mattress she was hiding under, questioning Barnes for an hour.

Some North Carolina officials wanted Little declared an outlaw, which under state law would allow any person to kill her on sight. Some advisers urged her to leave the country rather than stand trial. Instead, she sent word to lawyer Jerry Paul that she would turn herself in on the condition she wouldn't be held in the Beaufort County Jail. After a week at large, she finally surrendered.

When William Griffin, Jr., the Beaufort County district attorney, submitted Little's case to the grand jury, he presented a version of the fatal incident far different from Little's. The state claimed that Little had lured Alligood into her cell and then coldly stabbed him to death with the ice pick which she had taken from his drawer earlier in the evening when he had let her make a telephone call from his office.

Although the grand jury indicted Joan for first-degree murder, a capital offense, the case initially received little publicity outside North Carolina. Only after Wayne King's *New York Times* article on December 1 did the nation take note. Because of its racial and sexual overtones, the case made headlines and newscasts across the country and overseas. Outraged feminists and civil rights supporters came to Little's defense. To many, the case was proof positive that in America, white males held the keys to the kingdom as surely as Clarence Alligood had held the keys to Joan Little's cell. Suddenly, Joan Little was a hero to tens of thousands around the world.

Joan Little was an unlikely hero: a shy, quiet twenty-year-old who had grown up in rural Beaufort County, a hundred miles east of Raleigh. Poor blacks and whites often lived in shantytowns there, some farming tobacco, corn, or cotton. Others were employed as cheap labor on larger farms or worked in the phosphate mines of Texas Gulf Corporation or the yarn rooms of National Spinning. The prime real estate along the Pamlico River was primarily inhabited by well-to-do whites, many of them retirees who spent their leisure time sailing on nearby Pamlico Sound. Beaufort's county seat was the town of Washington, called "Little Washington" to avoid confusion with the nation's capital.

The oldest of nine children, Little had originally quit school at fifteen and moved north to live with relatives in Philadelphia. She resumed her education there and tried to continue when she returned the next year to Beaufort County, but eventually dropped out for health and economic reasons. After taking low-paying jobs in restaurants and a garment factory, she decided on a trade: sheetrock finishing.

To learn this traditionally male vocation, Little willingly apprenticed on several jobs without receiving any wages. She had finally started to earn a paycheck when she was arrested for a rash of trailer-home burglaries near Little Washington. Her brother, also linked to the crimes, turned state's evidence and testified against her. In June 1974, she was convicted of stealing, among other things, an air conditioner, and sentenced to seven to ten years in prison.

While appealing this conviction, Little had been held in the Beaufort County Jail. The jail, like many in small towns, was operated somewhat loosely. As the only woman prisoner, Little was given free run of three women's cells and the adjacent gallery. Still, she had little privacy due to the closed-circuit TV monitor across from her cell. She did not know when it was on or off. All of Joan's jailers were white men, among them the sixty-two-year-old Alligood, who had taken his job after giving up farming and driving a gravel truck.

Joe Levin and I had created the Center to take on cases like this. The trial promised to raise a number of important legal and social issues: the right of a woman to defend herself against a sexual attack; prison conditions for women (evidence was growing that sexual abuse of women inmates was a national epidemic); the discriminatory use of the death penalty against poor people and blacks; selection processes that failed to produce juries of true peers; and the right of a poor person to an adequate defense. But as important as these issues were, one motivation overrode all: We had to save Joan Little's life.

Dave Watson, a former Doubleday Book Club copy chief who left New York and the corporate world to join the Center, wrote a persuasive letter explaining the reasons for the Center's involvement. We added a photocopy of King's *New York Times* piece. Using several lists, including McGovern contributors and *Ms.* magazine subscribers, we then appealed to two million Americans for help in funding Little's defense.

The response was overwhelming. We eventually raised almost $350,000. With that kind of money—which, sadly, is available only to wealthy individuals or select clients whom a Center like ours comes to represent—you can mount a strong defense.

Our first task was to get a change of venue and ensure Little a fair trial. Racial tensions had run high in Beaufort County and its surroundings since Alligood's death. As Paul told the press, "It'd take them five minutes to convict her down there." District Attorney Griffin had offered to move the case to a neighboring county, a concession we viewed as purely cosmetic. We wanted to be far away from this rural part of the state—Jesse Helms country—where, we believed, whites were more prejudiced and blacks less outspoken than in the progressive urban areas.

North Carolina law mandated only a move to an adjoining county. To convince Superior Court Judge Henry A. McKinnon, Jr., that would be insufficient, we commissioned psychologists John McConahey and Courtney Mullin to prepare a survey of racial attitudes in the region. We also surveyed jury rolls in several counties and found racial imbalances.

The surveys, while costly, were persuasive. The judge ruled he had the power to go beyond the state statute, "in the interest of justice," and ordered the case tried in Wake County, where Raleigh was the county seat. We now had the urban area essential to give us a fighting chance.

After the North Carolina Supreme Court upheld Judge McKinnon's ruling, the psychologists helped us select the kind of jury that would most likely give Little a fair trial. There is nothing illegal, manipulative, or subversive about using experts to discern what prospective jurors really think. No prospective juror is spoken to outside the courtroom.

There would be little need for consultants if prospective jurors answered all questions truthfully. Instead, they deliver socially acceptable answers. *Yes,* they say, they will give the defendant the presumption of innocence. *No,* they say, they will not defer to the authority of the state and forget the prosecution's burden of proof. *Of course,* they insist, they are free from racial bias.

The truth is the vast majority of people sincerely believe that a person would not be on trial if he or she hadn't done something wrong, and that since the defendant was indicted, he or she is probably guilty. At the same time, many people do defer to those they see as representing "the system"—the judge and, most important, the district attorney. And there are certainly many prospective jurors who harbor racial prejudice.

Since prospective jurors won't generally tell me, as a defense attorney, any of this, I use indirect questions, intuition, and an experienced eye to weed out those who are predisposed to convict my client. A jury consultant can add information to my equation by creating a profile of the best juror for the case.

To determine the profile of our best jurors in Wake County, our psychologists, with the aid of Jay Shulman of the National Jury Project, conducted a scientific telephone poll of one thousand residents. When the survey was finished, the results were fed into a computer to correlate personal data with feelings about Little. Obviously our best jurors were those who felt Little was not guilty, that she had a valid self-defense claim, and that she did not lure Alligood into her cell. The survey showed that these individuals had other things in common besides sympathy for Joan, such as religious beliefs, racial attitudes, and educational background. Thus, a profile emerged.

Judge McKinnon requested he not be assigned to the trial for personal reasons. He was replaced by Judge Hamilton H. Hobgood, a man with more than twenty years' experience on the bench, described as a calm-mannered fellow and great storyteller. Outspoken in the area of prison reform, he had publicly urged better-funded systems for representing indigents. We felt we could have done a lot worse.

Judge Hobgood knew we had taken nearly a month on the change of venue motion and believed us when we said it would take nearly three months to pick a jury by asking tedious but critical background questions. To shorten the process, he allowed us, with the state's approval, to give all prospective jurors a questionnaire. There were no questions about the case, just about the individual's background.

We fed the answers into the computer, which then correlated the background information with the profile of the sympathetic juror developed through the phone survey. We then rated the prospective jurors on a scale of one to ten. Not surprisingly, blacks were found to be most sympathetic. We also wanted liberal, educated, urban Democrats, who were Episcopal, Jewish, or Unitarian, and read such publications as *Psychology Today, The Nation, Saturday Review,* and *The New York Times Book Review.* We did not want those who read conservative and simple-minded publications like *Reader's Digest,* attended conservative Protestant churches regularly, voted Republican, lived in rural or small-town areas, worked in humdrum jobs, read little, and generally had little education beyond high school.

When a prospective juror was queried, we skipped the background questions, save a few to make the individual comfortable and to allow us to watch body language (which our psychologists also used as an indicator). In North Carolina jury selection, the prosecutor asks questions first. If the state okays the individual, it cannot go back and rechallenge the juror, no matter what information the defense elicits. If a would-be juror was highly rated on our scale, we would verify our initial finding with a few soft questions and then okay him or her.

As helpful as jury consultants are, there remains no substitute for human interaction. Mrs. Hilda Lipscomb's answers on the questionnaire indicated she wasn't for us: a forty-eight-year-old white Presbyterian, a farmer's wife who lived on a rural route. She had a high-school education and read little.

Aware of her background, I wanted to find a reason to challenge her for cause—a challenge based on a juror's inability to be fair or impartial. I started by asking about racial bias. Most prejudiced folks will tell you they're not prejudiced, don't even think prejudice exists. This was the answer the survey suggested we'd hear from Mrs. Lipscomb when I asked her if she had ever seen minorities treated unfairly. Instead, she said, "Yes," noting it was a "shame how the tobacco farmers took advantage of migrant workers," how the children were denied educations, the workers underpaid, the housing unsanitary.

Mrs. Lipscomb began to cry as she related her feelings about this unfair situation. I handed her my handkerchief and quietly said, "Your honor, Joan accepts Mrs. Lipscomb. We feel she is a fair and honest person."

Because the black community was squarely behind Little, we wanted any black person on the jury list. The prosecution didn't want any. To eliminate blacks, the state asked: "Do you believe in the death penalty?" Predictably, most blacks answered no. This response had once been grounds for dismissing a would-be juror. But in 1968, the U.S. Supreme Court had ruled in *Witherspoon v. Illinois* that if a prospective juror admitted that he or she was not unequivocally opposed to the death penalty and would consider it in *some cases,* it would be error to grant the prosecutor's challenge for cause. Our job was to take these black prospects who initially said no to the death penalty question and elicit the *Witherspoon* exception from them—create a hypothetical situation in which they could in good conscience vote death or at least express some doubt about their opposition to capital punishment—so that the state would have to use one of its limited number of peremptory challenges (challenges requiring no explanation) to get rid of them. Soon the state had depleted those challenges, and we were assured of minority representation.

Between the jury consultants and the lawyers, we ended up with a terrific jury. There were seven whites and five blacks, seven women, five men. Of the whites, one operated a health food store; another was a young male lawyer, a former classmate of defense attorney Karen Galloway; a third was a prison counselor who said she wouldn't necessarily believe a jailer; and a fourth was a record store manager.

In heady moments, we told ourselves that the jury was so strongly disposed to Little that we couldn't lose. But the nagging fear remained that there were some holes in her story, that the state could build a solid case based on circumstantial evidence centering around the critical question: Why would Alligood, who was so much bigger and stronger than Little, need an ice pick to force himself on her?

The prospect of a conviction had been so strong before the Center entered the case and before the media focused on Little that, according to Griffin, Paul had discussed a plea bargain with the state. Paul indicated that if Little's conviction on the breaking and entering charges were upheld on appeal, he might have her plead guilty to second-degree murder if the sentences could run concurrently. Griffin said he would agree to this and, he remembers, he offered to dismiss all charges against Little if she passed a lie-detector test. Paul did not immediately take him up on this offer, and when Griffin renewed it a few months before the trial, he never responded. By this time the case had become so celebrated that there was no chance Paul would enter a plea of guilty.

In the weeks before the trial, I played the role of chief investigator. The Center's John Carroll and I unearthed a great deal of evidence that supported our case and a little that seemed potentially damning.

The positive evidence involved Alligood's actions, not only on the night in question, but before. John and I secured the names of more than a hundred women incarcerated during Alligood's tenure. We painstakingly tracked these women down, finding six (five former inmates as well as one visitor) willing to testify that Alligood had molested or attempted to molest them. Annie Jenkins was typical. When she had been an inmate-trustee in the jail in January 1974, she said, Alligood had tried to feel her breasts and put his hands on other parts of her body. She said he often talked about sex and that she had to "slap his hands to make him quit." Jenkins said he always approached her when no one was looking.

From a most unusual source, we learned that Alligood wanted to make sure no one would notice when he approached Little, too. I had asked my friend, Montgomery Sheriff Mac Sim Butler, to write a letter to Beaufort County Sheriff O. E. "Red" Davis telling him that I would visit the jail. I wanted this letter of introduction so I could avoid being associated with Paul, whose statements and tactics often antagonized law enforcement officials.

A big man, with large rough hands, Sheriff Davis was waiting for me in his small basement office down the hall from the cell where Little had stabbed Alligood. He appeared to be in his early fifties, with fiery red hair, freckled face, and watery blue eyes—well suited for a Norman Rockwell portrait.

The sheriff spoke slowly with an eastern North Carolina drawl, telling me that Mac had written him I was a good fellow. "These other lawyers, I don't know about them," he said. "No matter what you do, they call you 'pig' and say you're against them."

Sheriff Davis told me he was trying to look at Little's case fairly, and that the circumstances under which the jailer was found—dead in a cell with his pants off—suggested Joan might have an argument for self-defense. "You ought to go talk with Mrs. Beverly King, our radio operator," he told me. He went on to explain that Mrs. King had told him that Alligood had visited her in the radio room at about 2:55 A.M. and asked if all the deputies had gone in. "Beverly said Clarence asked for the information, but then he didn't make any request for assistance from any deputies," said the sheriff.

"Is that unusual?" I asked.

"Well, Beverly said it it wasn't unusual for Clarence to come into the radio room and ask about the deputies—we have two of 'em riding the county at night—but it was unusual to just inquire and then not request anything."

The sheriff brought me in to see Beverly King, a young, overweight black woman who looked uncomfortable in a deputy's uniform, heavy belt, and sidearm. She confirmed what Davis had told me: Alligood rarely asked about the deputies without a follow-up request for assistance. "Assistance" usually meant going to the Wagon Wheel Restaurant and getting sandwiches for the staff and inmates. This was obviously critical information. We could argue that Alligood wanted to know about the deputies' whereabouts because he was planning to visit Joan's cell and didn't want to be disturbed or caught.

After taking a statement from King, I thanked Sheriff Davis. "Mr. Dees," he said, "you know, we took Joan's personal property out of the cell that night. Let me show you." From a locker, he took a small sack full of clothes and other effects, including several puzzle books.

The sheriff also mentioned that in the confusion immediately following the stabbing, Little's cell and the bloody floor and mattress had been scrubbed. By the time the state's sophisticated traveling crime lab arrived the next morning, the whole site had been so thoroughly cleaned up that all evidence was gone—another factor in our favor, since the state had the burden of proof.

I left the jail armed with a statement from Beverly King and the knowledge that our case was stronger. Then I flipped through one of Little's puzzle books. "This book belongs to 'Taurus' Miss Joan Little," my client had written. In the margins, she had kept a diary. Most of the entries either professed her love for "Mr. J. Rodgers: Cancer"—her boyfriend—or described Alligood's actions.

The Alligood references were disturbing. On August 4, Little had written: "Mr. All. came back and talked odds and ends for about 20 min. I'm going home soon." On August 22, just five days before the stabbing, she had noted: "Alligood just came on duty. Pray to God I'll be out very soon."

What did these references to being out soon mean? Was she planning something? The prosecutor would certainly suggest this was the case. "Joan Little was counting the days before she killed Clarence Alligood," Griffin would no doubt tell the jury.

The state had tidied the cell and the mattress, but not Alligood's lifeless body. As the autopsy said, "extending from his penis to his thigh skin was a stream of what appeared to be seminal fluid . . . the urethral fluid was loaded with spermatozoa." This sperm confirmed Joan's story, didn't it? We thought so until some friends at the University of North Carolina Medical School said they had been approached by the prosecution to support a different theory, one that, if proven, could devastate our defense. According to these contacts, the state was trying to find an expert at the school to testify the sperm on Alligood's leg did not result from sex, but from traumatic ejaculation.

Traumatic ejaculation. The term was new to me. Apparently, there was a case or two in the medical literature in which a traumatic blow—a hanging, for example—had caused a man to ejaculate at death. I had heard of bowel movements happening under these circumstances, but not ejaculation. Now, rumor had it, the state was going to suggest that the ice pick to the heart caused the semen on the leg.

The list of witnesses the state intended to call revealed three doctors: Dr. Charles Gilbert, a noted pathologist who had conducted the Alligood autopsy; Dr. Page Hudson, the state medical examiner; and Beaufort County Medical Examiner Dr. Harry Carpenter, the first person to examine the body.

None of the doctors was under any obligation to talk to us, and both Hudson and Gilbert gave us the silent treatment. Fortunately, John Carroll had better luck with Carpenter, a 'Bama graduate who softened when he learned John had gone to law school in Birmingham and was now working for the Center in Montgomery.

I didn't expect to try the Joan Little case. Jerry Paul would handle that. I felt the Center could help by raising money to pay for the various experts and investigators needed to build the strongest defense. We would also absorb the cost of housing, travel, and other expenses for witnesses and the trial team. I also thought John and I could assist with the preparation and investigation. But it soon became evident that Jerry needed more than the Center's money and our legwork.

Jerry, a huge, lovable teddy bear of a man, was a "movement lawyer," skilled at making a case into a cause. Thirty-three years old with long, wavy brown hair and steel blue eyes, he saw the big picture and could manipulate the media into putting that picture in front of the nation. While such machinations can be important, sometimes "movement lawyers" are so concerned with the big picture that they don't want to bother with the details of representing a little client—details like uncovering evidence, securing experts, and preparing witnesses. This detail work, not grandstanding in front of the larger "court of public opinion," enables a lawyer to try a case in front of twelve people and invariably proves decisive.

Over the years, I've had more than my share of run-ins with some pretty prominent movement lawyers and movement people. It's not that we disagree on social philosophy, but rather on trial philosophy. I've always felt that my first responsibility lies with the client, not the cause. If a media blackout is best for the man or woman I'm representing, I won't talk to the press. And if a client will be better off if we settle a case before a precedent-setting verdict, I'll settle. We'll just have to find another case to change the world.

Jerry, who seemed strangely out of kilter during the months we worked together—something he attributed to medication he was tak-

172 Morris Dees

ing to fight back pain occasioned by an old football injury, prostate trouble, and the serious illness of his son—was not a detail person. To his credit, unlike some movement lawyers, he realized he needed assistance trying this case and did not let ego get in the way of providing Joan Little the best defense possible.

As a former college football player, Jerry saw himself as "head coach" of a team of lawyers with, as he put it, "assistants responsible for the actual work." Our team included Milton Williamson, an excellent country lawyer; Jim Rowan, Karen Galloway, and Jim Keenan, bright associates from Jerry's storefront law firm in Durham; Marvin Miller, a talented and delightful lawyer from Alexandria, Virginia; John Carroll; and myself. Our team headquarters was Raleigh's Lemon Tree Inn, where we reserved a whole floor. Continuing the football theme, Jerry set up a training table where fruits, nuts, and seeds were served to condition us for the ordeal ahead. I stuck with grits and biscuits.

In a pretrial "open letter to all persons who have helped put together the Joan Little defense," Jerry listed thirty-eight "team players" and their individual attributes. He described me as "the best investigator I have seen" and said I would be at the counsel's table "to give us all insights into the minds of those that oppose us." He closed the letter by saying, "When the book is written and film made, I will try to see to it that each gets the credit they so rightfully deserve."

The reference to book and movie deals was not an idle one. Raleigh and Little Washington, the home of legendary moviemaker Cecil B. DeMille, were crawling with writers and producers. Team members frequently speculated which Hollywood star would play them in the movie.

This seemed like putting the cart before the horse. There wasn't going to be much interest in a movie if we lost the case. I imagined that most of the team could accept the loss of a movie deal. It would be a lot harder to accept Joan Little getting the death penalty if we failed her because we were blinded by Hollywood spotlights.

The heat in Raleigh was intense, but that didn't stop crowds from lining up early outside the Wake County Courthouse for *State v. Joan Little.* Several of Little's relatives were present, as were numerous members of the Alligood family. The media, national and international, filled up many of the blond wood benches in Judge Hobgood's gold-carpeted courtroom. Jerry Paul's entourage occupied another twenty spaces.

Little, wearing a plain blue dress with a single strand of pearls, sat at our mahogany counsel table with Paul, Williamson, Galloway, and me. Other lawyers from the legal team positioned themselves behind us. Three prosecutors occupied an identical table across the aisle from us. The thirty-two-year-old, red-haired Griffin wore a seersucker suit and a nervous expression—thanks to the pressure from the folks back in Beaufort County to bring home a conviction. Griffin was joined by John Wilkinson, a Beaufort County practitioner in his sixties retained as special prosecutor by the Alligood family, and Lester Chalmers, another special prosecutor who normally worked in the North Carolina attorney general's office.

My mother's grandfather was a Wilkinson from North Carolina. I told John we must be kin. He wasn't willing to go that far, but at least it broke the ice. On the other hand, Chalmers bothered me. There was talk the Klan had pressed the attorney general's office to get involved in the case. I doubted those rumors, but I didn't doubt Chalmers himself was involved with the KKK. In private practice, he had represented United Klans of America Imperial Wizard Bobby Shelton. And that ring on his finger, which from a distance first struck me as a Sigma Chi memento with its Norman cross, reminded me a great deal of a Klan ring when I got a closer look.

I was to do more than *sit* at the counsel table. Jerry had decided that, as the only one who had talked to witnesses, I would handle the lion's share of direct examination and cross-examination, with one dramatic exception. He wanted to question Little.

The state's first witness was Beaufort County deputy Johnny Rose. He testified he had seen Alligood alive at 2:15 A.M. and had found him dead after being summoned by radio operator King at about 3:55. On cross-examination, I asked Rose to explain the proper procedures for contact between male jail personnel and female prisoners. He established that Alligood should not have been where he was found—in Joan's cell.

Dr. Carpenter, the friendly 'Bama pathologist who pronounced Alligood dead, took the stand next. The state called him merely to establish Alligood was dead in the cell. We weren't disputing that Little killed Alligood in the cell, but I had several questions for him.

When found, Alligood was holding the ice pick. The state was suggesting that Little had put it into his hand to make it look like he was after her. But under cross-examination, Dr. Carpenter testified that the ice pick was "firmly held" and in his opinion had not been placed in Alligood's hand after he died.

Dr. Carpenter also said he could clearly see Alligood's penis as the jailer lay in the cell. The state had suggested that Alligood did not have his shorts off, that Joan had stabbed him, then pulled off his pants and fled—the "no sex" theory. It was time to blow that out of the water with a preemptive strike. I showed Dr. Carpenter the medical report that mentioned sperm on Alligood's leg.

"How did it get there?" I asked.

"I assumed it indicated sexual activity."

"Have you ever had occasion to witness ejaculation of sperm caused by traumatic death?"

I knew the doctor's answer. John Carroll had asked Dr. Carpenter all the right questions.

"No, I have not." As a pathologist he had performed more than a thousand autopsies, many on trauma victims. Griffin had not bothered to ask.

Griffin's icy stare said he wished *he* had the ice pick. We had turned around *his* witness, making it difficult for Dr. Hudson or Dr. Gilbert to advance the traumatic ejaculation theory.

Beverly King was the state's next witness. As she approached the stand, neatly dressed in her deputy's uniform, I thought that the prosecution couldn't have done me a bigger favor by calling her. In a few minutes, I'd have her talking about Alligood's unusual behavior on the fateful night.

Special prosecutor Wilkinson asked King to describe jail activity and established that she had seen Alligood shortly before the stabbing. He surprised me by asking if Alligood's failure to call the deputies had been unusual. Beverly King surprised me even more by saying, "No," clearly contradicting the statement she'd given me, an important part of my cross-examination.

In its opening statement, the state had told the jury the evidence would prove that Alligood had innocently entered Little's cell with a sandwich and pack of cigarettes when she suddenly stabbed him. When Wilkinson had finished questioning King, I showed her a diagram of the jail. Then I handed her an enlarged photograph showing the hole that a jailer could pass food through into the cell area.

King testified that this was proper procedure and there was no reason for Alligood to have entered Joan's cell. She also noted that if a
jailer needed to go into a female's cell, the rules required a matron
to assist.

The prosecutors stirred uneasily as their witnesses helped our case.
It was time to establish that Alligood had wanted to make sure he
would be alone with Joan in the early hours of August 27.

Q: Has it not been Mr. Alligood's practice when he came in to . . . ask
you about the deputies? Was it not for the purpose of having you
call a deputy to come in and assist him at the jail?
A: Not always.

King again contradicted what she had told me when I visited the
jail. This wasn't the first time a witness had reversed a previous statement, but I hadn't expected Beverly King, a law enforcement officer,
to back off from what she had told me and Sheriff Davis. I looked to
our counsel's table. King's statement was sitting by my briefcase. It
would be simple to get it and then impeach her, show the jury she had
told me one thing a few weeks earlier and was now telling them
something else. But did I really want to impeach her, suggest that she
wasn't forthright? Did I want to embarrass a black woman, a law
enforcement official in front of this jury? Did I want to cast doubt on
the credibility of a witness whose testimony about the jail's layout and
procedures and about Alligood's entrance into the radio room that
night had already boosted our case?

If the testimony that Alligood's behavior was unusual had been
absolutely critical to our case, I would have taken the risk and im-
peached Beverly King. But it wasn't essential. King had, after all,
testified that Alligood was concerned about the deputies' whereabouts, yet he hadn't called them. Rather than retrieve King's statement, I asked the question again, in another way. But again she said
Alligood's behavior had not been unusual. Judge Hobgood suggested
I move on, then called the afternoon recess.

As the jury left the room and King came down from the witness stand, I did get her statement. When she passed between our
defense table and the prosecutors' table where Griffin and Wilkinson stood talking, I spoke. "Mrs. King, will you come over here
please?"

She walked over to the table.

"Mrs. King, you gave me a statement," I said. "You told me that it was unusual behavior on Mr. Alligood's part to ask about the deputies and then not ask you to radio them for assistance."

King said she didn't remember what she had told me.

I showed her the statement and read it to her, then told her that after the recess I was going to again ask her whether Alligood's behavior in the radio room was unusual. "You go ahead and say exactly what's in the statement," I said.

King left the room, followed by Griffin and Wilkinson. I told Paul the contradiction had been cleared up.

The recess took unusually long. "I wonder what's holding things up," I said to Paul.

When Judge Hobgood and the jury finally returned, Beverly King again took the stand. Confident she would repeat what she had previously told me and Sheriff Davis, I again asked her if Alligood's failure to ask her to call the deputies had been unusual. Again, she answered that it had not been unusual. Exasperated, I gave up.

Wilkinson asked a few questions on redirect examination. When he announced he had no further questions, Judge Hobgood asked the jury to leave the courtroom. He fixed me with a nasty stare, then turned to King, still on the witness stand.

"Mrs. King," Judge Hobgood said, "listen very carefully . . . because this is a serious moment to all concerned. I received a report before I came back in here that Mr. Morris Dees, the man who was talking to you, had a conversation with you . . . [and] insisted you tell something which was not true. Now is that true or not true? I want you to tell the court exactly what occurred."

My stomach tightened. What was going on?

King took a deep breath. "He asked me again did I say that it was unusual for Mr. Alligood to ask me where a deputy was. I told him, 'No,' and he said to go ahead and say it, that it would help Joan and it wouldn't hurt the state."

That wasn't what I had said at all. Had somebody actually suggested I had told this witness to lie?

Judge Hobgood's stare was even nastier now. The red veins in the rolls of fat around his neck bulged and his facial muscles twisted, pulling the corners of his mouth down to his chin. "I'll allow you to cross-examine," he said to me.

"I certainly will, Your Honor."

I walked slowly toward the witness stand. The courtroom was

deathly silent, but I could now feel the puzzled stares of the press, the gallery, my fellow defense attorneys, and the prosecution.

I asked Beverly King to read out loud the statement I had shown her during the recess: "This was abnormal conduct on his [Alligood's] part . . . and it was unusual."

I continued. "And is that what I read you standing right here in front of the bar?"

"Yes."

My heart resumed its normal rhythm.

But Judge Hobgood was not appeased. He focused on King's assertion that I had told her to "say it. It would help Joan."

I spoke up. "Your Honor, I told her to follow the statement she had given me."

"Regardless of her testimony here today?" asked the judge.

"No, sir, not regardless of her testimony. . . . I referred her to the statement and I said, 'Why don't you follow the statement you had given me?' "

I asked King one last question. "Didn't I insist that you tell the truth?" My voice was stern, almost commanding.

"Yes," she said.

There. I was satisfied that this misunderstanding was explained. Clearly I had done nothing wrong.

Judge Hobgood motioned me forward. "All right, Mr. Dees, you are out of the case as of right now, and I suggest you not say anything to me about it."

Jerry Paul jumped up and asked if we could offer evidence. Judge Hobgood said no, then he stretched out his arms and told me, "I'll give you five minutes to get out of the courtroom."

I felt dizzy as I gathered my papers. *What was going to happen to Joan's defense?*

Jerry was thinking the same thing. "May we have a recess, Your Honor, so we can—"

"Regroup," the judge interrupted.

"Replan," said Jerry.

I stood up. *What was going to happen to me?*

The press looked ready to devour me. I picked up my briefcase and hurried to our adjacent witness room.

I was sitting there by myself trying to figure out what had happened when Burley Mitchell, the local district attorney, walked in. A tall, handsome man whose blond hair was beginning to recede, he was not taking part in the trial. We had become friends over the past weeks, talking politics over pizza and beer.

"Burley, what in the world is going on?" I asked. "Is this judge crazy? I've got to get in there and try this case."

Burley looked down at his shoes. "Morris," he said, "I hate to tell you, but I got a warrant for your arrest right here."

CHAPTER 12

July 1975   **Raleigh, North Carolina**

Burley Mitchell held the warrant in his hand. Talk about swift justice. It must have been drawn up during the long recess.

"What are the charges, Burley?" I asked.

"Attempted subornation of perjury," he said, looking away.

What does subornation mean? I thought to myself. I knew it wasn't good.

"It's a felony," Burley continued.

A felony! I could picture myself in the same dark, ugly Central State Prison where the Tarboro Three had been held.

"Jesus Christ, Burley," I said. "Didn't Hobgood hear that woman say I told her to tell the truth? Didn't he hear her agree she had given me a different story in her statement?"

"This wasn't my doing, Morris," Burley said. "Griffin and Wilkinson went to Judge Hobgood, and he recommended charges be filed."

I slammed my fist into the table. The prosecution had gone to the judge behind my back, *ex parte,* and done this. The judge hadn't even given me the courtesy of explaining myself in chambers, and he certainly didn't pay attention to my questioning of Beverly King after the recess.

Burley started to hand me the warrant.

"Hold on," I said.

I called Sheriff Davis in Beaufort County, then asked Burley to come close to the phone. I didn't tell the sheriff about the day's events, just said I wanted him to confirm that Beverly King's signed statement reflected what she had told him about Alligood's actions. He did.

I put down the phone. "Now you know the truth, Burley. Tear up this warrant. You haven't served it yet. Go tell Hobgood I was right."

Burley took off his dark-framed glasses. He looked sympathetic. I sensed he knew I was being railroaded. Then he spoke: "Morris, Judge Hobgood is like a father to me." He handed me the warrant and left.

I stayed in the witness room as long as I could. I called Joe Levin and calmly asked him to alert Chuck Morgan. Then I started cursing Hobgood, Griffin, Wilkinson, Mitchell, the state of North Carolina, and, for good measure, the South. Joe said he'd be in Raleigh by morning and was sure Chuck would, too.

I phoned Maureene. I didn't want her or any family members to turn on the news and learn of my arrest. I told her I was convinced that someone from the state had persuaded Mrs. King to change her testimony, and that when I had called her on it during the recess, a plan had been hatched to discredit me.

"Why?" Maureene asked.

Clarence Darrow had once been unjustly accused of tampering with a jury in California and had spent the better part of two years trying to clear his name. "I guess they figured if they could keep me busy fighting their fire, I couldn't start any of my own." I explained the two big reasons the state might want me out: First, I was making their witnesses look bad and promised to try a strong case. Second, the state was angry at the outsiders who had come in and raised questions about justice in North Carolina. By portraying me as one who would encourage perjury, the state could adopt the posture that we outsiders were a bunch of unethical, felonious agitators.

Jerry Paul came into the room, looking worse than I did. The trial had resumed and he was being forced to cross-examine witnesses without any preparation. So I coached the coach.

After court was adjourned, I prepared a statement for the press and hurried into the hallway, where a podium held dozens of television and radio microphones. "It was clear as crystal I was attempting to get the truth from a witness who was reluctant to tell the truth. I hope I'm back at the defense table in a day or two," I said, trying to sound upbeat. Beverly King's testimony that I told her to tell the truth, "vindicated anything I could possibly be accused of," I added.

I closed by saying I felt sorry for King. This was true. Someone from the state had persuaded her to change her story.

I had been using the Raleigh law offices of Terry Sanford, the former governor of North Carolina who had become a friend during the

Above: Johnny Harris, shown here with me at Alabama's Holman Prison, was senenced to death for the murder of a prison guard. Work I did at his first trial was the basis for a reversal. Louisville attorney William Allison and others were ultimately successful in winning his escape from death row.

At right: Center attorneys John Carroll, Dennis Sweet, and I represented Marine Sgt. Roy Patterson, shown here, in his successful twelve-year capital case. He shot two Georgia lawmen in self-defense. He now lives in North Carolina.

At left: Clemmie Moultrie, seated, faced South Carolina's gas chamber for killing a deputy sheriff who was forcibly evicting him from his home. Center attorney Dennis Balske, right, jury expert Cathy Bennett, and volunteer South Carolina attorney Mike McCloskie won Moultrie a reduced sentence.

Clockwise from top right: Texas Gra[nd]
Dragon Louis Beam, with Bible in han[d]
proclaiming that Galveston Bay belongs [to]
white shrimpers. • Training at a sec[ret]
Klan paramilitary camp. • Klansmen [pa]
trolling the bay waters to scare away imm[i]
grant fishermen. • The burned boat o[f a]
Vietnamese shrimper.

Henry Hays

"Tiger" Knowles

Bennie Hays

Frank Cox

"Red" Betancourt

Bill O'Connor

Teddy Kyzar

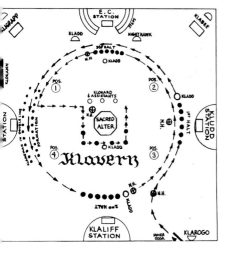

These members of Unit 900, a Klavern of the United Klans of America, met in this building in Theodore, Alabama, in March 1981 and made plans to "lynch a black man." Cox supplied the rope while Henry Hays and Tiger Knowles selected Michael Donald at random. At left is a secret diagram of a Klan meeting room I obtained for the trial. Kyzar provided vital evidence and was dropped from our lawsuit. Cox and Knowles are serving life sentences. Henry Hays is on death row.

Top left: Nineteen-year-old Michael Donald was lynched by members of the United Klans of America in 1981. *Above:* Beulah Mae Donald, shown here at her son's funeral, filed a suit that won a seven-million-dollar verdict and bankrupted the United Klans. *At left:* Sale of the Klan's headquarters provided money for the purchase of a new home for Mrs. Donald. She and I are shown here on the porch the day she moved in. *Top right:* Evidence from Beulah Mae Donald's suit resulted in the murder conviction of Klansman Frank Cox.

Clockwise from top: Daddy, top row center, holding me at a 1937 gathering in Mount Meigs. • My father at twenty-one. • My beautiful mother poses with my sister Carolyn and me. • My maternal grandparents in front of their rented farmhouse in 1913. My daddy is at far left.

Clockwise from top left: Picking cotton at fourteen behind our house. • Clarence Williams, our field hand and friend. I defended him in my "first case" at sixteen before a justice of the peace. • Democratic presidential nominee George McGovern and I discuss the campaign. As his finance chief, I used the mail to raise twenty-four million dollars. I also served as President Carter's National Finance Director in 1976. • Some of the many books I published before selling my company to the Times Mirror Corporation in 1969.

Clockwise from top left: First black Alabama State Troopers being sworn in after the 1972 court victory. • The Tarboro Three—left to right, Vernon Brown, Jesse Walston, and Bobby Hines—on North Carolina's death row in 1974 during my first visit. • Joan Little, center, in Raleigh's Central Prison, with North Carolina lawyers Jerry Paul and Karen Galloway.

Dear Poverty Law Center

Please try and understand what I'm about to explain to you. Please take out the time.

See I have know one else to help me. Please I need your help. I come from a very poor family, I don't know who my my father is. And my mother is getting welfare. I hurting and suffering Only if I had someone to hold my hand and walk with me I know I will make it. Please I beg you to help me and talk with me, I'm truly afraid to die, and Louisiana Penitentiary is a very dangerous place for a 16 year old to spend the rest of his life. Please help me. I'll wait to hear from you soon.

Sincerely,
Johnny M. Ross

Sixteen-year-old Johnny Ross was sentenced to Louisiana's electric chair for the rape of a white woman. He wrote to the Southern Poverty Law Center for help. Center attorney John Carroll won him a new trial—and, ultimately, freedom—based on scientific evidence proving his innocence.

McGovern campaign. I went into the "war room" established to defend Joan Little and prepared to defend myself.

A Dees defense team quickly formed. One of the senior lawyers in Sanford's firm, W. G. "Bucks" Ransdell, Jr., a prominent criminal defense attorney and former prosecutor, agreed to serve as lead counsel. We were soon joined by Richard Singer, a former Sanford firm partner and great trial lawyer whom I had met working on the McGovern campaign. I asked them the maximum sentence for attempted subornation of perjury.

"Ten years," Ransdell said.

"Jesus," I said. "Let's get going."

The task at hand was to get the transcript of Mrs. King's testimony. Under Judge Hobgood's thumb, the court reporter had already refused to transcribe a copy for Paul. Ransdell and Singer knew her. They contacted her at home and she promised a transcript of the exchange between Mrs. King and me and Hobgood after the judge had sent the jury out.

There was little we could do until morning. I returned to the motel. Most of the Paul "team" seemed no worse for wear despite the day's proceedings. The entourage was enjoying the "non–health food" beer bust held each night after court. Many of these people had little to do but hang around, eat at the Center's expense, and see who could get quoted by the press. I didn't fit in with these "cause groupies," and most had little sympathy for me.

Paul genuinely felt I'd been shafted and genuinely needed me back in court to examine and cross-examine witnesses. He told me he had called the famous activist lawyer William Kunstler to take my place.

I slept little that night. Early the next morning I prepared Paul and some of the other lawyers for the day's witnesses and then hurried to Sanford's offices, across the street from the courthouse. Chuck Morgan and Joe Levin had arrived. Several newspaper accounts of my arrest were sitting on the conference room table. "Dees Expelled from Little Trial; Named in Warrant," ran the front-page headline of the July 30 *Montgomery Advertiser.* I wondered how Maureene and the children and my mother were holding up.

The *Charlotte Observer's* front-page story on July 30 included an interesting piece of information: "It is known that before the trial the prosecution was told by Mrs. King: 'I knew there was something unusual when he asked me if the deputies had gone home.'" After noting the "rather fine point" was important because it might indicate that Alligood had plans to visit Joan's cell, the *Observer* continued, "Mrs. King's decision to change her story was unknown to many people involved in the state's investigation as late as [the night before she testified]."

The critical court transcript arrived. Ransdell told me he thought he could get the case dismissed at the preliminary hearing because the warrant information did not adequately state a crime. He added that since the state's true purpose had been served by getting me out of the case, there would be little reason to pursue prosecution.

His analysis did not soothe me. I didn't want to be out of the case, and I knew I'd go crazy waiting for the preliminary hearing, set for September 15, six weeks away. I also wasn't as confident that the state would drop the charges. "If the jury acquits Joan, who's to say those guys like Chalmers won't go after my ass," I said. "They can say they lost the Little case because her lawyers were unethical, out-of-state agitators, and Dees's conviction proves it."

I moved to the window and stared at the courthouse. I might as well have been back in Montgomery. "We have to get an affidavit from Sheriff Davis right away," I said. "He's King's boss. If he swears she told him the same thing she told me and he sent me to her, the jury will see I was just being a good lawyer, trying to nail down the truth." I walked back to the table. "If we got Davis's affidavit today, we could start a public relations campaign to show I'm innocent and get me back in the case."

Nobody jumped up and volunteered to get the affidavit.

"I'm on pretty good terms with the sheriff, maybe I should go and get it," I said.

Morgan, Ransdell, and Singer told me I was flirting with disaster by trying to persuade the sheriff to sign a statement that would embarrass a fellow worker. They didn't think Davis would help me. They also feared that at my trial the prosecution could coax Davis to testify I tried to persuade him to refute Beverly King and he refused to do it. They suggested waiting and then calling him as our witness at the trial.

"By trial time, he'll see his bread is buttered on the state's side and then he can just change or muddle his story like King so he won't hurt their case," I said. I looked at the *Advertiser* headline again. "Listen, it's my ass on the line here."

Joe was the only one who hadn't voiced any opposition. He knew how I'd gotten out of the YMCA mess and how I was hurting now. He spoke as a friend as well as lawyer. "Do it fast, Morris," he said.

Within an hour I had chartered a plane, prepared two affidavits for the sheriff, and arranged for Carol Sloane, a notary public, to fly with me to Beaufort County.

Joe's advice to move quickly was well taken. I wanted to return to the Little courtroom as soon as possible. Short of that I needed to be back by evening to help Paul prepare for the next day's witnesses.

When we landed in Little Washington, the pilot told me bad weather was rolling in. If I couldn't be back on the plane in two hours, he couldn't guarantee we'd make it back to Raleigh that day. We spent fifteen minutes driving from the airstrip to the jail and another hour waiting for Sheriff Davis. I began to wonder if I'd been foolish to make the trip.

When Davis finally arrived, he greeted me cautiously and showed me to his office. There was no need to bring him up to speed. My arrest was front-page news in the county.

I reminded him that I had gone to see King on his recommendation. "Sheriff," I said, "I need an affidavit from you because I want to quash this thing right away."

The sheriff got up from his desk and walked around the room. His back to me, he finally spoke. "Morris," he said softly and sadly, "I just don't believe I could do that. I could never get elected again in this county. But I promise you I'll testify at your trial."

That will be too late, I thought. I could see my career ruined, my law license lost, my family disgraced. *A felony! Central State Prison!*

The sheriff sat down at his desk. I looked at the photographs of his children on the wall behind him. "Sheriff," I said, "think about your own family. If you were in a fix like this, think how it would affect you and your children. I'm sure they love and respect you. I know you're a Christian man. You know what's right and what's wrong. You know this woman has changed her story."

I can't remember what else I said. All I remember is thinking that I had spent my whole life selling, and if I ever had to make a sale, now was the time.

We talked for the next hour. Time was running out to fly back to Raleigh, but I couldn't leave. We talked about everything on earth and beyond—philosophies of life, the Bible, Jesus. We laughed, we cried, we prayed. When we finished Sheriff Davis stood up and took a long look at the pictures of his kids. When he finally turned to me, tears were running down both sides of his face. "Morris, I'll sign your affidavit," he said.

I went to get Carol Sloane, the notary public. On the phone with the weather service, the pilot gave me a "we got to hurry" look.

"Now you read this affidavit to make sure it's right," I said to Sheriff Davis. I had prepared two—a strong one and a mild one. I gave him the strong one.

"Son, you read it for me."

When I was done, he said, "That's pretty good, but she told me more than that."

The typed statement said that Beverly King had told him it was unusual for Alligood not to request assistance after asking about the deputies. To this, Sheriff Davis added in pen that King "said he [Alligood] had never done this before without request for a deputies [sic] assistance." I couldn't have asked for more.

The pilot knocked on the door. "We have to be in the air in ten minutes, or we aren't gonna make it today," he said.

"That ain't no problem," said the sheriff. He stood up and put on his hat. "C'mon, let's go."

We rushed to the sheriff's car. He turned on the siren and the blue lights, and we raced through Little Washington. Turning into the dirt road leading to the airstrip, the car screeched and slid sideways, just like on "The Dukes of Hazzard."

Sheriff O. E. "Red" Davis pulled his car right up to the door of the plane. I shook his hand and told him he was a rare man, a hero. I meant it. The chief law enforcement officer of Beaufort county had just given me evidence that sabotaged the state's case.

Back in Raleigh, one of the lawyers in Sanford's office told me I'd been a fool to see the sheriff. "A pretty smart fool," Joe Levin said, smiling.

We stayed up most of the night preparing a motion to reinstate me in the case. Judge Hobgood refused to allow the court clerk to file it. Despite this, the press immediately picked up on Sheriff Davis's affidavit. I hoped Burley Mitchell would, too.

Judge Hobgood did allow me to use an office on the floor above the courtroom. On Thursday, Paul and the other lawyers beat a regular path to this room so I could prepare them for the state's parade of witnesses.

"This is torture," I told Joe when he came into the tiny white-walled room. "The trial of a lifetime, a trial I spent months preparing for, and I can't even walk into the goddamn courtroom."

Joe said two of Chuck Morgan's friends from the ACLU, Neil Bradley and Norman Siegel, were on the way to help us prepare a federal suit against Judge Hobgood, charging he had violated my civil rights and constitutional rights and my client's rights as well by dismissing me. Along with former U.S. Attorney General Ramsey Clark, a friend from my McGovern days, they would also help us with an emergency motion asking the U.S. District Court to order Hobgood to reinstate me. (It would be denied in short order because the federal courts are reluctant to intervene in ongoing state criminal prosecutions.) In support of these motions we cited the *Charlotte Observer*'s claim that the state had a statement from Beverly King consistent with the statement she had given me, and we asserted that the prosecutors had knowingly allowed her to testify falsely. We could play hardball, too.

Maureene showed up on Thursday night. She had been bitten on the heel by a neighbor's dog. The sight of a brunette beauty queen on crutches in the courthouse cafeteria on Friday caused a lot of long glances and hushed talk. Burley Mitchell walked by our table, and I asked him to join us. He acted as if nothing had happened. We talked about trivial things—farming, the weather in Alabama, children, the weather in Raleigh, Maureene's dog bite.

Maureene sensed immediately that Burley was the key to getting the case dropped. By this time he knew of Davis's affidavit. She told Burley I was highly ethical and had an excellent reputation in Alabama, told him how proud she was of the cases I had handled, and how this arrest would ruin my career, not to say what it was doing to our family. Tears trickled down her cheeks.

A big lump came into Burley's throat as he fought a surge of emotion. He left the table with a lot on his heart and mind.

I persuaded Maureene to go home for the weekend and leave the worrying to me. I passed the time discussing trial strategy with Paul and his group, my guts so torn up I couldn't concentrate on anything for long.

Joe and I thought and rethought the case. "I think if I can convince Burley to do the right thing, he'll drop the charges," I said. "But we need a way for him to save face."

I couldn't broach this idea with Morgan, Singer, or Ransdell. Lawyers don't want their clients talking with the prosecuting attorney. Joe also thought talking to Burley would be risky. "Mitchell's a politician," he said. "And he's tied tight to Hobgood."

Hobgood had already demonstrated his intransigency by refusing to reconsider my motion to be reinstated, saying I was "superfluous" to the defense—despite the fact that I was the only member of the team who had interviewed witnesses and was prepared for cross-examination.

While Joe and I brainstormed, Morgan was working behind the scenes. He had taken the transcript of Beverly King's testimony and Sheriff Davis's affidavit and paid a visit to an old friend, Claude Sitton. Claude, formerly the *New York Times*'s Atlanta Bureau chief during the height of the civil rights movement, was now editor of the highly respected *Raleigh News and Observer*.

On Sunday, August 3, the *News and Observer* ran an editorial titled "Murder Trial Takes a Bad Turn." It read in part:

> Judge Hamilton H. Hobgood's actions in summarily excluding one of Joan Little's defense attorneys from the case and then refusing to reconsider that step are regrettable. . . . The appearance of injustice is compounded by the grandstanding of Burley Mitchell, Jr., the Wake County district attorney. He raced in with a felony charge of subornation of perjury against Dees. . . . The nation and the world may be pardoned for believing that Dees is the hapless victim of hometown justice.

The editorial noted that ethics experts did not find anything wrong with interviews like the one I had with Beverly King after she left the witness stand.

I saw Burley Mitchell in the courthouse the next day and asked if we could talk. Once in his office, I asked him to drop the case. "I know it would be hard, Burley. But it's the right and honorable thing to do." I said that North Carolina had suffered unnecessarily from the bad publicity of the Little case. "This is a progressive state, but if you try me and some of the country's top lawyers come to my defense, you're gonna have even more bad publicity." I told him the editorial in the Raleigh paper showed the establishment in town didn't support my prosecution and that soon the *New York Times* and networks would follow. I added that if he lost the case, it might hurt his future political career.

Burley's eyes pleaded, "I agree. Help me out."

I did. I told him I'd agree to drop my federal suit seeking reinstatement (which I knew I couldn't win), that I'd withdraw as Joan Little's counsel of record (I knew Hobgood would never let me back in the courtroom), and that I'd leave the courthouse (if necessary I could work from across the street in my new, restricted capacity).

Burley called my lawyers the next day and told them he would dismiss the charges if I agreed to these concessions. Singer and Ransdell, unaware of my visit to Burley Mitchell, were delighted. A week of hell was finally over.

After preparing Jerry Paul for the remaining witnesses, I left for Montgomery. Of course I followed the case closely. Paul and Williamson did an excellent job examining the remaining witnesses. Paul's cross-examination of the state investigators concerning the destruction of evidence in the cell was particularly devastating. With Center funds, Jerry was also able to bring in a crime-scene reconstruction expert who corroborated Joan Little's version of the events.

Evidence I had previously secured also proved helpful. There were no crime scene photographs. We had learned that a local television station had heard the first police radio call about Alligood's stabbing and rushed to the jail. The TV camera crew had scanned the cell area as the body was being removed. I persuaded the station to provide me the outtakes and had an expert photographer make stills from the film. These color photographs showed Little's nightgown and robe tangled in her cell door. From this Jerry was able to tell the jury that the door must have been closed when Alligood approached the cell and that he pushed it open (these were not the clothes she had worn that night).

Little's two-day appearance on the witness stand was the highlight of the five-week trial. Speaking so softly jurors had to strain to hear her, Little said that Alligood had come to her cell three times in search of sex between 10 P.M. and the 3 A.M. stabbing. When he finally entered the cell, he dragged her to the floor, held the ice pick to her face, and forced her to engage in oral sex. "I didn't know what he was going to do, whether he was going to kill me," she said, her voice faltering.

Griffin's cross-examination was unrelenting. Forced to abandon its "no sex" theory, the state now insisted that Little had lured Alligood into the cell with the promise of sex.

"Why didn't you report Alligood's earlier advances?" Griffin asked.

"In Washington, North Carolina, coming up as a black woman, it's different saying what you did and having your word come up against a white person's," Little answered.

I heard later that Jerry's closing argument was weak, that he ranted and raved about all the world's problems and how the poor like Joan

Little were downtrodden. Observers described Karen Galloway's close as brilliant. The jury took less than ninety minutes to find Joan Little not guilty. "The burden of proof was on the state, and they didn't come close," explained one juror.

Immediately after the verdict, Judge Hobgood slapped Paul with a contempt citation for his conduct during the trial, sending him directly to jail. When the "Today Show" called and asked him and Joan Little to come to New York, he asked me to take his place. We were joined on the trip by Larry Little (no relation), an activist associated with a radical black group.

After arriving in Manhattan, Joan and Larry excused themselves, explaining they wanted to visit one of Joan's relatives in Harlem. I never saw either of them again.

When the "Today Show" limousine arrived the next morning, I went alone. Joan Little didn't show up at the studio. I did the interview solo, explaining I had no idea where "Miss Little" was.

I was still in the dark after I returned to Montgomery. Several days later an aide to Angela Davis, the radical black Berkeley professor, called and told me that Joan Little had joined the People's Liberation Movement and wanted nothing else to do with "the white lawyers who had been using her." Apparently Larry Little had been Ms. Davis's liaison. I reminded the aide that Karen Galloway was black and it had been an interracial legal team that had freed Joan Little. I was told the system itself should be tried for trying Little and that we lawyers were irrelevant.

I hung up the phone and laughed. In the same case, both the trial judge representing the state and an avowed enemy of the state had said I was irrelevant.

Joan Little stayed with the People's Liberation Movement only briefly. Apparently they quickly determined she was a money-hungry bourgeoise and kicked her out. Eventually she had to serve the balance of her sentence for the air conditioner burglary. She was on work release when another inmate asked her to cash a cashier's check or money order. Little cashed it and left town. She called me from somewhere in southern Georgia and wanted me to wire her two thousand dollars. I refused. When the authorities caught up with her, she said that she left because the North Carolina prison system had been so punitive. Paul and his team were unsuccessful in mounting this defense when it was learned that Joan Little really feared facing the black woman whose money she failed to deliver.

The last I heard, Joan had been arrested in 1989 at the New Jersey entrance of the Holland Tunnel on charges including possession of a weapon and stolen property. Jerry Paul did not defend her. He had been suspended from practicing law in North Carolina on two separate occasions unrelated to the Little trial.

It's not my role to judge Joan Little. I provide this epilogue only to make the point that Joan was no Martin Luther King, Jr. That certainly was not the reason I represented her. She was just a poor woman caught in the middle of the racist currents that flowed in the South, just a poor woman who needed a lawyer. Those who tried to make her into a hero did her and the cause a great disservice.

CHAPTER 13

July 28, 1983   **Rolling Hills Ranch**

The ringing telephone jarred me from a deep sleep. My eyes searched for the clock as my hand fumbled for the receiver. It was a few minutes shy of 4 A.M. My stomach tightened.

"This is the Montgomery Fire Department, Mr. Dees. The Law Center is on fire."

Our building on Hull Street, a former dentist's office, was an old frame and brick structure filled with wooden furniture. Tons of combustible pleadings, depositions, and other documents overflowed from cardboard boxes. I had always worried that the place might catch fire. We had recently put in fireproof filing cabinets to hold sensitive documents and installed a fire detection system. We had even hired a guard to watch the Center at night. Obviously, our precautions weren't enough.

Pulling on a pair of jeans, I tried to imagine what had happened. Could the guard have started the blaze with a carelessly placed cigarette? Could a faulty wire have triggered an electrical fire? I stuck a gun into my hip pocket, stepped into the cool night air, and ran for my car. It was twenty-five miles to town. I was doing a hundred miles per hour on the blacktop farm road before reaching the main highway, my mind racing even faster.

Could someone have set the fire on purpose?

Since the Little case, particularly since the creation of Klanwatch, the Center and I had made a lot of enemies. Earlier in the year, an old nemesis had renewed my acquaintance. A letter had arrived at the Center from the former Grand Dragon of the Ku Klux Klan.

January 21, 1983

Mr. Dees:

It has been brought to my attention that you are still travelling the country practicing perfidy. . . . I personally feel this behavior should no longer be allowed to go unchecked. . . . I therefore challenge you to a dual [*sic*] to the death. You against me. No federal judges, no federal marshals, no F.B.I. agents, not anyone except yourself and I.

We go to the woods (your state or mine) and settle once and for all the enmity that exists between us. Two go in—one comes out.

For a White America,
Louis R. Beam, Jr.

As ridiculous (yet tempting!) as the challenge was, I could not dismiss it. Beam had written on Aryan Nations stationery from the Hayden Lakes, Idaho, compound of the violent neo-Nazi Richard Butler. When our lawsuit on behalf of the Vietnamese fishermen had destroyed Beam's Texas Emergency Reserve, he had headed north. For months he had written articles in the Aryan Nations newsletter viciously attacking me as a race traitor.

Some of the Klansmen-defendants in Klanwatch's civil suit arising from the violence-marred march in Decatur would also have liked to see me and the Center out of the picture. We were scoring some telling blows that might lead to a victory in our case, as well as criminal indictments. Only hours before the fire, I had returned from Birmingham with Klanwatch's Randall Williams and Bill Stanton after meeting with the Justice Department's Dan Rinzell, one of his aides, and an FBI agent. We had shown them evidence gathered over the past three years in the Decatur case. The FBI had conducted its own investigation for six months immediately after the Klan attack in 1979 and concluded no Klan conspiracy existed.

We had taken depositions and signed statements from Klansmen whom we had convinced to turn on their former friends, dozens of incriminating photographs identifying participants, tape recordings of admissions of guilt, and the name of a Decatur police officer who we believed was too friendly with a Klan buddy. We felt we showed them enough proof to warrant criminal indictments. They promised to get back in touch.

Yes, this was arson.

Speeding through the early morning light to the fire in Montgom-

ery, I weighed motives, personality, style, and opportunity. Halfway
to town, I hit the brakes, pulled into Merle's Truck Stop, and called
Mac Sim Butler, the sheriff of Montgomery County.

I woke him up.

"Mac, you know the Center's on fire," I said.

"I didn't know," he said sleepily. "I'm sure we've got some people
over there."

"I think I know who burned it, Mac."

"Who, Morris?"

"Joe Garner and that Tommy Downs who lives with him in Snowdoun."

"I see." I couldn't tell if he believed me or was humoring me.

"Listen, Mac, I'm on my way to town. Why don't you send a deputy
out to Garner's to see if his car engine's still warm."

If Garner and Downs were questioned later and said they had been
home all night, they'd have some explaining to do if the engine was
warm.

Mac said, "Will do," and I sped on to Montgomery.

Joe Garner. It was just a hunch. Earlier in the week I'd received a
phone call from Bobby Taylor, a friend in Snowdoun, a farming
community ten miles south of the city limits. Taylor, who ran an auto
repair shop across the street from Garner's crossroads store, had overheard Garner call me a "son of a bitch" and complain that I was "after
him."

I had taken Garner's deposition six weeks earlier as part of the
pretrial investigation in the Decatur case which had been expanded
to claim an ongoing statewide Klan conspiracy to harm blacks. Klanwatch received a complaint that Garner and twenty-year-old Tommy
Downs were harassing a white Snowdoun youth who had befriended
a black girl by giving her rides to school. Someone had seen Tommy
Downs put sugar in the youth's gas tank and slash his tires.

Our investigators had learned that Garner was deeply involved in
a major Klan group, serving as a member of its national Imperial
Board, and had posted bond for a Klansman arrested in New Orleans
on a gunrunning charge. The childish prank of cutting car tires
seemed trivial, but knowing more about a secretive Klan leader living
so close to our base was worth a deposition.

Garner, a short, balding man in his late thirties, had run for sheriff
against Butler in 1982, telling the press that if elected he could be a
liaison between blacks and whites. Confronted by a reporter with a

photograph showing him speaking at a 1980 Klan rally, Garner denied being a Klan member, claiming instead to be a moderating voice trying to cool racist tempers. The picture later appeared in the *Montgomery Advertiser* with a photo credit to Klanwatch. We had given that photograph to the media along with a special report on Garner. After his defeat, Garner had called the Center and asked what we had against him.

At his deposition, I had peppered Garner with questions about Louis Beam and Don Black, the leader of his Klan faction whom he had probably met at national meetings. He denied knowing them. He also refused to acknowledge any connection to the harassment of the white youth in Snowdoun. He seemed concerned that I knew about Tommy Downs. He had taken Tommy and his nineteen-year-old brother, Bodie, products of a troubled home, under his wing, allowing them to live in the back room behind his store. My questions about other friends who hung around the Snowdoun Volunteer Fire Department—Garner was chief—also troubled him. We suspected some were Klansmen, too.

Our Klanwatch file also referred to Garner's lack of mental stability, a note that this man, who asserted he was a peacemaker between blacks and whites, was subject to violent outbursts. Before taking his deposition, I had warned Bill and Randall, both eager to add information to our data base, that it would be risky questioning Garner, that he might harm us in some way. The closer I got to the Center, the more certain I was that tonight he had done just that.

The Center had been cordoned off by the time I got there. Only police and fire investigators were allowed inside. Three fire trucks and two squad cars blocked the street, firemen and officers scurrying over hoses.

The fire was no longer burning, but smoke hung low and thick over Hull Street. Approaching the building I realized, much to my relief, it was still a building. Other Center staffers huddled together silently, looking shell-shocked, small and helpless against the backdrop of the Center. I imagined I looked the same. I straightened up.

I tried to talk my way inside, but the police were adamant. No one was allowed in. I went off by myself, sat down on a curb, and rested my face on my knees. I felt sick.

An investigator found me a few minutes later. He stated the obvious: arson. A petroleumlike accelerant appeared to have been poured throughout the building and then ignited.

The arsonists had been amateurs. The fire had consumed the air in the building quickly, and then, starved for oxygen, burned itself out just about the time the fire department (alerted by the detection system) arrived. If the arsonists had knocked out or opened a few windows, the building would probably have burned to the ground. "We found these," the investigator said, showing me a cloth glove and a piece of glass pane from the back of the building where the arsonists had apparently entered. The pane was covered with duct tape. The investigator said I could go inside.

The office was a mini-Pompeii. Soot swirled around my eyes and into my throat. A telltale trail where the fire had eaten the accelerant was charred into the blackened carpet. Computers had melted. Plastic ceiling grates that once covered fluorescent lights hung twisted to the floor. The aluminum handles of filing cabinets were warped from heat. Half the law books were burned beyond use.

Bill, Randall, and I moved through the smoke to the Klanwatch area. We feared the worst. On the drive home from Birmingham, we had joked about not giving the FBI copies of our files, playing their game of one-way-street. It had been after 9 P.M.—seven hours before I received the phone call—when we placed the leather briefcase stuffed with our evidence next to Randall's desk. We were too tired to sort out the statements and photographs and place them in their respective folders in the new fireproof files.

A big desk sign Randall's wife had given him, *Klanwatch,* announced to all where our investigative team was located. If the arsonists were trying to burn this area, they scored a direct hit. Files had been pulled out and sprayed with gasoline, a few burned beyond recognition. The heat in Randall's office had been so intense that his venetian blinds had melted. The ceiling had collapsed onto the floor.

For a frightening moment we could not see the briefcase. Had it burned? No, there it was! The leather was charred, but the contents were undamaged. A fireman told us that tightly packed paper won't burn easily. We congratulated ourselves for taking so many documents to Birmingham, then carefully opened the fireproof file drawers that contained thousands of Klan photographs, reels of videotapes of white supremacy activity, and a computer backup disk containing thousands of Klan and neo-Nazi members' names and addresses gathered by our staff over the last three years. The hot metal drawers burned our fingers, but the contents were safe.

Dual emotions tugged at me. I was glad that things weren't worse, that nothing irreplaceable had been destroyed. At the same time, I was angry—as angry as I have ever been. Thirteen years of hard work had almost been destroyed. I walked from one end of the seven-thousand-square-foot building to the other, going into each office and sharing my regrets with the occupants, who were sorting out personal items, trying to piece together singed work in progress, and determining whether they could continue with a specific case or business task without obtaining duplicate material from outside sources. The smell of gas fumes and burned plastic penetrated everything. Everybody retreated into his own world, talking very little. Shock set in.

I wished my friend Joe Levin were there. Our staff was close, but none so close to me as Joe. He now lived in Washington, D.C. Not too long after the Joan Little case, with the 1976 presidential campaign beginning to heat up, most of the leading Democratic candidates had sought my help in raising funds. My choice was Senator Ted Kennedy. I visited him and urged him to run. After he refused, I agreed to become Jimmy Carter's finance director. Joe doubled up for me at the Center while I spent six months based in Atlanta.

After Carter won the primary, I returned to Montgomery because the new campaign finance law provided federal funds for the general election. Joe then joined the campaign in the issues department. When Carter was elected, he named Joe as chief counsel to the National Highway Traffic and Safety Administration.

Joe had left the Carter administration in 1979 to become a partner in Chuck Morgan's Washington law firm. He was happy in the big city. I missed his wise counsel and funny stories. We met at Center board meetings, which he chaired, but our busy schedules otherwise kept us apart.

President Carter had offered to find a place for me in the White House or some government agency. He appointed Maureene to the National Endowment for the Arts board, but I had no interest in going to Washington. I had become good friends with Hamilton Jordan, the president's new chief of staff, and Jack Watson, another trusted White House aide. My entire primary campaign finance staff found key positions in the administration. All made sure I received invitations to White House functions, such as the signing of the Camp David Accords by Israel's Menachem Begin and Egypt's Anwar Sadat.

My principal interest was to convince President Carter to set up a national commission to study the death penalty. Death rows were filling up. Governors would soon be faced with signing death warrants. Something had to be done to slow the process.

After he secured the nomination, Carter told me at breakfast in his Plains, Georgia, home that he was in favor of the death penalty only when a law enforcement officer was murdered. Since the Tarboro and Little cases, I was hardening my views against capital punishment, but this one exception would account for few of the nearly one thousand occupants on death rows. John Carroll, who had worked so effectively on the Little case, had taken Joe's place as the Center's legal director. He helped me draft a memorandum to the president proposing the commission.

Ham Jordan arranged for the president and me to have lunch alone in the Rose Garden. Over cucumber soup, tuna fish sandwiches, and Coke, I explained that few civilized countries had a death penalty and that some nations considered less democratic than the U.S. had long ago abolished state-sanctioned murder. I said that it would not be long before the world would watch in horror as our states executed one person a day, maybe three or four, without reducing the growing death row population.

This was grim talk in such a beautiful setting, but I had the attention of someone who could form a blue-ribbon panel to examine the merits of execution. I explained that minorities, mainly blacks, bore the brunt of this penalty, and that states were not willing to provide adequate counsel to poor defendants. I closed by sharing Clarence Darrow's view that intelligent people should study those who commit horrible crimes, not execute them, in hopes of finding scientific ways of predicting violent criminal behavior in others. The president thanked me for my views, took the envelope containing my proposal, and promised to give me an answer.

About a month later, Stuart Eizenstat, the president's domestic affairs adviser, called and said that the president had rejected my proposal because he felt capital punishment was an issue for the states, not the federal government. Stuart also said Carter favored the death penalty for all the offenses covered by the Georgia law he had signed as governor. This law covered far more than the death of police officers. I reminded Stuart there were national commissions studying all kinds of things best left to the states and wondered aloud if fear of conservatives in the 1980 reelection campaign might have played a part in the decision. He assured me it had not.

Back at the Center, John Carroll assembled a trial team to develop a strategy for training lawyers trying capital cases. He brought in Dennis Balske, a criminal lawyer teaching at Ohio State University Law School. We jointly handled over fifty death penalty cases over the next seven years, among them several highly publicized proceedings in which we kept inmates from death or secured their freedom. John's work on behalf of Johnny Ross, a sixteen-year-old black sentenced to Louisiana's electric chair for the rape of a white woman, won the young man a new trial and ultimate freedom based on scientific evidence proving his innocence. Alabama prisoner Johnny Harris, sentenced to death for killing a prison guard, received a reduced sentence due to our efforts. So, too, did South Carolinian Clemmie Moultrie, who faced the gas chamber for killing a deputy sheriff who forcibly evicted him from his home. It took twelve years, but the Center's defense of Marine Sgt. Roy Patterson, who shot two Georgia lawmen in self-defense, finally resulted in his removal from death row and release from prison. John, Dennis, and I published four trial manuals using the experience from these and other cases, and distributed them to lawyers appointed to defend indigent capital defendants.

Other Center lawyers were winning precedent-setting cases, gaining new rights for powerless citizens. Steve Ellmann (now a law professor at Columbia) litigated a highly publicized case involving inhuman conditions in Alabama mental institutions. Harvard-educated Ira Burnim broke new ground in obtaining financial benefits for cotton mill workers suffering brown lung infection caused by excess cotton dust. He also conducted a one-person crusade against police shooting of suspected felons.

We had never had a more qualified litigation team; everybody worked well together. Our fund-raising had gone so well that, with nearly five million dollars set aside, we stopped sending out appeals in 1978. I was sure we could operate the Center on the five hundred thousand dollars yearly interest from the endowment fund.*

With four good lawyers in charge of the caseload, I was feeling restless for a new challenge. Senator Kennedy provided it. In mid-1979, Paul Kirk, a Washington lawyer and former Kennedy Senate aide, asked if I would be Kennedy's finance director. He said that Kennedy had finally decided to challenge Jimmy Carter. Paul remembered my 1976 visit encouraging the senator to run, and knew that Kennedy and I shared similar views on such key issues as the death penalty and abortion rights.

I told Paul I was supporting Carter. I had not planned to take the same active role in the campaign, but had promised to advise. Still,

---

*After we stopped fund-raising in 1978, inflation hit over 12 percent in 1979 and 1980. With rising prices and wages, our endowment fell far short of providing adequate funds for operations and to ensure future growth. It therefore became necessary to resume fund-raising.

I didn't want to rule out working for Kennedy. Carter's rebuff on my death penalty proposal had disturbed me. I also felt that because I had raised one million dollars for his impoverished campaign just before the critical Florida primary, the president could have at least honored my modest request for a blue-ribbon commission.* I asked Paul to wait, wanting to see what the president would say about another key issue before making a final decision.

I flew to Washington that night. Although the president's schedule was busy the next morning, he squeezed me in prior to his weekly cabinet meeting. I got straight to the point. What was his position going to be on the right of indigent pregnant women to receive Medicaid funds for abortion? Congress had passed the Hyde amendment prohibiting such payments, and, in an effort to keep both the pro-life and pro-choice groups on his side, Carter had not spoken out clearly on the issue. Without disrupting his smile, he told me he was against using federal funds to pay for abortions.

He invited me into the cabinet meeting. I paid little attention to the proceedings. The president had told me in 1976 that he personally did not favor abortion, but felt it was a woman's choice. In the Iowa caucus he had begun to waffle, but had managed to keep his pro-choice supporters satisfied. Now he was making a clear political decision. I felt betrayed. I also felt like a traitor sitting in the midst of his inner circle knowing now that I was going to accept Kirk's offer to raise money for Kennedy. I excused myself and gave Ham Jordan the news.

John Carroll agreed to pick up my Center caseload. Born in downtown Washington, D.C., John said he had rarely seen a blade of grass before joining the marines and coming South. His easygoing ways had won over the doctor in Joan Little's case and endeared him to the Center staff. A confidant and close friend, he had counseled me through a bitter divorce with Maureene and now thought a change of scenery would do me good. He assured me that I'd one day find a compatible woman.

On October 26, 1979, I went to Washington for the announcement of the formation of a committee to explore a Kennedy run for the presidency. The formal announcement of his candidacy would be November 7 in Boston. My job was to raise five million dollars in two months. This seemed possible, as Kennedy was leading Carter by some fifteen points in the polls.

---

*Carter ended up beating George Wallace in Florida, and with the momentum from that victory, went on to win the nomination.

With the Iowa caucus and New Hampshire primary only a few months away, I quickly planned a series of fund-raising dinners in ten key cities, each budgeted to raise five hundred thousand dollars. Carter wasn't popular with the party regulars, and they smelled blood. Front-page stories announced my defection from Carter to Kennedy, and before we had the campaign phones connected, offers of help were pouring in at the Senate office. Steve Smith, Kennedy's brother-in-law and campaign manager, gave me his list of Kennedy faithful dating back to JFK's days in the White House. Nothing, it seemed, could derail this new train to Camelot.

On November 3, just eight days after the campaign committee had been formed, the Ayatollah Khomeini's forces captured the United States embassy in Tehran and imprisoned sixty-three American hostages. President Carter adopted his Rose Garden strategy, wrapping himself in the American flag and suspending his campaign so that he could secure the hostages' release, a brief hero in a national crisis. His popularity rose; suddenly Kennedy trailed by fifteen points. My ten fund-raising dinners were scaled back to five as ticket sellers refused to return calls.

I wrote a fund-raising letter for the senator with the help of my McGovern collaborator Tom Collins. We mailed one million pieces to carefully selected lists of progressives and liberals, such as ACLU members: prime Kennedy territory. For every one contribution, we received eight negative letters with no money. There were a few tasteless diatribes from kooks—*A Blond in Every Pond* bumper stickers—but most were well-reasoned letters from people who sincerely respected Kennedy. The message was the same: We agree with your views, we think you do a great job in the Senate. We simply do not trust you to be president.

Ted Kennedy always kept his word to me. Chappaquiddick robbed our nation of a great leader. We are so human and erring in our personal lives, yet so pious and unforgiving when it comes to our public figures.

We settled the election by choosing a second-rate movie actor who couldn't remember the names of cabinet members and whose administration was so corrupt I've lost count of those who were convicted or had to resign. As his main legacy to the legal profession, Ronald Reagan gutted the Legal Services program and appointed scores of poorly qualified judges insensitive to human rights. The results of the 1980 campaign were so discouraging, I knew it was time to come back to Montgomery and the Center.

*   *   *

As the smoke cleared in the building, I could see a rising bitterness in the faces of some of my colleagues. I felt it wasn't directed so much at the perpetrators as at me. While Carroll had stood squarely alongside me in setting up Klanwatch, other Center lawyers had been opposed to the effort. They argued that the Klan was nothing more than a symptom of a sick social order. What we needed to focus on, they contended, were the conditions that had always fueled the Klan—poverty and ignorance. In many ways I agreed with this assessment. But I found it hard to turn my back on the real-life victims of Klan intimidation.

I could not content myself with the idea that, in the long run, the Center's traditional civil rights work would help eliminate these conditions. Part of the reason for the Klan's rise in the late 1970s and early 1980s was bound up with some of the gains of the civil rights movement. In a climate of economic stagnation, certain segments of the white community attributed their financial troubles to government handouts to "welfare mothers" and affirmative action plans—programs that were well publicized but actually few and far between. The Klan had capitalized on this resentment to build its ranks. If we were going to continue marching toward full equality, we needed to protect ourselves against a backlash from groups like the Klan along the way. In developing the Klanwatch project, I was not turning my back on traditional civil rights cases. (Such cases still make up most of the Center's docket.) I just was not willing to sit back while our side suffered casualties.

The fire scared the hell out of some staffers, putting them in the shoes of those we represented—and they didn't like it. They had come to work for the Center with the best of motives; they could certainly have earned more money in private practice. No one had told them it might be this dangerous. July 28, 1983, marked the end of their age of innocence.

I tried to ignore the cool stares coming through the heat. My mind raced in a hundred directions. Reporters somehow reached me, asking what was going to happen. I told them that nothing significant had been destroyed and we weren't backing down. Then I asked Jo-Ann Chancellor, our invaluable administrator, to call a professional photographer so we could take pictures of the destruction right away.

I picked up the charred clock that the Vietnamese fishermen had given us two years earlier and set it on a soot-covered desk. It made

me think of Louis Beam. I wondered if he might have joined Garner
in the arson.

I'm sure the same fear that had gripped me ninety minutes earlier
gripped Roger Craver when I phoned him at his McLean, Virginia,
home. Roger and I had met during the McGovern campaign. A
masterful fund-raiser with a keen sense of social justice, he had built
the citizens lobbying group Common Cause from scratch, attracting
150,000 members in just eighteen months. We communicated regularly.

I was fighting back tears. "Roger," I said, "I need your help. I'm
too emotional to do anything right now. Will you write a letter to our
supporters and tell them what happened? We'll include a picture of
the fire. I want you to tell them we aren't going to quit. We're not
going to back down."

I told Roger that we did not want to ask for money. Our nearly one
hundred thousand donors knew the risk we were taking, and they felt
a part of our victories. I wanted to let them see the damage and feel
our pain, thank them for standing with us, and assure them we would
not back down. We would need funds for a safer building, but there
would be time for that later.

Roger assured me he'd have a letter out before the week was over,
then said, "You sound terrible. Go home and get some sleep, Morris."

"Soon as I catch the son of a bitch who did this," I said.

Every morning when I get to the office, I pull out a yellow legal pad
and write a things-to-do list. The day after the fire, I didn't have an
office. Still, I found a legal pad and wrote *Get Joe Garner* at the top of
the list. I then asked Bill Stanton to canvas the neighborhood to
determine if anyone had seen anything unusual in the days and hours
before the fire. When he finished that assignment, Bill would drive
to Snowdoun and see if my friend Bobby Taylor had observed anything suspicious around Garner's store before or after the fire.

Preparing for Garner's deposition in June, I asked Taylor about his
neighbor. Taylor told me how devoted Tommy Downs was to Garner. I figured if Garner was behind the fire, Tommy had probably
done the dirty work. Taylor told Bill Stanton that when he heard
about the fire, he thought of Garner, but he had not seen anything
unusual. Bill also talked to another Garner neighbor who remem-

bered he had seen one of the Downs boys building a wooden cross shortly before a cross-burning on the lawn of a black Montgomery County commissioner.

While Bill was in Snowdoun, I sat in a coffee shop on Montgomery's Southern Bypass, talking to an old friend, sharing a plan that had begun cooking before the fire trucks had pulled away from the Center. James Killough was tall and wiry with long, dark, slicked-back hair. We had been running buddies in high school. His reputation as a tough guy was well deserved. He'd hit you first and ask questions later. He had a long arrest record for assaults and had done time in prison. Some of these assaults had been racially motivated. In the 1960s James had moved in a circle that included members of Bobby Shelton's United Klans of America, but he had never joined the organization himself.

We had gone our separate ways, but in early 1983 he came to me when his wife had legal problems. He said he was no longer sympathetic to the Klan and was trying to make ends meet as a carpenter. I believed him and helped the couple out. Afterward James and I would occasionally meet to shoot pool. I liked and trusted him.

I had called James right after talking to Craver. Convinced that I wouldn't get much help from the local police or fire officials in nailing Garner right away—I had no evidence of Garner's involvement, only my intuition—I had decided to conduct my own investigation.

"I need your help, James," I said over eggs and grits.

I told him about the fire, how I suspected Garner and Tommy Downs. The Center was offering a twenty-five-thousand-dollar reward. If he carried out my plan, he stood a good chance of earning that. His big brown eyes lit up.

The Downs brothers liked to play poker behind Garner's store. Perhaps James, with the three-hundred-dollar stake I would give him, could join the game, earn their confidence, and get the goods on Tommy. James said he was certain he could and that he might even bring a woman along to seduce Tommy, encouraging him to talk.

The week after the fire was a busy one:

Jo-Ann Chancellor found us temporary quarters in a former clothing store on a busy commercial strip, and we quickly moved in.

Our insurance representative put the damage of the fire at over $140,000.

The *New York Times* ran a front-page story about the fire and the Center's work.

Craver's letter went out to our supporters, and we were immediately flooded with unsolicited checks to rebuild.

On the investigative front, the federal government sent in Bureau of Alcohol, Tobacco, and Firearms (ATF) agents to conduct an investigation. (ATF, not the FBI, has jurisdiction over explosions.) Uninterested in my hypothesis about Garner, these agents focused on physical evidence. They thought they might find fingerprints on the duct tape the arsonists had affixed to the glass pane to reduce noise when they had broken in. The glove found in the building would also be examined.

We talked to the guard who had been on duty when the fire started. He admitted he had left the premises to work another job that night.

Bobby Taylor called and told me Tommy Downs had been in his shop. Tommy had unwittingly left a garden pump sprayer that smelled of gasoline. I asked Taylor to hide the sprayer so that we could compare its contents to the fire accelerant. (He refused, but did pour out some of the liquid; we handed it over to the ATF agents, but its value as evidence was diminished once it left the sprayer linking it to Downs.)

Stanton linked Tommy Downs to the Klan. Taylor had given Bill the name of Downs's former landlord, who also happened to be a friend of mine. When Downs had moved, he had left some belongings behind, including a certificate of Klan membership that the landlord now gave Bill. Tommy had signed his name on the document.

With this good news came the bad news from Killough that he was unable to round up a poker game with the Downs brothers. Undeterred that plan A hadn't worked, I asked James to meet me at The Limit, a roadside bar on the highway to my farm. There I unveiled plan B.

"You really want these guys, don't you?" said James when I was finished.

"No." I smiled. "I just want to make you rich with the reward money."

Two days later work began on a new shed on Bobby Taylor's property. The carpenter in charge of building this modest structure was James Killough. His two assistants, employed by Taylor at our suggestion, were Tommy and Bodie Downs. Unbeknownst to the Downs brothers and Joe Garner, who watched the work from his store across the street, the lumber and the labor were being provided free to Taylor, courtesy of the Southern Poverty Law Center.

Not long after the men started work, a big Cadillac drove by. "Did you see that?" James asked Tommy Downs.

"See what?" asked Tommy, a pimply-faced, moustached blond of medium build.

"A big nigger driving that Seville and a white woman next to him. What sorry sons of bitches," James said.

The Downs brothers agreed that the mixing of races, even if only in the front seat of a Cadillac, was indeed disgusting. The three men appeared to have something in common—hatred of "niggers" and "nigger lovers."

As the discussion heated, James put down his hammer and said, "It ain't nothin' but that damn Morris Dees. That's the son of a bitch who's causing our trouble."

After work James continued the discussion with Tommy over several beers at the Silver Dollar, a working-class bar on Montgomery's south side. Suddenly Tommy said, "You know we took care of that Dees fellow."

"What do you mean?" asked James.

"This guy I work for, Joe Garner, we went down there and burned that office."

James had done his work well to this point. My instructions on what to do next had been clear: "If Tommy talks, don't jeopardize the operation. Call me and we'll get you wired up. We'll have a van nearby. We'll do it by the book."

I had kept Glen Kibler, the sharp ATF agent in charge of the investigation, up to date on my use of James. Glen believed my Garner theory and helped me run down a number of leads. He told me it would take an act of Congress and a pair of scissors that could cut through tons of red tape to get federal approval for a body mike. He suggested I talk to Jimmy Evans, the local district attorney. Jimmy, an old school pal, had been skeptical about James's credibility, but out of friendship had agreed to equip James at the appropriate time.

James and Tommy moved down the street to Shoney's, a quieter place where you could conduct a serious telephone conversation. It was almost midnight when James called me.

"I got somebody who wants to talk to you, Bubba," he said.

"Who's that?" I asked.

"Tommy Downs. He confessed everything. He wants to tell you all about it."

Damn, I thought. This isn't the plan. We should be talking to Kibler and Evans and getting James fitted with a body mike.

"James, I don't think—"

"He'll tell you everything, Bubba. You got to slap him to shut him up he wants to talk so much."

"Put him on the phone," I said. Part of me was reluctant, the other part excited.

James went to get Tommy. It was a long time before he returned. "He decided he doesn't want to talk to you right this minute," he said.

Goddammit, I thought. Now Downs knows we're on to him. "James," I said, "take him to your house. Don't whip anybody. Don't kidnap anybody. Don't get me in trouble. But see if he'll go to your house."

"Okay."

I grabbed my tape recorder and drove ninety miles an hour down U.S. 231 to the south side neighborhood where James rented a house. James stood alone in the yard, smoking a cigarette.

"Where's Tommy?" I asked.

"He said he wanted to talk to his brother, and he'll talk about this tomorrow."

I shook my head. "James, you lost him. He knows you know me. It's over with. Let's go to his house right now."

"He asked me to drop him at his mother's," James said.

We climbed into our cars. I followed James to a small farmhouse in Snowdoun that sat a few hundred yards back from the road in the middle of a big field. James drove up the dirt trail to the house while I moved my car out of sight. I took a pair of binoculars out of the glove compartment.

James was back in a few minutes. "His mother says he ain't there, but I know he is. I saw his brother's old car back there." James told me Tommy depended on Bodie for transportation.

Together, we waited to see what Tommy would do next. About twenty minutes later—it was almost 2 A.M. by now—Tommy and Bodie came out of the house and drove off. James and I followed them in separate cars.

They went straight to the back of Garner's store. James and I parked down the road, so we couldn't be seen. We tried to figure out our next move, a onetime Klan sympathizer and a civil rights lawyer with a pair of binoculars on a stakeout. My pistol was on the seat. Hollywood couldn't have thought up anything more preposterous.

James thought we should call the police. "Tommy's no hero," he said. "A cop could get him to talk."

"If he did confess, it probably wouldn't be legal," I said. I thought for a moment. "You get out and watch the place. I'm gonna make a phone call."

I drove down the road, found a pay phone, and woke up Jimmy Evans. "You've got to subpoena these Downs brothers before the grand jury this morning," I pleaded. (Since Bodie was so close to Tommy and Garner, I felt he might know something about the fire.) I told Evans about our discovery and where the suspects were holed up. James's word wouldn't be enough to persuade the grand jury to indict them. The jurors would view him as an ex-con trying to get a twenty-five-thousand-dollar reward. If they knew him as I did, they would have realized he was telling the truth.

The sleepy district attorney said he would authorize a subpoena.

I rejoined James and waited . . . and waited. An hour passed. An hour and a half. I went back to the pay phone and called the assistant DA whom Evans had said would draw up the subpoena. "Where are you guys?" I asked. "I don't want Downs to skip town."

The assistant DA reminded me that a nighttime subpoena required the signature of the grand jury foreman. A staff person had gone to the foreman's house to wake him. James and I kept watch for the next hour. The Downs brothers were definitely in their room. It had no toilet. We saw each of them come out and pee off the porch.

The DA's man and a deputy arrived with the sun. James and I remained out of sight as they went to the back of the store and knocked. Nothing happened. They knocked again. Again, no answer.

The deputy finally returned to his car. He made a call on his radio. Soon there were a half dozen patrol cars and a state trooper as well. The deputy knocked on the door, and again, there was no answer.

"Shit," James said. "Why don't they just bust the fucking door in?"

I was so frustrated I almost agreed with him.

After pounding on the door for about ten minutes, the mini-battalion got into their cars and left. I was calculating how long Tommy and Bodie could hold their water before they had to come back out on the porch again when a squad car returned. This time when the officer knocked, the door opened. Bodie Downs stood on the porch in his undershirt and boxer shorts scratching his head. The officer served him with the subpoena, leaving one for Tommy as well.

James and I were getting ready to leave when Joe Garner drove by in his Cadillac, smoking a big cigar. He made several passes before driving off. Obviously, somebody had alerted him that the police had been there.

A few minutes later, Sherry Rhodes, a close friend of Garner, drove up in her yellow Pinto. She knocked on the Downses' door. The brothers came out, looked around, and drove off with her.

Later that morning Evans told me the Downs brothers had appeared before the grand jury, testifying they knew nothing about the fire. Tommy had also denied saying anything to Killough. I thanked Jimmy, then immediately subpoenaed Tommy and Bodie Downs and Joe Garner to give depositions as part of the Decatur investigation.

Kibler and Evans put Killough on the polygraph and determined he was telling the truth about Tommy Downs's confession. Two Justice Department attorneys had come to town and offered their help with the investigation. As the next federal grand jury was not scheduled to convene for sixty days, I asked them to persuade the local U.S. attorney, John Bell, to convene a special federal grand jury. We had a long list of suspected Klansmen from the Snowdoun area and information on the cross burning at the black Montgomery County commissioner's house. With all this, we felt Tommy Downs would crack.

At a meeting with the Justice Department lawyers, Bell, Kibler, and several FBI agents, I made my pitch for a special grand jury. Kibler called back later that day and said he had heard there would be no such grand jury; it was too expensive to call one. I phoned Bell and offered to pay all costs. Bell correctly said that would be improper. Still, I felt that if the offices of a mainstream law firm involved in federal cases had been burned and evidence pointed to a culprit, a special grand jury would have been called. Now we would have to wait two months.

I was still fuming about Bell's intransigence when Randall Williams came in and told me he had received a phone call from a *Montgomery Advertiser* reporter. The paper was about to run a story that the city fire marshall considered me a suspect in the arson and was going to ask me to take a polygraph. The marshall suggested I might have set the fire for insurance money or publicity.

I hit the ceiling. A story like this would cause people to think the worst, regardless of the polygraph test. I was furious that I was being considered a common criminal by this man who had done absolutely nothing to find the arsonist. After the fire trucks left, no investigator from the fire department or the city police ever returned to the Center to ask any of us questions. I never told any city law enforcement agent what we had learned about Garner because we found out he had friends in the police department.*

Williams called Kibler and the FBI. They apparently believed Killough's story and promised to contact the *Advertiser*'s city editor and inform him I was not a suspect. Randall told me the story would not run in the paper. No one ever asked me to take a polygraph test.

Meanwhile, the official investigation had bogged down. The fingerprints found on the sticky side of the duct tape removed from the pane of glass were unreadable. The test on the liquid from Downs's spray bottle had been inconclusive. No one had ever checked Garner's engine as I had requested.

Unless we got an unexpected break, the depositions were my last hope. Along with Garner and the Downs brothers, I had subpoenaed Charles "Dink" Bailey, a twenty-year-old friend of Tommy Downs who I learned occasionally spent nights behind Garner's store with the Downs brothers.

Garner and the Downses were remarkably cool, insisting they knew nothing about the fire. Tommy denied being in the Klan and said that he had been at a girlfriend's apartment most of the night Killough and I had observed him. Since we had the Klan certificate with his signature, I thought he should be subject to perjury charges for denying his affiliation. But when I approached the government investigators, they said the signature on the certificate could not be verified. I hired a handwriting expert from the Alabama Department of Toxicology who provided such verification, but he was ignored.

Bailey, a scrawny six-footer with a patch of fuzzy blond hair on his chin, was clearly the most nervous. He, too, denied any involvement, but when I looked him in the eye, I could tell he was lying. A vein in his neck started pulsing the minute he sat down and was throbbing so fast that for a while I thought he might have a stroke.

I asked the court reporter to leave the room. I knelt by Bailey's chair, put my hand on his shoulder, and tried to calm him, explaining I had a son his age and understood how easy it was to follow someone and get in trouble. I told him to trust me. If he knew anything about the fire, I would see that he was protected, if he would just be honest.

---

*I was not on good terms at the time with the Montgomery police. I had recently posted a five-hundred-thousand-dollar property bond for several blacks arrested for shooting and wounding two policemen. From what I could tell, the blacks had been defending themselves when the police mistakenly raided a gathering after a funeral. The Center had also accused the city of police brutality in other cases.

The words formed in his throat. I coaxed. He relaxed. I felt I had him, but he could not bring himself to talk.

Maybe we could get him or one of the Downs boys to turn in the future, but for now we had reached a dead end. I had never felt more frustrated or helpless. There was little to do except check in with my private sources and agent Kibler—and write *GET JOE GARNER* at the top of my yellow legal pad every morning.

In October 1983, the *White Patriot,* the news monthly of the Alabama-based Knights of the Ku Klux Klan, published an editorial titled "An Act of God?" The piece suggested that the fire was "Divine judgement" because the Center had "a history of legal harassment against the Ku Klux Klan and has been unrelenting in its campaign of terror against White Christian America." The editorial concluded: "It is now obvious that with their building destroyed by fire their activities have received a major setback."

Falser words have never been written. It would take over a year to finally bring those who burned the Center to justice. In that time, however, we would hardly rest on our charred laurels. By the end of 1984, Bobby Shelton's United Klans of America and Glenn Miller's Carolina Knights of the Ku Klux Klan—the established old guard and the rising new guard—would be subjects of our "unrelenting" campaigns.

We raised the stakes now, trying to put out of business these violent hatemongers, some of whom were advocating the overthrow of the United States government. As we played the game harder, so did our opponents. Character assassination was no longer enough. Assassination—as in murder—seemed the only solution for people like Denver talk-radio host Alan Berg and Morris Dees.

T. J. Hendricks, our black neighbor from Mount Meigs who took me hunting when I was a boy and remained a close friend, once said, "Lawyer Dees survives because God has his arms wrapped around him."

I'm not so sure I believe in the Divine judgment that the *White Patriot* or T. J. talked of. But I do know I'm glad I'm still around to tell the story of two of the Center's most important cases, *Bobby Person v. Carolina Knights of the Ku Klux Klan, Glenn Miller, et al.* and *Beulah Mae Donald v. United Klans of America, Robert Shelton, et al.*

CHAPTER 14

December 1983   Mobile, Alabama

Pretending we didn't know each other, Bill Stanton and I passed by the sheriff's deputies and entered the small courtroom. Bill, undercover as a truck driver sympathetic to the Klan, took a seat on a bench populated by like-minded men and women. I sat several feet away from him, directly behind the family of Michael Donald, the young black man hanged in Mobile two and a half years earlier.

Not all the family members were present. Beulah Mae Donald, Michael's mother, had told friends and relatives she would not come to the courthouse. Mrs. Donald was a brave woman. She had insisted that her son's casket be open at the funeral so the world could see his battered body, reviving memories of the Emmett Till funeral twenty-five years earlier. However, the thought of watching the trial of one of the men accused of murdering her youngest child, her baby, was too much to bear.

The courtroom filled up quickly. A hum of anticipation ran through the crowd. The bailiff called for order. Judge Braxton L. Kittrell, Jr., took the bench and then summoned the jury. The panel of eleven whites and one black entered somberly. *State v. Henry Hays* was again in session.

In the abbreviated opening session the day before, the man who happened upon Donald's body and the policeman who first examined it had testified. The first witness on this day would be the most important of the trial. Assistant District Attorney Thomas Harrison, who had inherited the case when District Attorney Chris Galanos took a medical leave of absence, rose and called James Llewellyn Knowles to the stand.

The door behind Judge Kittrell opened. Two U.S. marshalls, their

210

eyes coolly scanning the gallery for danger, escorted a short, fat man into the courtroom. James "Tiger" Knowles marched confidently to the witness stand, looking older than his twenty years with a dark moustache, long, dark sideburns, and dark hair combed neatly to one side. He wore blue jeans and a brown sport shirt.

Harrison wasted no time getting to the point. He asked Knowles if he knew Henry Hays and could identify him. Knowles nodded, motioning toward the defense table. Hays, a fresh-faced twenty-nine-year-old with dark hair, stared impassively. Harrison then showed Knowles a photograph of Michael Donald hanging from the tree and asked if he knew how the body got there.

Knowles's response was short and devoid of emotion—perhaps because he had delivered it so many times to state and federal grand juries; perhaps because it was the only way he could deal with what had happened. "Henry Hays and I abducted Michael Donald on Friday night in the latter part of March 1981 and took him to Baldwin County where he was beaten and strangled to death and later on early that Saturday morning he was hanged from this tree on Herndon Avenue."

There it was. After a two-year investigation by city, state, and federal law enforcement agencies that had included several wrong turns and several dead ends, the public was finally hearing the true story of what had happened to Michael Donald. The young man had not been murdered in a drug deal. That was the theory first advanced by local authorities, who initially had arrested three men described as "junkies." Instead, as the black community had suspected from the moment the hanging corpse was found, Michael Donald had been the victim of Klan violence. Both Knowles and Hays were members of the United Klans of America, Bobby Shelton's group.

Why had they committed the murder? "Simply because he was black," Knowles testified matter-of-factly. He went on to explain that two or three days before the murder, he had engaged in a "casual discussion" with Henry Hays and Henry's Klansman father Bennie "as to what people would think if they found a nigger hanging from a tree in Mobile County." After Shelton, Bennie was the highest-ranking UKA official in south Alabama—an organizer, or Grand Titan, in Klan parlance. His territory included thirty of Alabama's sixty-seven counties.

After describing the "casual discussion," Knowles added almost parenthetically, "Bennie Hays made the statement not to do anything until after Friday because he was selling his apartments on Herndon

Avenue." Those apartments were across the street from the tree from which Donald had been hanged early Saturday. A dead body in a tree before the sale might scare off the buyer.

The three Klansmen were talking about a lynching because of a trial taking place in Mobile. Josephus Anderson, a black man, stood accused of murdering a white policeman. Because the jury was composed of eleven blacks and one white, Knowles and the Hayses anticipated a verdict of not guilty. Hanging a "nigger" was one way of demonstrating their disgust with blacks, who were appearing on juries in increasing numbers because of cases like the one Joe Levin and I filed in Montgomery County in 1972.

Knowles testified that on Friday, March 20, he was at the house at 117 Herndon Avenue that Henry rented from Bennie Hays. Several members of Unit 900, the Mobile UKA chapter, or Klavern, were there, as were some "aliens," the Klan's term for non-Klan.

Not long after arriving, Knowles left the party with Henry Hays and Frank Cox, Hays's brother-in-law and the Exalted Cyclops, or president, of Unit 900. The three men drove to Cox's mother's house in Theodore, a rural suburb ten miles west of Mobile. There they borrowed a rope, saying that they needed it to tow Knowles's mother's car. They then went to the trailer home of Johnny Matt Jones, another Unit 900 member, and borrowed a gun. On the way back to Hays's house, Knowles tied a hangman's noose in the rope. There were thirteen loops in the knot—standard Klan operating procedure.

Back at the party, they watched the ten o'clock news with the rest of the guests to see if there had been a verdict in the Anderson case. *A hung jury.* Tantamount to acquittal in the Klansmen's eyes. After "a discussion amongst the various people in the apartment," Tiger Knowles and Henry Hays excused themselves.

In his emotionless voice, Knowles then described in graphic detail how he and Hays had cruised the city looking for a black person to kill. They first spotted a middle-aged black man using a pay phone. *Too far from the curb,* they thought. Then they saw Michael Donald. Donald, who went to technical school and worked part-time in the mailroom at the *Mobile Press Register,* had gone out to buy a pack of cigarettes, promising his family he would be back in a few minutes. The Klansmen saw him walking alone on the dark, deserted street and pulled over. They asked him directions to a nightclub. When Donald leaned in toward the window to help them, Knowles pulled out Jones's gun and ordered Donald into the car. Hays then drove to an isolated wooded area in adjoining Baldwin County. Knowles remembered that on the way there Michael Donald begged, "Please don't kill me."

The abductors pushed Donald out of the car. As the three men stood in a small clearing, Donald knocked the gun away from Knowles. A shot discharged when the gun hit the ground. Donald ran. The Klansmen caught him, and after a considerable struggle, they pushed him to the rough, damp ground, beating him with tree limbs.

Donald continued to struggle. "[He was] . . . like a crazed madman all of a sudden," said Knowles.

You are the madman, you bastard, I wrote on my legal pad.

Eventually, the beating was too much for Donald, and he collapsed, barely conscious. Knowles and Hays looped the rope around Donald's neck. Hays put his boot on Donald's forehead and pulled the rope, and pulled and pulled. Donald didn't seem to be breathing, but the Klansmen weren't sure if he was dead. To make sure, Hays "cut Donald's throat three times," recounted Knowles.

Michael Donald's family was crying now. So was I.

Bennie Hays and his family were not moved. They stared daggers at Knowles. In their eyes, he was the great betrayer. When federal officials had finally cracked the case, Knowles had been accused of violating Donald's civil rights, a federal crime with a maximum penalty of life in prison. Fearing that the state of Alabama would soon file murder charges—charges that carried the possibility of the death penalty—Knowles quickly cut a deal. He pled guilty to the federal charges, accepting a life sentence that carried the possibility of parole. He agreed to testify against Hays on state murder charges with the understanding that he himself would not be subject to state charges. In a show of cooperation not common in the 1960s, federal and state prosecutors had agreed for the Mobile district attorney to prosecute Hays. If Henry Hays had cut a deal instead of "Tiger," then he may have been the star witness, not the defendant facing the death penalty. Knowles had simply beaten his friend to the punch.

Oblivious to the stares of the Hays family, Knowles described how he and Henry had loaded Michael Donald's mutilated body into the car trunk and brought it back to Herndon Avenue. Cox came out from the house to see the body and then, with another Klansman named Teddy Kyzar, burned a cross on the lawn of the courthouse.

These other people—Bennie Hays, Cox, Jones, Kyzar—why hadn't the district attorney indicted some or all of them, too? Alabama law makes an accomplice as guilty as a principal.

When Harrison's examination of Knowles was over, everyone in the courtroom knew what had happened and who had done it. Cross-examination revealed even more.

Bubba Marsal, who represented Henry Hays, was one of the best criminal lawyers in Mobile. But the more Marsal asked, the deeper Knowles buried the knife in Hays. Was the sole reason for the killing "because Donald was black?" Marsal asked.

"Yes . . . and to show the strength of the Klan . . . to show that they were still here in Alabama," Knowles responded.

Bingo! I turned around and made eye contact with Stanton. He nodded. This was what we had hoped to hear.

If Michael Donald had been the victim of a drug deal gone sour, Bill and I would not have been in Mobile. If Donald had been murdered by a crazed white man with no ties to the Klan or any other extremist organization, we would not have considered becoming involved in the grisly affair. While we would have mourned his death, the Center could not have taken legal action.

When the Klan connection was finally confirmed with the indictments in June, I alerted the staff at the Center about a potential lawsuit. I didn't know whom we would sue or exactly what our theory would be, but that really didn't matter. This was the most gruesome racially motivated murder in almost twenty years. We'd find something.

As the Hays trial approached, my desire to nail the Klan had grown stronger. Klanwatch was gathering startling information that demonstrated the Klan's lethal force. Each deposition we took in the Decatur case gave evidence of deadly past abuses and plans for future violence. Information about Beam's activities in Idaho was equally ominous. And Klan violence and paramilitary activity frightfully reminiscent of Beam's now-defunct Texas Emergency Reserve were dramatically increasing in North Carolina under former Green Beret Glenn Miller.

In October, members of Miller's Carolina Knights terrorized Bobby Person, a black man trying to get a promotion in the state prison system. We had been looking for an opportunity to go after Miller. When Person's lawyer called to see if we would consider helping him, Randall Williams headed to North Carolina to investigate.

One more factor motivated me: The torching of the Center had made my battle against the Ku Klux Klan personal as well as philosophical.

*   *   *

Beulah Mae Donald, as executor of her son's estate, would have to be a willing plaintiff if we were to sue Klansmen and Bobby Shelton's UKA. Before the Hays trial, I called Michael Figures, the Donald family lawyer. Along with ace federal civil rights prosecutor Barry Kowalski, Figures's brother, Thomas, an assistant U.S. attorney, had steadfastly refused to let the stymied murder investigation die. I told Michael Figures that I was coming to the Hays trial. If it looked like we could prove the UKA and others were involved, I explained, we wanted to file a civil suit on behalf of Beulah Mae Donald. Figures had then talked to Mrs. Donald. She agreed to cooperate.

After Knowles testified, the basis for a civil suit took shape. *"To show the strength of the Klan . . . to show that we were still in Alabama."* My mind raced back to a conversation with Bobby Shelton just weeks earlier. I had called him in connection with the Decatur case, hoping he might want to help nail the coffin of his rival, Bill Wilkinson of the Invisible Empire of the KKK, the group that disrupted the Tommy Hines march. We had learned that an Invisible Empire Titan had rejoined Shelton's group. We suspected the man would be indicted for his actions in Decatur. I suggested to Shelton that this man should offer to help federal prosecutors, thereby assuring the indictment of all of Wilkinson's Alabama leaders.

Shelton told me how much he disliked what he called the "public antics" of Wilkinson, considered along with David Duke and Louis Beam as one of the new breed of Klansmen. Wilkinson's frequent press conferences made it difficult for the Invisible Empire to maintain its invisibility, rankling the tight-lipped Shelton.

No doubt Shelton also disliked hearing from his lieutenants that the UKA was losing members to Wilkinson's more modern, upbeat Klan. Klanwatch had determined that two thousand members paid dues to Wilkinson in the Decatur area alone, while Shelton and his group were hurting. The Invisible Empire was besting the United Klans in other states as well. I could see the lynching as the work of a weak Klan group trying to prove itself in the only way the UKA knew how—through violence.

A number of witnesses supported or added to Knowles's story. Frank Cox's mother testified that her son, Knowles, and Hays borrowed a rope early that Friday evening. Teddy Kyzar testified that Knowles and Hays had left the house on Herndon Avenue after seeing the news story about the hung jury, and that he and Cox burned a cross on the Mobile County Courthouse lawn after Knowles returned with blood on his shirt. Kyzar also identified someone named Bill O'Connor as present at the house. I added the name to my growing list of people to check out.

Kyzar, in his early twenties, nervous, fat, and slow-witted, refused to say where he lived " 'cause I done been threatened three times to die already since [the murder]." The first threat had come from "Bennie Hays hisself." The way Kyzar said "hisself" made it clear that he considered Bennie the boss, the big man you tried not to cross. Teddy Kyzar struck me as honest, not sinister. I felt pity for the young man.

Later, Judge Kittrell recalled Kyzar to the stand, an unusual move. He wanted to know more about Bennie Hays's threats. I suspect he realized the prosecutor was traveling too narrow a path. More extensive questioning might finger other criminally culpable figures. Kyzar explained that Bennie Hays had told him that if he took the fall for the murder and went to jail he would be well taken care of, "far as money-wise when I come out."

Bill O'Connor, who had not been identified as a Klansman, took the stand. Six months after the murder, he testified, Henry had told him "we hung that nigger," giving him details.

I seated myself so I could observe all the players. If this was a Klan conspiracy, the body language of those who had something to hide might betray them. Bennie Hays, gray-haired, in his mid-sixties, slightly stooped, with thick black glasses, presented himself to the media as a kindly, innocent old man in need of a cane. But now he became angry, silently mouthing obscenities to O'Connor, bursting to keep the lid on something. I could hardly wait to take some depositions.

Already at work trying to get the names of more witnesses, Stanton used the cover story that he was a long-haul truck driver whose rig had broken down in Mobile. Being a Texas Klansman, he had read about the case with great interest and wanted to show his support for Henry Hays. Dressed in jeans, a blue work shirt, and a baseball cap, Bill looked the part of a Klansman, a role he had played many times in going undercover at rallies. Before the first day was over, he was talking freely with Bennie Hays, Frank Cox and his wife, and a woman named Donna.

Donna, who lived across the street from Henry Hays, quickly took a liking to Bill. She sat next to him at the trial, and every time I looked back, she was snuggling closer. I'd wink at Bill and his full cheeks would turn beet red. Bill was a good-looking young man with slightly shaggy brown hair down to his collar. More than one female Center intern had found him appealing. Donna, however, was not exactly his type. She was a heavyset woman with stringy brown hair on both her head and her upper lip. Her crooked teeth looked like they had opened one too many beer bottles. She wore tennis shoes and stockings that were always falling down.

Back in our room at the stately Malaga Inn, Bill told me that Donna had invited him to her house. I could tell he wanted to avoid the woman. There was really no reason to go—Donna didn't know anything—but I thought I'd have some fun. "Well, partner, sometimes you gotta bite the bullet and do what's necessary to get the facts. Old Donna's real close to the Hays family. You get intimate with her, there's no telling what you'll find," I said.

When I said the word "intimate," Bill looked like he had just eaten a lemon. "I'll go along with this to a point, Morris," he said, "but dangit, I'm not gonna sleep with her."

I reached into my pocket. "Here," I said, tossing him a pack of Certs.

"What if I make her angry by saying I won't sleep with her?" he asked.

"Don't want that to happen, do we?" I grinned.

Bill picked up the phone to call Donna. "I don't think—" he started to say.

Donna interrupted him. "Listen, honey," she said. "I like you, but I've got some rules. First of all, I'm not into any leather straps or kinky sex."

Bill almost fainted. After a speechless moment, he assured Donna that she would not have to worry about that because he had to help repair his truck. He threw my Certs back at me.

In the end, Bill learned a lot of names, but no additional information about the crime. Opal Hays, wife of Bennie and mother of Henry, kept silent. Bennie insisted that Henry had not been involved in the murder.

Anxious to free his son, Bennie Hays told the same story on the witness stand when he testified for the defense. He said some of his best friends were black and that he had even sold an apartment to a black person. He denied Knowles's testimony that he said to hold off on "hanging a nigger" until he sold his Herndon Avenue property. But he failed to convince; his answer was too glib. I doubted Knowles had made up such an unusual story about selling property.

I watched Bennie Hays's face and body carefully. The veins in his neck (like Dink Bailey's) pulsed wildly. His hand partially covered his mouth as he testified, a mannerism our jury consultants say often indicates untruthfulness. His eyes darted around the room as he tried to oversell the jury.

On cross-examination, Harrison showed Bennie Hays the property deed he executed on the eve of the murder. I couldn't understand how he had escaped being indicted.

The prosecutor delved into the background of Hays senior. Acknowledging he was Grand Titan of the Klan in south Alabama, Hays said Unit 900 meetings were always on Wednesdays, admitting, too, that a unit meeting had probably taken place in the week preceding the murder.

Did his son Henry attend the meeting on the Wednesday before the Friday night murder? Yes, Bennie Hays said, for Henry was "Kligripp," or secretary, of Unit 900.

What was Knowles's role? While not a member of Unit 900, he was, Hays stated, "a member of this organization . . . he was under me." I knew what that meant: Knowles, then seventeen, served as a state or national officer, next in command in the region after Bobby Shelton and Bennie Hays.

I was already drafting the civil suit in my mind. Any lawyer could do the obvious here and file a civil rights or wrongful death suit against Tiger Knowles and Henry Hays on behalf of the Donald estate. Such a suit would have little effect. Hays and Knowles were probably judgment-proof—unable to pay any monetary damages. Equally important, such a suit would allow the other perpetrators to escape. Any suit should include them. But even that was not enough. We should use a murder of this magnitude as the starting point for a suit against the United Klans of America itself.

Bill Stanton and I headed back to Montgomery when the jury began its deliberations. On our way out of town, we drove to the 100 block of Herndon Avenue. After locating the Hays house, we crossed the street to the camphor tree on which Michael Donald had been hanged. We stood in silence for a long time before slowly walking back to our car.

During the three-hour drive back home, Bill and I discussed what shape a lawsuit might take. Prosecutor Harrison, a capable man, had taken the position that the murder was a terrible act committed by two individuals who just happened to be Klansmen. "I'm not sure this was a Klan case," he said.

I saw it differently. Tiger Knowles and Henry Hays had not acted merely as individuals. This was a classic Klan murder down to the thirteen knots on the hangman's noose, a murder that Knowles, Bennie Hays, Henry Hays, and probably Frank Cox—not just Klansmen, but all of them Klan *officials*—had discussed, plotted.

"These bastards were agents of the Klan," I said to Bill. "Why can't we sue the Klan like you'd sue any corporation liable for the acts of its agents?"

"I've never heard of the Klan being sued like that," said Bill.

Neither had I.

I didn't know whether a court would allow us to hold the Klan responsible for the acts of these so-called agents. My gut reaction told me that we would have to prove the UKA was an organization that had engaged in acts of violence over the years to carry out its white supremacy goals and that the Klansmen who planned and carried out the murder were acting in the line or scope of their authority. This seemed obvious at first glance. But how do you establish the line or scope of authority for the Klan? Finding actual evidence to prove Klan goals, policy, and operating procedure would be very difficult. Even Klanwatch—which now utilized informants and received Klan literature through phony subscriptions—knew virtually nothing about the UKA's internal policy. The UKA didn't publish fancy annual reports trumpeting its deeds. Shelton ran one of the most secretive Klan groups around.

Some information was known: Members of the UKA had beaten the Freedom Riders in Birmingham and Montgomery in 1961, had bombed the Sixteenth Street Baptist Church in 1963, and had killed Viola Liuzzo as she drove Selma marchers in 1965. All three events had been crucial in my personal education. The Freedom Riders case brought me in contact with the young black man who questioned my values; the Birmingham church bombing led to my split from my old church and neighbors; the Selma march marked my first involvement in the civil rights movement.

But my involvement began at the same time the UKA's involvement seemingly ended. How could we argue there was a history of violence if the time line of UKA terror was empty between the 1965 shooting of Liuzzo and the 1981 lynching?

*   *   *

By the time Bill and I returned to the Center, the jury in Mobile had
convicted Henry Hays.* We immediately pulled John Carroll and
Steve Ellmann into my office, where I advanced my agency theory.

"Novel, but unlikely," John said.

"Can't be done," said Steve. "You'll never clear the legal hurdles
so a jury can consider the Klan's liability. Corporations are not usually
liable for the criminal acts of agents. You'd have to prove it was the
UKA's official policy, or at least a practice encouraged or condoned
by high officials, to commit criminal acts to carry out UKA goals," he
concluded in his wordy but scholarly analysis. He was sure that a
judge would throw out the agency claim.

I disagreed. I argued that if we could show the past record of units
and members committing violent acts, the court would allow the jury
to determine whether Bennie Hays, as the Klan's top person in southern Alabama and its agent, had bound the UKA corporation by his
acts.

John and Steve remained skeptical, particularly since the violent acts
seemed to have ceased in 1965. "Bill, you gotta find us something
more recent," I said.

He did. In 1979, Bill learned, thirteen UKA members were convicted in federal court in Birmingham for shooting into the home of
Charles Woods, NAACP president in Childersburg, Alabama. A top
klavern member had testified for the government. Without determining whether we could find any witnesses or the turncoat, I decided this
was the missing link we needed to file our lawsuit.

Pretrial investigation, not clever cross-examination or stirring closing
arguments, wins most lawsuits. I dreaded the investigation it would
take to put the Donald case together. Bill had already spent the better
part of three years on the Decatur case, identifying involved Klansmen and tracking them down with photographs of the march as a
starting point. Here, Hays's criminal trial and the identification of a
handful of witnesses would start the process. But what did these
witnesses know? Would they talk to us? Who else was involved? And
could we find these witnesses?

Maybe we could find a shortcut. I called Mobile County District
Attorney Galanos, now back on the job, and told him about our idea

---

*The jury would go on to deliver a sentence of life without parole. Judge Kittrell overruled
this sentence, as was his right, and imposed the death penalty. This marked only the second time
in Alabama history that a white person was sentenced to death for murdering a black person.

for a civil suit. "Chris, it would be a big help if we could see what you had in your files."

I wasn't surprised that Chris cooperated. A first-generation Greek-American, he was in the tradition of progressive North Carolinians like Terry Sanford. Black voters had helped elect him. As a prosecutor, he was also concerned about the rights of victims. Why shouldn't he help Michael Donald's family pursue its legal recourse? He invited me to meet with his investigator, Bob Eddy.

Eddy greeted me warmly in his office, a mile away from the DA's headquarters. His reputation as a Klan-hater was well earned. In 1977, he helped Alabama Attorney General Bill Baxley finally indict and convict Robert Chambliss, the UKA Klansman who had bombed the Sixteenth Street Baptist Church fourteen years earlier. In a windowless conference room, he presented me with two large file drawers marked *Donald* and wished me luck.

I quickly glanced through the file tabs. O'Connor, Jones, Betancourt, a name I hadn't heard at the trial.

I pulled out the file. Jesus! "Red" Betancourt had told authorities that he read aloud a newspaper clipping about the Anderson trial at the Unit 900 Wednesday night meeting two days before the murder. He mentioned that Henry and Bennie Hays, O'Connor, Cox, and Kyzar were present. He denied knowing about plans to kill anyone—of course, he would deny that—but reading the clipping could easily have ignited discussion about coming up with some Klan response to the Anderson trial.

Betancourt also said he had turned over the Klan's scrapbook, book of rules, and regulation book to Bennie Hays after deciding to leave the Klan. These books could help us pierce Shelton's veil of secrecy. I searched the files, but the books weren't there. Maybe Bennie Hays still had them.

After almost three hours of reading the files without taking notes, I realized the bulk of our investigation had already been accomplished. The office was closing. I didn't want to leave this wealth of information behind. What if Galanos or Eddy decided they didn't want me to come back? I asked if I could stay and let myself out later. Eddy showed me the copy machine and extra paper. "Stay as long as you want," he said.

It was almost midnight when I left, my briefcase barely containing all the copies. Heading back to my hotel, I realized I was in the same neighborhood in which Michael Donald had been abducted. I tried to imagine the terror he must have felt when Knowles pulled the gun on him. *"Please don't kill me."*

The street was dark and quiet. A light rain fell. I shivered and locked my car door.

Steve Ellmann's Decatur and Vietnamese fishermen complaints served as models for the Donald complaint. I added my agency theory and a catalog of past UKA events. Although aware that, as Steve and John Carroll had noted, there was a serious question whether the applicable civil rights statutes allowed liability for the acts of agents, I did not bother to research the point. I just put it in and decided to cross that bridge later.

Legal precedent aside, my common sense continued to assure me the agency theory was valid. If a loan company's business is to make and collect loans, it would not be liable if a collector used violence against a debtor; but if the company had a practice of encouraging strong-arm collection tactics, criminal assaults would result in civil liability. I suspected Shelton and UKA officials knew from past experience that UKA members resorted to violence in carrying out the UKA's goals, and that they encouraged it. In his capacity as Grand Titan, Bennie Hays knew of and encouraged the act in question here—the murder of Michael Donald.

While working on the complaint, I asked Bill Stanton to investigate UKA property and corporate status, remembering from my college days that Shelton had owned a small concrete-block building on the edge of Tuscaloosa. Bill returned with photos of a newer brick building, perhaps worth more than $250,000. He and Randall also discovered corporate papers in the secretary of state's office.

We filed the complaint in federal court in Mobile on June 14, 1984, seeking $10 million in damages from the United Klans of America, Inc., Bennie Hays, Henry Hays, Tiger Knowles, Frank Cox, Teddy Kyzar, and other as yet unidentified Klansmen. We wanted to wait until we took the depositions of Betancourt and O'Connor to decide if we should add them. Bobby Shelton was named a defendant in his capacity as Imperial Wizard of the UKA.

It was a tough decision to sue Bobby because I knew it would cut off a helpful line of communication. I didn't view this old man as a threat like Beam, Miller, and Wilkinson. The two of us went back a long way. Although he knew I did not share his views, I felt he grudgingly respected me. He had built the UKA partially to spread his ideology, but mainly, I believed, to make money. In the 1950s and

'60s, he mailed out over two hundred thousand issues of the *Fiery Cross* monthly and sold a ton of Klan paraphernalia. He eventually ran his own private press. Dues poured in.

He felt our motives were similar. Once he commented how much I must be bilking out of Northern liberals. He saw my Klan suits much like my ultra-liberal detractors did—as vehicles to gain dollars. To maintain communication, I did not tell him what I really thought of his actions.

I called Beulah Mae Donald and explained we had a greater likelihood of succeeding against the Klansmen than the Klan itself. Unfortunately these lowlifes probably wouldn't provide very much money if the jury awarded damages. On the other hand, the UKA had a major asset, the building. "Mr. Dees," she said. "No amount of money is going to bring back Michael or make my heart ache any less. That's not why I agreed to this suit. You just find all the people who killed my baby, and let the world know, and I'll be able to go to my grave."

Winning money for Mrs. Donald was not my principal aim, but I felt it important. If we could jump the legal hurdles surrounding the agency argument, if we could persuade the jury that a conspiracy existed and that Benny Hays and Tiger Knowles and Henry Hays were acting as agents, and if we could show the history of Klan violence by finding credible witnesses to testify to past acts—three big, big ifs at this stage—a jury might award huge damages because of the defendants' heinous acts. Prosecutors might also indict Bennie Hays, Frank Cox, and others if we uncovered new evidence.

Driving into work the morning after filing the suit, I fantasized about a jury returning a verdict that would bankrupt the United Klans of America. I honked my horn in excitement and pressed my foot down on the accelerator.

A black state trooper pulled me over for doing 80 miles per hour in a 55-miles-per-hour zone. The Center's lawsuit had resulted in the integration of the troopers. The officer glanced at my license.

"Attorney Dees," he said in recognition.

"Yes, sir."

"You slow down and watch yourself," he said, handing me back my license with a smile.

CHAPTER 15

October 1983   Moore County, North Carolina

Bobby Person had been luckier than Michael Donald. The robed figure standing in the back of the pickup truck that pulled in front of his house at 4 P.M. on October 12, 1983, didn't fire the rifle he was holding; he merely held his arm out in a Nazi-style salute as the truck drove off. Person recognized him as Jerry Michael ("Mike") Lewis, a fellow guard at the Moore County, North Carolina, Correctional Unit.

The truck returned again at dusk, with Lewis and two additional passengers, speeding up to Person's double-wide trailer home at the end of a dirt road next to a black church. One of the men in the back of the truck, dressed in camouflage gear and brandishing a .22 rifle, called for Person to come out. While Person's terrified wife and three children hid in the house, Person, a stocky ex-infantryman, grabbed his shotgun and ran outside. According to Lewis, the man with the .22, later identified as Klansman Gregory Short, yelled, "Come out from behind that tree, nigger, and I'll whip your ass." Holding up his gun, Person cursed the night riders, and challenged them to come into his yard. The truck, driven by Joan Short, Gregory's wife, veered away as one of the men vowed to "keep coming back until you straighten up."

This wasn't the forty-one-year-old Person's first encounter with the Klan. The threats and intimidation had begun in March of 1983, when Person and fellow employee Jimmy Pratt had applied to become the first blacks in supervisory positions at the prison facility. On May 30, a cross was burned in front of Person's house. Later, Klan literature was strewn in his yard and inside the neighboring church; the letters "KKK" were scratched into the hood of Person's father's pickup; and while driving to town, Person's wife and children were harassed by another driver.

Other incidents had occurred in the area. A cross was burned in the yard of a white woman suspected of dating a black man; a black woman worker at a convenience store was given a Klan calling card; a black man who worked at the prison with Person was visited by Klansmen; a Klansman visited a local business and told the owner to stop hiring blacks.

Klanwatch was monitoring this activity. Eastern North Carolina was rapidly becoming a Klan hotbed, thanks to one Glenn Miller, the forty-two-year-old former Green Beret. According to Miller, he was forced to retire from the service because of Klan-related activities.

Settling on a twenty-seven-acre farm outside Angier, North Carolina, approximately twenty-five miles south of his native Raleigh, Miller had become a leader in the pro-Nazi National States Rights party. He had witnessed the infamous 1979 Nazi-Klan counter-demonstration that led to the shooting deaths of five white Communist party workers in Greensboro, and claimed that he was more proud of being in the caravan with the instigators of that eighty-eight-second gun battle than anything he had accomplished during his two decades in the military. All five men arrested for the shootings were acquitted; Miller was not indicted. Concluding that swastikas turned people off, he had resigned from the Nazis in December 1980, to set up the Carolina Knights of the Ku Klux Klan.

Miller anointed himself Grand Dragon, just as Louis Beam had named himself Grand Dragon of the Texas Knights. The title and Vietnam experience were not the only similarities between the two men. Miller sounded like Beam when he announced his goal was the creation of the Carolina Free State, "an all-white nation within the bounds of North and South Carolina. Separation is the key." "Niggers" and Jews (also "nonwhite") were the enemy, Miller told the *Duke Chronicle* in 1981. Noting (inaccurately) that "over 90 percent of the murders [in 1980] were committed by niggers," Miller warned, "It's pretty obvious that white people are going to have to use their weapons."

Like Beam, Miller had created a KKK heavily influenced by his military background. Klanwatch had received reports of paramilitary-type training going on at the farm in Angier, and Miller had allegedly boasted that he had supporters at Fort Bragg, the forty-thousand-man U.S. Army base twenty-five miles to the southwest. Total membership in the Carolina Knights ran about fifteen hundred, the Grand Dragon estimated. These members, who paid annual dues of twenty dollars, were spread among several "dens" in the Carolinas.

Miller's vitriolic newspaper, the *White Carolinian,* reported Knights' activity and railed against blacks, Jews, and other enemies of good white Christians.

Dressed in army fatigues more often than Klan robes, Miller and his followers held numerous rallies and marched somewhere on the eastern seaboard almost every week. Mike Lewis was an assistant den leader in Chatham County. When Lewis went to court in November 1983 on charges related to the harassment of Person, Miller and other members of the Knights, all in army fatigues, were there to support him. Having pointed a gun at Lewis and the others in the truck, Person had also been arrested on the same charge: communicating a threat. The judge threw out the charges against both men.

After the court appearance, the incidents at Person's house stopped until March 31, 1984. On that day, while Person was at work, Lewis appeared at about 1 P.M. and began cursing and yelling racial epithets at Person's wife and children.

This was a particularly busy time for the Carolina Knights. Since the beginning of the year, the organization had tried to provide an armed patrol at a school in Sanford where a white girl had been raped, supposedly by a black man. The North Carolina Human Rights Council and the state attorney general's office had tried to keep the Klan off school property, but Miller's men were always in the area.

When I talked to Bobby Person in the spring of 1984, he was adamant about suing the Klan.

"If you file suit, they might come back and burn your house down," I warned. I didn't think they would, but I needed to test his resolve. We couldn't have him quit on us in the middle of the lawsuit.

"If I'm going to have to live like I'm living, I might as well live with it burned down," he said.

The Center had a client.

May 1984   Boise, Idaho

Robert Mathews and the "Inner Circle" of his radical group, the Order, debate whether they should plan an assassination. Randy Duey says the army they are forming is not strong enough to withstand the pressure brought on by an assassination. Denver Parmenter agrees: It would be best to wait until the Aryan Academy training camp is in full swing. It is one thing to rob pornographic bookstores and even pull off Brink's truck heists like the one that netted $230,000 in March; it is something else to actually pull off a hit.

Mathews and his trusted aides Bruce Pierce and Gary Yarborough disagree.
The Turner Diaries *clearly states that political assassinations are necessary
to begin the revolution. A novel written by National Alliance for the Advancement of White People leader William Pierce (under the pseudonym Andrew
Macdonald),* **The Turner Diaries** *serves as the group's revolutionary manual. In the book, an underground white supremacist terrorist organization
executes a worldwide revolution through assassination, bombings, sabotage,
mass murder, guerrilla warfare, and nuclear explosions.*

*The thirty-one-year-old Mathews founded the Order in September 1983,
during an Aryan Nations meeting in Idaho. A handful of young, radical
racists swore a secret vow with him to "One God, one race, one nation." Since
then, they have armed themselves, studied guerrilla warfare, and conducted
robberies.*

*Now Mathews pulls out a folder full of newspaper clippings and other
documents. He holds up a piece of paper on which he has written three names:*

> *MORRIS DEES*
> *NORMAN LEAR*
> *ALAN BERG*

*Parmenter and Duey restate their objections to killing anyone of note at this
point.*

*"Well, this is a situation that will be taken care of by those who want to
do it," says Mathews.* *

The harassment of Bobby Person offered a good chance to stop Glenn
Miller just as we had his ideological clone, Louis Beam. We would first
try to halt the Knights' intimidation. If we could find evidence of
paramilitary training that violated the North Carolina criminal statutes, we would try to halt that, too.

Outside of Mike Lewis's membership in the Carolina Knights, nothing linked Miller to the campaign against Person. Strategically, it
seemed best to wait to file the suit until we knew more. I explained
to Person we could take the depositions of Mike Lewis, Glenn Miller,
and others under the broad sweep of the ongoing Decatur case,
alleging a national Klan conspiracy to harass blacks.

"Others" included James Holder, a former Klansman out on bond
awaiting trial for the murder of another Klansman, David Wallace.

---

*I was not aware of the events described in this and other italicized sections until well after
the events took place. My descriptions are based upon eyewitness accounts in *The Silent Brotherhood* by Kevin Flynn and Gary Gerhardt (New York: Free Press, 1989) and *Brotherhood of
Murder* by Thomas Martinez and John Guinther (New York: McGraw-Hill, 1988).

On May 29, Bill Stanton, Randall Williams, and I met Holder, a short, slight man of about thirty, for his deposition in Sanford. After serving with the Eighty-second Airborne paratroopers out of Fort Bragg, he left the service and became a pipe fitter. He had also joined the Carolina Knights, heading the Lee County den. His official title in Miller's militaristic organization was staff sergeant.

Now disenchanted with Miller's policies and practices, Holder told me he had been a member of what Miller called his "elite fighting force." Explained Holder: "He says they're the toughest out of his whole organization. They are trained better. Ninety-nine percent of them are ex-military soldiers, and they are able to train the ones that come in that's not."

"What is he training them for?

"Total civil disorder."

Holder then described training the elite forces in communications and first aid. Well armed, dressed in combat garb, they engaged in various training maneuvers. "AR-fourteens, thirty-caliber carbines, twelve-gauge shotguns, forty-five-caliber semiautomatic Thompsons [submachine guns]."

Enough here to support a complaint that Miller was running a paramilitary operation, I told Randall and Bill.

Mike Lewis, whom we deposed immediately after Holder, said that he, too, had served in the Knights' special forces. "[It] is an elite force," he said. "Not everybody can be in the Klan special forces. You have to go through military training, like jungle training. It's a tough outfit, just as good as the field special forces at Fort Bragg."

I would not ordinarily have associated Mike with the word "elite." The Klan was probably the only organization he could join where he would feel special. A gangly six-foot misfit with boyish features, he had spent four years in the military, then five years as an officer with the Department of Corrections, guarding a chain gang with a shotgun. He was fired after his arrest for threatening Person. He now worked as a warp attendant at a rug factory. I imagine he could have buffaloed the folks on "What's My Line" with that job title.

Angry that blacks were promoted ahead of supposedly better-qualified whites in the Department of Corrections (himself included), Mike joined the Klan because "I busted my butt and it came down through [the governor] in Raleigh they had to give special privileges to minorities. . . . That's racial discrimination against the white people."

His version of the two truck rides past Person's house was almost laughable.

Q: So the only reason you went up that road was to go up to his house with your Klan uniform on and stand in the back of your truck?

A: Well, see . . . the Pope wears a white robe. My church, we wear white robes to sing in the choir. . . . I use my same robe I go to the Klan meetings with at the church where I sing in the choir. It's the same thing.

Q: Have you got any symbols on it, blood drops or anything?

A: We've got the blood drop patch, but you can take that off. . . .

Q: When you were riding in the back of the truck that day, were you singing in the choir? Were you out there as a Klan member?

A: No . . . I was just practicing a parade, because we had Klan parades coming up and down, pretty soon.

Q: So you went out there as a Klansman?

A: As a Klansman.

Lewis insisted Person had been the aggressor, drawing his shotgun first and cursing before anyone in the truck did anything. He also refused to acknowledge any involvement in other incidents. No, he had not burned the cross near the house of the white woman, Sue Goodwin; had not strewn Klan literature in Person's yard or the black church; had not vandalized Person's father's truck. He refused to implicate Glenn Miller in anything.

We had hoped for a stronger link to the Grand Dragon. Still, Lewis was a member of the Carolina Knights, and our investigation showed that despite his testimony, he had been involved in these incidents. He also reiterated Holder's description of the paramilitary nature of the operation.

Although I had tested Person by suggesting the Klan might retaliate if he brought a lawsuit, my experience has shown that once a suit was filed the intimidation usually stopped. The Klan didn't want to stir up more trouble for itself. On the other hand, if we kept taking depositions and didn't file a suit in Person's name, the Klan might do something nasty. Since Bobby Person was brave enough to come forward, we owed it to him to sue now. With any luck, future depositions would reveal more. On June 5 we filed suit in federal court in Raleigh against Glenn Miller, the Carolina Knights, Mike Lewis, Gregory and Joan Short, and unnamed, unknown other Klan members to stop intimidating blacks and operating a paramilitary organization.

After receiving his summons as a defendant, Lewis called me. I turned on my tape recorder, as Lewis said he didn't have a lawyer and couldn't afford one. I said that if he were willing to cooperate, we might drop him from the case. That appealed to him because he was trying to start life over by going to Tennessee Temple University, a Christian school in Chattanooga.

"You know it's but a week ago I got saved. And it changed my whole outlook on life," he said.

"Well, I think some of the things y'all did up there [in North Carolina] weren't too Christian," I said.

"I agree with you a hundred percent now." He went on to tell me he had been at fault in the Person incident, had come out to intimidate Bobby Person. He insisted Miller didn't know of his plan, but several other Klansmen had known and had offered to go shoot Person's house. While Miller wasn't connected to this, Lewis did link him to the cross-burning at Sue Goodwin's house. He said he heard David Wallace call Miller and tell him about "a white bitch shacking up with a nigger buck down the road . . . and Wallace wanted to make a little demonstration."

Wallace wanted to use Miller's flags. Miller gave him permission. Lewis felt certain Miller knew a cross would be burned.

I clicked off my tape recorder. The case against Glenn Miller and the Carolina Knights had just strengthened.

June 18, 1984 Denver, Colorado
Alan Berg, the liberal Denver radio talk-show host who has long infuriated the political right, pulls his Volkswagen into his driveway.

"Okay," says Robert Mathews, sitting in a Plymouth just down the street, "let's move." Driver David Lane speeds the Plymouth to Berg's driveway. Mathews jumps out and holds the door open for Bruce Pierce.

Berg grabs a grocery bag, then starts to get out of his car.

Pierce fires his MAC-10 automatic. The .45-caliber cartridges pummel Berg to the ground. He dies instantly. A can of dog food from his grocery bag rolls down the driveway as Mathews and his accomplices wheel off. The Order's first assassination is a success.

Had Teddy Kyzar and Johnny Matt Jones, the first two witnesses we interviewed in the Donald investigation, been asked to join an American Legion outpost or tavern bowling team or any other mainstream social group that would have made them feel wanted, they might not have felt the need to join Unit 900 of the UKA. Teddy and Johnny, like so many in the Klan, just wanted to belong to something. The Klan happened to ask these wallflowers to dance when no one else did, and as a result of such "kindness," was able to have its way with them.

Some Klan and white-supremacist leaders like Louis Beam and Richard Butler said they found the basis for their anti-black, anti-Semitic activities by reading history or scripture. Jones was reading the menu at the Colonel Dixie fast-food restaurant in Theodore when Frank Cox's wife Gail suggested he join Unit 900. Jones explained to me that Gail Cox, who was Henry Hays's sister and Bennie Hays's daughter, had told him "it was a good thing to join and I wouldn't be getting into anything that was wrong or anything like that."

A few weeks after the Donald suit was filed, Teddy Kyzar also said that he had been told there was nothing wrong with joining the Klan. Stanton and I had driven down to Mobile to ask Kyzar about the events leading up to Donald's murder. We were particularly interested in learning what had happened at the Klavern meeting on the Wednesday before the lynching. Teddy Kyzar, like the rest of the defendants save Shelton, had not hired a lawyer, but was willing to see us.

I haven't seen too many snowmen in the South, but Kyzar—with his blank expression, round head set on top of his round body, with hardly any neck—made me think he should have a carrot for a nose and coal for buttons. He was in danger of melting at any time.

He proved a cooperative snowman, telling us that Unit 900 had discussed the Anderson trial at its meeting on Wednesday, March 18. At one point, he recalled, Bennie Hays had said no black man should get away with killing a white man. Others present, including Henry Hays, had agreed.

This was good stuff. We wanted to know more about the meeting: What happened next? Who said what? But Kyzar's mind was as blank as his stare. He insisted he couldn't remember anything else. Bennie Hays had become angry at the meeting and at that point, said Kyzar, "I kicked back in the chair and started daydreaming." I believed Kyzar, although I couldn't imagine what kind of daydreams ran through his mind. We'd gone as far as we could with the snowman.

Jones's memory was better, but it took time and patience to get his version of the Wednesday night meeting. A few months after the murder, Johnny Jones had sold his trailer home and left town. We tracked him down in Houston where he was working as a mechanic.

The Jones file in the Mobile DA's office was thin. Investigators had cut short their interviews because they suspected he was mentally retarded. Over the course of several telephone conversations with him in early July, I learned Jones wasn't retarded, but epileptic. He spoke slowly, and the greater the pressure, the less articulate he became. He said he remembered the Klan meeting on the Wednesday before Michael Donald was hanged, but he was reluctant to talk about it. He feared the Klan might retaliate if he cooperated with me. I told him we could sue him because he provided the gun, but if he was truthful and provided a statement we might not. He finally agreed.

A frail young man with damp hands and deep-set dark eyes, Johnny Jones escorted me and a court reporter from the muggy Houston morning into his tiny, neat apartment in a large, characterless complex. We sat at a small, round table. His whole body shook.

I tried to ease him into his story by beginning with simple questions. He was so nervous he got his age wrong. He stumbled while trying to remember his Social Security number, too, but when I suggested he could look it up in his wallet he calmed down. Then slowly, painfully slowly, his tale unfolded.

Jones had lived in the "gold trailer with brown trim" next to Frank and Gail Cox's trailer. When his car broke down in 1980, Gail Cox had driven him to work and started talking about the Klavern that her husband, brother, and father belonged to. Jones was nineteen at the time, an ideological blank slate. He began attending weekly meetings in the Klan building on Bennie Hays's Theodore property. After going to several meetings, Jones was named the Klavern's "Kludd." His responsibilities included reading "the big old oath" at the beginning of every meeting and taking measurements for Klan robes and hoods sewn by the women. Jones said that he had participated in several cross-burnings and that Tiger Knowles and he had once picked up a long-haired hitchhiker, pulled out their knives, and cut his hair.

At the March 18 meeting, Jones recalled, Bennie Hays stood up and told Henry Hays, Unit 900's secretary, to "get this down." Referring to the Anderson trial, Bennie said, if a black man could get away with killing a white man, a white man should be able to get away with killing a black man. In the discussion that followed, Henry Hays said "a nigger ought to be hung by the neck until dead to put them in their place" and Tiger Knowles suggested a lynching. This had been met with enthusiastic support. Another Klansman, Frank Ginocchio, had said, "We gonna kill a nigger." Red Betancourt mentioned that blacks were so dumb they should all be killed.

At this Wednesday night meeting, Knowles also asked if he could borrow Johnny Jones's .22 pistol. Jones checked with Cox, who had bought him the gun. Cox said to lend it to Tiger. Driving home from the meeting that night, Jones noted, Cox supported the idea of killing a black person if the jury failed to convict Anderson. On Friday night, Cox and Knowles and Henry Hays came for the gun. Tiger returned it several days later, with sand in the barrel and one shell missing.

The number of conspirators was widening; the role of Bennie Hays, Klan officer, was becoming more prominent. The next step—much more difficult—would be to establish the formal business connection between Bennie Hays's Unit 900 and the United Klans of America and to show these conspirators had been acting as agents of the UKA.

August 1984   Angier, North Carolina
Glenn Miller and Stephen Miller of the Carolina Knights and Robert Mathews and Richard Scutari of the Order cruise down Interstate 85. "We're thinking about killing Morris Dees," says Mathews. "What do you think about that, Glenn?"

"It doesn't matter to me one way or the other," replies Miller.

Mathews gives Glenn Miller a paper sack with $75,000 in cash. Miller doesn't know it, but the money came from a $3.8 million Brink's armored truck robbery pulled off by Mathews and the Order in Ukiah, California, on July 19. Mathews is on a whirlwind tour around the country giving money to his allies. Miller will shortly receive another $125,000. On the elaborate organizational chart Mathews has drawn up, Glenn Miller—code name, Rounder—will head the South and Southeast after the revolution. Louis Beam—code name, Lone Star—will head the Southwest.

Mathews tells Miller that there are no strings attached to the money, but he has several recommendations. Miller should put six people on the payroll and purchase two vehicles. "One more thing," adds Mathews. "Train one of your men to play the bagpipes in your marches."

Both the Donald case and the Person case had attracted the media's attention, but Bill Stanton was surprised when our receptionist buzzed him and said there was a three-man television crew in the lobby. They had asked for me, but I was out.

When Bill came into the lobby, his surprise, then terror, was evident.

"I see by the look on your face you know who I am," said Louis Beam, dressed in a gray pin-striped suit, a tiny microphone clipped to his blue tie. "I'd like to interview Mr. Dees." The cameraman was videotaping. The third member of the "crew" also looked familiar:

Thom Robb, national chaplain of the Knights of the Ku Klux Klan.

Having witnessed Beam's behavior in Texas and read the letter in which he had challenged me to a duel, Bill initially thought that Beam had come to the Center to kill some or all of us. He scrutinized the men, sighed his relief when he couldn't see any weapons, and then excused himself. He called the police, then raced back to the lobby where Beam was delivering an off-camera voice-over while the cameraman focused on an artist's rendering of the proposed new Center.

"You're going to have to leave here immediately," Bill said.

"You want us to leave?" Beam said, mimicking aggressive TV reporters who are turned away by unwilling subjects. He took his crew to the sidewalk outside, continuing to speak to the camera. Thinking quickly, Bill used his own camera to record Beam's intrusion. For a moment the duel Beam had envisioned took place—with cameras as weapons and Bill as my stand-in.

Bill ordered Beam to leave again. As the three men headed for a red Lincoln Continental, Beam retorted, "Sir, we will no longer be intimidated. We are bringing the war to you." He climbed into the car and instructed the driver, "Gentlemen, start your engines."

Bill jotted down the license number as the car raced off, then ran inside and called the ATF's Glen Kibler.

When I arrived at the Center, Bill explained what had happened. A few minutes later, an anonymous informer called to say Beam was in Montgomery, making a film about me and the Center for "propaganda purposes." Earlier in the day, Beam had apparently filmed at Rolling Hills Ranch. "He's lucky I wasn't there," I told Bill. "If I'd have seen him, I would have shot first and asked questions later." I learned another interesting fact from the informer: Beam had spent part of the day with Joe Garner. The pair had asked questions about me.

Louis Beam and friends had been able to walk in off the street and start "shooting." Despite the fire, the Center had continued to operate in a casual fashion. Our door was open to anyone. We had no choice but to change that after the visit, however; the next day a security firm installed an electronic door system. No one could get in without buzzing the receptionist. Entry was by appointment only, requiring sign-in.

The attorneys and rest of the staff didn't like this any better than I did, but realized there was no alternative, since our enemy played with fire and, most probably, firearms.

Late September 1984   Boise, Idaho
Robert Mathews tells Gary Yarborough, "I want you on our assassination squad."
"Who's next?" asks Yarborough.
"Dees. We're going to start tailing him in Montgomery. We'll kidnap him, interrogate him, and then flay him."
"Flay him?"
"Right, we'll peel that fucker's skin from his body before we kill him."
A few days later Alabama Klansman Billy Riccio flies to Boise to be initiated in the Order. "What do you have on Dees?" asks Mathews.
Riccio provides important information for the assassination squad.
"We'll be sending someone to trail him," says Mathews. "Just like we trailed Berg."

The security system lasted less than a month. Ten days after Beam's visit, a telephone call came from Garry Nungester, a paid informer who had been feeding us accurate information about the Klan since the early days of the Decatur case. "It looks like somebody's gonna try and knock off Dees," he told Stanton. Wolfgang Droege, a Canadian neo-Nazi and cocaine smuggler living illegally in the U.S., had been asking questions about me, Nungester explained. What kind of car did I drive? What route did I take to work? Where did I spend my time outside the office?

Nungester said he thought I was on the hit list of a new, violent, right-wing extremist group, plotting a race war and the overthrow of the government. Within a few days, the FBI called with a cryptic message: "We have information of a serious threat on your life," said the agent. "I'm not authorized to tell you more."

I put the phone down. Death threats issued on electronic bulletin boards and in white supremacist circulars seemed less ominous. From my office, I could see the new glass in the window the arsonist had broken. I imagined the sound of glass shattering, then the crack of a sniper's rifle. When I was a boy, my dad had explained that sound travels more slowly than a bullet, that the dove we saw crumple in the sky across the corn field did not hear the blast that killed it.

I asked to see John Carroll immediately. Although he had left the Center to join Howard Mandell's law firm in downtown Montgomery, John still served on our board of directors. He remained the person I felt most comfortable with discussing personal matters and Center business.

John knew of the earlier threats. After he closed his office door, I told him I had verified the FBI's call. "It was for real, man," I said nervously. We had priced wall-to-wall security for me. I had refused it, based on the eighteen-thousand-dollar-per-month cost and the personal intrusions it entailed. The thought of high-tech security devices, protective fencing, and a new lighting system at the farm violated both nature and the Center's treasury.

"Dees"—John always addressed me by my last name in his deep marine drill-instructor voice—"if they kill you, all the money you got from Times Mirror and the Center's endowment will serve little purpose." He convinced me we should beef up security quickly, not just for my sake, but for my family and the Center. We consulted Joe Levin in Washington and he agreed.

I left John's office and sped away on my motorcycle for a two-hour ride to nowhere, my last bit of freedom for a long time. I had always been aware of the danger presented by high speeds. In the past, when I would take the bike to 90, 100, 120 miles per hour, I felt fear mixed with exhilaration. Death could be calculated as the distance from my head to the asphalt.

I felt no fear on this final solo run. I was in control out here, the master of my destiny, not some unseen assassin's target.

By the end of the first week in October, we had hired National Security, a highly regarded firm run by former Montgomery police captain Don Terry, to protect us. He transformed our not-for-profit legal and educational center into a fortress. An armed guard kept watch outside the front door around the clock. Shotguns were placed in the office at carefully selected spots, reminding me of Beam's old bookstore in Texas. Klanwatch staffers Williams and Stanton, the most likely targets after me, were issued guns. Panic buttons, similar to those used by bank tellers and linked directly to the police, were installed throughout the office. I was assigned personal bodyguards.

I can't discuss here, for obvious reasons, some of the other comprehensive security systems that remain in place even today and that will be a part of my life for years to come. The FBI, regardless of what critics say about Hoover's actions during the civil rights movement, has earned my deep respect and eternal thanks.

Early in October, bodyguards in tow, I traveled back to Mobile for pretrial motions in the Donald case. We ran into Bobby Shelton and his lawyer, John Mays, in the courthouse elevator. "I thought you were a friend, Morris," the Imperial Wizard said.

"I did what I had to do, Bobby."

A few spectators were scattered throughout the courtroom. The Donald family had come, as had Bennie and Opal Hays. After the hearing, I chatted with the Donalds, then introduced myself to Mr. and Mrs. Hays. They had aged considerably since the trial. Not only was their son on death row, they had recently been indicted for insurance fraud in connection with a fire that destroyed their home in July, shortly after Henry Hays had been charged with Donald's murder. The government alleged that in order to raise fifty thousand dollars for Henry's defense, they burned the house themselves and then filed a phony claim.

I offered my hand to Bennie. He did not take it, but he wasn't hostile. I sat down on the bench in front of them. "Mr. Hays," I said, "I'm sorry about your son being on death row. I've got problems with the death penalty. I've got kids of my own. I know how you must feel."

I meant what I said. Some folks have a hard time when they hear I'm courteous to Klansmen. I don't jump on them like some civil rights lawyers do. However misguided, these Klansmen are human beings. What purpose does treating them as dirt serve? Over the years I've had dozens of Klansmen, as young as Johnny Jones and as old as Bennie Hays, decide they trust me enough to talk, tell the truth, cooperate.

A few days after returning to Montgomery, I received a letter from Bennie Hays. Enclosed was the tattered Charter of Klavern 900 issued in 1973 by Bobby Shelton, who had signed it "his lordship." We had always suspected the Klavern was a chartered unit of the UKA, but this was the first physical evidence we had, something essential to proving our agency theory. This piece of paper allowed the national office of the UKA to authorize its local units to conduct business in the name of the UKA.

Bennie wrote that he had paid seventy-five dollars for the charter, but no longer wanted it because he "found out the kind of people I was working with." He said he hoped the charter would help me "in doing the work that kneeds [sic] to be done," adding, "I am sure I have a lot of helpful information. . . . I will be glad to work out any deal with you and get my life straighten [sic] out. I am told that I can not get a fair deal from you people without a atty. You talked very nice to me and my wife. Much different than I expected after being told about you."

John Mays, a criminal defense attorney from Decatur who had long served as UKA counsel, had told me at the hearing that Hays was an old fool who ran the Mobile unit as he wanted to and that Shelton had been trying to get rid of him. Bad blood between these two defendants, clearly. Stanton and I scheduled an appointment to see what "helpful information" Bennie had. Before our visit, Bennie sent us another letter listing some of the documents in his possession. The letter confirmed his dislike of Shelton. "I saw him burn things in barrels just so it wouldn't be available," he tattled.

After spotting the two-story iron cross, Bill and I pulled off the asphalt and onto the gravel trail leading the hundred yards to Bennie and Opal Hays's trailer home in Theodore. Along the way we passed a small frame building with a tin roof.

"That must be where Unit 900 met," said Bill. He spoke in the past tense because the unit had dissolved after the arrest of Henry Hays and Tiger Knowles.

The trailer home sat on flat, sandy land within a few hundred yards of the burned-out house that Bennie and Opal allegedly torched. We parked near the trailer by a large live oak draped with Spanish moss, then climbed out of the car cautiously. I had persuaded our security team to stay away. In Alabama, a man who shoots an "intruder" in his own home is rarely convicted. Bob Eddy had told me that Hays was a mean SOB. There was a real possibility that this was a trap, but I felt it worth the risk. I had my gun under my coat.

Bennie and Opal invited us in. According to a prearranged plan with Bill, I immediately asked to use the bathroom. While Bill occupied the Hayses, I inspected the house, even looking in closets and under beds. I could see that these were simple, poor people. All the furniture in the house probably wouldn't have brought two thousand dollars. No one waited to ambush us. The only faces I saw were those of grandchildren in photographs decorating every table and dresser.

I rejoined everyone at a Formica table in the kitchen. Bennie brought a cardboard box almost a yard long full of documents.

"You know, I turned in my Klan membership," Bennie claimed.

I leaned over to thumb through the box, but he pulled it back. Apparently he wanted to deal first.

"What can you do for my son on death row?" he asked.

"Nothing, sir. But Bubba Marsal is a very fine lawyer. He'll probably get the sentence reversed."

Bennie fingered the documents in the box. "What would it take to let me out of your lawsuit?"

"I don't know, Mr. Hays. We'll have to talk some before I can answer that question." I shifted in my chair to make sure my gun couldn't be seen. "Mr. Hays, why are you so mad at Bobby Shelton?"

Bennie stood up, with that same mean glare he had flashed at Tiger Knowles and Bill O'Connor in the courtroom. He spit out that Shelton had promised financial and spiritual support during Henry's legal ordeal, but had broken that promise. Opal Hays, gaunt and tired, looked down and played nervously with a button on her sweater. Her son's death sentence and the arson of her home had taken a heavy toll. Her family was slowly being destroyed by the bitter racism that her husband preached would save the white race.

I reached for the box again. This time Bennie did not stop me. "Lucky those weren't burned in the fire," he said. He insisted that anti-Klan forces had burned the house. There were several books entitled *Kloran Klan in Action Constitution.* I picked one up and handed another to Bill. I had never seen such a document (few "aliens" had, I reckoned). It contained the bylaws, rituals, an outline of the Klan's structure. We had to have it.

"Well, let me take a look at this and I'll get back in touch with you," I said trying to conceal that I was holding an important key to our case.

Bennie was not as foolish as Mays and Shelton thought. He took the constitution from me. Before we could have anything, he had to know what we could do for him.

"Without looking at this box real close, I can't make any deal, Mr. Hays. Why don't you let me take it, make some copies, and get it back to you in a day."

"No, sir," he said, taking the box away.

I wasn't ready to make a deal. "Call me, if you want," I told him and parted on friendly terms.

On the ride back to Montgomery, Bill and I discussed how to get the critical items. We considered dropping the money claims against Bennie Hays and settling for an injunction preventing him from harassing blacks. No, we decided, this would let off one of the guiltiest parties and confuse the jury.

"Let's wait him out," I said.

"What if he destroys the documents?" Bill asked.

"He won't. Those are the only bargaining chips he has."

CHAPTER 16

November 1984   Raleigh, North Carolina

Randall Williams, Center attorney Deborah Ellis, and I tightened our bulletproof vests, looked to Don Terry and our bodyguards for approval, and quickly exited our rental car. We rushed into the Wake County Courthouse to an elevator that would take us to the conference room where we would take the first depositions in the Bobby Person case.

"Well, that wasn't too bad," I said when our entourage was safely in the elevator.

Terry did not respond. He had not favored the trip. A few days after the visit with Bennie Hays, we had received another call from informant Garry Nungester. Wolfgang Droege, Louis Beam, and Billy Riccio were all planning to be in North Carolina at the same time we were. Beam was apparently helping Glenn Miller start a computer bulletin board similar to the one he had operated first in Texas and most recently in Idaho.

Klanwatch had been monitoring the bulletin board, called the Aryan Nations Net, for months. Sometimes the messages were quite personal. One day Bill called me into his office, pressed a few keys on his computer, and suddenly, courtesy of Beam, my name was in lights.

ACCORDING TO THE WORD OF OUR GOD, MORRIS DEES HAS EARNED TWO (2) DEATH SENTENCES. . . . THY WILL BE DONE IN EARTH AS IT IS IN HEAVEN.

Beam, Droege, and Riccio—the prospect of encountering this unholy trinity did not excite me. I called the FBI and spoke with an agent who agreed with Terry that I should not go to Raleigh. He suggested

240

that if I wanted to travel, I should leave the country until things cooled down.

I was concerned, but it was important we get the Person case moving forward. We were paying a small fortune for security. Don Terry's boys could earn their money in Raleigh. We flew into the city on the eve of the depositions and registered at our hotel using pseudonyms. Now, riding up in the elevator, confident that no enemy would be foolish enough to attack in a county courthouse, I told myself I'd made the right decision by going ahead with the trip.

The elevator door opened. We followed our bodyguards out. The hallway was crawling with soldiers in army fatigues and combat boots, Glenn Miller's elite. Terry and his crew formed a wedge and led us through some twenty Klansmen. Most snarled obscenities, some photographed us.

Once we were safe in the conference room, Terry phoned the county sheriff and requested protection. The sheriff, a black man who we assumed would be sympathetic, said he couldn't help us. The death of the Communist organizers in Greensboro and subsequent acquittal of the neo-Nazis and Klansmen accused of murder had made most state lawmen suspicious of both extremes and wary of involvement. The sheriff apparently associated us with the Communists.

"I can't believe Miller's got the balls to pull this in the county courthouse," I said.

"After Greensboro, these guys think they can get away with anything," replied Travis Payne, Bobby Person's lawyer and our local counsel, as he came in the room, followed by Mike Lewis and two men in military garb. I recognized Glenn Miller and Stephen Miller (no kin), his chaplain and second in command, from Klanwatch pictures.

Glenn Miller, about six feet two inches, lanky, with dark hair and a dark moustache, reminded me of Rollie Fingers, the Oakland Athletics' great relief pitcher. A pack of cigarettes bulged in the front pocket of his shirt. Stephen Miller, almost as tall as Glenn, was broader and more handsome. He, too, had a dark moustache. His hair was neatly styled and parted in the middle.

Glenn wore a Green Beret–type hat and a uniform with sergeant's stripes on each side of his shirt collar. On his left front pocket were stitched the initials CKKKK, for Confederate Knights of the Ku Klux Klan (he had recently changed the name of the group, dropping the regional "Carolina" in favor of the all-encompassing "Confederate");

he wore combat boots and a cartridge belt. Stephen Miller was dressed similarly.

As a defendant, Glenn Miller was entitled to be present at all depositions. When I questioned Stephen Miller's right to attend, Mike Lewis said that both Stephen and Glenn were serving as his counsel. Mike, who had been so cooperative after his visit from God in June, had apparently experienced another conversion after visiting with the two Millers.

He constantly conferred with his "counsel" and answered almost every question the same, "I neither admit or deny or do I recall at this time the answer to your question." This was his response to my question about our telephone conversation in June. The Klan had apparently won out over Tennessee Temple University.

Often contentious, Glenn Miller and Stephen Miller made a game of raising baseless legal objections. At one point, they tried to question Randall Williams on the record. I told them to take his deposition if they wanted to ask him questions.

The tension inside the room multiplied outside. Whenever the door opened for a new (and uncooperative) Klansman, the Confederate Knights in the hallway tried to barge in and take photographs. Whenever we went out, we were followed and bothered.

Eating lunch in the courthouse cafeteria, I looked up and found Glenn Miller looming over me. With a mean stare, he handed me a motion seeking to halt the depositions. He and Stephen Miller then marched off to the clerk's office in the federal courthouse across town to file the motion. The young woman responsible for taking motions was apparently so frightened by the sight of two "Green Berets" that she almost fainted. The FBI was called, but the Millers had done nothing illegal. Their frivolous motion was registered at 12:23 P.M. and denied by the judge at 12:27.

We persuaded courthouse officials to transfer the afternoon session to a room that didn't allow such easy access to outsiders. When we were settled, Randall went out in the hall, where a Klansman attempted to take his picture at close range. Randall stuck up his hands. The move knocked the camera into the face of the Klansman, who claimed that Randall had attacked him.

The afternoon closed on a more positive note. After deposing a number of uncooperative witnesses, we went to a friend's law office and took a private statement from David Wallace, the son of the Klansman who had been shot dead by James Holder in November. (Not too long after we had deposed him, Holder was convicted.)

Randall had spoken to this young former Knight earlier about the group's paramilitary operations. I followed up:

Q: I believe you told Mr. Williams, my assistant, that the marines directed much of the paramilitary training.
A: Marines and Steve [Miller] both. They was in there together.
Q: Now these were active-duty marines where?
A: At Jacksonville, North Carolina, marine base.
Q: Now, also I believed you said they supplied some equipment?
A: Some supplies, you know, like canteens, pistol belts, and uniforms.
Q: And I believe some of the training that you talked about was—you said combat techniques. . . . What did that consist of?
A: Shooting rifles, crawling on the ground, hand-to-hand combat.

This was explosive information. Active-duty marines were leading a white supremacist group in paramilitary maneuvers, teaching combat techniques, and giving government issue supplies to an organization committed to setting up a Carolina Free State—no blacks or Jews allowed, similar to Louis Beam's operation in Texas. Unfortunately, David Wallace would not make a terribly strong witness for us, since he had not observed CKKKK activity for some time and his credibility was suspect. He had a bone to pick with Glenn Miller; the Klan had killed his daddy.

Back in the hotel that evening, the thought of the elite, special forces Klansman attacked by his own camera was the only thing we found funny about the day's tense proceedings. Even that ceased to be funny the next morning. After we had charged through the omnipresent swarm of Knights, a sheriff's deputy came with a frivolous warrant signed by the Klansman and arrested Randall. Randall was booked and freed on his own recognizance.

Stephen Miller was our first deponent.

Q: What type of work do you do?
A: I work for the Almighty.
Q: Well, where is this company located?
A: He runs the universe.
Q: Give me a little more information. I've never met this fellow. . . . What do you do for this person?
A: Whatever he tells me to do.
Q: So you're unemployed? Is that what you're trying to say?

Actually, according to our information Stephen Miller had a commercial pilot's license. When he wasn't working for the Almighty or Glenn Miller, he worked as a crop duster.

Miller took the Fifth Amendment when I asked him about his Klan involvement. There was no point in pressing forward. We ended the deposition.

The Klansmen became bolder, more aggressive, thinking they had the upper hand. Not only were they stonewalling us in the depositions, they'd managed to get one of our guys arrested. At lunchtime, as we walked down the hall toward the elevator, they closed in on us with taunts and elbows.

A Klansman pointed a camera in my face. I brought my elbow up and gave him what football players call a forearm shiver. I call it a whack upside the head. His cap flew through the air. As he started to protest, Terry moved us out.

"It's time to leave town," Terry stated flatly at lunch.

I agreed. Besides, the depositions scheduled for the afternoon promised to be as fruitless as the ones we had already taken.

However dangerous it was to stay, it seemed even more dangerous to leave. We'd make better targets out on the open road, away from the courthouse. It wasn't too hard to imagine our car followed by a convoy of armed Confederate Knights. We were armed, too. A shootout seemed quite possible. Greensboro redux.

Placing calls to the state troopers, the county police, and the city police, we requested an escort to the airport. After these agencies told us they couldn't get involved, we asked friends in high places to call for help. The response was the same: Until something actually happened to us, these bodies did not have the authority to intervene; the CKKKK's threats were not enough. It seemed like we, instead of Miller's forces, were being viewed with suspicion. We were "outside agitators" poking our noses into North Carolina business. I pulled Terry aside and ran an idea past him.

Several short depositions were scheduled for the afternoon. The first one, as useless as all the previous ones, ended at about 2 P.M. Glenn Miller, whose presence caused acute memory loss to deponents like Mike Lewis, smiled as another silent foot soldier marched from the room. I told him our team would be back for the next deposition in a few minutes—we just needed to chat privately. The court reporter stayed in the room.

Terry had located a back way out that led to a service stairwell. We moved quickly to our car, already packed with important documents in anticipation of our "escape." Miller and his men could have the legal pads we'd left in the conference room. As we drove out of town, I couldn't help wondering if the Wake County Courthouse might be jinxed. I'd left the building under unusual circumstances in the Joan Little case, too.

From what we later learned, Miller sat patiently at first, then became restless waiting for us to return. About ninety minutes later, when we were safely in the air on our way back to Montgomery, the court reporter, who had been in on our plan from the beginning, told the Grand Dragon she had just received word that we weren't coming back. Miller cursed. The enemy had slipped through his lines.

CHAPTER 17

November 1984   Mobile, Alabama

Bennie Hays, dressed in a blue prison shirt, loose-fitting white pants, and sandals, shuffled into a conference room in the Mobile City Jail. The Titan had fallen since our meeting at his house just two weeks earlier; a federal jury had convicted him of insurance fraud in connection with the burning of his house. Unable to post bond, he was behind bars awaiting sentencing.

Hays's deposition in the Donald case was scheduled for 2 P.M. It was not yet noon. I hoped to plant an idea that might grow over the next few hours. If it did, old Bennie might put the noose around his own neck.

According to Johnny Matt Jones, Bennie had stood up at the Klavern meeting two days before Michael Donald was lynched and suggested a black should be killed if Josephus Anderson wasn't convicted of murdering the white policeman. We knew Benny Hays wouldn't admit this, but we wanted him to admit that the lynching had been discussed at the Wednesday night gathering, something he had denied at his son's murder trial.

I had a plan to get the truth out of him.

"Bennie," I said, "you know I'm gonna be taking Bill O'Connor's deposition, too. He's a sorry excuse for a man, isn't he?"

Bennie had made clear his feelings about O'Connor at the trial: He hated the man who testified that Henry admitted killing Michael Donald. As I had hoped, Bennie now started ranting and raving about O'Connor. I let him spew his venom for a while, then said, "Now look, Bennie, it ain't no skin off your back if you tell the truth on O'Connor about what he might have said at the meeting. What did he say about a black being killed?"

Bennie saw his chance to turn the tables on O'Connor. He told me that after Red Betancourt read the clipping about the Anderson trial, O'Connor raised his hand to be recognized. According to Hays, O'Connor then said, "There ought to be a damned nigger hung if this guy is turned loose."

If Hays would repeat this at his deposition, we'd have what we wanted—corroboration of Jones's testimony that a lynching had been discussed at the meeting. Teddy Kyzar's description of the events was helpful, but Kyzar was feebleminded and had not specifically mentioned a lynching. It didn't trouble me that everybody was pointing a finger at somebody else—Jones at Bennie Hays, Hays at O'Connor—as long as they were blaming someone in Unit 900. The similarities in the stories, not the differences, were critical. It didn't matter who spoke first.

I had no idea whether Bennie Hays would repeat his story when I walked into his tiny cell for the deposition ninety minutes later. In close quarters, we sat on opposite ends of his bunk, his metal cane between us. Shelton/UKA attorney John Mays didn't attend this or any other deposition, save Shelton's—foolishly, in my opinion. Because Bennie was in jail, the judge might not allow him to testify in court. In that event this deposition would be read into evidence before the jury. By forgoing the deposition, Mays yielded the right to cross-examine Hays and negate damaging testimony. Perhaps I had coaxed Mays to sleep. Whenever I had the chance, I told him, "Don't worry, John, I probably don't have a case against the UKA, but my clients want me to make the claim, and I'm going through the motions."

Hays was testy from the outset. I asked if he owned his own home. "Hell, no," he said, "I'm having to give every goddamn thing I've got for lawyers' fees. I can't even understand why in hell this is going on."

He picked up his cane from the bed, started swinging it menacingly. Where was the cooperative man I'd visited earlier?

After showing him the charter he had sent, I apologized for not knowing more about the Klan before he had given me information. "Well," he said, "that's because you've dealt with goddamn liars and thieves out here that has finked on decent people, who has costed me every goddamn thing I got."

The veneer of the kindly old gentleman was wearing off fast. If only the jury could see him like this, there would be little doubt that he was capable of suggesting a black man's hanging.

Hays said he had been elected Titan over a number of Klan units in Alabama, including Unit 900, gratuitously adding that UKA attorney Mays was himself a Klansman and enjoyed hitting new members during initiation "on their toes with a damn two-by-four."

I asked him about the Klan's secrecy oath I had seen while glancing through his documents. I would want the jury to see that this was a secret, hooded group that did bad things behind closed doors. If what the Klan did was legal, then why take the oath?

Hays acknowledged there was an oath, "and now I have broken it." Then, apparently to justify his position, he added, "No, I haven't. Because I'm talking about sons of bitches that's no good."

Moving on to the Wednesday Klavern meeting, I referred to "one of the hothead members of your Klan raising his hand to get recognized." Hays piped up, "Bill O'Connor," and after delivering a diatribe about him, he gave me the hoped-for line: O'Connor had said, "There ought to be a damn nigger hung."

Had Bennie Hays disavowed the plan? What had he said to O'Connor?

"I didn't say a damn thing. It wasn't none of my business."

Opal Hays was waiting for us at the federal courthouse when we walked in after Bennie's deposition. She, too, had been convicted of insurance fraud, but the judge had suspended her sentence. We had set her deposition for this day as well.

After subpoenaing all the documents we'd seen at her house, I had phoned Opal earlier in the week, afraid she might tell Bennie about the subpoena and that he would tell her to destroy everything. He had, after all, seen Bobby Shelton burn records. And, recalling the burned house in Theodore, we knew Bennie liked to play with fire.

"If you destroy any of the documents, ma'am, or don't bring everything in that box, you might go to jail for contempt of court," I warned her.

The box was now sitting on a table in a federal grand jury room. We like to use these rooms for depositions to impose a sense of truthfulness on the witness. Bill and I took all the originals, and left copies with the reporter. We had no intention of letting anything happen to this material, planning to store it safely in a fireproof vault at the Center.

We went through the box on the drive back to Montgomery like kids going through Christmas stockings. There were fifty-five separate presents: Klan membership applications, newspaper clippings, copies of the *Fiery Cross,* a Klan manual giving lessons and duties of various offices, a program from the 1981 convention commemorating the UKA's twentieth anniversary autographed by Henry Hays's KKK heroes, the secrecy oath, and financial forms to be filed by each Klavern. These financial forms were important because they reflected a money tie between Unit 900 and the UKA. In their depositions, both Bennie and Opal said they filled out these forms, forwarding money to the UKA.

The *Kloran Klan in Action Constitution* was the most critical document. Bill and I looked at each other as if we'd found the Holy Grail. To Shelton and his followers, unholy folks like us were not supposed to see it. "The *Kloran* is . . . a sacred book . . . and MUST not be kept or carried where any person of the 'alien' world may chance to become acquainted with its sacred contents," read a "greeting" from Imperial Wizard Shelton on page three.

At first glance, one might have thought this sacred book described the inner workings of a church group or civic organization, with numerous references about loyalty to God and country. The suggested structure of units—athletic committees, funeral committees, even a committee to visit sick members—seemed harmless, but a closer reading revealed the purpose of the organization. According to the Ku Klux Kreed: ". . . we shall ever be true in the faithful maintenance of White Supremacy and will strenuously oppose any compromise thereof. . . ."

A "lecture" on the "noble achievements of the Ku Klux Klan" explained how the Klan had overcome the threat of compromise after the Civil War, when, "the chastity of the mother, wife, sister, and daughter was imperiled and their sacred persons were placed in jeopardy to the licentious longings of lust-crazed beasts in human form. . . . The very blood of the Caucasian race was seriously threatened with an everlasting contamination."

The *Kloran* explained that the purpose of the local units was to carry out the goal of the national organization: maintaining the supremacy of the Caucasian race. The detailed description of the UKA's military-like structure also established that a chain of command existed from the top man, Shelton, through his second in command, Bennie Hays, all the way down to the officers of the chartered units (such as Unit 900). "The officers of the local Klans . . . are the line officers and the fighting leadership of the Klan. . . . It is the total of the power of the individual Klans which makes the strength and effectiveness of the National Klan. It is they who are in contact with the enemy; it is they who must carry out the strategy of the high command," read the constitution.

The ties that bound Bobby Shelton and the UKA to Unit 900 were tightening. The Titan, definitely an agent of the UKA, had participated in the talk of the lynching. We had everything we needed about the corporation itself—its purpose and chain of command, who was who, and the role of national officials like Bennie Hays working at the local level. But crucial questions remained to be answered. Was violence used to advance white supremacy or was the UKA just a political group that made speeches, burned crosses, and backed political candidates for office? Nothing in any of the Klan documents suggested the organization encouraged or condoned violence.

We had to prove that the UKA fulfilled its goal of the "God-given superiority of the white race" through violence. We had to convince a jury that Shelton knew about this and, in the face of such knowledge, continued to charter units, collect their money, hold training meetings, conduct business as usual.

When drafting the complaint, I'd given little thought to the fact that we must provide live witnesses to prove this. Who could we find to testify about the Freedom Rider riots, the Liuzzo murder, and most recently, the Childersburg shooting? Shelton wouldn't admit the UKA was involved. Newspaper articles suggesting the connection, even old court testimony, weren't going to be admissible. Although familiar with Gary Thomas Rowe, the controversial FBI informant present at the Liuzzo shooting who had testified against the murderers, we had no idea where he was or if he would cooperate.

Without Rowe and other witnesses, all the Klan documents in the world weren't going to be enough to nail Shelton and the UKA.

November 25, 1984   Portland, Oregon
Tom Martinez sits in room fourteen of the Capri Motel with Robert Mathews. Martinez has come west from Philadelphia, apparently to join the Order. "I'm going to tell you about your first assignment," Mathews says. "Tom, it's a big one! You're going to be part of a cell on the Morris Dees thing. We've gathered good intelligence on him, and what we're going to do, we're going to kidnap him and then we'll torture him and get as much information out of him as we can, and when we have that, we'll kill him, and bury him, and pour lye over him."
After Mathews leaves, Martinez goes out for a walk. A man in a black

Buick pulls up. Martinez gets in the car, rides to the rear of a nearby darkened car wash. Martinez exits and climbs into the back of a Lincoln Continental.
"You won't believe this," he begins.

On the eve of another round of depositions in the Donald case, my security guard and I took turns with a bottle of bourbon in room twelve at the Malaga Inn. I was leafing through the Yellow Pages looking for one of the seafood restaurants at the edge of Mobile Bay when the phone rang. It was Danny Welch, chief security director for Don Terry's outfit.

"Morris, don't leave the room. I'll be down there as soon as I can."

I put down the phone book. "What the hell's going on, Danny?"

"I'd rather not tell you. I'm not sure the line you're using is secure."

I looked at the phone. "Shit, man, nobody but you knows I'm staying here. I registered under the name Bill Wilkinson. Tell me what's going on."

"The FBI just called and said to find you ASAP."

"The FBI has called before," I said.

"I know," said Danny. "But this time they say they've got reliable info that some white supremacist group has assassins on its way to Alabama."

"Oh, shit."

"I'm on my way," said Danny.

If this was the big one, I was glad that Danny, a thirty-five-year-old, wiry, tough former homicide detective would be coming. Blond hair cropped short, one eye drooping a bit, Danny was as restless as a hill of fire ants, but extra-cautious when it came to his work. Few men ever got the drop on him. I'd seen him grow up around his family's store at the crossroads near my farm; we'd hunted together in Catoma Creek Swamp. I trusted this home boy.

My guard and I ordered our seafood dinner from room service. After picking at my food, I lay on my four-poster bed, fingering the fourteen-round clip of my pistol. The guard fell asleep, snoring so loudly that anyone lurking outside the room would have thought I had a flock of guinea hens protecting me.

I tried to sleep, but couldn't. Who was it? Joe Garner? Bobby Shelton? Bill Riccio? No, all these guys were local. They wouldn't be heading here from out of state. Wolfgang Droege? Bill Wilkinson? Glenn Miller? Louis Beam? It struck me that I didn't have to count sheep to fall asleep. I could count potential assassins.

*   *   *

No one came for me that night except Danny Welch. A week later, on December 3, an outer-perimeter night patrol team spotted two men with small flashlights in the back pasture's high grass. The trespassers ran before they could be apprehended.

On December 9, I read in the newspaper that a man named Robert Mathews had died in a fiery shootout with the FBI at Whidbey Island, Washington. According to the newspaper, Mathews had shot an FBI agent in late November. He was also suspected of heading an organization that had robbed a Brink's armored truck of almost $4 million in Ukiah, California, and murdered Alan Berg, a radio personality from Denver. The organization, called the Order, was supposedly priming to overthrow the United States government.

Like everyone else in the country, I had never heard of the Order. I had seen Mathews's name in some Klanwatch material about Aryans Nations members and visitors, but he was not high on our list. It didn't occur to me reading the news reports that Mathews might have been the one behind some or all of the death threats the FBI and Nungester had communicated to me. It did occur to me you could buy a lot of weapons with four million dollars.

On December 10, two days after Mathews died, two armed intruders interrupted our Christmas-tree trimming, sending Ellie and me to the dark closet. I sat holding my brave fourteen-year-old daughter and my pistol, wishing to God that I could be outside with the guard, catching the bastards who were doing this, putting an end to the psychological terror that had gripped me, my family, and my colleagues at the Center.

I received one big present before the end of the year.

Bill Stanton's desk was stacked high with photo contact sheets and pictures of Klansmen taken by our undercover informant, Nungester. As we sifted through some of these, I glimpsed a familiar figure dressed in his Klan robe at a rally identified as "Birmingham, 1980."

"Bill, that's Joe Garner," I said.

Bill picked up the photograph.

"Who's that with him?" I asked.

"Let's enlarge it," said Bill.

A day later we had our answer: The figure next to Garner, also in a Klan robe, was Tommy Downs, the same Tommy Downs who had insisted at his deposition and before the local grand jury in the arson case that he had never been in the Ku Klux Klan.

"Let's take the picture over to Jimmy Evans," I told Bill.

Within a week Evans called Downs before the local grand jury, asking him whether he had ever been a member of the Klan and whether he had ever worn a Klan robe. Downs answered each question as he had before the regularly scheduled federal grand jury more than a year earlier: "No." Evans then stopped the proceeding, brought Downs back to his office, and revealed the picture of the Birmingham rally as well as the same certificate the feds had shown him. "Son, you just perjured yourself before a grand jury. You're going to jail for five years if you don't tell us the truth about that fire."

Downs, married now and no longer so dependent on Garner, broke down, confessing that he and Dink Bailey had been hired by Garner to burn down the Center. He said his brother Bodie had not been involved.

We were halfway there. Under Alabama law, Evans still needed corroborative evidence to make a case against Garner. "What about Sherry Rhodes?" I asked.

We had long suspected that Garner might have confided in this close female friend. Evans had learned from Downs that Sherry's husband Buster had been involved with Garner and other Klansmen in a plot to steal and store explosives to be used against future civil rights demonstrations.

The DA summoned Sherry and told her Buster was facing a long stretch in prison with the information uncovered about his recent criminal activities. Sherry could shorten that stretch by telling what she knew about Joe Garner and the Center fire. From what we heard, Sherry's loyalty to Garner almost overcame her loyalty to her husband, but Buster eventually won out. Sherry agreed to testify against Garner, and Evans agreed to recommend a light sentence after Buster Rhodes pleaded guilty to charges related to receiving stolen property.

It had taken eighteen months for me to get Joe Garner, but the photograph in the next day's *Advertiser*—the meek Klansman being taken into custody by two of Sheriff Butler's confident black deputies—almost made the wait worth it. Times were changing in Montgomery County.

Garner, Downs, and Bailey were all indicted, by both the state and the federal government. The FBI now asserted the fingerprints on the duct tape belonged to Tommy Downs. All three men pleaded guilty before their trials. The state court sentenced Garner to fifteen years, while Downs and Bailey received three-year terms. Garner also pleaded guilty to federal civil rights violations. The sentences would run concurrently and be served in federal prison. The federal sentence

may have been the smartest thing Garner ever agreed to. He might
not have lasted too long in the state penitentiary with its large black
population.

When the FBI interviewed Joe Garner several weeks after his arrest, he told them that Louis Beam and Thom Robb had visited him
in March of 1983 and asked questions about me. Garner said Beam
had called me "scum" because I had not responded to his January duel
challenge. Garner mentioned he had also met with Beam and Robb
when they were making their "documentary" about me in September.
"It's a damn shame that a man like Morris Dees can jog up and down
these streets and still breathe this air," Beam had told him.

Why had Garner orchestrated the fire? The main reason, he said,
was to retaliate for the Decatur case by destroying records. I've often
wondered whether a friend in the local law enforcement community
had tipped him off that we had just shared important information with
federal officials.

Garner gave the FBI another reason. He was "tired of Dees ag-
gravating the hell out of me and all the harassment, depositions, and
subpoenas." This aggravation had become so intense that at one point
he offered Dink Bailey one thousand dollars to kill me. He had taken
Bailey out to my house twice. Armed with a gun, Bailey hid out
watching for me.

Garner told the FBI that on the night of the fire Downs and Bailey
met him at his store, bringing a small bag that contained Garner's bug
sprayer and a tire tool. They filled the sprayer with gas from the store.
Garner then dropped them off four blocks from the Center.

As children Downs and Bailey had lived near the area where the
Law Center stood and had often explored the sewers in the neighborhood. They crawled through the sewer system toward the Center—
they painted a yellow line along the walls to avoid getting lost—then
broke in by putting duct tape on the window to reduce noise and
breaking it out. While Bailey stood lookout, Downs went inside,
splashing gasoline on the walls as he walked through the Center.

They left by sewer, too. It seemed only fitting.

Garner is still in prison. Not too long ago, I received a letter from
him. Like so many inmates, he claims to have seen the light and found
God. He asked that I put in a good word for him with the parole
board. I wrote back and said that I was happy he had found religion
and that if he could find some information about Louis Beam and
others coming after me, I might forgive him. He hasn't written back.

*   *   *

With Garner's name scratched from my things-to-do list, I could concentrate on the two names that remained—BOBBY SHELTON and GLENN MILLER. Shelton's deposition was not scheduled until April 1985, Miller's for early January. This time we would avoid the Wake County Courthouse. We had received permission to use the grand jury room in the federal courthouse, knowing U.S. marshalls would not allow Miller's men to show force. It worked. Miller came alone.

Although Miller did not have an attorney of record, he was generating a good deal of paperwork. On November 29, the court granted our motion for a protective order filed after the Klan intimidation and harassment in the courthouse on November 1 and 2. At the hearing on the motion, we also showed the federal judge, Earl Britt, a computer printout from Beam's network in which he said I was going to be in North Carolina and that anyone knowing my hotel should report it. On December 10, Miller filed his own motion for a protective order, citing Randall Williams's "assault" on the Klan photographer (even though Randall had been acquitted of the preposterous charge after a brief trial on November 30). Miller also asserted that when he and his family attended a peaceful CKKKK rally on August 28, 1984, "someone" broke into his home and stole "most of the files pertaining to the CKKKK." According to Miller: "It is felt that this break-in and theft was the work of Attorney MORRIS DEES and others working in concert with Mr. Dees and the Southern Poverty Law Center, and other ultraleftist organizations such as Klanwatch. . . ." Miller also suggested that we might be connected to two shotgun blasts fired into his home in the early hours of November 17.

I began Miller's deposition by asking what files were missing.

"I don't remember," he said.

With prodding Miller said that financial files and membership records had been stolen. Then the circus began. When I asked him if past issues of his *White Carolinian* and *Confederate Leader* publications had been stolen as well, he took the Fifth Amendment. I explained that *he* couldn't take the Fifth Amendment in response to a question about documents he had accused *me* of stealing. I told him if I had to ask Judge Britt for an order compelling him to answer my questions, I'd ask for a fine, attorney's fees, and court costs.

The alleged break-in to his house was obviously an excuse for him to avoid providing certain records. To call his bluff, I again asked what was missing. Had cancelled checks of the CKKKK been stolen from the house? Miller refused to answer. I'd had enough. "Let's both go to the judge," I finally said.

Judge Britt, in his fifties, patient but stern, told Miller that if he didn't answer my questions in the deposition the judge would dismiss the motion for a protective order and put him in jail for contempt of court.

Some Klan leaders like Bill Wilkinson had a sense of humor and were easy to talk to. Miller, on the other hand, was cool and humorless, always the tough guy trying to stare me down.

The hearing in front of Judge Britt changed all that. As the deposition was about to resume, I noticed the fear in Miller's eyes. He fidgeted nervously in his chair, hands shaking. Was he afraid of going to jail? Was he trying to hide something? If I had known at this time that Miller was afraid we might find out Robert Mathews had visited him twice in 1984 and had given him two hundred thousand dollars in cash, I might have understood why the Grand Dragon looked like a mouse. All I knew was that a window of opportunity had opened.

"Glenn," I said quietly, "let's just get this whole thing over with. I think we can settle this case. Don't you?"

"What do you want to do, Morris?" he asked, his voice uncharacteristically submissive.

On my legal pad I wrote an agreement that he wouldn't operate a paramilitary organization in violation of various sections of the North Carolina statutes and that he wouldn't harass, intimidate, or threaten blacks. I said we'd bear our own court costs and waive our claims for damages. Bobby Person would agree to this; Travis Payne, Bobby's personal lawyer, endorsed the proposal wholeheartedly. If we went to trial and all the issues were presented, we couldn't get an order any better than this. At best we might obtain a small money judgment for Bobby against Mike Lewis and Gregory and Joan Short, all of whom were judgment-proof. As for Miller and the Knights, the court might order what I had just written, but certainly no more.

I showed Miller the proposal and he agreed to it. Randall typed it before Miller changed his mind.

Would Miller actually give up the Confederate Knights paramilitary activity? I didn't think so. He didn't seem to believe the agreement prevented him from operating.

Knowing this, why did I settle? Because if Miller violated the settlement agreement, we could bring a criminal contempt action against him and exact a stronger penalty than we could with a civil suit. We could put him behind bars, if only briefly. I already had some ammunition here—the testimony of James Holder and young David Wallace. Why waste it in the civil suit?

*   *   *

I flew into Raleigh the next week to appear with Miller before Judge
Britt for the final order in *Person v. Carolina Knights.* Miller arrived
without his troops. I came without my bodyguards. I felt that Miller
was appeased and wouldn't feel the need to parade his soldiers.

The settlement agreement was a simple one, only a page and a half.
For a moment, I wondered if it was too simple; a Philadelphia lawyer
would have drafted something much more technical. Judge Britt detailed the proposed consent decree: Miller agreed not to operate a
paramilitary organization and do other acts prohibited by two North
Carolina statutes. One statute prohibited furthering civil disorder.
The other statute made it illegal to "band together, muster, drill, or
practice any military evolutions" without the state's authority. The
judge asked Miller if he understood what he was signing. Miller asked
all sorts of questions and then signed.

As Miller and I walked out of the courtroom, something—perhaps
the impulsive risk-taker that often seizes control in me—moved me to
ask him for a ride back to the airport. He said he'd be happy to make
the half-hour trip.

As we climbed into his old Ford Pinto, I thought about my ride
twenty years earlier in Bobby Shelton's white Cadillac. I had felt no
danger with Shelton. Here, I was at Miller's mercy.

The backseat of the Pinto was filled with stacks of Miller's Klan
newspaper. Apparently he would drive through neighborhoods and
throw them on every lawn, hoping to find one or two discontented
or lost souls willing to join his cause.

"Glenn," I said, as he pulled into traffic, "there's something I've
been meaning to ask you. I've been reading all your stuff about the
superiority of the Aryans. Now, I've got blond hair and blue eyes and
you've got brown hair, almost black eyes. Does that ever bother you?
Have you ever wondered about yourself?"

"You don't have to have blond hair to be an Aryan, Morris," he
said seriously. He paused. "You know, you really should rethink your
position. This country's in real danger. The Jews are taking it over.
The mud people. They are behind the music that's breaking down our
morals; they're behind drugs. They control everything."

I glanced back to see if we were being followed. It didn't look as
if we were. "Glenn, you look back in history, the Jews have made
some pretty important contributions."

"Yeah, only if they could make a dollar."

We cruised through the countryside now. I told him about growing up on a farm, working with blacks and getting to know them as people. I told him, too, that I didn't represent people because of their color. I mentioned the reverse-discrimination case on behalf of the white school employees. Could I show him I was fair, not some radical, and create a dialogue that would be useful later? If Glenn Miller's attitude could change, maybe his ardor for violence would diminish. It was my Baptist evangelism, ingrained from childhood, trying to convert the lost.

We were approaching the entrance to the airport. I was glad I'd asked him for a ride. The conversation gave me hope.

Oh, shit.

He had driven right past the entrance. Suddenly, we were driving down a dirt road.

Did he just miss his turn, or is this it for you, Dees?

Unarmed, I braced myself to hit him if he made a move.

The only move he made was to turn the car around. He had simply missed the entrance.

"Morris, you know, I kind of like you," he said as he pulled into the airport. "I'm going to tell you something. There are some people out there who want to kill you. You better be careful, friend." Little did I know how much he knew, what "Rounder" had been part of over the last months with Mathews and the Order.

On the way to my plane, I stopped in the gift shop to bring something back for Ellie. At the counter, I noticed a little ballpoint pen painted with the same camouflage colors Glenn and his men wore. I bought it, and when I arrived home I sent the pen to Glenn with a note: "Remember, the pen is mightier than the sword."

I wish he'd paid attention to that message.

CHAPTER 18

April 1985   Tuscaloosa, Alabama

What does evil look like? The fifty-six-year-old man sitting across the table from me could only be described as ordinary—ordinary height, ordinary weight, ordinary amount of gray in his hair and lines on his face for someone his age. The kind of person you don't even notice walking down the street, sitting at a bar, riding on an airplane.

The realization that evil could come wrapped in so ordinary a package frightened me for a moment. Better to have lived centuries ago, when the harelip or scarlet letter singled out the devil's children. I looked at my notes to remind myself that there was nothing ordinary about the deeds attributed to Bobby Shelton over the last quarter of a century.

Shelton once told my friend Patsy Sims, author of *The Klan,* "I think actually a person is really born a Klansman, and it just works out of him as he develops." Shelton's racist attitudes developed when President Harry Truman integrated the military. Having grown up in segregated Tuscaloosa, his contacts with blacks had been limited. Integration created those same sexual anxieties in him that Southern preachers and politicians had voiced before the Civil War. "The black soldiers forced themselves in with the white German girls [overseas]," Shelton explained. "This was very irritating. . . . I began to realize we were going to have the same problem in this country."

When he returned home from the service in the early 1950s, Shelton determined he could best fight integration by joining the Klan, specifically the U.S. Klans in Alabama. It was a busy time for the KKK, its membership burgeoning in direct proportion to the growing civil rights movement. Shelton, a rubber worker at a B. F. Goodrich factory by day, rose through the Klan and built a substantial power base—a base that included more than Klansmen. He marshalled support that helped elect two governors—John Patterson in 1958 and George Wallace in 1962—and worked closely with each to advance the shared segregationist agenda.

By the time Wallace was elected, Shelton had split with the U.S. Klans, forming the Knights of Alabama in 1960. In July 1961, five hundred Klansmen from various groups met in Indian Springs, Georgia, to discuss a merger. Shelton, who had distinguished himself three months earlier by orchestrating the attacks on the Freedom Riders, emerged from the "Klonvention" as the Imperial Wizard of the new United Klans of America.

The campaign of terror waged by the Klan in the period between *Brown v. Board of Education* in 1954 and the Voting Rights Act of 1965 is well known. According to the Justice Department, over that period the Klan was responsible for seventy bombings in Georgia and Alabama, thirty Negro church burnings in Mississippi, the castration of a black man in Birmingham, ten racial killings in Alabama, and the much publicized murders of Michael Schwerner, James Chaney, and Andrew Goodman in Mississippi, Viola Liuzzo and Reverend James Reeb in Selma, and Lemuel Penn, a black army colonel killed by a sniper outside Athens, Georgia.

Shelton expressed little remorse when he talked to Patsy Sims several years after these murders. "It's unfortunate, really, there wasn't more violence. . . . Had there been enough violence it would have stopped all this [the civil rights movement]," he said.

The UKA had held rallies in honor of the two law enforcement officers accused of the Mississippi murders and the three men arrested for Liuzzo's murder. Shelton had sat at the counsel's table during the trial of one of those accused of killing Liuzzo. The Imperial Wizard, by all accounts a devoted husband and loving father, had no sympathy for the victim. "They portrayed her as being the mother of five lovely children and a community worker. . . . The fact is she was a fat slob with crud that looked like rust all over her body. She was braless," he said. As for Reeb, a white Unitarian minister from Boston clubbed to death on a Selma street: "He had been dying of cancer before he even came to Alabama."

Shelton had not made many headlines since that time, having been eclipsed by the militaristic Louis Beam and Glenn Miller and the pinstripe-suited Bill Wilkinson and David Duke. While this new-wave Klan may have been adept at terrorizing blacks, Asians, and Jews, and their allies, it didn't sit well with the traditionalist Shelton. "I don't even consider Bill Wilkinson a Klansman, or David Duke,'' he said. "They have no knowledge of Klankraft. They don't have any bylaws or constitution, any disciplinary procedure, organization structure.''

It was the UKA constitution, procedures, and organization structure that I wanted to interrogate Bobby about at his deposition in a conference room in Tuscaloosa's federal courthouse. Klan lawyer, or Klonsel, John Mays sat at his side.

Unfortunately, but not unsurprisingly, Shelton's own knowledge of Klankraft and procedures seemed to have gone up in smoke. He conceded that he had chartered Unit 900 in Mobile and that Klan revenues were generated by monthly dues, but beyond that his command of the facts was less than imperial.

I asked if he held custody of Klan records.

"I don't have any records," he replied. "I learned my lesson about that and I announced there would be no more records and I destroyed them and that is that.''

Shelton was making it difficult to find a paper trail linking the UKA to Unit 900, but we did have the charter and the cancelled checks the Hayses had sent to the national headquarters. He denied, however, that Bennie Hays had held the important supervisory position of UKA Titan.

He also provided little help tracking the trail of blood leading from Birmingham, Selma, Childersburg, and Mobile to the UKA's doorstep.

After several questions, Shelton did stipulate that Gene Thomas, one of those in the car from which the shot that killed Liuzzo was fired, had been in a UKA unit. He was less forthcoming about events in Birmingham and Childersburg. When confronted with information that Robert Chambliss, the Klansman convicted of the Sixteenth Street Baptist Church bombing, had been in the Eastview 13 Unit of the UKA, Shelton said he didn't know anything about that. He also said he could not truthfully answer whether any of the thirteen men convicted of the 1979 shooting into NAACP president Charles Woods's home in Childersburg had been members of the UKA.

Mays had represented some of the defendants in the Childersburg case. I asked him if any had been in the UKA. Even though I wasn't deposing him, I figured he might want to impress me with his knowledge. He conceded only that the three men who had turned state's evidence had publicly admitted that they were members of the United Klans.

I closed the session by reminding the Klonsel and the Wizard that we would be taking the deposition of Gary Thomas Rowe on April 27. We had found Rowe hidden in a federal witness protection program a few weeks earlier. I'd struck a nerve when I initially had phoned Mays to tell him of Rowe's deposition. "I will, will, will not be in the same room with that ma-, ma-, ma-, man," he had stammered.

Mays was true to his word. Neither he nor Bobby came to Montgomery for Rowe's deposition. They should have.

"Tommy" Rowe was part racist Klan sympathizer and part cop. In the South of the 1960s, there often wasn't too much difference—except badge holders had wider public acceptance. Each often got away with violence.

Rowe's role in the Liuzzo murder has long been a mystery. In testifying against Thomas and the two other Klansmen convicted in federal court of violating Liuzzo's civil rights, Rowe had said he was present for the murder in his capacity as an FBI operative. Over the years, a number of individuals—some reputable, some not so reputable—have suggested that Rowe encouraged the murder. "He was a federal agent provocateur," said Mays. The Liuzzo family had sued the federal government, saying that Rowe knew about the possibility of an attack and had failed in his duty to warn about it. (The Liuzzos lost.)

Gene Thomas, acknowledged by Shelton as a UKA member, had long maintained that Rowe actually fired the shots that killed Liuzzo. After Thomas, accompanied by Shelton and Mays, repeated those charges on television in 1979, Rowe was indicted for the murder by an Alabama district attorney some fourteen years after the fact. The charges were eventually dropped. Suffice it to say, however, Rowe was not on the Christmas card list of the FBI or the KKK.

The Christmas cards wouldn't have been delivered, anyway. Given a new identity, Rowe had been in witness protection since 1965. The story of how we located him is a fascinating one. Unfortunately, it cannot be told in detail without breaching several confidences. Someone who knew of Rowe's whereabouts contacted him, paving the way for a phone call.

Rowe, under an assumed name, was managing a security guard firm in a southern state when we reached him. From our research, we knew that despite his need for protection, he liked publicity. He had written a book about his experiences and appeared on a few talk shows. I told him about the case we were trying to build against Shelton and the UKA and said we wanted him to be the key witness. A dramatic account of the Liuzzo murder and the UKA's role would have an important, lasting effect on the jury.

Rowe was unenthusiastic about testifying. "That part of my life is behind me," he said.

"Man, if you believed what you professed in 1965 when you helped the FBI, then it's even more important now to stop these Klansmen," I said. After playing on his small conscience I massaged his large ego. "You're the only one who can do it, Tommy. You'll be the star of the show."

He finally agreed to talk with us. Stanton and Williams met him for breakfast in Montgomery, where they conducted an in-depth interview. They filled me in on the details before I talked with him. Since none of the defendants or Shelton or Mays was coming, I had a long conversation with Rowe before beginning the deposition. It seemed likely that this would be my only opportunity to examine him, that he would not come out of hiding and testify at the trial. In his absence we would have to read the appropriate parts of his deposition to the jury.

Beefy, with closely cropped blond hair, Tommy seemed a short version of the actor Aldo Ray. He arrived wearing a white short-sleeve shirt over an old-fashioned undershirt and brown khaki pants. His ample gut hung over his belt. He looked like the stereotypical Southern sheriff; central casting couldn't have picked a better bully.

Tommy conducted himself with the bravado of a bully, too. I promised him a starring role, and from the moment the deposition began it was clear he'd come to perform—a loud, bragging, know-it-all thug who had been made a hero for what would have sent most men to prison.

He described how an FBI agent had recruited him in 1958 to go undercover and inform on the Klan. His contact with Shelton had begun before the UKA was formed and continued until 1965. One of his earliest missions on behalf of Shelton had taken place around 1960 in Birmingham when blacks attempted to get service at a segregated Woolworth's food counter. "Members of the Klan went in and jumped on and beat up some, what we called 'sinners' at the time," Rowe said.

Not too long after this, Rowe met with Shelton and a handful of other Klansmen as well as Birmingham police Lt. Tom Cook and

Detective W. W. Self at Ivan's Restaurant in Birmingham. Shelton ran the meeting, which centered on the anticipated arrival of the Freedom Riders on Mother's Day 1961. Said Rowe:

> The discussion was for the Klan to intercept the Freedom Riders when they were coming into Birmingham and that the city officials would allow the Klan fifteen minutes, quote from Detective [*sic*] Cook, "you have got time to beat them, kick them, burn them, kill them, I don't give a shit, we just don't care. We don't ever want to see another nigger ride on the bus in Birmingham again."

Under Shelton's direction, Rowe stated, the Klan had indeed beaten and almost killed the Freedom Riders. The police had shown up late as planned; the FBI, informed by Rowe in advance of the attack, merely watched. The FBI later explained to Rowe, who was injured in the riot, that it felt it had done its job by giving advance notice to Alabama Governor Patterson and other state and local officials—none of whom did anything. Their informant Rowe did take action. We had a photograph of him striking a helpless Freedom Rider with an iron pipe as he lay on the pavement surrounded by UKA members. Rowe now identified several of these Klansmen by name. We marked the photo as an exhibit.

I was surprised to get proof of Shelton's *personal* involvement at a lunch counter sit-in beating and the Freedom Rider beatings. I had never heard the story of the sickening deal struck between the Birmingham Police and the UKA. It didn't surprise me.

We moved from Birmingham, 1961, to Birmingham, 1963. Rowe confirmed that Chambliss had been a member of the UKA when he bombed the Sixteenth Street Baptist Church. We now jumped to Selma, 1965. I asked Rowe to tell me what had happened on March 25. His detailed description of Viola Liuzzo's terror-filled last minutes made me shiver and feel deep sorrow at the same time. I thought about Bobby Shelton's cruel words about Liuzzo, and Michael Donald looking his murderers in the eye just as she had.

After an hour of questions, I turned the spotlight off Tommy Rowe. He had played his starring role well, demonstrating that Shelton had advocated violence. I wrote the letters UKA on my legal pad, sketching a hangman's noose around them.

Two weeks later we were back in Tuscaloosa deposing Bobby Shelton for a second time. The uneventful deposition centered on tax records that we had subpoenaed. One of my questions appeared to be a throwaway. I casually asked about the *Fiery Cross* newspaper and showed him several copies, including one of a 1979 issue with the headline: "Thomas Again Says Rowe Killed Viola Liuzzo."

He acknowledged that the *Fiery Cross* was the official publication of the UKA, that he was the publisher, and that it was distributed to members. I marked them as exhibits without objection from Mays, also pictured on the cover of the 1979 issue.

Bill had found these papers on a trip to the Anti-Defamation League (ADL) headquarters in New York. We had obtained the paper since forming Klanwatch in 1980. The ADL, a longtime and effective foe of the Klan and other extremist groups, had monitored Shelton much longer. Going through microfilm after microfilm of past issues of the *Fiery Cross* to find statements promoting violence, Bill had found a picture worth a thousand words. Shelton didn't even bother to look at it.

It was a big mistake.

CHAPTER 19

May 1986   Butner, North Carolina

The man with the scarred face, the metal arm, and the blown-off testicle had heard of me. "Glenn and Steve Miller told me there's a price on your head and someone's going to kill you," he said.

"That's old news," I replied. "I'm here to talk to you about something else."

Sliding his molded plastic chair forward with his good arm, Robert Norman Jones took a pack of cigarettes and a book of matches out of his pocket. I offered to light his Marlboro, but he shook his head. He lifted the cover of the matchbook with his good hand, then held the book with his hook, pulled off a match and struck it, lighting his cigarette. Danny Welch and I watched in amazement as he performed this delicate task. "I got blown up pounding a fuckin' rocket in my garage," he said after taking a long drag. "My hearing's shot, too. You're gonna have to speak up."

"I want to talk with you about Glenn Miller," I said.

Jones heard me fine. "Shit," he said. "I got nothing to say to you."

Danny, who had left National Security to become Klanwatch's chief investigator, and I had come on a hunch to the Federal Corrections Institute in Butner, a small town twenty-two miles north of Raleigh. We hadn't phoned ahead, so we had no idea whether Jones would talk to us or what he had to say if he would talk. My curiosity about this former marine and munitions expert—it was a bit difficult to think of him as an expert considering his physical state—had been triggered by a news item from almost a year earlier.

In the summer of 1985, Jones was arrested by an undercover agent in Fayetteville, North Carolina, for conspiring to buy stolen military

266

weapons and explosives. Ordinarily such an arrest would not have interested Klanwatch. But, in searching his home, authorities had found White Patriot Party literature.

The White Patriot Party (WPP) had been formed by Glenn Miller in March 1985, two months after we settled the Person case. We had carefully watched Miller's activities since the settlement, and his press release announcing the new organization was ominous.

Effective March 15, 1985, I officially disbanded the Confederate Knights of the Ku Klux Klan, and formed the WHITE PATRIOT PARTY.

The lying subversive and unAmerican JEWISH CONTROLLED liberal media has never and will never tell the truth about the Klan. . . . That is why we have become the WHITE PATRIOT PARTY.

Though our tactics will change, our goal remains the same. That goal is the UNIFICATION OF WHITE PEOPLE. . . .

We will work legally and peaceably within the system, as long as the federal government does. When the federal government returns to the "dirty tricks" tactics of the 1960s . . . then, of course, we will be forced to adopt the tactics of our REVOLUTIONARY FOREFATHERS. . . . Our contingency plans are already made. . . .

The federal government is at this minute plotting to frame myself and possibly other leaders within our organization. . . . They have been ordered by their Jew masters to stop Glenn Miller. . . .

When they take away our constitutional rights . . . , we as FREEDOM LOVING Patriots have no choice but to resort to UNDERGROUND REVOLUTIONARY TACTICS . . . with the armed resources at our disposal.

This threatening tone matched other Miller statements as well as the public and private activities of the WPP. On May 11, 1985, Miller publicly announced the party was planning to "conduct murder and treason trials of selected defendants," including "ultraliberal federal judges, neocommunist congressmen and senators, neocommunist professors, and neocommunist newspaper and television magnates." Miller vowed that if these "murderers and traitors" were convicted, they would be sentenced to death "immediately following the victory of the White Patriot Party, which will be complete by the year 1992."

Eight days later, Miller and members of the WPP had "convicted" Bernard Nathanson, a Jewish doctor from New York, in absentia. Nathanson's crime? "Treason against the U.S.A. and conspiracy to commit genocide against the White Race" because he supported the pro-choice movement. Either Miller's knowledge of current affairs was poor or he didn't believe a Jew could be redeemed; at the time the WPP's court was trying him, Dr. Nathanson was making the rounds on the pro-life circuit, promoting a movie called *The Silent Scream* and claiming his past support for abortion had been wrong. The WPP newsletter's account of the trial concluded: "Many more Jews and their puppets will be tried . . . and subsequent judgments will be carried out . . . even if it requires the use of every telephone and light pole on every interstate highway across the length and bredth [*sic*] of the united rebel states."

In November, Miller announced that the WPP was "a citizens' militia," adding, "It is our irrevocable goal to create a White Republic within the geographical bounds of the Southern United States, consisting of a minimum of one million square miles." To accomplish this, his leaders would "organize the White masses into political and military units."

In February, Miller publicly threatened "to resort to armed revolution," replacing North Carolina's duly elected political leaders if the state's legislators refused to respond to his written questionnaire on racial issues. And on April 4, he contacted Johnson County, North Carolina, law enforcement officials and offered the services of "one thousand armed and uniformed" members of his organization to quell what he termed "a black insurrection" in an interracial school dispute.

The presence of Miller's armed and uniformed men on the streets in a North Carolina town would have been nothing new. Ten days after Miller drove me to the Raleigh airport, three hundred of his men had conducted marching drills on the streets of the city. Since then, at least five similar marches had occurred in other cities.

Miller's public statements were constitutionally protected, and I would be the first to defend his right to make a fool of himself. The WPP's secret activities worried us, however. Our investigation—led by Danny Welch and aided by certain law enforcement officials in North Carolina—revealed paramilitary activities far more extensive than we had been aware of when the settlement agreement had been executed. These activities included training in the use of sophisticated firearms, river crossings, map usage, escape and evasion, and hand-to-hand combat.

Was the federal government in real danger from Miller and the WPP? No, but Glenn Miller constituted a real danger to society. Those who dismissed him as a crackpot—and there were many in the media and law enforcement community in this category—were dead wrong. This man had an extensive military background. This man had two hundred thousand dollars in cash thanks to the late Robert Mathews, according to the testimony of a surviving member of the Order at the 1985 trial; two hundred thousand dollars could buy a lot of weapons. This man had approximately twenty-three hundred followers, according to our information. And, perhaps most frightening, this man had recruited former military officers and active-duty marines to train party members.

The WPP was not your stereotypical Klan group of beer-drinking rednecks with a few shotguns in their arsenal, but rather a group with a military structure, military leaders, military weapons, and military drill instructors capable of doing great harm and itching to go to war.

We had garnered information supporting young David Wallace's claim that he had seen active military men helping Miller's forces. Danny and his sources secured two color photos of active-duty marines training WPP "soldiers." The sight of these United States military officers working with a militia committed to Miller's goals shocked and sickened. I saw it as a call to arms for us. Any tendency that we might have had to dismiss Miller as a buffoon flew out the window the moment we saw those photographs. Not only was it morally wrong for U.S. soldiers to be involved with the WPP, it was dangerous. Further professionalization of Miller's "elite forces" could prove deadly.

Active-duty marines. That intelligence was so distressing that I sent Secretary of Defense Caspar Weinberger a letter requesting immediate action. I enclosed the photographs and asked him to prohibit active-duty members of the United States Armed Services from holding membership in the Ku Klux Klan and Klan-related groups, and from taking part in KKK activities. I requested he publicly identify active-duty marines from Camp Lejeune shown in Klanwatch intelligence to be participating in WPP paramilitary activities. And I asked him to make public a list of all military hardware, such as guns and explosives, that had been lost, stolen, or misplaced from any North Carolina military facility over the past five years. Our information suggested that a great deal of hardware was missing and much of it had gone to groups like the WPP.

"It is simply intolerable that members of the U.S. armed forces, sworn to uphold and defend the Constitution of the United States, be allowed to hold membership in an organization which seeks to overthrow the federal government through violent means . . . and to actively participate in such groups' armed paramilitary exercises," I wrote.

There was, I realized, a First Amendment question here. Didn't these marines have a constitutional right to assemble with whom they pleased and espouse whatever beliefs they wished? At the same time I wrote the letter to Secretary Weinberger, Richard Cohen, the Center's new legal director, prepared a memorandum on the constitutional issues raised by our demands. A graduate of Columbia University and the University of Virginia Law School, Richard, thirty-one, had replaced Dennis Balske, who had left to pursue his longtime dream of building a criminal law practice. Richard had worked at Chuck Morgan's Washington, D.C., firm before joining us. Chuck had described him as "brilliant." The memorandum confirmed that assessment, convincing me we stood on firm legal ground to call for Pentagon action.

My observation of the federal bureaucracy during the Carter years made it clear that letters written by private citizens to cabinet members raise a variation of the old question: If a tree falls in the forest and no one hears it, has it made a noise? The noise most cabinet members listened to came from the *New York Times.* I called Bill Schmidt of the *Times*'s Atlanta bureau, and told him we had an important story for him.

Schmidt's exclusive, "Soldiers Said to Attend Klan-Related Activities," ran the same day that we held a press conference for the rest of the media. The military promised to look into the matter immediately to see if any civilian laws or military regulations were being breached.

Glenn Miller phoned me at home after learning of the press conference. I hung up on him before he could finish his angry message. A few days later, Cecil Cox, one of Miller's inner circle, phoned to tell me it was "the Führer's birthday" and that he wanted to wish me a happy birthday, too, on this "special occasion." I hung up again.

A few days before the press conference, we had filed a motion to hold Mike Lewis in criminal contempt of court for calling Bobby Person's home and making threatening remarks in violation of the year-old court agreement not to harass Person and other blacks. The day after Cox's call, we filed a motion to hold Miller and the WPP (which Judge Britt had already ruled was a successor to the CKKKK) in criminal contempt for operating a paramilitary organization in violation of the agreement. If we could prove that Miller had violated Judge Britt's order reflecting the terms of the settlement agreement, the judge had the power to put Miller in prison. The sentence for contempt of court was a mild one, but if we could cut off the head of the WPP, there was a good chance the body would die. At the same time, if we could demonstrate that Miller was a real danger, we might persuade state or federal law enforcement officials to prosecute him for more serious crimes. As private citizens, we had no power to bring any criminal charges against him except contempt of court.

We filed a motion for a protective order as well, concerned again for our safety inside and outside the Raleigh courthouse. We didn't want threatening phone calls. And we didn't want Miller's men to visit us as they had Mike Lewis.

Lewis called me a week after we filed the contempt action against him, explaining that his "memory loss" at his November 1984 deposition, when he had denied previously making admissions to me about Miller's knowledge of a cross-burning and other activities, resulted from Miller's intimidation. He also related a terrifying story of a late-night visit early in 1985 from four men wearing paramilitary uniforms. He had recognized one of the men as a member of Miller's Confederate Knights.

I taped our conversation:

Q: What did they have at your head?
A: A three-fifty-seven.
Q: And tell me exactly what they said now.
A: "If you keep talking to Morris Dees, you're gonna end up like David."

David Wallace was the Klan member killed by another Klansman, James Holder, in 1983.

Our May 1984 conversation with Holder had persuaded us to file the Person suit in the first place. Now, two years later, Holder was serving eighteen years in Sampson County Prison for second-degree murder. Stanton went to talk with him about our criminal contempt action against Miller. Although reluctant to talk at first, in due course Holder reaffirmed his previous testimony about paramilitary activities and disclosed critical new information. Miller did everything by the book, Holder said, and that book was *The Turner Diaries*. The Grand Dragon and Commander-in-Chief of the WPP had instructed unit leaders like Holder to read this 211-page blueprint for revolution and to order members serving under them to read it.

I reread *The Turner Diaries*. The Great Revolution, the subject of the novel, had started in late 1991. As part of that revolution, the paramilitary soldiers who overthrew the U.S. government conducted extralegal trials and executions of Jewish business and media leaders, federal judges, liberal congressmen, and others who had betrayed the Aryan values of America, hanging guilty parties from telephone poles along the streets and highways of America. A look at Miller's statements and the account of the WPP's "trial" of Dr. Nathanson made it clear that the book was Miller's bible, just as it had been the bible of Robert Mathews and the Order.

Having learned I was at the top of Mathew's hit list, I followed the September 1985 trial of the surviving members of the Order with great interest. Two dozen of them had been charged with conducting a criminal enterprise for the purpose of overthrowing the federal government. Thirteen had pleaded guilty.

At this trial in Seattle, the full extent of the Order's activities had been detailed. A revolutionary band of some thirty men and women had robbed businesses and armored cars of more than four million dollars, stockpiled vast supplies of high-tech, military-type weapons, trained as a paramilitary organization, held extralegal trials of traitors, handed out death sentences, and murdered Alan Berg.

In December, the jury found ten of the eleven on trial guilty of various charges. They received lengthy prison terms.

Tom Martinez had testified for the government. Mathews had thought he was recruiting Martinez for the Order, but in fact, Martinez was an informant for the FBI. At his secrecy-shrouded late-night meeting at the darkened Portland car wash, he had told agents of the plot on my life. They had relayed the information to Montgomery, and when Welch had heard of the threat he had immediately called me in Mobile. Martinez's testimony at the trial marked the first time I heard the full extent of Mathew's plans for me. I later thanked him for saving my skin, quite literally.

Three weeks after the verdict in the Order case, Miller and the WPP marched through the streets of Raleigh holding a large sign reading WE LOVE THE ORDER. The day before I went to Butner to see Robert Norman Jones, we filed an amended complaint adding material about Miller's support of the Order, reliance on *The Turner Diaries,* and intent to overthrow the U.S. government by 1992.

Miller's defense, like that of Louis Beam in Texas, contended that he and the WPP were doing nothing more than exercising their constitutional rights to assemble, to speak freely, and to bear arms. We were mistaken, he insisted, in describing his activities as paramilitary training in violation of the applicable North Carolina statutes. He and his friends and followers had the right to gather on private property for target practice or shooting competitions. They also had the right, he said, to learn how to protect themselves, to engage in defensive maneuvers. They weren't doing anything illegal and didn't have any illegal weapons, Miller said. I was hoping Jones might tell me a different story.

Sitting in the canteen at the Butner Correctional Institute, Bob Jones told me he had become a religious man since going to prison. "I've read the Bible cover to cover two or three fuckin' times," he said. "I'm putting all the shit in my past behind me."

I wanted to know about that past, but Jones seemed hesitant to talk about it. "Fuck, man, they'd kill me in a minute," he said, raising his metal arm. "I'm not as good as I used to be at defending myself."

I sized up Jones, as I had sized up sales prospects, clients, jurors, and witnesses my whole life. He had only fourteen months left to serve. A promise to help him obtain early release—always a liability when it came to witness credibility at a trial anyway—was of little value. How could I win over this profane ex-marine and find out if he knew any valuable information?

"Bob, do you really read the Bible?"

He took a drag on his cigarette and nodded.

"You know, I used to preach a little," I said. "I think the most important passage in the whole Bible is Romans, chapter eight, verse twenty-eight. You know that verse?"

He shook his head.

"Let's see if we can't get us a Bible," I said.

It's easy to find the Good Book in a penitentiary. I paraphrased the passage before opening the Gideon's a guard brought us: "Everything works for the good of those who love the Lord."

I handed Jones the Bible. "I really believe that," I said. He scanned the passage as I continued. "Bob, I don't know what you were into with Glenn Miller, but he's a bad man. Say those explosives you tried to sell the cop had gotten to Glenn. The man wants to start a race war. Could you live with yourself if Glenn and his boys put some of that C-four shit under a school bus that carried black kids and then blew it up by remote control? Seventy-five kids dead just like that."

We were afraid of this. Miller had the knowledge, capability, and perhaps the weaponry, to take out a school bus, synagogue, or predominantly black school, triggering widespread disorder that would afford his men the opportunity to fire guns on public streets, not just on private property. This probably wouldn't topple our "Zionist Occupation Government" that *The Turner Diaries* constantly referred to, but it could lead to death and destruction.

Jones didn't respond. I continued. "If you really believe in the Bible, man, tell me what you were up to. Tell me about Glenn. Believe me, everything works to the good of those who love the Lord," I said.

Jones glanced around the canteen. The warden had told me there were no private conference rooms available. We were sitting in a public area; there was a chance that we might be overheard. I understood Jones's fears. It would be dangerous if someone sympathetic to Miller found out he snitched. He stubbed his cigarette and quickly lit another one. "Okay, man," he said.

I don't know if his heart was pounding when he finished fifteen minutes later, but mine was. "Bob, that is an incredible story. You have to let a court reporter write that down. This man has to be stopped. There are innocent lives at stake here." I was not exaggerating. Jones's story, along with our knowledge about active-duty marines and Miller's ties to the Order, made it clear the Center had to win this lawsuit. If we were going to win, Jones's testimony would be essential.

Hoping for the best, we had brought a court reporter along. We'd left her in the waiting room so Jones wouldn't feel intimidated. I now suggested we call her in.

"I can't testify, man," Jones said looking anxiously around the canteen again. "They will fuckin' kill me in a fuckin' minute."

"I understand you're scared," I said. "I would be, too. But I've got an idea." We would seal the statement the moment we got it back from the court reporter. The only ones to see it would be Judge Britt and, possibly, someone from the Justice Department who could arrange protection. After I took his statement about his relationship to Miller, I'd take another statement about his fear for his safety and show that to the government.

He agreed. I called in the court reporter, and Bob Jones, the man who had, as I'd suspected, supplied Glenn Miller with weapons and trained his forces, provided us with vital information.

It took a while for everything good to come to Jones. Two days after meeting with him, we filed an *in camera* motion (literally, in chambers; only Judge Britt would see this) asking the court to devise a witness protection plan for him. We attached Jones's statement. The next day in Washington, D.C., Stanton and I went to see Linda Davis, chief of the Criminal Section of the Civil Rights Division of the Justice Department, and two of her aides. After sharing our information with them, we requested the Justice Department assist the court in providing a witness protection program for Jones. They agreed to look into it.

Ten days later, the Justice Department informed the court that it couldn't provide a program. We were shocked. Jones's explosive story should have launched a federal investigation. We were suddenly in danger of losing our star witness. Jones would not testify without a guarantee that he would be safe after his release from prison.

Okay. He needed protection? We'd supply it. There was nothing in the law prohibiting a private body like the Center from arranging with a private firm like National Security to protect a private citizen like Bob Jones. I told Jones the Center would create and pay for a witness protection plan. He was skeptical at first, but after I told him Don Terry's outfit had kept me alive and protected the Saudi Arabian royal family on its visits to the United States, he agreed. We filed the plan, again *in camera*, with Judge Britt.

With Jones set to testify, it was time to visit another important witness sitting in prison, James Holder. He, too, had seen the light, telling me that he had interpreted Bill Stanton's recent visit as a message from God to straighten out his life. Toward that end, and with the hope that we would put in a good word for him with the governor, he was willing to testify and to provide photographs of WPP training sessions, taken for the *White Carolinian*, Miller's official publication.

We were interrupted by a guard who said I had an important call from the Center in the warden's office. On the short walk from the prison conference room, I thought to myself that with Jones and Holder as our key witnesses, we'd have a pretty strong case if the jury could be persuaded to believe a born-again bombmaker and a born-again murderer trying to curry favor for an early release.

"Are you sitting down?" Stanton asked over the phone.

"What is it?" I asked.

"Judge Britt just ruled on Bill Martin's motion to disqualify you."

My stomach churned. Martin was the talented federal public defender assigned to represent Miller after Miller claimed no North Carolina lawyer would take his case. He had moved to disqualify me as the plaintiffs' lawyer, arguing that as a private citizen I could not stand in the government's shoes and prosecute Miller for the alleged crime of criminal contempt of court; only the U.S. attorney could prosecute this action.

Judge Britt, Bill told me, agreed with Martin in part, ordering that the case be turned over to the U.S. attorney in Raleigh, Sam Currin. The judge had ruled that I could continue as a special prosecutor to assist Currin. This was hardly encouraging. Currin could drop the case if he wanted. And even if he didn't drop it, we would no longer be in charge. The U.S. attorney would call the shots.

I had never met Currin. I did know, however, that he'd been an aide to Senator Jesse Helms, and that Helms had sponsored him for his current position. Right-wing Jesse Helms! Case dismissed. I hurried back to Raleigh to see if I could prevent that from happening.

I walked into Sam Currin's office, wondering if I would have to use Romans 8:28 on him, too. He was a pale, soft-faced man of thirty-eight with horn-rimmed glasses and every hair combed in place Sunday-school fashion. In spite of the gallery of Helms and Reagan photos on his wall and the *Report of the President's Commission on Pornography* (on which he had served proudly) on his desk, I liked him. He was a soft-spoken straight shooter.

Over lunch at a downtown tearoom, we got to know each other, one ex–Southern Baptist and the leading deacon of Raleigh's prominent Hayes Barton Baptist Church. In his distinct eastern North Carolina dialect, Currin told me he had grown up in the country outside Raleigh and then attended Wake Forest University and the University of North Carolina Law School before signing on with the country's most conservative senator.

He confessed he didn't know too much about Glenn Miller or our case. "Let's go back to my offices and you can show me what you've got," he said.

I spent two hours reviewing my files with him, building the case against Miller, building the case to let me help him vigorously prosecute the Grand Dragon. Clearly a sharp guy, Currin sat patiently through my sometimes emotional presentation, asking several good questions.

When I had finally finished, he stood up. "You've opened my eyes, Morris," he said. "I'll stand behind you a hundred percent on this one. Where do we start?"

I told my new law partner that I wanted him to meet Bob Jones first, and then talk with a half dozen other key witnesses.

"Fine," he said, looking over the case files spread out on his conference table. "We'd better find you an office. You'll need a key to the federal building, an electronic access card, and the code to our suite." In just a few hours, conservative Sam Currin had placed more trust in me than many liberal civil rights lawyers and prosecutors whom I'd known for years. Labels don't mean a damn thing.

The next day Richard Cohen and I moved our files into the "pig room," the office where Currin and his colleagues stored important evidence for a current pornography case. Apparently they considered the evidence there so much pig slop: stacks of girlie magazines, eight large boxes full of "pornographic" videotapes, a television, and VCR.

The Miller trial was less than two weeks away, but I told myself if I had time I'd watch a couple of these and see what the federal government was calling objectionable these days. I couldn't imagine it was any more obscene than what Glenn Miller and the White Patriot party were doing.

CHAPTER 20

July 1986   Raleigh, North Carolina

Grabbing his submachine gun, my brother Leslie poked his head out the motel door into the already steamy morning air. He, more than anyone, had inherited Daddy's looks. More important, he had also inherited Daddy's uncanny eye for shooting.

Leslie looked the parking lot over, then moved quickly outside and scanned it again. After thirty seconds, he came back to the door and silently motioned for us to follow him to the cars. Flanked by Danny Welch and two heavily armed National Security bodyguards, Richard Cohen, Bill Stanton, and I hustled across the hot pavement. Lt. Tommy Coleman, an Alabama state trooper given an official leave so he could protect us, closed the door and brought up the rear. He, too, carried a submachine gun—courtesy of Leslie, a licensed firearms dealer. The sophisticated radio equipment in our three cars—the more automobiles in your convoy, the better, Don Terry had advised—had also been provided by an Alabama law enforcement agency.

We snaked our way through the main streets and side streets of Raleigh. This "evasive counter-terrorist driving" meant it would take twice as long to reach our destination. That was fine with me, as long as we reached it. I fingered my gun. Richard tapped his fingers nervously on the seat. "Helluva way to try a case, huh?" I asked. He didn't answer.

The tall glass building glistened in the early morning light. Our convoy pulled up to the curb in front of the main entrance. As we had hoped, the sidewalk was empty. The courthouse would not open to the public for another half hour; we had beaten the White Patriots to the punch.

Leslie and the bodyguards guided us to the door. A U.S. marshall, advised by Sam Currin that we were on our way, let us in. The color returned to our faces. Once in Sam's suite, we went over *Person v. Miller* one last time.

By the time we reached the hallway leading to Judge Britt's courtroom, the doors to the building had opened. The people we had successfully avoided on the street crowded the corridor. Their commander had ordered them to wear civvies instead of combat fatigues, wisely reasoning that when you're on trial for operating a paramilitary organization you don't have your men dress as if they were preparing to invade Grenada. Although out of uniform, the White Patriots were not out of character. When they saw us, they swarmed in our direction, as loud and determined as bees. Leslie and Danny positioned themselves in front of us as we pushed our way to the courtroom, stung only by words.

A traditional federal-courthouse metal detector stood in the lobby. Another metal detector was positioned directly outside the courtroom. I confessed I'd rarely seen this kind of security. "Only once," said Richard, grimacing, ". . . outside a Mafia trial in Chicago."

As I entered the courtroom, someone in the hall shouted, "One shot is all it takes, Dees." I was delighted to see ten federal marshalls (some brought in from out of state, we later learned) stationed strategically to prevent any shots. "Only six marshalls at the Mafia trial," Richard whispered to me.

Like his men, Glenn Miller was out of uniform, looking uncomfortable in an ill-fitting tan suit with no tie. His court-appointed lawyer, Bill Martin, sat with him at the counsel's table, along with Stephen Miller, whom we had added as a defendant after hearing Bob Jones's account of WPP events. Stephen appeared quite comfortable in tan pants, a blue blazer, and tie. The self-assured second-in-command had turned down Judge Britt's offer of a public defender, saying he felt he could defend himself. Just in case he could not, the judge had taken the precaution of appointing him an advisory lawyer, called stand-by counsel.

By the time Judge Britt took the bench, the Patriots had taken most of the seats in the courtroom. Glenn Miller's ex-wife and their four children sat in the front row. The children were cute. Their presence would humanize their father, the man we were trying to portray as a hate monger. I was sorry they'd come.

The prosecutor's table was closest to the jury—one of the many perks for the government since the ball game is played on its field. I

felt odd sitting there, and for a moment I pictured myself a traitor to
the criminal defense bar. Sam Currin's opening statement put an end
to that foolish thought.

Sam had been the perfect partner since entering the case. He had
told Richard and me that, although he retained ultimate responsibility
for the case, *Person v. Miller* was ours to try. He would provide
whatever legal and technical help we needed and would assist in the
courtroom. Naturally, as U.S. attorney, he would have final say. We
had agreed that we would divide the opening statement: He would
explain the charges to the jury and provide an overview. I would
outline the specifics of our case.

> Ladies and gentlemen of the jury . . . this is a very serious matter,
> and this is a very important case. It's important for the United
> States. . . .
>
> Some of the evidence may shock you. You will see and hear preju-
> dice, bigotry, and hate. You will learn about a Klan paramilitary force
> that obtains stolen military arms and explosives and uses active-duty and
> ex-military personnel for training. You will hear evidence as to how this
> Klan army plans to take power by force. And you will see the absolute
> disdain that the defendants have for the United States government and
> the rights of minority citizens. . . .

Sam delivered exactly what was needed. The jury had to hear the
United States attorney, not the executive director of the Southern
Poverty Law Center, emphasize the importance of the case to the
United States as well as the disdain of both Millers for the govern-
ment.

Our pretrial strategy sessions resulted in a twenty-three-page case
outline. I took one last glance at the section titled "Opening Statement" before following Sam to a lectern just a few feet away from the
jury box. "The jury will find it hard to believe that a bigmouthed
publicity hound like Miller is seriously planning to do in the government and kill blacks and Jews. We must be extremely serious and
thorough when outlining the evidence," read our outline.

I did not need to remind myself that Glenn Miller had to be taken
seriously. There was no doubt in my mind that this was the most
dangerous Klansman in America. Apparently, the Justice Department
finally agreed with me; it had sent several observers to the trial. If we
could prove our case, the federal government might be encouraged
to indict the Millers for more serious crimes.

Proving our case was no sure thing. The Glenn Miller the jury had heard of or seen was the self-appointed sergeant who marched his uniformed men down city streets to bagpipe music; the perennial candidate for governor or senator, whose assertions about Jews and blacks and the leaders of the United States were so outrageous that they almost seemed harmless. It was this prejudice—prejudging of the Millers—we as prosecutors would have to overcome.

I scrutinized the jurors: eleven white faces, one black one. That didn't bother me. In using all its peremptory challenges to exclude blacks, the defense had let a number of open-minded, progressive whites remain. I began:

> There are two sides to the White Patriot Party. If you happen to be in the street when they come marching by, you see the public side— protesting, exercising First Amendment rights.
>
> That public side is not what this case is all about. This case is also not about distributing hate literature, even though it might be repulsive to you. This case is not about unpopular views.

As I said this, I thought to myself how far we'd come since I'd been a young boy sitting in front of my uncle Lucien's country store, listening to the popular talk about the "niggers." Now it was Glenn Miller's views that were unpopular. I continued:

> These defendants and their members operate a dangerous paramilitary organization. They meet in secret. Their conduct violates this court's order. That's what this case is about.

The Millers and the WPP, the successor to the CKKKK, had violated the court order in three ways: They had operated a paramilitary organization, and they had violated two North Carolina statutes. The first statute made it illegal to "band together and muster or drill, or practice any military evolutions, except by virtue of the authority of any officer recognized by law or of an instructor in institutions or schools in which such evolutions form a part of the course of instruction." The second statute barred teaching or demonstrating to any person "the use, application, or making of any firearm, explosive, or incendiary device or technique capable of causing injury or death to persons, knowing or having reason to know that the same will be employed for use in or in furtherance of a civil disorder."

If these statutes appear confusing or unclear on the printed page, imagine what they sound like when presented orally to the jury in an opening statement. Bill Martin's well-conceived defense played on the difficulty of understanding the meaning of the settlement agreement and the statutes. Don't look at the uniforms, *The Turner Diaries,* the weapons, he told the jury in his opening statement. Look at the word "and" in the settlement agreement. Glenn agreed not to operate a paramilitary organization *and* violate two statutes. Operating a paramilitary organization by itself was permissible under the agreement, as long as the statutes weren't violated, insisted Martin. This is like someone agreeing not to drink *and* drive. It's okay to drink as long as you don't drive. Glenn Miller, Martin accurately noted, had struck the word "or" in my original draft of the agreement and inserted the word "and." He never would have allowed Judge Britt to enter the order if he had thought he'd have to cease those activities now being characterized as "paramilitary," Martin told the jury.

As for the statutes, Martin said, they were also confusing. The official heading of the first statute read "Secret Political and Military Organizations Prohibited." Glenn didn't knowingly or willfully violate this because he operated his organization in public, not secretly. And he didn't violate the second statute because he and his men engaged only in legal, defensive training.*

The battle lines had been drawn with more than a little irony. We were trying to blow our opponent away with military hardware, munitions experts like Bob Jones, and *The Turner Diaries.* The Millers were using the dictionary and the *Elements of Style.* For this trial at least, I hoped I had been wrong when I'd written Glenn that the pen was mightier than the sword.

We began our assault with a former eighty-second Airborne paratrooper, James Holder. In naming Holder a "Klansman of the Month" several years earlier, Glenn Miller had written:

> [James] is the type white man with the courage, the willpower, perseverance, and the out-and-out gumption that will one day arrive from our race by the millions to fight the holy battle against the Jew-led Communist mongrel herds and will create out of the ashes a great White nation.

The new James Holder was fighting the "holy battle" on our side now. After establishing that Holder was Glenn Miller's man in charge

---

*Bill Martin had previously filed a motion to dismiss the case based, in large part, on the confusing nature of the statutes. At a hearing shortly before the trial, Richard Cohen had argued that both Glenn and Stephen Miller, with their extensive military backgrounds, knew what the statutes meant. Indeed, said Richard, the two men had actively lobbied against one of the statutes. Richard can quickly master facts and develop devastating legal arguments few opponents have successfully countered. Judge Britt had denied the motion.

in Sanford, I focused on *The Turner Diaries,* which Holder described as Miller's bible. He outlined the plan for revolution in the book, noting that Miller had distributed the book to new members.

Q: Did Glenn Miller do anything to carry out the plan in this book?

A: Yes. We were organizing small groups throughout the state of North Carolina . . . putting them in uniform, getting them weapons and getting them trained in paramilitary-type tactics.

Q: Did Glenn Miller tell you the purpose for having this paramilitary organization?

A: When what was known as "when the balloon goes up," we will use these small groups to go against the United States government to bring an economic as well as psychological downfall.

Q: Did Glenn Miller tell you what, if anything, his organization . . . would do to black people when he took power?

A: We were to get the blacks to disarm themselves, give themselves up to us. . . . We were supposed to put them on ships, supposedly leaking ships, send them back to Africa. And to help them leak we would blow them up.

Q: What, if anything, did Mr. Glenn Miller tell you his paramilitary army would do with Jews when he took power in 1991?

A: Lynch them.

As I'd hoped, the jury was stunned, not amused. It was important now to show them the steps Glenn Miller had taken to put this horrifying plan in action. Holder obliged by describing Miller's army as "an underground elite fighting force." Among the elite, he said, were active-duty military personnel he had recruited from Camp Lejeune with both Glenn and Steve Miller's blessing. He named names and described the paramilitary activities: "seek out and destroy missions, search and ambush, counterambush, river crossings." They used U.S. Army and Marine Corps manuals obtained from the National Guard armory in Sanford, said Holder, "the same thing a United States Army soldier would have to know or use."

Q: Did Glenn Miller have an occasion to discuss with you his description of training as being defensive training?

A: . . . Mr. Miller indicated to me that we were not doing paramilitary training for the fact that the law would come down on us. He said, "We got to tell each time we give a class that this training is just for defensive-type training only and not to violate anyone's civil rights." Then, later on when none of his people was around, he would laugh and say, "We are doing this to cover our ass. We have to say this."

Holder recalled a visit from Joseph Momier of the North Carolina State Bureau of Investigation. Glenn Miller had told Momier that the group only engaged in defensive training. "After Momier . . . left," said Holder, "it was a big laugh. We sat and joked about it because we had blew a smoke screen."

Using photographs taken for the *White Carolinian,* Holder detailed a variety of maneuvers, such as ambush training. I introduced the photographs into evidence, showing them to the jury. Now we brought in the weapons that the former Klansman of the Month maintained were used on the maneuvers. Judge Britt assured the jury that these exhibits were not loaded, adding that he had taken the additional precaution of instructing lawyers and witnesses not to point them. The jurors sat up straight as the federal marshalls brought in a Mini-14 rifle and semiautomatic AR-15.

Glenn Miller had discussed with Holder the need to find a place to hide explosives, weapons, and fuel in Holder's den area, Sanford/Lee County. This area had been designated a stronghold for the revolution because of two major power plants, an airport, four intersecting U.S. highways, and a large hospital. "It was easy for a small group of men to seize and hold." Holder and Steve Miller flew over the region in Miller's plane, checking out its strategic assets.

Those assets would be used during that magic period 1991–1992.

Q: Did Glenn Miller tell you whether that had any connection with *The Turner Diaries?*
A: Glenn Miller and Stephen Miller both told me and other members of the organization that the sequence of events were falling into place just like *The Turner Diaries.*

Holder's testimony, delivered sincerely if not articulately, had exactly the impact we had hoped. It opened the juror's eyes, wide. We didn't think any ambiguity existed in the settlement agreement or the applicable statutes, but even if there was, such ambiguity seemed meaningless after this talk of weapons and lynchings conducted by an elite force trained by active military personnel.

One glaring weakness showed in Holder's testimony, and Bill Martin didn't miss it. "He has not participated or been a participant of the

White Patriot Party since 1983," Martin told Judge Britt after cross-examining Holder. "[I] would like to move to strike his testimony on the basis of irrelevancy."

Martin's point, which we had anticipated, had some merit. The criminal contempt charges centered on activity that took place after Glenn Miller and I settled the original *Person* case in January of 1985, almost two years after Holder left the organization. Holder had been in prison since his conviction in the summer of 1984. We responded that we were trying to sketch the overall plan being implemented by the Millers, and we could link Holder's testimony with that of other witnesses who had participated since 1985.

Judge Britt denied Martin's motion, but added, "I will wait and see how it develops. I may entertain it later."

Holder had testified that Steve Miller had attended weapons training sessions and helped conduct maneuvers. Not only a sergeant of the elite forces, Steve also served as the party's chaplain. Cross-examining Holder, Steve Miller tried to cloak himself in religious robes rather than Klan robes or combat fatigues. "Did I advocate following the Bible more than *The Turner Diaries* or *The Turner Diaries* more than the Bible?" he asked.

Holder's answer made me smile: "In my opinion, both."

We had told the jury that the evidence would show that active-duty marines helped instruct the Millers' elite forces. It was time to call in the marines and army. We had intended to begin with Ward Erik Frazier, a soldier in the U.S. Army, currently stationed at Fort Bragg. Although a low-level member of the WPP, Frazier had used an M-14 to patrol the perimeter in uniform at a WPP rally. He was an important witness because he demonstrated that the Millers still had the same aims and operating procedure as when James Holder had been active.

Frazier, however, could not testify. He was incommunicado . . . literally. Someone had broken his jaw on the eve of the trial. His mouth was now wired shut—one way of making sure his words couldn't hurt the party or its leaders. This assault not only weakened our case, but our knees, too. There was little question that the White Patriots would use violence to win in court.

Fortunately, no one had silenced Richard Pounder.

Q: [Mr. Pounder,] did your discharge [from the U.S. Marine Corps on April 14, 1986] have anything to do with your membership in the White Patriot Party?

A: It was the reason for my discharge.

Q: Were you given a choice of staying in the United States Marines or staying a member of the White Patriot Party?

A: I stayed with the White Patriot Party.

A recent U.S. Marines advertising campaign was built around the slogan "We're Looking for a Few Good Men." Glenn Miller found one of those men in Richard Pounder, who had been forced to decide between the Klan and the USMC after the *New York Times*'s Bill Schmidt had called Camp Lejeune. On learning of Pounder's ties to Miller, the marine brass had told the soldier he could not serve two masters. He chose to serve Glenn Miller. According to the *Confederate Leader,* the successor publication to the *White Carolinian,* Pounder was named Soldier of the Month by Miller, assisting Steve Miller in fire-arms training while still a member of the Marine Corps. He was our first actual link between the Millers' presettlement and postsettlement paramilitary activities.

A hostile witness—perhaps this was why his jaw was still function-ing—Pounder was a roommate of Cecil Cox, another former marine now third in command in the party. He didn't want to divulge any-thing more than the proverbial name, rank, and serial number. Photo-graphs of the Millers and others in action were too hazy for him to identify. His own memory was equally hazy.

We knew he would not be cooperative, but we managed to elicit a few facts from him: He described the uniforms and military aspects of the current WPP; he admitted obtaining an M-14 with an extended thirty-round clip that he practiced with at the WPP headquarters training camp (Glenn Miller's farm); he said he had received a copy of *The Turner Diaries* at Miller's farm; and he said he had heard Glenn Miller make speeches about "an all-white South," and was aware of the WPP goal of creating a "Southland . . . free of other racial influence." Perhaps most important, he admitted that since joining up with the Millers in July 1984, there had been no change in firearms training and that neither Glenn nor Steve told him there would be any changes after the January 1985 court order that put the settlement agreement into effect.

Although we scored points by getting Pounder to acknowledge that it had been business as usual after the court order, Martin scored points on cross-examination by establishing that such business did not violate the statutes in question. Pounder maintained that the so-called firearms training was nothing more than a marksmanship contest with

participants shooting .22-caliber rifles at National Rifle Association–
type targets—perfectly legal. He said he had never seen any illegal
weapons at any WPP event. And he dutifully read certain paragraphs
from a letter Glenn Miller sent to new recruits.

Martin had carefully selected these paragraphs. More important,
Miller had carefully written them.

> Members who engage in illegal activities will be subject to involun-
> tary termination from the White Patriot Party.
>
> Our militia is totally defensive. We are not out to violate anyone's
> civil rights or cause civil disorder. Offensive violence is counterproduc-
> tive to our movement.
>
> We're not out to overthrow the government like the Communists
> are.

What was rhetoric and what was reality? We contended that, to
quote James Holder, these words were a "smoke screen." *The Turner
Diaries* and Glenn Miller's statements that paralleled events in the
book were reality. The view from the defendants' table was exactly
the opposite. In the end it would be the view from the jury box that
mattered.

The jury didn't see the events that added more tension to the proceedings a few minutes before the trial was resumed on the second morning. Richard Cohen walked over to the counsel's table where Stephen
Miller was already seated. As Richard was about to talk to Miller on
a procedural matter, another man also attempted to speak. Richard
recognized him as Ed Fields, the Atlanta-based publisher of a virulent
anti-Semitic newspaper, *The Truth at Last,* and a long-time supporter
of white supremacist causes. Fields had distributed pamphlets outside
the court personally attacking me as a sexually perverted Antichrist
Jew who was seeking to use this trial as a stepping-stone to the office
of attorney general.

Despite his "credentials," Fields was not a party to this action and
was not supposed to be behind the rail or bar reserved for lawyers and
court officials.

"Excuse me, Mr. Fields," said Richard.

"Get the fuck away from me," snarled Fields, explaining that he had
something important to discuss with Miller. Richard, six feet two
inches and not easily frightened, wisely walked away from the pair.
Fields then looked up and told Richard in an ominous tone, "I'll see
you later."

A U.S. marshall reported the incident to Judge Britt, who immediately charged Ed Fields with criminal contempt of court. After a hearing, Judge Britt found Fields guilty.

The Turner Diaries is a frightening work. I wanted the jury to hear as many passages from the book as possible, showing them that this was not just a novel, but had already been used as a revolutionary manual by Robert Mathews and the Order and was currently being used by the Millers, whom the FBI had linked to Mathews's group. We had a witness prepared to say just that—Don Wofford, an FBI special agent who had investigated the Order and was an expert on domestic terrorism.

Judge Britt let Wofford read some portions of *The Turner Diaries*, but beyond that, the judge severely limited his testimony, saying it was irrelevant and prejudicial. Prejudicial perhaps, but not irrelevant. In a hearing outside the presence of the jury, Wofford told the court he was prepared to testify that both Millers had been part of the Order's hierarchy. The FBI had found Mathews's records which included coded telephone listings and secret names of regional leaders: "Lone Star" (Louis Beam), "Rounder One" (Glenn Miller), "Rounder Two" (Steve Miller). What could be more relevant than evidence conclusively connecting the Millers to the violent Order? The WPP had marched with a banner proclaiming WE LOVE THE ORDER. Glenn Miller had printed the same words across the masthead of the *Confederate Leader*. Wofford could tell the jury what we already knew: The Millers were playing in the big leagues, were running the best funded, best trained, and most revolutionary Klan group in the nation. But Judge Britt said no. One way or another, the mouths of our witnesses were being shut.

Had the jury decided the case at this point, I'm not sure how it would have ruled. As powerful as Holder's testimony had been, it did not relate to events after the signing of the settlement agreement. Wofford had effectively drawn parallels between *The Turner Diaries* and Glenn Miller's words and deeds, but his most telling points were disallowed. As a result, his appearance had done little to convince a jury to convict. Cross-examination had blunted Pounder's testimony about firearms training.

It was time for our star witness. Robert Norman Jones placed his metal hook on the Holy Bible, raised his good hand, and promised to tell the truth.

Q: Tell the jury what type of military explosives you were attempting
to purchase [when you were arrested by the undercover agent].

A: They were C-four plastic explosives and some blasting caps, couple
rolls of time fuse.

Q: Did you request of this [undercover agent] to join any organization
[at the time you tried to buy the weapons]?

A: The White Patriot Party.

Q: What did you request of him to do?

A: To help train members of the White Patriot Party.

Q: Could you tell the jury whether or not any military items were
found in your home [after your arrest]?

A: Yes, sir. I guess that there were quite a few military-type items.
Among them were military radios, night vision scopes, gas masks,
CR grenades, hand grenade fuse assemblies, some plastic explosives, booby-trap simulators, an assortment of gear packs, load-
bearing equipment, seven weapons, ammunition.

On my cue, the marshalls brought in these items. A silence fell over
the courtroom. As the gallery and jury looked on in awe, the marshalls
piled the startling number of weapons on the courtroom floor between the counsels' tables and the witness stand. I had to tiptoe my
way through this mine field to get close enough to ask the hard-of-
hearing Jones more questions.

Q: Sir, what was this material being held for?

A: Delivery.

Q: To whom?

A: White Patriot Party.

I glanced back at our counsel's table as Jones answered this and saw
Bobby Person shaking his head in amazement. What a long way we
had come since Mike Lewis had driven down that dead-end road and
tried to intimidate him.

Speaking in a soft, sure drawl, Jones described how he had begun
his association with the WPP by selling military supplies to three
members of the elite forces—Robert "Jack" Jackson, Doug Sheets,
and Tony Wydra. He had obtained some of these supplies from members of the U.S. Army stationed at Fort Bragg. What did he give them
in return?

"Well, I traded just about everything I could: drugs, weapons, depending on who I was dealing with at the time. Some individuals preferred marijuana, some preferred cash, and some preferred weapons," Jones testified.

Through Jackson, Sheets, and Wydra, Jones met Steve Miller in 1984. Miller gave him some issues of the *Confederate Leader* and a copy of *The Turner Diaries,* described by Miller as "a plan for revolution in America in 1992." Soon Jones was training WPP members in explosives handling and transportation and making recommendations about weapon procurement. Then, "I commenced gathering up a small training staff which was comprised of some active-duty individuals at Fort Bragg."

After meeting with the Millers to suggest changes "necessary to improve the organization," Glenn Miller asked Jones to acquire military weapons while Steve Miller handled the payments. Who supplied Jones with these weapons?

"The major part were active-duty military individuals, Special Forces supply sergeants. The military intelligence captain was an excellent source," Jones said.

Jones identified the military intelligence captain as William Mason Roberson from Fort Bragg, mentioning he had bought a pistol for Steve Miller from the captain. I made a mental note to send Secretary of Defense Weinberger another letter.

Jones said he had started supplying these weapons in 1984, before the January 1985 settlement agreement. How long had he continued?

"It ended on July 8, 1985, the day of my arrest."

"Would you tell the jury whether the items that you supplied became more frequent or less as the time went on before your arrest?" I asked.

Scratching his head with his hook, Jones thought for a moment. "They became more frequent I would say. Around January, February of 1985, much more money was supplied."

It sounded like old Glenn Miller had dropped me off at the airport and then gone and bought himself some heavy-duty weapons.

"Would you tell the jury approximately the amount of money you obtained from the White Patriot Party for this?"

"I would estimate somewhere close to fifty thousand dollars."

Some of that fifty thousand dollars went toward the purchase of Cobra M-11 pistols. "What is that used for?" I asked.

"Death, close range."

Some of the money went for AR-15s. Purpose?

"Death, long range."

TNT, C-4 plastic explosives, hand grenades, Claymore mines, LAW rockets. What was a LAW rocket?

"It's a lightweight antitank rocket, heat high-explosive antitank, sixty-six millimeter. It's portable. It's armor-penetrating up to eleven inches."

Steve Miller had asked Jones to see if he could come up with something even more explosive, a Stinger rocket—a surface-to-air weapon. Jones told him "nobody I knew could get them."

I asked: "What reason did Mr. Stephen Miller give for wanting something of this nature?"

"Well, he told me directly about an incident that happened with an Order member, the leader, Bob Mathews, that a helicopter rocketed his house, that if they had had some type of weapon against that, that wouldn't have happened."

Jones said he supplied thirteen LAW rockets at approximately one thousand dollars apiece. I knew the jury had to be wondering where Glenn Miller got the money to pay for all of this. Jones described flying to Eastover, North Carolina, with Steve Miller. There, they joined Doug Sheets and the Order's David Lane, later identified as the driver of the car in the Alan Berg murder. Said Jones: "[Sheets] produced a duffel bag full of money which let me know there would be no more problems."

That money paid Jones to train WPP members in "paramilitary activity" from October 1984 to July 1985.

"Was this activity that you did secret or public?" I asked.

"It was about as clandestine as we could make it under the circumstance."

Steve Miller paid him one hundred dollars a day to conduct sessions in night training, land navigation, map reading, rocket firing, ambushes, "how to stay alive and how to kill." With the help of his active-duty military staff, he created small, ten-man training units with Miller participating in the training.

Q: Did Stephen Miller ever tell you what the purpose of this training was?

A: To create a paramilitary guerrilla unit for later use in creating a White Southland is what he called it.

The training's secretive nature was evidenced by Glenn Miller's remarks to Jones a few days after the July arrest. In the middle of a cornfield near Steve Miller's house, Glenn "told me not to say shit,"

Jones testified. "He also said they would try to square me away as best as possible."

What did that mean?

"It meant thirteen hundred dollars for every month I spent in prison."

He didn't get the money while he was at Butner, but he did receive a supportive note from Steve Miller. How had the chaplain closed the note?

"Death to the enemy."

Bill Martin is the best lawyer I have faced in a Klan case. His cross-examination of our witnesses had been extremely effective up to this point. He had his work cut out after Jones's testimony, however. All he could really do was try to paint Jones as a self-serving liar hoping to get out of prison early for his testimony.

Q: You made a lot of statements regarding the matter for which you were arrested, didn't you?

A: [Nodding]

Q: And you admitted here that your plea bargain called for you to fully cooperate; is that correct?

A: Yes, sir.

Q: But you didn't fully cooperate, did you?

A: No, sir. At that point I was still protecting the White Patriot Party.

Martin established that a week before his arrest, Jones had told the undercover agent, Chuck Alexander, that he was training six ten-man teams for the WPP. The conversation had taken place at Alexander's home.

"And there you smoked marijuana, took Quaaludes, and drank beer all afternoon?" asked Martin.

Jones shrugged. "Lord have mercy."

"Is that true?" Martin asked.

"Yes, sir."

Lord have mercy, indeed. Our star was falling.

Martin asked if the talk about the ten-man teams had been "BS."

"No, sir, not all of it," said Jones.

"You didn't tell ATF during your four-hour interview on October 2, 1985, that all that stuff about the six ten-man teams was BS?"

"I did make that statement," said Jones. "As I told you before, I was trying my best to cover as best I could."

Jones admitted flunking a lie-detector test administered by ATF

agents three weeks later. When they accused him of embellishing the
amount of explosives he had delivered, he had shrugged and said,
"You're probably right." He admitted telling ATF that the only time
he had met Glenn Miller, Steve Miller, Tony Wydra, and Robert
Jackson was for beer and a game of pool. "That wasn't true, was it?"
asked Martin.

"No, sir, not totally," Jones said.

Martin cited several other instances where Jones had told the undercover policeman something different than the ATF agents and had
told the ATF agents something different than he had testified when
I questioned him. There was no doubt that Jones had lied a good deal
over the last year. The jury would have to decide if he was telling the
truth today.

His consistent explanation of his inconsistent statements made perfect sense to me. He had initially lied after his arrest to protect the
WPP; as he said, Glenn Miller had told him to keep quiet, promising
to pay him for the time he spent in prison. He may have played loose
with the truth—embellishing some things, downplaying others—in an
effort to get the best possible plea bargain; in other words, he lied out
of self-interest. But there was nothing to be gained from lying to this
jury: No deal had been cut for early release from prison. The federal
government had even denied him witness protection.

When Steve Miller stood up to cross-examine Jones, I breathed a
sigh of relief. Gordon Widenhouse, Steve Miller's stand-by counsel,
a solid lawyer from Raleigh, could have continued the onslaught on
Jones's credibility by further exploring his drug use. But the cocky
Miller had no intention of yielding the floor. As a result, the cross-
examination soon deteriorated into an argument between two former
friends who seemed oblivious to the fact that they were in a courtroom, not a bar. The judge frequently cautioned Jones to stop asking
Miller questions and warned Miller to refrain from testifying. Each
time Miller tried to correct Jones's memory of happier days, Jones
corrected him. Each man looked ridiculous, but Jones emerged the
winner.

Q: Bob, we were friends, were we not?
A: At one time we were.
Q: We went shooting together a few times, did we not?
A: Quite a few times.
Q: I told you I wanted nothing to do with [guns and explosives], did
   I not?

A: No, sir, you did not. Definitely you did not. The very first day I met you, you purchased a nine-millimeter automatic pistol. I don't think, you know—how can you sit there and say—

Q: That was a totally legitimate transaction.

A: That one was. The very first one. If you remember, the very second one, it was not legitimate. Some five thousand rounds of .223 ammunition.

Q: Other than a little bit of ammo, I never purchased anything else from you, did I?

A: Yes, you did. In fact, I believe you got one of those gas masks that came out of the armory. . . .

Two former friends arguing, one man reminding his holier-than-thou ex-pal about past transgressions. In its own way, the exchange between Jones and Steve Miller was as explosive as any weapon we could have shown the jury. When Jones blurted "How can you sit there and say . . ." there was no doubt that his indignation was clearly genuine, his honesty completely apparent. Martin's earlier effort to discredit him was damaged when Steve Miller stuck his combat-booted foot into his own mouth.

The crowd outside the courtroom at the close of the day acted more angrily than earlier. Raised fists threatened to become flying elbows, but Leslie, Tommy, and Danny kept us out of harm's way. As we drove back to the motel, I told Richard that the Patriots' bellicose behavior was a good sign. "They must be worried that we're sticking it to Glenn and Steve," I said.

"Great," he said sarcastically. "Let's eat in."

July 1985   Raleigh, North Carolina
"This Dees is a thorn in the side of the White Patriot Party," Steve Miller tells WPP member Simeon Davis. "He needs to be plucked out."

Bill Martin began his defense with a law enforcement officer, odd as that seems. The jury had already heard James Holder mention the name of Joe Momier, the special agent of the State Bureau of Investigation of North Carolina taken in by Glenn Miller's smoke screens. The WPP invited Momier to public rallies and even some of its private meetings, where Miller always reminded his men not to do anything illegal. When Momier left, the Patriots would laugh at how they were snookering him.

Martin proceeded on the theory that the jury could find his client guilty of violating the first statute in question only if the WPP had operated as a secret organization.

Q: Has [Glenn Miller] invited you to rallies?
A: Yes, sir.
Q: Has he ever denied you entry to any rally or activity of the White Patriot Party?
A: No, sir.
Q: Has he been cooperative with you?
A: Yes, sir.

Our cross-examination quickly made Martin's decision to call Agent Momier backfire.

Q: Are you aware that the White Patriot Party has a secret or clandestine paramilitary training operation?
A: I've had reports that there was training. Again, the semantics I'm not sure of, but there has been training camps and a number of things reported to me.
Q: These are training camps that are supposed to be secret?
A: I have had reports that some of them have been secret, yes, sir.

It would take more than the ineffectual Agent Momier to persuade the jury that the Millers were legitimate. Only one person could explain away the damaging testimony of Holder and Jones. Glenn Miller took the witness stand in his own defense.

Martin began by trying to contradict the most damaging testimony against his client.

Q: Mr. Miller, do you know Robert Norman Jones?
A: I never in my entire life ever seen that man until he came in the courtroom yesterday.
Q: Mr. Miller, have you ever authorized Doug Sheets to buy illegal weapons for the White Patriot Party?
A: No, sir.
Q: Have you ever given anyone fifty thousand dollars to purchase items for the White Patriot Party?
A: No, sir.

With Jones a nonfactor now, Martin concentrated on the firearms training sessions described by our witnesses. According to Miller, these were nothing more than shooting contests: "As I recall, I still had cows in the pasture, and we had to lock them up in the barn," he said innocently. "We set up bull's-eye targets in the woods and got up on the hill behind my house and conducted . . . shooting contests with twenty-two [caliber] rifles."

We had already introduced into evidence several issues of the *Confederate Leader.* In those issues, Miller had written that different WPP units were engaging in such activities as hand-to-hand combat, night training, and firearms training. He now admitted writing up reports of these sessions sent to him by WPP den leaders, but he said he had not attended the activities and had no real knowledge of them.

With the paramilitary activity a nonfactor now, Martin focused on *The Turner Diaries* and the goals of the WPP. Miller said he hadn't read the book since 1978 or 1979, but did distribute it to his men because "it describes things that may or may not happen in the future that I think people should think about"—innocent enough, as were, he insisted, the goals of the WPP. The party never intended to overthrow the U.S. government or the state of North Carolina; the Southland, he "hoped and prayed," would come about through the political process. He pointed out that he was running for governor of North Carolina again in 1988.

With *The Turner Diaries* now a nonfactor and Miller's inflammatory speech only rhetoric, Martin moved on to the statutes Miller had agreed not to violate. Miller said that to his knowledge he had not violated them. The WPP was not a secret organization, was engaged only in defensive training, and had refrained from causing or furthering civil disorder.

Martin showed Miller the same portions of his letter to recruits that he had shown Richard Pounder, and Miller duly noted that he had advised newcomers that activities must be legal and that the militia was purely defensive.

The examination ended as it had begun. "Do you have any knowledge of training activities that Mr. Jones testified to yesterday?

"No, sir," Glenn Miller said with a straight face.

Cross-examination. Under Martin's questioning, Miller had made a favorable impression, appearing more like the Green Beret sergeant he had been than the fanatical, militant extremist he now was. The jury might be lured into thinking he was an innocent victim of legalese—a babe in the woods who had signed a document without completely understanding it and who had tried to adhere to it, upholding the law. My job was to expose the private side of Sergeant Miller, proving he was no babe in the woods, but rather a soldier in the woods.

I came back to the war manual, *The Turner Diaries.*

Q: Is the year 1992 significant in any way in *The Turner Diaries?*
A: Yes, sir, I believe it is.
Q: And you used 1992 several times saying that's when the White Patriot Party will take power over the United States. Is there any reason why you picked 1992 and 1992 appears in *The Turner Diaries?*
A: I don't believe that I stated that we were going to take power over the United States. I might have mentioned the South. . . . That's the year I'm going to be elected governor of North Carolina. That's an election year, Mr. Dees.

Still the innocent.

Q: Mr. Miller, do you know any other candidate for governor in this state that has a citizen's militia, that trains men in firearms, hand-to-hand combat, ambush, counterambush, river crossing?
A: No, sir.

The question didn't trouble him. He spoke confidently. I asked him about "the balloon going up."

A: There's a good possibility, in my opinion, that law and order is going to break down in our country and the National Guard and police departments won't be able to handle it. It will be too big for them, at which time we will be organized, and we are going to restore law and order and protect our people.
Q: So when this civil disorder comes you are going to further this civil disorder by taking over, aren't you?

This was what the key statute prohibited.

A: No, sir.
Q: You will just take over the country from—from who?
A: I don't know. I can't paint the exact picture for you, Mr. Dees, of what will take place. I do know that when that period comes, when there is a breakdown of law and order, when the Communists

attempt to take over our country, it will be more to our benefit, our country's benefit, for some people to be organized and prepared and willing to try to combat it.

The country's benefit? Did the jury see the danger in this man?

Q: Mr. Miller, have you printed in the masthead of your newspaper the title, "We love the Order"?
A: Yes, sir.
Q: Is this not the same organization, the Order, that used *The Turner Diaries* that you heard Mr. Don Wofford testify about earlier?
A: Yes.
Q: Is this the same organization whose members have been accused of and convicted of criminal conspiracy to violate laws to overthrow the United States government?
A: Yes, sir.
Q: Government's Exhibit 38, which you wrote on March 19, 1985. Did you write this:

In short, if the federal government follows through on their present plot to imprison myself or other leaders within our organization, then the fifteen hundred White Patriots of the White Patriot Party will commence underground guerrilla warfare against the federal government, which will include the punishment of federal tyrants and their puppets.

We will declare war on the federal government if they take away our constitutional rights. It's as simple as that. And I have never made a more serious statement during my twelve years in the American White Movement.

Did you write that?
A: It sounds similar to what I believe I wrote. . . . I was bluffing, though, Mr. Dees.
Q: You were *bluffing?* . . . Who were you trying to bluff, Mr. Miller?
A: I'm trying to bluff those who would conspire, scheme, plot, use perjury, or, for example, go to prison and find an inmate and pay him money, promise him a transfer, a good word to the Parole Board to come and lie on people who are simply trying to execute their constitutional right. It's those type people that terrify me . . . that cause me to bluff and tell them to please allow me to continue exercising my constitutional right to unite and organize

my people so that I can work for the right and for the survival of
my rights.

So it all boiled down to this: Glenn Miller—Grand Dragon of the
Confederate Knights of the Ku Klux Klan; first sergeant of the White
Patriot Party; Rounder, the Order's man in the Southland—was just
bluffing. A kind of (Imperial) Wizard of Oz, full of bluster, spitting
out marching orders from behind a curtain, who when exposed immediately confessed that it was all an act. Tell that to Bobby Person or
the next black citizen with a gun held to his or her head by a Klansman.

*Ladies and gentlemen of the jury, please don't convict me, don't even take
me seriously. I was just bluffing.* I savored the thought that after hum-
bling himself, no, after denying the very principles that he had told
his followers they should be prepared to die for, Glenn Miller might
still have to go to prison. He'd had the opportunity to stand up for
himself but instead he had whined that he was just bluffing.

There was only one problem: It would be difficult to prove Glenn
Miller hadn't been bluffing. He sentenced Jewish abortionists to die;
but he didn't carry out the sentence. He threatened to take arms
against the government; but he didn't attack. Robert Jones's military
hardware notwithstanding, our greatest weapon against Miller was his
words. Paper, not rock or scissors. If the jury decided he was more
credible than Jones and less dangerous than we said—a paper tiger—
then he would march out of the courtroom the victor.

The jurors might dismiss Glenn's threats as hot air, but what would
they make of the active-duty marines training his men? Nothing,
Martin had insisted. To prove it, he called Corporal Russell Bordelon.

We had a photograph of Bordelon leading a White Patriot drill
taken when he was stationed at Camp Lejeune. We had intended to
call him as our witness, but he proved less than forthcoming when we
interviewed him, so we dropped him from our list. Martin picked him
up, and he testified like a good soldier on behalf of his former leaders,
the Millers. No, he said, he had never seen WPP firearms training or
any other kind of training. The WPP was more a social club than
anything else, he said.

Benson, North Carolina: 555-5230. I looked at the number on Robert
Jones's telephone bill one more time. While leafing through Jones's
ATF file looking for ways to explain his seemingly inconsistent state-

ments, I'd come across the bill by accident—555-5230, Glenn Miller's number. I was sure of it. Here it was in black and white, Jones had called Miller, the man who claimed he didn't know Jones from Adam—on July 9, the day after Jones's arrest. Jones had never told me about the call. Up to this point, Miller was probably leading Jones in the crucial game of credibility. Perhaps this bill would change the score.

To introduce the phone record as evidence, we would have to subpoena a phone company representative or persuade the defense to acknowledge, or stipulate, its authenticity. It was too late in the trial to subpoena phone company records. I asked Sam Currin, who dealt with Bill Martin on a regular basis, to play upon their friendship and ask for the stipulation.

If I were Glenn Miller's lawyer, I would have said, "No way. Get the phone company to verify it." If the response had then been, "That will take too long," I would have retorted, "Good." Martin, however, was not as disagreeable. Either being nice to Sam or feeling comfortable the document was not important, he made the stipulation.

Perhaps he felt comfortable because he believed his next and final witness would torpedo whatever credibility remained in Jones's earlier testimony. "The defendant Glenn Miller will call William Roberson to the stand," said the lawyer.

We had been surprised when, during a break fifteen minutes earlier, Martin had told us he was calling Roberson. "What the hell do we have on this guy?" I asked Richard frantically. All I knew was that Jones and he had apparently transacted a little business together.

While Richard searched through our files, I ran to the lockup area where Jones was being held. "Tell me all you know about this guy," I said. Five minutes later I returned to the courtroom. Richard had found some information that ATF had recorded after Jones was arrested and said he had traded weapons with Roberson. I tried to read it and listen to Martin's examination of Roberson at the same time.

Thirty-four-year-old William Mason Roberson, Jr., had served as a military intelligence officer, a captain at Fort Bragg before his retirement. Jones had testified that he had purchased weapons from and traded weapons with Roberson when the captain was still in the army. Roberson's account differed. He testified that Jones came to him with a night-vision device Jones said he had stolen from an armory. Jones wanted to trade the device for Roberson's canoe and a few other things. "I said I didn't think it was a good idea. . . . A friend of his pulled a gun on me and Robert said, 'What we are going to do now is shoot you and bury your body in the woods.' "

According to Roberson, he took the night-vision device from Jones in trade, fearing for his life. He then drove the device from his home in Fayetteville to his mother-in-law's home in Winston-Salem. He later "went straight to ATF" and turned in the weapon.

This story delivered by U.S. Army captain with an honorable discharge made Jones look like a liar again. We couldn't have the jury going off to make its decision with this witness's damaging testimony fresh in its mind. I looked through the file for any holes in Roberson's account. The ATF file indicated that Roberson had told the agents he had suffered three nervous breakdowns. I began my cross-examination by asking why he had left the army. He explained that he received a medical discharge because of cataracts, cluster headaches, and a perforated ulcer. He denied receiving psychiatric treatment or suffering nervous breakdowns, but then acknowledged he had seen a psychiatrist for evaluation of the headaches.

The story of the deal just didn't ring true to me. Why would Robert Jones and friends force an army captain and weapons source at gunpoint to trade a stolen night scope for a canoe? Roberson's cool military manner slowly melted as I questioned him about the specifics of the evening. "So you didn't take the night scope now until after Mr. Jones pulled the gun on you and forced you to take it; is that what you are telling us?" I asked.

"I don't know. I'm not sure."

Roberson maintained he went straight to ATF with the night scope. I went back to the counsel's table and looked at the file. "Isn't it a fact that you didn't even call ATF until after Jones was arrested, some forty-two days later?"

At that time, after the arrest, Roberson had given ATF a statement. I took the statement from the file and asked Roberson to read it. In it he had admitted doing several deals with Jones. There was no mention of the canoe. If he had planned to turn in the night scope to ATF, why had he driven the weapon to his in-laws over one hundred miles away? It was clear that Jones was telling the truth. He had traded with Roberson and, when push came to shove, Roberson had traded Jones for his own freedom.

Roberson seemed to have shrunk since he had first taken the stand and answered Martin's questions so confidently. He was babbling; I honestly thought he might have a breakdown on the stand as he tried to explain that he had been at Walter Reed Hospital—no, he admitted, he couldn't have been—when the deal was made. Richard sensed the breakdown, too. As I passed by the table, he pulled my coat as if to say, "Enough. If you go any further, you'll make the jury feel sorry for him." The left side of my brain told me to sit down. The right side said there was one more question to be asked. The left side responded that you should never ask the other side's witness a question if you don't know the answer. I went on intuition. "Mr. Roberson, didn't Agent Kalco [of ATF] tell you that based on your mental and emotional condition, they weren't going to bring charges against you?"

Roberson's voice was barely audible. "That's probably what it boiled down to."

The defense had ended its case with a whimper, not a bang.

July 1985   Raleigh, North Carolina

Steve Miller introduces Tony Wydra and Robert Jackson to Simeon Davis and Wendell Lane. The chaplain wants to know if the four men will commit illegal acts to get money for the movement. Later, Miller and Lane drive around Raleigh looking for a certain car with Alabama plates, then motor along Interstate 95 looking for people to rob. They can't find a suitable victim.

When Miller learns a powerful stolen army LAW rocket or even more powerful Dragon rocket might be available, he says to Lane, "Wouldn't it be neat if a Dragon rocket went through Dragon Dees's office?"

In many ways this was the most important case I had ever tried. I thought long and hard about how I would finish my closing argument to the jury.

This is a nation which just celebrated a pretty important time, just dedicated the refurbished Statue of Liberty. A nation that's built from the good people that came from every country on earth: the Jews, blacks, Orientals, Italians. I don't know what a white person is. Blond hair and blue eyes? I don't know.

There have been people in history who have had the same dream of an all-Aryan nation. They started out real little, too, and ended up real big. And they caused us a lot of damage.

You have an opportunity here today to protect our community, to protect the citizens of North Carolina, and you have an opportunity today to stop Stephen Miller and Glenn Miller.

After six hours, the jury reached a unanimous verdict: Glenn Miller, Stephen Miller, and the White Patriot Party were guilty on all counts.

Judge Britt scheduled sentencing for September 8, but we didn't have to wait that long to hear the WPP's death rattle. Immediately after the verdict, the judge set the conditions under which the Millers could remain free on bond. Each had to "disassociate himself completely from the White Patriot Party in every manner." They could have no contact with past or present members or others in the white supremacist movement. That list of some two dozen "others" was hastily scribbled by Bill Stanton as the judge spoke. We had beheaded the monster. Without Glenn's charisma and doggedness and Steve's style and aggressiveness, the beast would collapse. It might flail a bit, but it would die.

The monster was already flailing in the hall outside the courtroom. I didn't care how many bodyguards we had, we weren't risking an armed battle with the now leaderless White Patriots. In Sam's office, we congratulated ourselves and talked to a reporter until late into the evening. Sam was expansive, and afterward Richard swore he'd heard him utter the first cussword since we'd met him—"damn." By the time we left, the courthouse and the streets below were empty. The ride back to the motel was blissfully uneventful.

Judge Britt sentenced Glenn Miller to the maximum one year in prison and three years' probation. He then suspended six months of the sentence. Steve Miller was sentenced to six months in prison and three years' probation, with a six-month suspended sentence.

Shortly after the trial, Secretary of Defense Weinberger announced a crackdown on military personnel joining the Ku Klux Klan and similar groups. For the first time, commanders had "the authority to order the facilities or events sponsored or controlled by such groups 'off-limits.' "

With the Millers banned, Cecil Cox took over the WPP. In the first *Confederate Leader* published after the trial, Cox ran an article stating that the Millers had been "railroaded" by the "Troika" of Cohen, Dees, and Currin. According to the article, Richard Cohen represented "all Jews and their hatred of White Christian America." I was described as "a brilliant Southerner with no sense of racial identity who has sold himself to the Jewish Sanhedrin for thirty pieces of silver." Sam Currin represented "the masses of white people: ignorant and gullible, they work to bring their own destruction."

Cox's rhetoric matched Glenn Miller's, but he lacked the charisma or skill at marshalling the troops. Within a month he announced that he was disbanding what had been the fastest growing, most militant racist organization in the United States.

CHAPTER 21

September 1985   Montgomery, Alabama

The tension followed us back to Montgomery, hanging in the air, invisible as cotton dust and just as stifling. After the sentencing, we heard rumors that I was again at the top of somebody's hit list. I felt more secure this time around. The new Center that we had built on Washington Avenue and moved into in May 1985 had structural safeguards to withstand a bombing and a state-of-the-art security system. My house and grounds were also fortified. And a couple of guardian angels from the FBI hovered closely. Still, I kept my gun with me at all times and I never moved outside without giving the landscape or pavement a good look-see.

I was feeding the horses when Danny Welch drove up in his Bronco. "The Fayetteville PD busted three White Patriots last night," he said before opening the door.

"And?" There must be more to warrant a visit this early on a Sunday morning.

"You're not gonna believe this," Danny said. "They were apparently planning to rob a Pizza Hut so they could buy some explosives to bomb the Center and kill you."

I let out a laugh that was too loud to have come just because this sounded funny. This news unsettled me, but, damn, it did sound funny—starting the revolution at a Pizza Hut.

Danny filled me in on the details. A few days earlier the Fayetteville police had received a tip about the overall scheme. When they learned the robbery was going down, they converged on the three men just as they were leaving for the restaurant. Apparently the Pizza Hut did a booming business with the thousands of servicemen stationed in the

area, and the robbers hoped for about ten thousand dollars from a
target a lot less secure than a bank.

The cops confiscated two pistols, a shotgun, ski masks, dark clothing, and chemicals apparently used to make bombs. One of the suspects had mentioned they were going to buy a Dragon rocket—an
antitank assault missile used by the army and marines—to blow up the
Center.

"Do we know any of these guys?" I asked.

"Simeon Davis," said Danny.

Davis was extremely close to Stephen Miller.

"You thinking what I'm thinking?" I asked Danny.

He nodded.

There was plenty to do at the Center while we waited for the Fayetteville police and the ATF to link one or both of the Millers to the Great
Pizza Hut Robbery. Richard Cohen and I assembled a new legal team.
Ira Burnim, Deb Ellis, and Dennis Sweet had left shortly after the
Miller verdicts because of "philosophical differences." The tension
that started with Klanwatch and was inflamed by the fire had increased
after the Decatur, Miller, and Donald cases heated up. The Center
wasn't heading in the direction these well-meaning and dedicated
attorneys wanted. Although sorry to see them leave, I made no apolo-
gies for taking on the likes of Bill Wilkinson, Bobby Shelton, and
Glenn Miller.

Richard also immersed himself in the Alabama State Troopers case.
His first appellate argument would be against the solicitor general of
the United States in the U.S. Supreme Court. In its fifteen years, this
case had taken more twists and turns than the Appalachian Trial. The
issue now in appeal was novel: Could racial quotas be applied not only
to hiring, but to promotions as well? President Nixon's Justice Department sided with us originally. Now President Reagan's lawyers opposed us. This switch paralleled the rise of white supremacist groups,
a point not lost on civil rights leaders.

I spent my time readying the Donald case for trial. The case had
been put on hold months earlier pending the appointment of a new
federal judge for the district that includes Mobile. Finally confirmed
by the Senate, Judge Alex Howard scheduled our trial for February
1987.

"We've got us a problem," I told Bill Stanton one morning as we
reviewed a list of potential witnesses. "We've got Tommy Rowe's

testimony about the Freedom Riders, the Sixteenth Street Baptist Church, and Selma, and Johnny Matt Jones and Bennie Hays and the rest will talk about the lynching, but man, there's sixteen years between Mrs. Liuzzo and Michael Donald."

Too wide a gap. We had to prove that Bobby Shelton and the UKA continued their violent ways of the 1960s into the '70s. "Find me the missing link," I told Bill.

"The Childersburg man," Bill replied, smiling.

Within a few days, the Childersburg man had a name—Randy Ward. Bill and Center investigator Joe Roy went to the federal courthouse in Birmingham and dug up the six-year-old transcript from the trial of the Klansmen who had shot up two homes in the Childersburg area in 1979. It was apparent from the transcript and a conversation with Henry Frosin, the government prosecutor, that the case had centered around the testimony of Ward, the Exalted Cyclops (EC) of Unit 1015, the UKA Klavern in Talladega County.

In private practice after serving as chief assistant U.S. attorney in Birmingham, Henry was a longtime Klan fighter. He offered to help us in any way he could, but confessed he had no idea where Ward was; the ex–Exalted Cyclops had slipped into a federal witness protection program after putting thirteen of his fellow Klansmen behind bars. "Locating him could take a year," said Henry, "and even if you do find him, there's no telling what he'll say about the UKA."

On that discouraging note, I asked Roy, who had spent eight years as a criminal investigator for the Montgomery PD and six years as a private detective, to find the man last known as Randy Ward. Joe's quick wit, intellect, and unassuming manner had opened many doors in past investigations. He would need all this and more to find Ward.

In 1978, Ward had joined the Klan in Childersburg, a town of five thousand in central Alabama that advertised itself as the home of De Soto Caverns, the first officially recorded cave in America. He had quickly impressed Great Titan Les Suttle, who had named him EC. Suttle felt the Klavern had become too much of a social club and wanted someone who could forward the Klan's white supremacy agenda. He liked the twenty-two-year-old Ward's aggressiveness.

Shortly after he and nineteen other Klansmen were arrested for shooting into the homes of the local NAACP president and a white woman thought to be dating a black man, Ward became a government witness, partly to save his skin and partly because he regretted his actions. After the trial he and his wife had disappeared into witness protection. His parents, too, had left town.

Joe Roy's initial effort to track Ward down through his Social Security number or driver's license failed. Visits with Ward's old neighbors, friends, preachers, and teachers in Childersburg and the surrounding counties proved just as fruitless. Many of these folks told Joe it was the NAACP who should be investigated, not the Klan.

The breakthrough came when Joe told a former neighbor of Ward's parents that he was trying to locate the family because they were potential heirs to an estate. The neighbor said he thought he knew where the senior Wards had moved. After checking property records, Joe hit pay dirt.

Randy Ward's parents were, understandably, reluctant to talk, but Joe's boy-next-door charm eased their suspicions, and they invited him into their modest house. Soon they were telling him how they feared for the safety of Randy, who had made a new life for himself in "another state." Communication was difficult. Not wanting his phone number to appear on their bill, they always called Randy collect from a pay phone. They always held reunions in a "neutral" city.

Joe talked with the Wards for a couple of hours, sizing them up as hardworking, honest people happy to have their Childersburg days behind them. They quoted the Bible to him—sometimes referring to scripture about the importance of protecting family, sometimes citing chapter and verse about doing the right thing. As they debated whether or not to help us, Joe talked about the Donald case, describing how at the time of his death, Michael was working and going to school just like Randy. Misty-eyed, the Wards talked about the horror that Mrs. Donald must have experienced.

Joe sensed they wanted to help, but also realized how fearful they were that helping might spell death for their own son. "I promise we won't reveal his new identity or whereabouts, and we'll do everything possible to protect him," Joe said, explaining that the Center had become expert at protection over the last few years. The Wards finally promised to talk with Randy.

"If it will make him feel better, have him call Mr. Froshin in Birmingham to check us out," said Joe.

Henry phoned a few days later. "Randy will meet you in my office," he said.

Henry Froshin looked uneasy, realizing he was now using his status as a former prosecutor to influence Randy Ward. His introduction seemed as neutral as possible. "Randy, this is Morris Dees, the man I told you about. He wants to ask you some questions. I'm not recommending that you help him or even talk to him. Just listen to him and make up your own mind."

Henry left the room, leaving Ward with Joe and me. Chunky and baby-faced, with sandy blond hair, Ward was wearing a pair of blue jeans and a plaid flannel shirt. With callused hands and grease under his fingernails, he looked out of place in this huge conference room with antique furnishings and an oriental carpet under his work boots. I took off my coat, rolled up my sleeves, and loosened my tie to downplay the formality of the room and Froshin's cool introduction.

I told Ward what had happened to Michael Donald and showed him the photo of the lynching. He winced, then shook his head sadly. "Did you realize this stuff was still going on today?" I asked.

"No, sir. But I guess with Bobby Shelton at the top I'm not surprised."

"You ever meet Bobby?"

"Yes, sir." Ward explained he had been very involved in Klan politics, attending as many meetings as he could at the UKA's national headquarters in Tuscaloosa. "I was hoping to take over from Bobby after he retired."

At ease now, he told us the story of what had happened in Childersburg, explaining how the Titan had approved the shootings. Almost as an afterthought he then told us about the time Bobby Shelton visited Unit 1015—our missing link.

My mind raced. Getting Randy Ward to come to this private meeting was one thing. How could we compel him to come out of hiding and testify in Mobile? I could take his deposition instead of asking him to testify in person. But if I did that, Mays would have the opportunity to examine him and try to trip him up. The element of surprise would also be gone and the Klonsel would have time to find witnesses to discredit Ward or rebut his testimony.

The downside was even greater if I didn't take his deposition and relied on him to testify at the trial. What if he didn't show up? We'd lose one of our most important witnesses.

Play it safe and tell him you'll take his deposition, Dees. Ward picked up the picture of Michael Donald hanging from the camphor tree. Again, he shook his head in disbelief. *No deposition. Develop a bond with him, make him feel part of the team. He'll show up.*

"Randy, I'd like you to come to the trial and testify for us," I said. The blood drained from his pink face. He thought we had only wanted to talk to him about some old history. "I'm afraid," he said.

I understood. We had just shown him proof positive of the UKA's violent 1981 methods and now we were asking him to expose himself for no gain. The glory trip I had used on Rowe would not work here. Joe and I promised him we would sneak him in and out of Mobile with top security, paying for all his expenses.

He was skeptical. Unhappy about his treatment in the witness protection program, he said that the government had reneged on almost all of its promises. All he had was a passport with a new name, not even a Social Security number.

Joe calmed his fears about security, then I tried to take the matter to higher ground. "Son, most people live and do very little for their fellow man," I said quietly. "Other folks are gonna die at the hands of Bobby Shelton's men unless someone like you has the courage to step forward. Not too many people have the opportunity to be somebody, do something important. You do. This is between you and your God. I'll be praying you make the right decision."

"I'll have to think about this," Ward said. He promised he would call us with his answer.

There was no sense pressuring him. I asked him what he was doing for the rest of the weekend. He said he was planning on catching a bus in Birmingham to visit his parents. I offered to rent him a car that he could return to the airport when he flew back home, showing I trusted him with a car checked out on my credit card. I felt this trust might be repaid later. He gratefully accepted the offer. After Ward had rented the car, Joe got his address from the driver's license data on the rental receipt—just in case we had to find him for a deposition. It looked like that wouldn't be necessary. Randy Ward called and said he would testify.

Sam Currin phoned a couple of days later. It had taken almost four months to put all the pieces together, but the government was finally ready to indict five WPP members for various crimes arising from the Pizza Hut arrests. The names were familiar: Simeon Davis; Wendell Lee Lane, a leader of WPP den 79; Tony Wydra and Robert "Jack" Jackson, identified by Bob Jones at the Miller trial as involved in weaponry; and, as Danny and I had suspected, Steve Miller. All were charged with conspiracy to obtain stolen U.S. Army weapons, explosives, and equipment. Miller was also indicted for making an illegal firearm.

According to the indictment, during the criminal contempt trial in July, Miller had told Davis that I was a "thorn in the side of the White Patriot Party" that needed to be "plucked out." At the same time

Miller gave Lane my address in Alabama. The two then staked out the home of our local counsel in Raleigh where they thought I might be staying. Next, Miller and Lane drove along Interstate 95 looking for people to rob.

Miller wanted money for weapons. The Dragon rocket to kill Dragon Dees would cost seventy-five hundred dollars. Miller, Davis, and Lane cooked up the Pizza Hut plan to finance the transaction, and then Davis and Lane enlisted another WPP member to participate in a plan to come to Alabama and kill me.

Sam Currin said the other Miller had not been involved in the plot. Glenn had kept a low profile since the sentencing hearing. "I imagine it won't be too long before we hear from him," I said.

Unfortunately, I was right.

CHAPTER 22

February 1987   Mobile, Alabama

The Imperial Wizard slid his wire-rimmed glasses up his nose as I handed him plaintiff's exhibit seventeen, a 1979 copy of the *Fiery Cross*.

"Mr. Shelton, I ask you to look at this document here. . . . What is this a picture of?"

He looked the paper over and gave me an angry look.

"It's a picture of an individual looking out. Apparently it's a white man," he said impatiently.

"Okay. And what does it say?"

He lowered his eyes to the page. "[It says], 'It's terrible the way blacks are being treated. All whites should work to give the blacks what they deserve.' Then it says, 'Turn page.' "

"What do you see on the other page?"

Several jurors were straining to see the document Shelton held in his hand.

"And it is a black with a rope on it—" he stopped abruptly, moved up in his chair, then raised his voice "—which was printed in Louisiana. When it came out, I called—with concern about it. I was told that it was used as a fill-in, for space."

"Yes?" I asked, wanting to give him every opportunity to hang himself.

"And I was assured it would never happen again." His voice was rich with authority. This was, after all, the man who had earlier acknowledged signing Klan documents "His Lordship."

"Is that right?" My voice was rich with incredulity. "Now this came out of the *Fiery Cross* dated 1979, and it says down here 'Robert Shelton, editor and publisher.' Is that right?"

311

"Yes."

I took back the drawing found by Bill Stanton at the Anti-Defamation League and fed it to the hungry jury. In my opening statement, I had apologized that much of my examination of Shelton would be less than exciting, and the jurors had seemed bored while I went over the Klan constitution, the Klavern Unit 900 charter, and financial records with Shelton. "This is not your typical social club like the Kiwanis or Rotary," I had said of the UKA in my opening. But looking at Shelton—wearing a conservative gray suit, not purple robes—and listening to him explain how his organization worked, the jury could be forgiven in these early moments of the trial for thinking the UKA was indeed a social club and wondering why it and its leader were parties to the lawsuit.

Only Judge Howard had appeared interested in the paper trail. Before opening statements, he called the parties and the lawyers into his chambers. There, among other things, he told Richard Cohen and me that he disagreed with our position on what was necessary to hold Shelton and UKA, Inc., liable for the deeds of the Klansmen. Greater proof than recounting old Klan atrocities would be required, he warned us. I thought back to the dire predictions made by Steve Ellmann and John Carroll about the difficulty proving our theory to a judge.

As plaintiff's exhibit seventeen made its way around the jury box, I could see the jurors were no longer bored. One by one they looked at the top page, then turned it over to see the lynched black man. Several shook their heads in disbelief. Life had imitated art two years later when Unit 900 gave Michael Donald what they thought he deserved. I waited for each of the jurors to examine the drawing before I turned my first witness over to his lawyer for cross-examination.

I returned to the counsel's table, taking my seat next to Beulah Mae Donald. Nodding, she patted my pale white hand with her weathered brown one. She looked considerably older than sixty-four: diabetes, high blood pressure, and Michael's death had taken their toll. She moved slowly but proudly, a daughter or niece always at her side, the matriarch of a close-knit family. Beulah Mae Donald had reared seven children from two marriages almost singlehandedly, working as a hotel maid, living in public housing. Michael, her youngest and pride and joy, was still living at home when Henry Hays and Tiger Knowles assaulted him.

Now Knowles sat no more than thirty feet from the woman whose son he had lynched. Isolated from the other defendants, next to the wall across from the jury, he was flanked by U.S. marshalls assigned to guard him under the federal witness protection program. Knowles had qualified for this special treatment by sacrificing his friend Henry Hays.

Tiger Knowles's presence was essential. Normally, when a witness is in jail, he or she does not attend the trial; his or her deposition is read into evidence. But I wanted the jury to see and hear this man, to *feel* the murder as he described it. I had prevailed upon Judge Howard to make an exception and let Knowles come, agreeing that the Center would pay the two thousand dollars in travel expenses and the cost of the marshalls.

Judge Howard refused to order that Henry Hays and Bennie Hays be brought from their respective cells. Fortunately, Bennie was released just a few days before our trial. Cane across his lap, the Titan now sat at the defendants' counsel table with Exalted Cyclops Frank Cox, Red Betancourt, Bill O'Connor, and the snowman, Teddy Kyzar. I looked at Bennie, but he didn't see me. He was too busy evil-eyeing Knowles and Shelton.

The defendants' table was no farther away from Beulah Mae Donald than the length of rope that lynched her son. Mrs. Donald never looked over, her gaze fixed instead on the witness. She leaned forward in her chair to hear every word. It seemed to me she had concluded that this was the only way to understand, to absorb, what had happened to her son. To stray from the witness and stare at the men who had planned and carried out Michael's murder was a waste of precious energy. I marveled at her willpower. If one of my children had been killed, I would have crossed over the line that separated me physically and morally from the murderers and fixed them with more than my eyes.

Richard handed me a note. "Nice job, Daddy." I turned toward the packed gallery, almost evenly divided between the Ku Klux Klan and the Donald clan. Ellie, seventeen now, sat in the first row between one of the Donald nieces and Danny Welch, a pad of paper in her hands. She wrote as Bobby Shelton told John Mays how distressed he felt when he saw the drawing of the lynched black man in his own newspaper. On rebuttal I'd have to ask him if he had printed a retraction in the next issue of the *Fiery Cross.* I already knew he hadn't.

When Ellie looked up, I caught her eye and smiled. Trial lawyers, the story goes, make bad husbands and fathers. We seem to keep our files in good order, but not our homes, attending to the needs of star witnesses like Tommy Rowe or Bob Jones—no matter what despicable acts they've committed—more than the needs of wives or sons or daughters.

On the December night that bodyguard E. T. Davis had pushed Ellie and me into the darkened closet, Ellie had asked me why I did what I did, an accusatory edge to her voice. I did what I did without feeling accountable to anyone. She deserved an explanation. "Ellie, it's a lifetime commitment," I had said. "I doubt if I can really tell you why. I'd like for you to come with me to court some day so you can see for yourself." I'd had the Donald trial in mind.

With the Donald case, I did not feel the same sense of urgency I had felt in North Carolina, yet this was clearly the most important case of my life. There was one more corpse here than in the Miller trial, but that wasn't the reason. The UKA was not, in the 1980s, in the same league as the White Patriot Party. Tiger Knowles and Henry Hays used tree limbs and a rope, not LAW rockets and Claymore mines. But this case was not about a present or future danger. It was about history, about accountability for past sins, murderous sins.

Some individuals had been punished for those sins—although not nearly enough—but the Ku Klux Klan itself had never been held accountable. And of all the Klan groups, the most powerful, the one that had symbolized hatred and violence most during the civil rights movement, was Bobby Shelton's United Klans of America. The assault on the Freedom Riders, the bombing of the Sixteenth Street Baptist Church, the murder of Viola Liuzzo—the most famous, most vicious attacks of the era could be traced to the lead pipes, matches, and bullets of the UKA. Justice delayed is better than justice denied.

Ellie had not even been born when Dr. King was shot in 1968, but the events of the civil rights era were a part of her geography, her heritage, her blood. I wanted her to know that and, by knowing, come to know me, too.

She had been excited about coming to the trial. I went over the facts of the case with her before we left for Mobile. I wanted her emotionally involved in the proceedings.

With Shelton's dry explanation (or lack of explanation) about how the UKA operated out of the way, I moved on to Klavern Unit 900. If a witness lives more than one hundred miles from the courthouse, an attorney can choose to read his or her deposition into evidence rather than call the witness to testify in person. Knowing the nervous Johnny Matt Jones, still in Texas, would make a poor and unreliable witness in person, I happily exercised this option. I read aloud the questions from the two-year-old deposition and Welch, considerably more effective than Jones, read the answers most convincingly. The first inklings of a conspiracy to kill Donald now lay before the jury. As Jones noted, after hearing Betancourt read the clipping about the trial of Josephus Anderson, Bennie Hays had risen to his feet and ordered Henry to "get this down. . . . If a black man could kill a white man, a white man should be able to get away with killing a black man." Henry had then added: "A nigger ought to be hung by the neck until dead to put them in their place."

I glanced over at the all-white jury. As in the Miller case, the defendants had used their peremptory challenges to exclude blacks. Cathy Bennett, the country's foremost trial consultant, had volunteered to help me pick this jury, and despite the absence of blacks, we were pleased with the results. Justice would be best served if an all-white jury found the Klan guilty for its past deeds. During those same years when the UKA had been leading the reign of terror, all-white juries had shamelessly refused to convict obviously guilty Klansmen and other white defendants of horrendous deeds, from the murder of Emmett Till to the murder of Medgar Evers to the murder of Viola Liuzzo.

As Danny read Jones's answers, some jurors scribbled notes, some shook their heads. One older man looked skeptical. One younger woman smiled at me. What did that mean?

I do not subscribe to trial lawyers' view that *they* are on trial and the case will rise or fall on whether the jury likes *them.* The courtroom dynamic is more complex. I see my role as background music, the kind that you don't really hear, but you hum when you leave the theater.

Trying to make music to a smiling juror during the trial is tempting, but it doesn't always work. In one death penalty case I tried, an attractive young woman from Birmingham's finest neighborhood caught my eye. During jury selection, I made a note to myself: "I feel good vibes about Valerie Martin." She ended up on the jury and sat in the front row, left end. I began to notice that Valerie was watching me a lot when she should have been watching other things in the courtroom. Her interest in me became a running joke with the defense team. I was careful not to overplay my "relationship" with Valerie, but I held out enough promise to her to make her vote our way. I thought.

I was wrong. The jury rejected our insanity plea and found my client guilty of murder. He was sentenced to death. I learned that by themselves, good looks and charm—at least my good looks and charm—would not win a case.

When Danny finished reading Jones's deposition, I took my eye off the smiling female juror and called Tiger Knowles to the stand. Knowles had undergone a major transformation over the last three years: He had shed a good twenty pounds, cut his sideburns, and styled his hair, losing the young punk image he had swaggered to the witness stand with at Henry Hays's murder trial. If it is possible to feel sympathy for someone who has done something so brutal, I did. At the Hays trial I had been shocked by the coolness with which Tiger Knowles recounted the murder, but at his deposition and in subsequent conversations, I found he truly regretted what he had done. A teenager, younger than his nineteen-year-old victim, he realized he had also destroyed his own life with this one senseless act. There was no going back, he told me, but he hoped he could go forward.

I wanted three things from Knowles at this trial: a logical explanation of Klan structure and hierarchy to strengthen our agency theory, testimony that this was a Klan killing, and a detailed account of the murder itself that would horrify the jury, leave it gasping, move it to tears, and convince it that someone had to pay.

Q: How did the Klan operate structure-wise?
A: On a military basis. . . . Each person carried out the orders that was given to him from his commanding officer.
Q: Was Mr. Robert Shelton the Klan official directly above you that you took orders from, or was it Mr. Hays?
A: Mr. Hays is who I took orders from.
Q: Okay. And then Mr. Hays took orders from whom?
A: Mr. Shelton.

We could now focus on the murder, beginning with the plan. Knowles explained that the racial makeup of the Anderson jury had triggered his discussion with Bennie and Henry Hays about hanging a black man. What was the reason for killing a black person?

"Because he was—black people shouldn't be on juries . . . it was strictly white supremacy," said Knowles.

From the back of the gallery, I heard the testifying that goes on in some Southern black churches, an emotional commentary in response to Tiger Knowles's testimony.

Why had the murderers decided to hang the body out on the street?

"To get the message out to, not just the state of Alabama, but the

whole United States that the Klan didn't want black people on juries,"
Knowles answered. They had wanted to emphasize the Klan connection, he said—thus they burned the cross on the courthouse lawn.

Knowles described Michael Donald's abduction. Donald had asked
what they were going to do to him, Knowles remembered, and then,
"Henry said, 'You know all those little nigger kids that's been getting
killed up in Atlanta? Well a lot of people think the Klan is behind it.
But we are not. You know the same thing could happen to you.' "
Tiger Knowles paused for a moment. "And then he started pleading
for his life. He said, 'Please don't kill me. You know you can do
whatever you want to, beat me or anything else. But just don't kill
me.' " It was impossible not to feel Michael Donald's terror.

I looked back at Mrs. Donald. Sitting silent, she squeezed the hand
of Michael Figures, our co-counsel, her tearless eyes holding
Knowles's.

How had hatred based on skin color been so thoroughly ingrained
in these two young men that they could carry this out. *They didn't even
know Michael.* "And finally Donald just fell," Knowles told the silent
courtroom. "And then Henry rushed over to the other end of the
rope and grabbed the rope and started pulling it and it was like he was
enjoying this. And then he was pulling it and then I finally said, 'Well
he's dead.' And so we got him and we put him in the trunk of Henry's
car. And then Henry took a razor knife and cut his throat and I asked
him what for. He said: 'To make sure he was dead.' "

Somebody from the Donald family said, "Dear Lord." Mrs. Donald, tears in her eyes now, rocked back and forth in her chair, fighting
to maintain her composure. The jury sat frozen in horror.

Knowles told how he and Henry Hays returned to the Hays house
to show Donald's body to Frank Cox, and how Teddy Kyzar had given
him a friendly punch and said, "Good job, Tiger." At the break of
dawn, Knowles said, Henry Hays called a television station to tell
them a body was hanging from a camphor tree on Herndon Avenue.

I wanted the jury to know more, to feel the rope around their own
necks until they delivered a verdict. I asked Knowles to come down
in front of the jury box and show how Henry Hays had put his boot
on Donald's head for better leverage when pulling the rope. Referring to a police photograph, I asked, "If you can look at his head right
here, do you see across here what's basically a waffle print where
somebody's had an object pressing into the head of this person?"

"Yes, sir, I can." He explained that the waffle-patterned underside
of Hays's army boot had left that impression on Donald's head hours

after the murder. *The anger that Henry must have possessed.*

I thought about another client of mine, Willie Truitt, a middle-aged black man from Lafayette, Alabama, a small town that the civil rights movement had passed by. In the early 1980s, Willie had come upon a Klan gathering by accident, and without being provoked, fired a couple of shots in the direction of the Klansmen. No one was hurt, but Willie, who had never been in serious trouble before, was arrested for attempted murder.

My first question was: Why did you do it? Willie explained that when he was a young boy some forty years earlier, he and a friend had been playing in the woods when they heard a commotion at a nearby house. They moved to the edge of the clearing and watched in silent terror as hooded Klansmen pulled a black man from the house, then threw him on the front of a pickup truck and beat him until his clothes turned completely red. "Completely red," Willie told me, shaking his head. Then, in front of the man's wife and small children, the Klansmen looped a rope around his neck and hung him from an oak tree in the front yard. "Just left him to swing," said Willie. He said that when he had seen the Klansmen at their gathering, he had suddenly flashed back to that forty-year-old scene and some unknown force had taken over and caused him to shoot his gun. He claimed he had only shot into the air. We got Willie off with a short work-release sentence.

I put into evidence another photograph of Michael Donald dangling from the tree. The jury could see the eerie similarity between the photo and the drawing in the *Fiery Cross,* the noose and heads in each positioned at virtually the same angles. I asked Tiger Knowles about the drawing.

Q: Now when you saw this piece of information, how did you interpret that coming from Robert Shelton, editor in chief, as a Klan official?
A: That's what blacks deserved—to be hung. And that we should go out and since this was a publication of the Klan telling us what we should do and telling the Klan's beliefs, that's what we should do, go out and hang black people.

In his opening statement, Klonsel Mays had told the jury that the people at the national office of the UKA found the murder of Michael Donald "sickening and disgusting." He then said there was no way that we could prove the UKA "conspired, endorsed, encouraged, or assisted in this atrocity." Knowles's testimony about what the drawing meant to him helped establish that there had been encouragement and an endorsement. Mays knew this and began his cross-examination by trying to control the damage. Knowles admitted that this was the only drawing of its nature he had ever seen in the *Fiery Cross.* Mays then asked: "Did Mr. Shelton himself ever give you an order or directive remotely suggesting that you or anyone else should commit an act of violence?

"Not directly. He instructed us to follow our leaders. And I followed my leaders which got instructions from Mr. Shelton."

A good question, and an even better answer. Knowles's leader was Bennie Hays, directly accountable to Bobby Shelton.

Mays tried to make the point that Tiger Knowles, Bennie Hays, and Henry Hays—good friends and drinking buddies—had hatched their plan to lynch a black man the day before the weekly Unit 900 meeting. Like Mobile Assistant DA Harrison, Mays suggested that this was not a Klan murder, but was instead a murder committed by men who happened to be in the Klan. Knowles acknowledged the three friends had indeed talked about the lynching in advance of the meeting, but this did not negate the testimony that they had followed through on that initial conversation and discussed the murder at the meeting. Why bring it up there if it wasn't a Klan matter? As Knowles said, the whole point was to show the Klan's displeasure with the jury system.

While none of the other defendants were represented by counsel, they each had a chance to cross-examine the witnesses. Bennie Hays's rambling interrogation centered on the fact that Knowles had told him he hadn't committed the murder, but had just hauled Donald's body for a friend. Knowles denied this, but Bennie Hays said he remembered it clearly because the discussion had come when Knowles borrowed twenty dollars from him. Now Knowles denied borrowing twenty dollars and the exchange deteriorated to a quarrel not over a murder, but a debt.

Following Bennie Hays, Frank Cox raised an important point. Tiger Knowles had described numerous versions of the Donald murder to various people and had lied under oath several times. Indeed, said Cox, Knowles had admitted he was a liar at Cox's recent trial for conspiracy to commit murder. Cox's indictment resulted from information we had given to Mobile DA Chris Galanos. Chris had done a fine job at the trial in the face of Cox's excellent defense attorney, who crucified Tiger Knowles over discrepancies in his prior statements. In most of these statements, Knowles had said only he and Henry Hays planned and carried out the murder.

Just before the case went to the jury, Cox's attorney checked the statute of limitations on conspiracy and found it had expired before the arrest. The judge threw the case out. The possibility of trying Cox for murder, which has no statute of limitations, still existed. We hoped this trial might lead to those charges. On my redirect examination Tiger Knowles admitted he had initially lied "out of allegiance to the Klan." He was telling the truth now, he said, because he wanted to "come clean."

Michael Figures and I had told Beulah Mae Donald that she would have the opportunity to testify. We wanted someone from the family to fill in the time period directly before the abduction. More important, we wanted to show who Michael Donald was, breathe life back into the battered corpse. We were asking the jury to award damages because Michael's life had been taken. As impossible as the task seems to place a monetary value on a shortened life, it cannot be avoided in these cases. We also wanted to demonstrate the impact of Michael's death on the family.

Mrs. Donald chose not to testify. In her place, Michael's twenty-nine-year-old relative Vanessa Wyatt told the jury about Michael's last hours with his family. After watching a basketball game on television with two of his brothers, Michael had borrowed a dollar to buy a pack of cigarettes. "We all assumed he was going up to the service station and coming right back," she said in a quiet voice.

"When did you next see him?" asked Figures.

"At the wake."

An answer as abrupt as the end of Michael's life.

Vanessa Wyatt established that Michael had never been in trouble, that he was working nights at the *Mobile Press Register* and attending technical school to become a brick mason.

Figures showed Wyatt a photograph far different from the one I had shown Tiger Knowles: Michael smiling at a wedding reception.

"Is that Michael?" asked Figures. Vanessa Wyatt allowed herself a brief smile. "Yes," she said firmly.

Frank Cox took the Fifth Amendment. His mother, Sarah Cox, and Tiger's mother, Beatrice Knowles, were more forthcoming, each substantiating Tiger's account of the events of March 21. Mrs. Cox in particular was a lovely, classy woman, and as she spoke I thought: These poor mothers; they sent their boys, innocent as Adam, into the world where history and human snakes corrupted them.

*   *   *

The snakes took the witness stand the second day, every snake for himself. Beefy Bill O'Connor testified that on the morning Michael Donald's body was discovered, he and several Klansmen, including Bennie Hays, had stood across the street, watching the police begin their investigation. Bennie Hays had commented that the scene was "a pretty sight or pretty picture."

When it was Bennie's turn on the stand, he testified O'Connor had suggested hanging a "nigger," a statement consistent with what he had told me at his deposition in the Mobile County jail. He denied virtually everything else he had said at the deposition, particularly anything negative about Shelton. When I showed him the deposition and asked him to read certain passages that contradicted what he was now saying, Bennie protested that his mind "was in a swirl" and he could not read. He insisted that Knowles, O'Connor, Teddy Kyzar, and other witnesses had all lied when they had implicated him in the discussion or plan to lynch a black. It was one of the meanest performances I have ever seen: Bennie Hays spit out each denial, and whenever he had the opportunity to drop a name he did—just so he could step on it. Hate had eaten away Bennie's heart, and, sadly, hate was keeping him alive.

Teddy Kyzar's memory of the Klavern meeting two nights before the lynching was clearer than Bennie Hays's. He recalled that Exalted Cyclops Frank Cox had given him fifty lashes with a five-inch strap at the sacred altar for getting drunk and spending a new applicant's initiation money. Like Johnny Matt Jones, he also remembered Bennie saying that a black man shouldn't be allowed to get away with murdering a white man and something should be done.

His recollection of the period after the murder was also better. He said that several weeks after the lynching, Bennie had told him that if he took the fall and went to prison "when I came out, my pockets would be padded with money and I wouldn't have to worry about working. . . . But if I opened my mouth about the Klan, that I was going to die within eight hours, twenty-four hours at the most."

Kyzar took Bennie Hays's threats seriously. After Tiger Knowles and Henry Hays had been arrested in 1983, Bennie came looking for him. Kyzar said he had been so scared he had changed into dark clothes, taken his gun, and hidden behind his living-room couch.

The last of the conspirators to testify, Kyzar seemed a fitting finale for the pathetic procession of finger-pointers. Little doubt remained that we had proven the case against these individual Klansmen, under-scoring how the murder was sanctioned by Bennie Hays, the man who reported directly to Shelton. We were through with the events of 1981. It was time to take the trip back to 1961, 1963, 1965, and, finally, 1979.

Although I had promised Tommy Rowe a chance to star at the trial, I didn't want him anywhere near the courtroom. Just as Johnny Matt Jones would make a bad witness because of his lack of confidence, Rowe would make a bad one because of his overabundance of ego. I also didn't want to give Mays the chance to cross-examine him. Rowe had enough skeletons in his closet to make him suspect, and if anybody knew about those skeletons it was Mays and Shelton. They had blown their opportunity to question him by refusing to come to the deposi-tion. The time for accountability had arrived.

Joe Roy stood in for the absent witness. We began with Rowe's description of how Shelton and the Birmingham police had made a deal before the Freedom Riders had arrived and how Shelton person-ally had taken to the street and directed traffic for his club-wielding UKA thugs.

I showed Rowe a 1961 newspaper photo of the violence that day. He identified one of the men in the picture as Robert Chambliss, a member of his own UKA unit. Yes, he said, this was the same Robert Chambliss convicted of the 1963 bombing of the Sixteenth Street Baptist Church that left four little black girls dead.

From Birmingham, 1963, to Selma, 1965: How had Shelton re-sponded to the march to Montgomery in support of the Voting Rights Act? Rowe said the Imperial Wizard had come to his Klavern and said, "If necessary, you know, just do what you have to do." Later, Robert Creel, Alabama Grand Dragon of UKA, phoned Rowe and said, "Tommy, this is probably going to be one of the greatest days of Klan history." Creel said they were going for a ride.

Rowe was in a car with UKA members Gene Thomas, William Eaton, and Collie Leroy Wilkins outside Selma when Viola Liuzzo accompanied by Leroy Moton, a black teenager who had taken part in the march, pulled alongside them at a stoplight. "I believe Eaton was the one that said, 'Goddamn, look over there.' And Wilkins said, 'I'll be a sonofabitch, look at that. Let's take them.' "

The chase exceeded ninety miles per hour. As the Klan car gained on Liuzzo, Thomas said to Wilkins, "This is it. Let's do it." Rowe said Thomas pulled out a pistol and handed it to Wilkins. Wilkins shouted to Rowe, "When we get that motherfucker . . . I'm going to get that sport coat for you. It will just about fit you." Moton was wearing a green sport coat.

Rowe continued:

> We got pretty much even with the car and the lady just turned her head solid all the way around and looked at us. I will never forget it in my lifetime, and her mouth flew open like she—in my heart I've always said she was saying, "Oh God," or something like that. . . . You could tell she was startled. At that point Wilkins fired a shot. . . . He fired three or four more shots.
>
> I saw a black man kind of fall over toward the dash. . . . At that point she just kind of fell right down toward the wheel. . . . The car went straight as a board, I bet you, for five hundred feet. It didn't turn, it didn't stop, it went down the road. . . . Gene Thomas said, "Goddamn, I don't believe it." At that time the car just very casually . . . went and ran off the road into some bushes.

The FBI arrested the four men within twenty-four hours. (Interestingly, it was a month before a reporter thought to ask FBI Director J. Edgar Hoover how they had solved the crime so quickly. Rowe came out from undercover and testified against his three companions, who were acquitted of state murder charges by an all-white jury of their peers, but convicted on federal civil rights charges.)

Tiger Knowles's graphic description of the Donald murder. Tommy Rowe's equally vivid account of beatings, bombings, and the Liuzzo murder. The beginning and the end of the trail were red with blood spilled by the UKA. It was time to fill in the gap.

One week before the trial began, we still weren't sure whether Randy Ward would make good on his promise and testify. "I know if he ever gets to the stand, we can count on him," I told Joe Roy.

"*If* he ever gets to the stand," said Joe. "He's terrified of what the Klan may do to him."

When Ward finally said he would come, we made elaborate security arrangements, having him drive from his home to another city and then fly to Mobile. We registered him under an assumed name at his hotel. As the trial began, Joe and Danny went to several hotels and motels in the Mobile area and picked up matchbooks and notepads. They "carelessly" left these on the counsel table or flashed them so the Klan defendants could see. We even made reservations under the name Randy Ward in one hotel.

If the Klan looked for Ward, they never found him until he walked into Judge Howard's courtroom as our final witness.

After describing his membership in the UKA and his role as Exalted Cyclops, Ward recounted the Childersburg shootings, admitting he had fired a twelve-gauge shotgun into NAACP president Woods's house. He then told the story that had persuaded me he was essential to proving that UKA violence had continued between the Liuzzo and Donald murders. Shelton, he said, had personally visited the Klavern to give the membership a pep talk. The Imperial Wizard regaled his troops with old war stories, including an account of the deal made with the Birmingham police before the attack on the Freedom Riders and the violence used by UKA members.

> Q: From his talking to you about that and the story he gave you, how did you interpret this example he was giving you about what he had done as to what you should do as an official of the local unit of the UKA?
>
> A: To use any means necessary to carry out this, you know, the prior directive, to maintain the white race.
>
> Q: Well, did it fire you up?
>
> A: Oh, yeah. Definitely.
>
> Q: What about the other members in there?
>
> A: Everybody was fired up. When Mr. Shelton came around, people would follow him through hell if it came to it.

I was hoping it would come to just that.

The plan used in the attack on Woods's house bore one huge similarity to the Freedom Riders attack eighteen years earlier. The police, Ward testified, agreed to look the other way.

We rested our case. Judge Howard summoned us into chambers, where Mays moved that the court direct a verdict in his client's favor because we had failed to prove our case. The other defendants made the same motion on behalf of themselves. Judge Howard denied them all. I smiled at Richard. We had made it past the judge to the jury.

Before we went back into the courtroom so the defense could present its case, I told the judge we were dismissing Teddy Kyzar as a defendant. Poor Kyzar didn't even understand what Judge Howard meant when he gave him the good news.

"Do I have to come back tomorrow?" he asked.

"No," said the judge, smiling.

Teddy Kyzar had Ellie to thank for his good fortune. She had become more excited and involved as the case progressed. By the time we recessed for lunch the first day, I had a stack of notes that said a lot more than "Nice job, Daddy." Now it was "Ask this . . ." or "What about this . . . ?"

During lunch Ellie was so full of suggestions that she forgot to eat. I had always hoped she would want to be a lawyer, but had vowed never to push her. The questions she was asking and the suggestions she was making proved she had the skill. "Ellie, you come sit at the counsel table with Richard and me," I told her. "If you're gonna help try this case, you're gonna try it from where the lawyers sit." When we returned to the courtroom, she proudly moved her note pad to the table. I felt even prouder later that afternoon when Judge Howard asked if Ellie was a secretary. "No, Your Honor, this is my daughter," I said, beaming.

That evening Ellie was leaving the courthouse with Joe Roy and Klanwatch's Pat Clark when she saw Teddy Kyzar standing on the street corner. She started talking to him and learned he had to wait until nine for his mother to pick him up. There was no other way of getting to Prichard, the low-income, mostly black community outside Mobile where he lived.

Ellie felt sorry for Kyzar and asked Joe to offer him a ride home. On the drive to Prichard, Kyzar confessed he'd never had a girlfriend. On the only date he ever had, he said, the girl stood him up. "I'd gotten flowers for her and everything," he said.

Back at the hotel, Ellie asked me if I could drop Teddy Kyzar from the case. She'd read his deposition and was convinced he had not been a part of the conspiracy. I had already been thinking about finding some way to dismiss him without hurting our case. It would, however, be complicated to explain to the jury why we were dropping a defendant. I told Ellie I would wait to hear his testimony before making a decision and that if we did drop him, it would be at the end of the case.

When Kyzar left the witness stand, Ellie wrote me another note: "You heard him, Daddy. Please drop him."

I should have trusted Ellie's intuition from the start. Before my closing argument, I crossed Kyzar's name off the big chart listing the defendants. One of the female jurors sighed in relief.

The time for closing arguments arrived faster than I had expected; Mays had surprised us all by resting his case without calling a single witness. Apparently he felt the case against Shelton and the UKA was so weak it didn't require a defense. The rest of the defendants also rested, save Bill O'Connor, who made a statement to the jury denying Bennie Hays's accusations.

I had been thinking about my closing argument even while watching Henry Hays's trial almost four years earlier. I had outlined it, parts at least, on the way back from Mobile after seeing the Klan constitution and its talk of the "God-given supremacy of the white race," adding more after seeing the *Fiery Cross* drawing of the lynched black man.

Drifting into sleep the night before, I thought about a line from one of Mrs. Donald's favorite hymns—"O what peace we often forfeit, O what needless pain we bear." I thought about closing with a verse from the Old Testament prophet Amos, paraphrased by Dr. King: "We will not be satisfied until justice rolls down like waters . . . and righteousness like a mighty stream."

I arose at dawn and did a half-hour workout of sit-ups and other calisthenics to get the oxygen flowing. My close would begin the day's proceedings, to be followed by closing arguments from each of the defendants, and then Michael Figures. I had previously heard Michael's eloquent recitation of John Donne's "No Man Is an Island." These moving words, delivered by a black man to our white jury just before deliberations began, would, I was certain, be most powerful. In my presentation, I would review the facts of the case and make a pitch for a large monetary verdict.

After finishing my exercises, I woke Richard and asked if he'd come on a walk so I could get his input on the major points I should cover. It was a cool, damp morning: The mist hugged the fishing boats and leisure craft moored on the waterfront, while the sun fought to poke through the haze. Richard cleared away a lot of my mind's clutter, and I thought how fortunate I'd been over the past sixteen years to have friends and counsel like him, Joe Levin, and John Carroll.

After a quick breakfast, the Center contingent headed for the courthouse. Unfortunately Ellie had a test she couldn't miss at school. She had gone back to Montgomery, but not without outlining my argument, of course. She felt I should emphasize that Bobby Shelton and Bennie Hays were the true villains—the general and his next-in-command who sent young, unsophisticated soldiers like Teddy Kyzar and Tiger Knowles out to fight their wars. Richard, on the other hand, wanted me to make sure I explained our agency theory in very simple terms—if Tiger and Henry and the rest of the conspirators had been acting in the scope of their authority as dictated by the UKA, Inc., and its leader Shelton, then the UKA, Inc., must be found liable.

When we reached the courtroom, I put my briefcase on the counsel table and then went out in the hallway to find a quiet spot where I could be alone. Before facing a jury, I need this private time. I need to get in touch with my feelings about the case, need to remember why I have become involved. It was not difficult to remember why the Donald case meant so much to me. My personal history and the history of the South were inextricably woven into the rope with which Michael Donald had been hanged. It was time to put that rope to rest forever.

I don't review my argument during this quiet time. I think about the simpler times of my life. On this day, I remembered as a small boy walking along Line Creek with Daddy to check the catfish lines, riding my horse into the late evening sun at Rolling Hills Ranch, holding my children in my arms when they were born.

I also thought about my very first public speech as a sixteen-year-old contestant in a Future Farmers of America oratory competition. I'd written every word, memorized and practiced it for weeks, and then fainted flat out in front of five hundred students when I lost my place—perhaps the most embarrassing moment in my life. Today the words I wanted the jury to feel were etched in the last twenty-five years of my life, not typed on paper.

I stood before the jury for a long time before beginning. I wanted the jurors' attention and anticipation. After summarizing the facts and making the points Ellie and Richard suggested, I slowed the pace and lowered my voice.

> We told you when we started this case that we would show you that a conspiracy existed. And I believe we've shown you that the defendants conspired to kill a human being to retaliate against a jury for returning a verdict that was contrary to what they believe in. And what they believe in is white supremacy. God-given white supremacy. . . .

I walked over to the Klan's table and continued.

> But I do not want you to come back with a verdict against the Klan because they have unpopular beliefs. In this country you have the right to have unpopular beliefs just as long as you don't turn those beliefs into violent action that interferes with somebody else's rights. . . .

I raised my voice and motioned directly toward Bennie Hays and Bobby Shelton.

But they put a rope around Michael Donald's neck and treated him to an awful death on a dirt road in Baldwin County so that they could get out their message.

I walked back to our table and stopped beside Beulah Mae Donald.

You have an opportunity to send a different message. A message that will ring out from the top of this courthouse and be heard all over Alabama and all over the United States—that an all-white jury from the heart of the South will not tolerate racial violence in any way, shape, or form. . . .

No amount of money can ever truly compensate Mrs. Donald for her son's death. But if you return a large verdict—a very large verdict—you will be telling Mrs. Donald and this nation that her son's life was as valuable and as precious as anyone's.

I put my hands on Mrs. Donald's shoulders, then returned to the jury, tears trickling down my face. I felt Mrs. Donald's pain and the hurt and outrage of a civilized society for what these barbarians had done. I was not ashamed for the jury to know.

I paused, cleared my throat, and looked each juror in the eye.

No matter what you decide, Michael Donald will take his place in history along with others whose lives were lost in the struggle for human rights. And when the final roll is called in heaven—when they call Dr. Martin Luther King, and Medgar Evers, and Viola Liuzzo— they will also call Michael Donald. I hope the verdict you reach will also go down in history on the side of justice.*

I returned to my chair. Still rocking slowly, Mrs. Donald nodded.

The defendants were about to begin their closing arguments when I got word that Tiger Knowles would like to see me. I hurried to the tiny cell where he was being held when court was not in session.

"Do you think I should say something, Mr. Dees?" he asked.

"That's up to you, Tiger," I said.

"I'd like to," he said.

"Then do it."

"What should I say?" he asked.

"I can't answer that, Tiger. Just say what you feel."

*   *   *

*My ninety-minute closing argument has been edited and revised for clarity and emphasis.

The young man who had murdered Michael Donald addressed the court: "Everything I said is true," Tiger Knowles began. "I was acting as a Klansman when I done this. I hope that people learn from my mistake. I've lost my family. I've got people after me."

Tears filled Knowles's eyes and I began to feel them again well up in mine. Knowles pivoted and faced Beulah Mae Donald. "I can't bring your son back, but I'm sorry for what happened." He was sobbing now. Mrs. Donald rocked back and forth. "God knows if I could trade places with him, I would. I can't. Whatever it takes—I have nothing. But I will have to do it. And if it takes me the rest of my life to pay it, any comfort it may bring, I hope it will. I will."

Knowles paused to compose himself. I looked at the jury, Judge Howard, the Donald family. There were no dry eyes. Knowles gave up trying to fight his own tears. "I want you to understand that it is true what happened and I'm just sorry that it happened."

Beulah Mae Donald stopped rocking. "I forgive you," she said softly.

Knowles turned back to the jury and told them he hoped they'd "decide a judgment against me and everyone else. . . . Because you people need to understand that this can't happen."

John Mays was not impressed by Tiger Knowles's speech. Knowles was a murderer and a liar, the Klonsel reminded the jury. If they believed that Tiger had been moved to violence by the "disgusting cartoon" of the lynching in the *Fiery Cross,* then, "I've got a gold mine in downtown Prichard I'll sell you real cheap."

The conspiracy to murder Michael Donald did not extend to Robert Shelton and the UKA, Mays insisted. "There is a total lack of evidence in this case that the national organization, United Klans of America, had anything to do with this. They did not encourage it. They did not approve it. They didn't congratulate anybody."

Mays suggested that if organizations with such goals as attempting to stop pornography or abortion were punished for the acts of wayward members, those organizations would, sadly, cease to exist. Holding a national organization responsible for acts committed by members without the organization's knowledge would mean "no more freedom of association in this country."

He added, "Perhaps it's an inappropriate comparison, but . . . nobody attempted to hold the NAACP, the Southern Christian Leadership Conference . . . or any other such organizations pecuniarily liable for . . . riots and fires and busted heads."

Michael Figures succinctly showed the error in Mays's premise. "It could be persuasive if we were talking about pornography . . . or prayer in public schools or abortion. All of those things strike at the heart of Americans this hour in our history. But we aren't talking about that. We're talking about a murder," Figures told the jury.

He closed with the wisdom of Donne: "Any man's death diminishes me, because I am involved in Mankind; and therefore never send to know for whom the bell tolls." Stately, handsome, black, Figures looked into the white faces in the jury box. "They toll for Mrs. Donald right now. But one day they may toll for thee."

The jury retired early in the afternoon. It returned with a verdict four and a half hours later. Judge Howard instructed the clerk to read it. "We the jury find for the plaintiff and against defendant United Klans of America. . . . We the jury find for the plaintiff and against the defendant Bennie Hays." It was the same with respect to the remaining defendants—judgment for the plaintiff. After the final defendant's name was read, the clerk concluded: "We fix plaintiff's damages at seven million dollars."

There were gasps from both counsels' tables and both sides of the gallery. Mrs. Donald grabbed my hand and Michael Figures's hand. Richard quickly scribbled a note to me. "Thank you for letting me be a part of this."

The verdict's size did not sink in immediately. I was more excited that the quest to get Shelton and the UKA had succeeded. History would show that an all-white Southern jury had held the Klan accountable after all these years. The healing could begin. Indeed, it already had when Tiger Knowles and Beulah Mae Donald had reached out to one another.

Shelton and Mays avoided my eyes. They rose and quickly left the courtroom.

Richard Cohen, Michael Figures, Mrs. Donald, and I eventually made our way to the packed press room. Mrs. Donald said: "I don't want no other mother to go through what I did." I said I hoped the verdict would mean just that.

After leaving the press conference, I called Ellie. "We won, sweetheart," I said.

"I heard," she said. "I'm really proud of you. I understand why you do what you do, Daddy."

A wonderful ending to a memorable day.

*   *   *

The verdict was a major news story for days. *Newsweek* wrote: "A court-ordered white sale will force the United Klans to sell off its assets, down to the last hooded sheet." Hundreds of editorials followed. The *New York Times* wrote:

> It's not unusual for corporations to correct dangerous practices because they fear civil damage suits. The risk of multimillion-dollar judgments attracts their attention in ways that even criminal charges against individual officers might not. What is unusual is for such a judgment to be rendered against a corporation called the United Klans of America— and for it to come from an all-white jury in Alabama. . . .
>
> The Alabama verdict gives a new meaning to the old slogan: those who sanction brutal crimes must pay.

The only major asset the UKA possessed was its new seventy-four-hundred-square-foot building that sat at the end of a dirt road on the outskirts of Tuscaloosa. Six weeks after the trial, the deed to the property and the keys to the building arrived at the Center in the mail. Beulah Mae Donald was the new owner. The Klan had decided not to appeal.

When Center staffers went to see the building, they found it barren. Shelton and his aides had taken everything except a wooden plaque that hung on a wall in the lobby. KKK YESTERDAY TODAY AND TOMORROW, it read.

The UKA, the most visible symbol of racial hatred yesterday, was bankrupt today. What tomorrow would bring for Bobby Shelton, I did not know. I did know that Beulah Mae Donald could look forward to a brighter future. She had already decided to sell the building and use the proceeds to buy a house. Pending the sale of the property, the Center loaned her the money to move out of the public housing project where she had lived with her son Michael and into the first home she had ever owned.

I was there the day she moved in, and for a moment at least, the sadness that had weighed her down these last six years seemed to lift. A smile of hope, of faith in the future crossed her face. Tomorrow *would* be a better day.

EPILOGUE

September 1990   Montgomery, Alabama

Beulah Mae Donald lived less than a year after moving into her new home. The pain of losing her Michael was too much for her heart to bear.

Before Mrs. Donald died, she and I were honored at the annual Alabama NAACP convention. I repeated to those gathered the portion of my closing argument about the roll call in heaven for fallen civil rights leaders. After my speech, a group of teenagers came forward for autographs. One young man asked me about some of the people I had named. "Who were Medgar Evers, Viola Liuzzo, and Emmett Till?" he asked.

During the drive home that night, I was troubled that today's young people, black and white, have no real sense of civil rights history. These teenagers, not even born when Dr. King marched to Montgomery in 1965, enjoy the movement's benefits yet have little knowledge of the necessary past sacrifices.

Data gathered by Klanwatch showed a rising tide of racial violence, more in the North than the South, and much of it coming from young people. Black demagogues, as well as white, were spreading racial hatred. Candidate George Bush, sensing fertile political ground, had shamelessly played on white America's fear and prejudice by running commercials about Willie Horton, a black convict on furlough who assaulted a white woman. Bush's flimsy excuse for this commercial was that it proved his opponent was soft on crime. In the previous campaign, candidate Jesse Jackson had referred to New York as "hymie town." Our nation needed to be reminded of the horrible price we paid so few years earlier in the civil rights movement.

I proposed to the Center's board that we build a Civil Rights Memorial honoring those slain in the movement. On November 5, 1989, more than ten thousand people gathered in Montgomery to dedicate this monument, designed by Maya Lin, the architect who also designed the Vietnam Memorial in Washington, D.C. At the dedication, Myrlie Evers spoke of seeing her husband Medgar drag his bullet-ridden body to their door. Chris McNair recalled the painful loss of his eleven-year-old daughter Denise in the Sixteenth Street Baptist Church bombing. Marie Till Mobley talked of her son Emmett as if he was sharing the podium with her; she tried to explain the inexplicable, then closed by saying, "Now the world will remember." Rosa Parks, the graying mother of the movement, said, "We must learn to love more than we hate."

This striking monument, with its curved black granite wall and unique granite table listing the names of the fallen, graces the plaza in front of the Southern Poverty Law Center. Water flows down the wall and across the table. On the wall are carved the words from Amos used by Dr. King: UNTIL JUSTICE ROLLS DOWN LIKE WATERS AND RIGHTEOUSNESS LIKE A MIGHTY STREAM. Each week hundreds of people come by and read and touch the forty names etched into the table. I watch them from my office window as they ponder the inscriptions describing how and why each man, woman, and child died.

The night before the memorial was dedicated, I received a phone call from former Governor George Wallace, my onetime hero who had lost my allegiance when he vowed never to be "out-segged" by a political opponent. He received the black vote in his third and last term as governor after publicly admitting he was wrong to support segregation. The governor, himself the victim of senseless violence, is seriously ill now. I had invited him to the ceremonies. "Morris," he said in his weak but unforgettable voice, "I'm not going to be able to come. I have to go into the hospital tomorrow. But tell everybody I wish I could be there and that I'm with you all in spirit. I think the memorial is a wonderful thing."

At a dinner for the families of those named on the memorial, I retold the story of Tiger Knowles's plea to Mrs. Donald for understanding and of her forgiveness. This, I said, is the most dramatic and memorable moment of my thirty years of jury trials. This was a higher justice, a love we speak so much of but know so little about. I thanked Beulah Mae Donald, present in spirit if not in body, for giving me the rare chance to experience it.

Justice of a more earthly kind befell Frank Cox and Bennie Hays. Using evidence we supplied, Mobile District Attorney Chris Galanos indicted the pair for Michael Donald's murder. Cox was convicted and given a life sentence. Hays had a heart seizure during his trial. Another trial is pending. Convicted or not, Hays, the architect of Michael Donald's lynching, is a broken man, and UKA Unit 900 is no more.

Opal Hays died as Mrs. Donald did, grieving over the tragedy that befell her family. In a sense, she, too, was a victim of Bennie's racism and hate. Before her death, Mrs. Hays became a leader of a group of mothers of death row inmates. These mothers, mostly black, joined hands with Opal, caring little about skin color. If Henry Hays, who still sits on death row, loses his appeals, I intend to ask our governor to spare his life. Mrs. Donald, I believe, would approve.

Steve Miller and his cohorts also sit in prison, convicted of the Pizza Hut robbery and conspiracy to murder me. Steve received a ten-year sentence.

Glenn Miller's whereabouts are unknown. In 1987, he went underground while on bond awaiting the appeal of his criminal contempt conviction, taking along Doug Sheets and Robert Jackson, the munitions experts fingered by Robert Jones. Miller had planned to kill me and others he targeted as enemies of the people. He mailed me a death threat and sent a letter to his followers saying I was worth 888 points dead.

Miller and his men were eventually flushed out of a rented mobile home near Springfield, Missouri, at dawn by an FBI swat team. The FBI found an arsenal of illegal weapons and explosives rivaling those described by Jones. Sheets and Jackson received long prison terms. Miller pled guilty to threatening me by mail and received a five-year sentence.

This light sentence was partial payoff by federal prosecutors for Miller's agreement to testify against Louis Beam and twelve other high-level white supremacist leaders charged with sedition. At this trial Miller admitted receiving two hundred thousand dollars of stolen armored-car receipts from Order founder Robert Mathews. He also testified that he had heard Mathews discuss killing me. Unfortunately, a white Fort Smith, Arkansas, jury acquitted all defendants, apparently not seeing them as a threat to overthrow the United States government and possibly agreeing with much of the men's philosophy. One female juror later married a defendant. Glenn Miller is hiding somewhere today in the government's witness protection program—a once proud savior of the white race turned informant to save his own white hide.

The Decatur case, filed in 1981, ended in January 1989 with a happier result than the sedition trial. The civil case was finally settled with a most unusual agreement that resulted in Klan leaders attending a course on race relations. The defendants also agreed to pay damages to the black marchers and refrain from participating in white supremacy activity.

The evidence we delivered to federal prosecutors in 1983, less than twelve hours before our building burned, resulted in the indictment and conviction of ten Invisible Empire officials in Alabama for violating the marchers' civil rights. All served jail terms.

I felt the Decatur case, our first attempt to use the civil court to stop Klan violence, had served its purpose. What more fitting conclusion to nearly ten years of painstaking investigation and arduous litigation than to have Klan leaders sit down with the black leaders whom they had assaulted. This novel remedy reminded me of Dr. King's words in his 1963 speech on the Washington Mall: "I have a dream that someday in the red clay hills of Georgia, the sons of slaves and the sons of former slaveholders will sit down around the table of brotherhood."

Dr. Joseph Lowery, Jr., the Decatur march leader and head of King's SCLC, conducted the class. His wife Evelyn, who was almost killed by a Klansman's bullet that day in 1979, also attended. When the private meeting ended, Klansman Terry Joe Tucker told the press that he had learned a lot about brotherhood. "We should have been talking more," he said.

Sometimes I think a great deal has been accomplished by our suits and the Justice Department's diligent prosecutions. Traditional Klan groups have been severely damaged. Recruits are scarce. But new extremist groups are emerging with the same message, only their uniforms are different. Their victims are still blacks, Jews, and other minorities. Their numbers are limited, and if we move quickly, we may be able to eliminate them also.

As I write, we are in the midst of a suit against Tom Metzger and his White Aryan Resistance (WAR) organization based in Fallbrook, California, as well as two skinhead members of Portland's East Side White Pride gang. These skinheads beat a black man's brains out with a baseball bat in November 1988. On behalf of the victim's family, we claim agents of Metzger and WAR encouraged these skinheads. The legal theory is similar to the one we used against Shelton's United Klans. A victory could destroy Metzger's group before he spreads his hate-filled message to other embittered young people confused and fearful of our complicated racial climate.

Portland is twenty-seven hundred miles from Montgomery. Gathering evidence for the skinhead case has taken more than one year, and I have traveled more than fifty thousand miles. I long to be home with my family rather than in strange motels whose names I can't remember. Some nights I am so tired that sleep will not come. As I settle back into my Delta seat somewhere in the air between Oregon and Alabama, I wonder how long I can keep up this pace and fight these battles.

It seems like only yesterday when Little Buddy and I were carefree, running barefoot down cotton rows. Or when I could quickly climb a hundred-foot oak while hunting with T. J. Hendricks. I'd scale the tallest tree in the swamp or even cut it down to keep from losing a raccoon.

In August I spoke at T. J.'s funeral. More than fifteen years ago we had gone to court to get the gravel road that ran in front of his house and the houses of other blacks paved, and we had won. As I took that road to the little church where he lay in state, I wished for those simpler times—times when Daddy and T. J. and their sons walked the hardwood forest, hunting game for the table. This hunting party never gave race a thought. Thomas Jefferson Hendricks and my father were friends, and when T. J. died, a piece of my past left forever.

I know the feeling of tracking a big buck, matching survival skills, and then, at the moment when I have the advantage, feeling a kinship—not wanting to triumph because he will lose. When I had Glenn Miller, Louis Beam, and Robert Shelton in my sights, I wanted to say, "Hey, fellows, let's go somewhere, sit down and talk." I'd tell them that if they knew T. J. or Clarence or Mrs. Donald or the Smith sisters as people, as I did, they could not hate them.

These men and others like them are bright and completely dedicated. With a change of heart, they could build bonds between the races. Sadly, they hate so deeply that their words and deeds destroy all they touch. I cannot give up hope that they may someday change.

Clients like Beulah Mae Donald keep my hope alive and refresh me, giving me strength to fight another day, or maybe a few more years. But I know there won't be that many more years because no one, not even Ellie's guardian angel, can slow the clock. My three grandchildren remind me that others, not just the victims of injustice, need to share my time.

An important other is my wonderful and beautiful wife Elizabeth. John Carroll was correct when he said that someday I would find the right woman. We met on a rooftop in New York City a few months before the Donald trial and were married in the courtyard at our country home on a beautiful spring day in 1989. Her roots, like mine, go four generations deep in Alabama's soil. We share each other's dreams. She has breathed new life into Rolling Hills Ranch and me. I have never been happier or more at peace in my adult life.

I'll always be a trial lawyer. No higher calling has come my way. I do not know when the next case will come or if I will be able to resist.

Clarence Darrow, the lawyer whose life spurred my decision to enter the arena, wrote words of wisdom I failed to notice two decades ago: "Nature treats all her children as she does the fields and forest; in late autumn, as the cold blasts are coming on, she strips us for the ordeal that is waiting. Our steps grow slower, our efforts briefer, our journeys shorter; our ambitions are not so irresistible, and our hopes no longer wear wings."

Postscript

November 1991   Montgomery, Alabama

Six weeks after I wrote this epilogue, a Portland jury returned a verdict of 12.5 million dollars for the family of Mulugeta Seraw, the Ethiopian student who was senselessly clubbed to death by three skinheads. Tom and John Metzger and their vicious, white supremacist organization WAR were to pay 11.5 million dollars of this award. Of course, the Metzgers do not have enough money to satisfy this judgment, but we immediately set the wheels in motion to collect all they do have. Tom Metzger's house was auctioned. Court-appointed representatives today monitor WAR's post office box for contributions and other monies. That money, as well as the proceeds from the sale of the Metzger home, will provide a legacy for the young son that Mulugeta left behind.

Under Oregon law, monies can be collected for up to twenty years to satisfy a judgment. We intend to do just that. Tom Metzger's hate business has been severely crippled.

The shadow of our treasured First Amendment hung over the Metzger case. The defendants argued that Tom Metzger's right to free speech protected him from liability for the acts of the skinheads who had been motivated by his henchmen. We responded that in America you have the right to hate, but not to hurt. The court agreed with us.

Unfortunately, while Tom Metzger's power has been greatly diminished, the hurt and the hate continue in our country. In 1990 there were more "hate crime" murders than in any year during the Civil Rights era. In 1991, the longtime white supremacist David Duke—his rhetoric reconstructed to appeal to the masses—emerged as a political force in his divisive campaign for governor of Louisiana. Although he lost, he captured a majority of the white vote. He then announced his candidacy for President.

The Center will continue to go to court against those in the hate business. But I have concluded that our time is equally well spent in the schools. We have launched a major new project, Teaching Tolerance. Our goal is to provide schools with quality teaching materials that can be used to educate a new generation of young Americans. White students born after the Civil Rights Movement often have little tolerance for minorities struggling to overcome hundreds of years of racial and economic discrimination. On the other hand, minority students enjoy rights won with blood and tears, sometimes with little respect for the sacrifice.

I believe that America can be a just nation with room for diverse views, races, and values. To accomplish this, our local and national leaders must speak out against intolerance at every turn. Our President must set the highest example by not resorting to racial politics. History has shown us in painful ways the high costs of pitting the people of our nation against each other for political and economic gain.

INDEX

Photo Credits

Page 2: *bottom*—Stanley Tretick; Page 3: *top left*—courtesy of Southern Poverty Law Center, *top right*—Morris Dees, courtesy of Southern Poverty Law Center, *bottom*—Jill Krementz; Page 4: Penny Weaver, courtesy of Southern Poverty Law Center; Page 5: *top*—Michael Mauney, *center*—Penny Weaver, courtesy of Southern Poverty Law Center, *bottom*—R. Williams, courtesy of Southern Poverty Law Center; Page 6: *top left*—*The Houston Post, top right*—Garry Nungester, *bottom left*—John R. Van Beekum, *bottom right*—Robert Dunnavant, Jr.; Page 7: *top*—Joe Roy, courtesy of Southern Poverty Law Center, *"Tiger" Knowles*—courtesy of *Mobile Press Register, Teddy Kyzar*—courtesy of *Mobile Press Register;* Page 8: *top right*—courtesy of *Mobile Press Register, center*—AP/Wide World Photos, *bottom*—Jo Ann Chancellor, courtesy of Southern Poverty Law Center

ABOUT THE COAUTHOR

Steve Fiffer was raised in the Midwest. He graduated from Yale University with a B.A. in American Studies, then earned a J.D. from the University of Chicago Law School. After practicing with a major Chicago law firm, he left to write full time. Over the last ten years, he has authored six books and numerous articles for publications ranging from *Sports Illustrated* to *The New York Times*. He and his wife, writer Sharon Sloan Fiffer, have three children.